THE
CULTURAL
CONTRADICTIONS
OF
CAPITALISM

DANIEL BELL

THE CULTURAL CONTRADICTIONS OF CAPITALISM

Twentieth Anniversary Edition

Basic Books
A Division of *HarperCollinsPublishers*

Permission to reprint excerpts from the following poems is gratefully acknowledged:

"Choruses from 'The Rock,' " in *Collected Poems: 1909–1962*, by T. S. Eliot, copyright 1936, by Harcourt Brace Jovanovich, Inc.; copyright 1963, 1964, by T. S. Eliot. Reprinted by permission of the publishers, Harcourt Brace Jovanovich, Inc., and Faber and Faber, Ltd.

"Adieu, Mademoiselle Véronique," in *Joseph Brodsky: Selected Poems*. Translated from the Russian by George L. Kline. English translation copyright © 1973 by George L. Kline. By permission of Harper & Row, Publishers, Inc., and Penguin Books, Ltd.

"Garden of Gethsemane," from *Doctor Zhivago*, by Boris Pasternak, translated by Max Hayward and Manya Harari, revised by Bernard Guilbert Guerney. Copyright © 1958 by Pantheon Books, Inc. Reprinted by permission of Pantheon Books, a Division of Random House, Inc., and Collins Publishers.

Designed by Vincent Torre

ISBN 0-465-01499-2

96 97 98 99 00 ❖/HC 10 9 8 7 6 5 4 3 2 1

For Pearl, with love

The endless cycle of idea and action,
Endless invention, endless experiment,
Brings knowledge of motion, but not of stillness;
Knowledge of speech, but not of silence;
Knowledge of words, and ignorance of the Word.

T. S. ELIOT
Choruses from *The Rock*

Contents

Foreword: 1978

I

THAT FABULOUS POLYMATH Samuel Johnson maintained that no man in his right mind ever read a book through from beginning to end. His own method was to glance rapidly through the pages, read only the parts that interested him, and skip all the rest.

This is one way of knowing a book, and for a clever reader it may suffice. But these days, many persons do not read a book but read of it, and usually from reviewers. Given the constraints of the media and the nature of the culture, this knowledge at one remove contains a peril. For one thing, even when a book has a complex argument, most reviewers, busy people they, sprint through a book seeking to catch a few lines to encapsulate the argument and to find a tag which can locate the author into the comfortable niches of the marketable vocabularies of conversation. Since the dominant bias in American culture is a liberal one, an argument that cuts across that liberalism makes some reviewers uncomfortable. And those whose work decries those aspects of contemporary culture which make cheap claims to "liberation," often find themselves labeled as "neo-conservative."

In its own terms, such a designation is meaningless, for it assumes that social views can be aligned along a single dimension. (What is ironic, in fact, is that those who decry the "one-dimensional" society, often hold such a one-dimensional view of politics.) In the larger historical context, the phrase makes no sense because the kind of cultural criticism I make—and I think of similar criticisms by Peter Berger and Philip Rieff—transcend the received categories of liberalism, and seek to treat the dilemmas of contemporary society within a very different framework.

Since an author's point of view is relevant to the understanding of his intentions, I think it not amiss to say that I am a socialist in economics, a liberal in politics, and a conservative in culture. Many persons might find this statement puzzling, assuming that if a person is a radical in one realm, he is a radical in all others; and, conversely, if he is a conservative in one realm, then he must be conservative in the others as well. Such an assumption misreads, both sociologically and morally, the nature of these different realms. I believe there is a consistency to my views which I hope to demonstrate in this Foreword. I will begin with the values I hold, and deal with the sociological distinctions in the following section.

About economics: the economic realm today is usually thought to be simply instrumental. One of the themes of this book is that capitalist society, in its emphasis on accumulation, has made that activity an end in itself. But no moral philosopher, from Aristotle and Aquinas, to John Locke and Adam Smith, divorced economics from a set of moral ends or held the production of wealth to be an end in itself; rather it was seen as a means to the realization of virtue, a means of leading a civilized life.

Modern economics has become a "positive science" in which the ends to be pursued are assumed to be individual and varied, and economics is only a science of "means," or of rational choice in the allocation of resources among competing individual ends. The price system, however, is only a *mechanism* for the relative allocation of goods and services within the framework of the kinds of demands generated. Yet these demands derive from the existing distribution of income. And moreover, what ultimately provides direction for the economy is the value system of the culture in which the economy is embedded. Economic policy can be efficacious as a means; but it can only be as *just* as the cultural value system that shapes it.

It is for that reason that I am a socialist in economics. For me, socialism is not statism, or the collective ownership of the means of production. It is a judgment on the priorities of economic policy. It is for that reason that I believe that *in this realm*, the community takes precedence over the individual in the values that legitimate economic policy. The first lien on the resources of a society therefore should be to establish that "social minimum" which would allow individuals to lead a life of self-respect, to be members of the community.[1] This

---

[1] The turning point in modern thought comes with Bentham. Bentham assumed that all men desired happiness, which he described simply as the maximizing of pleasure and the minimizing of pain. In practice this meant that whatever individuals defined as their own good was to be accepted as an "end" to be pursued. Adam Smith had written, besides *The Wealth of Nations*, a book entitled *The Theory of Moral Sentiments*, in which an "impartial spectator" represented the judgment of the community, which all right-thinking men would have to take into account. But for Bentham, in the *Introduction to the Principles of Morals and Legislation*, "the Community is a fictitious body" and the interest of the community is "the sum of the interests of the several members who compose it."

means a set of priorities that ensures work for those who seek it, a degree of adequate security against the hazards of the market, and adequate access to medical care and protection against the ravages of disease and illness.

I accept, and in this book reinterpret, the classical distinction between needs and wants. Needs are what all individuals have as members of the "species." Wants are the varied desires of individuals in accordance with their own tastes and idiosyncrasies. I believe that the first obligation of a society is to meet those essential needs; otherwise, individuals cannot be full "citizens" of the society. Admittedly, the word "needs" is ambiguous. Keynes once wrote: ". . . it is true that the needs of human beings may seem to be insatiable. But they fall into two classes—those needs which are absolute in the sense that we feel them whatever the situation of our fellow human beings may be, and those which are relative in the sense that we feel them only if their satisfaction lifts us above, makes us feel superior to, our fellows. Needs of the second class, those which satisfy the desire for superiority, may indeed be insatiable. . . . but this is not true of absolute needs.[2]

In this book, I pursue that difference through Aristotle's, and later, Thomas Aquinas's distinctions. As Aquinas pointed out, the desire for money knows no limits—which is why the Catholic Church placed restrictions on usury and the free setting of prices. But the needs represented in the form of food, clothing, shelter, and the like, have limits established by the capacities of the user.

Unwittingly, modern economics has established its own distinction between needs and wants: the concept of discretionary income. One part of a person's expenditure is relatively fixed—the amount necessary to meet one's self-defined basic (or, in Keynes's sense, absolute) needs. The other portion is variable: it can be postponed, used to satisfy different wants, and spent quite often in those pursuits that express the signs of status and the desires for superiority.

The social minimum I support is the amount of family income

Modern capitalist thought has accepted that argument to its own detriment, for a justification only or largely on the basis of individual interest is a weak moral argument. As my colleague Irving Kristol points out, economics is necessarily bound with normative considerations—the judgments whether the consequences of aggregated individual decisions are just and fair. No society can escape the necessity of making a reasoned judgment about what is proper and desirable, and of assessing the consequences of economic decisions in the light of those standards.

[2] J. M. Keynes, "Economic Possibilities for Our Grandchildren," in *Essays in Persuasion*, The Collected Works of J. M. Keynes, vol. IX (London: Macmillan, 1972), p. 326.

required to meet basic needs. And, since this is also a cultural definition, it will, understandably, change over time.[3] And I am a socialist, also, in that I do not believe wealth should be convertible into undue privilege in realms where it is not relevant. Thus it is unjust, I argue (see pp. 260ff), for wealth to command undue advantage in medical facilities, when these are social rights that should be available to all. In the realms of wealth, status, and power, there are principles of just allocation that are distinctive to each realm.

Yet I am a liberal in politics—defining both terms in the Kantian sense. I am a liberal in that, within the polity, I believe the individual should be the primary actor, not the group (be it family or corporation or church, or ethnic or minority group). And the polity, I believe, has to maintain the distinction between the public and the private, so that not all behavior is politicized, as in communist states, or left without restraint, as in the justification of laissez-faire in traditional capitalist societies.

The public realm operates under the rule of law which applies equally to all, and is therefore procedural: it does not specify outcomes between individuals; it treats people equally, rather than seeking to "make them" equal. The private realm—in morals and economics— is one where consenting parties make their own decisions, so long as the spillover effects (pornography in one instance, pollution in the other) do not upset the public realm.

I believe in the principle of individual achievement, rather than the inherited, or prescribed allocation of social positions. But I am not an egalitarian in the current, fashionable sense that the law should *make* persons equal—a situation which is not, in fact, equality but representation by numerical quota. One of the reasons that I distinguish between needs and wants is that I do not see how, in the economic realm, one can make incomes equal. The insistence on wage differentials—which is strongest among workers—reflects the moral intuition that differences in skill and effort should be rewarded differently. Once a social minimum is created, then what people do with the remainder of their money (subject to the principle of illegitimate convertibility), is their own business, just as what people do in the realm of morals is equally their own business, so long as it is done

[3] My colleague Lee Rainwater, in a number of empirical studies, has found that working-class individuals, in a wide variety of life settings and from diverse ethnic groups, when asked what it would take to give them a "decent" life, invariably converge on a common figure—about half the median income of the society. See Rainwater's *What Money Buys* (New York: Basic Books, 1976).

privately. And, if universalism prevails in social competition, then the criterion of merit, I believe, is a just principle to reward individual achievement in the society.

I am a conservative in culture because I respect tradition; I believe in reasoned judgments of good and bad about the qualities of a work of art; and I regard as necessary the principle of authority in the judging of the value of experience and art and education.

I use the term culture—as is evident in this book—to mean less than the anthropological catchall which defines any "patterned way of life" as a culture, and more than the aristocratic tradition which restricts culture to refinement and to the high arts. Culture, for me, is the effort to provide a coherent set of answers to the existential predicaments that confront all human beings in the passage of their lives. (See pp. 12–13.) For this reason, tradition becomes essential to the vitality of a culture, for it provides the continuity of memory that teaches how one's forebears met the same existential predicaments. (Which is why the psalmist says: "If I forget thee, o Jerusalem, let my right hand lose its cunning.")

The emphasis on judgment is necessary to fend off that indiscriminateness which regards all "meaningful" experience as good, and which insists that each group's "culture" is as valid as any other. The debasement of modernity is the emphasis on "*self*-expression," and the erasure of the distinction between art and life, so that the acting out of impulse, rather than the reflective discipline of the imagination becomes the touchstone of satisfaction. To have significance, a culture must transcend the present, because it is the recurrent confrontation with those root questions whose answers, through a set of symbols, provide a viable coherence to the meaning of existence. And since the appreciation of tradition in culture, and judgment in art (and a coherent curriculum in education) has to be learned, authority—in the form of scholarship, teaching, and skilled exegesis—is a necessary guide for the perplexed. And such authority can be earned only by study, not by speaking in tongues.

The triune positions I hold do have a consistency in that they unite a belief in the inclusion of all people into citizenship through that economic minimum which allows for self-respect, the principle of individual achievement of social position on the basis of merit, and the continuity of the past and present, in order to shape the future, as the necessary conditions of a civilized order.

II

In the broader sense, the theme of this book is not just the cultural contradictions of capitalism as such, but of bourgeois society: that new world created by the mercantile and fabricating guilds, the middle or bourgeois class that revolutionized modern society after the sixteenth century by making economic activity, rather than military or religious concerns, the central feature of society.

Capitalism is a socioeconomic system geared to the production of commodities by a rational calculus of cost and price, and to the consistent accumulation of capital for the purposes of reinvestment. But this singular new mode of operation was fused with a distinctive culture and character structure. In culture, this was the idea of self-realization, the release of the individual from traditional restraints and ascriptive ties (family and birth) so that he could "make" of himself what he willed. In character structure, this was the norm of self-control and delayed gratification, of purposeful behavior in the pursuit of well-defined goals. It is the interrelationship of this economic system, culture, and character structure which comprised bourgeois civilization. It is the unraveling of this unity and its consequences, which are the threads of this book.

I read the contradictions through two prisms: the first, a synthetic construct, is an "ideal type." It is "ahistorical" and treats the phenomena as a closed system. Thus it can be "hypothetical deductive" and specify the limits of the phenomena. Its virtue as an ideal type is the possibility of identifying the essential lineaments—what I call the axial principles and axial structures—of the circumscribed social realms which the flux of historical change sometimes obscures. Being static, however, the ideal type does not account for origins or future directions. For that, one needs the second prism of history and the detailed empirical complexity which is its content.

Using the ideal type, I see the contradictions of capitalism in the antagonistic principles that underlie the technical-economic, political, and cultural structures of the society. Now, the technical-economic realm, which became central in the beginning of capitalism, is, like all industrial society today, based on the axial principle of economizing: the effort to achieve efficiency through the breakdown of all activities into the smallest components of unit cost, as defined by the systems of financial accounting. The axial structure, based on specialization and hierarchy, is one of bureaucratic coordination. Necessarily, individuals are treated not as persons but as "things" (in the sociological jargon their behavior regulated by the role requirements), as instruments to maximize profit.[4] In short, individuals are dissolved into their function.

The political realm, which regulates conflict, is governed by the axial principle of equality: equality before the law, equal civil rights, and, most recently, the claims of equal social and economic rights. Because these claims become translated into entitlements, the political order increasingly intervenes in the economic and social realms (in the affairs of corporations, universities, and hospitals), in order to redress the positions and rewards generated in the society by the economic system. The axial structure of the polity is representation, and, more recently, participation. And the demands for participation, as a principle, now are carried over into all other realms of the society. The tensions between bureaucracy and equality frame the social conflicts of the day.

Finally, the cultural realm is one of self-expression and self-gratification. It is anti-institutional and antinomian in that the individual is taken to be the measure of satisfaction, and *his* feelings, sentiments, and judgments, not some objective standard of quality and value, determine the worth of cultural objects. At its most blatant, this sentiment asks of a poem, a play, or a painting, not whether it is good or meretricious, but "What does it do for *me*?" In this democratization of culture, every individual, understandably, seeks to realize his full "potential," and so the individual "self" comes increasingly into conflict with the role requirements of the technical-economic order.

A number of critics have objected to these formulations on the ground that "power" still lies primarily in the economic realm, principally in the hands of the large corporations, and that the impulses to self-expression in the culture have been "co-opted" by the capitalist system and converted into commodities, i.e., objects for sale.

---

[4] I use the word profit here in the specific economic sense of those gains that derive from productivity in the efficient use of resources, not in the sense of speculation or windfall gains arising, say, out of shortages or the exercise of a monopoly or cartel. To that extent, *any* economic system seeks profit, for its converse is waste. The sociological question asks what factors one takes into account in the calculus of profit. Until the last fifty years, capitalist enterprise tended to adopt a narrow calculus, and the social costs (from pollution to the effects of work on the health and safety of the worker) were borne by the workers or by society. But the situation is often no different in communist countries where the bureaucratic enterprise, in order to increase its own plants' funds (from which it builds houses or pays for vacations) will generate high social costs (e.g., the pollution of Lake Baikal by paper plants on the shore) in order to increase its profits.

Such questions are empirical ones that test particular assumptions, not whether this mode of analysis, i.e., the idea of the disjunction between the realms, is useful or not. The answers lie in the court of history, and I shall return to them at the close of my historical exposition, the second thread of my analysis.

III

Much of the prevailing view of capitalism (that of the last thirty years) was shaped by Max Weber through his emphasis on Calvinism and the Protestant ethic—the role of methodical work and the legitimation of the pursuit of wealth—as the doctrines that facilitated the rise of the distinctive Western organization of rational production and exchange. But the origins of capitalism were twofold. If one source was the *asceticism* which Weber emphasized, the other was *acquisitiveness*, a central theme of Werner Sombart whose work was almost completely neglected in that period of time.[5]

To emphasize the diversity of origins, Sombart in his *Der Bourgeois*, identifies six fundamental types of "capitalist undertakers":

---

[5] Sombart's main works were the extensive three volumes, *Der Moderne Kapitalismus* (the first two appeared in 1916–17, the concluding volume ten years later in 1927), and a series of earlier volumes on the Jews and capitalism, luxury and capitalism, war and capitalism, and the capstone of that series, *Der Bourgeois*, published in 1913.

The dramatic eclipse of Sombart's reputation is probably due to two reasons. Before World War I, Sombart was highly sympathetic to socialism and produced a number of works which won him a high reputation, beginning with his first major book, *Sozialismus und soziale Bewegung*, in 1896, which was translated into more than twenty languages. (His book on the United States, *Warum gibt es kein Sozialismus in de Vereingten Staaten*, published in 1904, became a standard explanation for the failure of socialist ideas to take root in the U.S.) After World War I, however, Sombart turned against Marxism, and, in 1934, vaguely embraced National Socialism in the book, *Deutscher Sozialismus* (translated as *A New Social Philosophy*) continuing with other works that espoused a cloudy, spiritual view of man, until his death in 1941.

The second reason, theoretical rather than political, is that Sombart's work on capitalism, while extraordinarily rich and diverse—he assembled more material on the subject than probably any other writer—is, in the end, an *olla podrida* in which a number of indigestible elements were combined in the thick stew, and no clear-cut causal connections ever clearly emerged. At different times, Sombart sought to emphasize the importance of one social group or another (e.g., the Jews or the Florentines), or one social fact or another (e.g., the new supply of precious metals, or technology), yet underneath all these was an underlying emphasis on the impulse of acquisitiveness.

There is no complete translation of *Der Moderne Kapitalismus*, though a free-hand version was done by Frederick L. Nussbaum, as *A History of the Economic Institutions of Modern Europe: An Introduction to Der Moderne Kapitalismus of Werner Sombart* (New York, F. S. Crofts, 1933). *Der Bourgeois* was translated and edited by M. Epstein under the title *The Quintessence of Capitalism: A study of the history* the Freebooters (the "ruthless sea-dogs who abounded . . . in England in the sixteenth century"); the Landlord (e.g., the capitalist farmers who turned to mining and the creation of iron works, as in France in the early eighteenth century); the Civil Servant (promoters of enterprise, such as Colbert, in France); the Speculators (such as the men behind the South Sea company, which took over the nation debt in England for overseas investment); the Trader (originally middlemen, they became entrepreneurs); and the Craftsman, or *fabricant*, who became manufacturers.

Sombart located the main areas of capitalist undertaking not in the Protestant countries, such as Holland, England, or the United States, but in the Florentine world, and he argued that the same kind of prudential bourgeois maxims associated with Benjamin Franklin (who in personal life was a *bon viveur*) could be found several hundred years earlier in the writings of Leon Batista Alberti, whose book *Del governo della famiglia* was a classic in its time, and whose views of middle-class virtues, the proper coordination of actions and the profitable employment of time, were adopted by large numbers of bourgeois entrepreneurs and *commercants* in Italy and France.[6]

---

and psychology of the modern business man (New York: E. P. Dutton & Co., 1915). Curiously, nowhere does the book state that it is a translation of *Der Bourgeois*. The fact that it was issued in London during the war may account for the lack of reference to a German edition. The most succinct statement of Sombart's views can be found in his article on "Capitalism," in *The Encyclopedia of the Social Sciences* (New York: The Macmillan Co., 1930) vol. 3, pp. 195–208.

[6] *The Quintessence of Capitalism*, pp. 104–113. For a discussion of Alberti as one of the key figures in establishing a rational esthetic of space and time, see pp. 108–111 in this volume.

Interesting support for the argument that the origins of capitalism are to be located in Catholic Italy, and that the Counter-Reformation, not the Protestant ethic, was responsible for the "trans-location" of capitalism has been offered recently by Hugh Trevor-Roper, *Religion, the Reformation and Social Change, and Other Essays* (London: Macmillan, 1967), pp. 23, 27–28. He writes:

For Marx, Weber, Sombart, who regarded medieval Europe as non-capitalist, the problem was to discover why capitalism was created in the sixteenth century. For us, who believe that Catholic Europe, at least up to the Reformation, was perfectly able to create a capitalist economy, the question is, why, in the sixteenth century, did so many essential agents of such an economy—not only entrepreneurs, but also workers—leave the old centers, predominantly in Catholic lands, and migrate to new centers, predominantly in Protestant lands. . . . They were expelled. And they were expelled for religion. . . .

It was not that Calvinism created a new type of man, who in turn created capitalism; it was rather that the old economic elites of Europe were driven into heresy because the attitude of mind which had been theirs for generations, was suddenly, and in some places, declared heretical and intolerable. . . .

For always we come back to this: the Calvinist and for that matter the Jewish entrepreneurs of northern Europe were not a native growth; they were an old growth transplanted.

Whatever the exact locations of early capitalism, it is clear that, from the start, the two impulses of asceticism and acquisitiveness were yoked together. One was the bourgeois prudential spirit of calculation; the other, the restless Faustian drive which, as expressed in the modern economy and technology, took as its motto "the endless frontier," and, as its goal, the complete transformation of nature. The intertwining of the two impulses shaped the modern conception of rationality. The tension between the two imposed a moral restraint on the sumptuary display that had characterized earlier periods of conquest. What is also evident—and it is one of the arguments in this book— is that the ascetic element, and with it one kind of moral legitimation of capitalist behavior, has virtually disappeared.

On the level of philosophical justification, the major attack on asceticism was mounted by Jeremy Bentham, who argued that asceticism ("miseries" inflicted by sectarians on unwilling others) violated the "natural" hedonism which rules men—the search for pleasure and the avoidance of pain. Its "mischief" is that, whatever its pure intention, asceticism leads to "despotism" over men. The principle of utility alone could serve as the regulating instrument of men's search to satisfy their diverse ends. Thus the notion of common ends was dissolved into individual preferences.

On the plane of history, the "economic impulse" has been constrained earlier by the rules of custom and tradition, to some extent by the Catholic moral principle of the just price, and later by the Puritan emphasis on frugality. As the religious impulses diminished, a complex history in its own right, so did the restraints. What became distinctive about capitalism—its very dynamic—was its boundlessness. Propelled by the dynamo of technology, there were to be no asymptotes to its exponential growth. No limits. Nothing was sacred. Change became the norm. By the middle of the nineteenth century, this was the trajectory of the economic impulse. It was, as well, the trajectory of the culture.

IV

The realm of culture is the realm of meanings, the effort in some imaginative form to make sense of the world through the expressiveness of art and ritual, particularly those "incomprehensions" such as tragedy and death that arise out of the existential predicaments which every self-conscious human being must confront at some point in his life. In these encounters, one becomes aware of the fundamental questions—what Goethe called *Urphänomen*—which frame all others. Religion, as the oldest effort to comprehend these "mysteries," has historically been the source of cultural symbols.

If science is the search for the unity of nature, religion has been the quest for the unity of culture in the different historical periods of civilizations. To close that circle, religion has woven tradition as the fabric of meaning and guarded the portals of culture by rejecting those works of art which threatened the moral norms of religion.

The modern movement disrupts that unity. It does so in three ways: by insisting on the autonomy of the aesthetic from moral norms; by valuing more highly the new and experimental; and by taking the self (in its quest for originality and uniqueness) as the touchstone of cultural judgment.

The most aggressive outrider of the movement is the self-proclaimed *avant-garde* which calls itself Modernism. The discussion of Modernism (see pp. 46–52, and Chapters 2 and 3) is the inner thread of this book, for I see Modernism as the agency for the dissolution of the bourgeois world view and, in the past half-century, as gaining hegemony in the culture.

The difficulties of defining Modernism are notorious. Schematically, I would specify three different dimensions:

1. Thematically Modernism has been a rage against order, and in particular, bourgeois orderliness. The emphasis is on the self, and the unceasing search for experience. If Terence once said, "Nothing human is alien to me," the Modernist could say with equal fervor, "Nothing inhuman is alien to me." Rationalism is seen as devitalizing; the surge to creativity is propelled by an exploration of the demonic. In that exploration, one cannot set aesthetic limits (or even moral norms) to this protean reach of the imagination. The crucial insistence is that experience is to have no boundaries to its cravings, that there be "nothing sacred."[7]

2. Stylistically, there is a common syntax in what I have called "the eclipse of distance." This is the effort to achieve immediacy, impact, simultaneity, and sensation by eliminating aesthetic and psychic distance. In diminishing aesthetic distance, one annihilates contemplation and envelops the spectator in the experience. By eliminating psychic distance, one emphasizes (in Freudian terms) the "primary process" of dream and hallucination, of instinct and impulse. In all this, Modern-

[7] I have elaborated this argument through an examination of major literary works in the nineteenth and twentieth centuries, in an essay, "Beyond Modernism, Beyond Self," in *Art, Politics and Will: Essays in Honor of Lionel Trilling*, edited by Quentin Anderson, Stephen Donadio, and Steven Marcus (New York: Basic Books, 1977).

ism rejects the "rational cosmology" that was introduced into the arts during the Renaissance and codified by Alberti: of foreground and background in pictorial space; of beginning, middle, and end, or sequence, in time; and the distinction of genres and the modes of work appropriate to each genre. This eclipse of distance, as a formal syntax, cuts across all the arts: in literature, the "stream of consciousness"; in painting, the elimination of the "interior distance" within the canvas"; in music, the upset of the balance of melody and harmony; in poetry, the disruption of the ordered meter. In the broadest sense, this common syntax repudiates mimesis as a principle of art.[8]

3. The preoccupation with the medium. In all periods of cultural history, artists have been conscious of the nature and complexity of the medium as a formal problem in transmuting the "pre-figured" into the "figured" result. In the last twenty-five years, we have seen a preoccupation not with the content or form (i.e., style and genre), but with the medium of art itself: with the actual texture of paint and materials in painting, with the abstract "sounds" in music, with phonology or even "breath" in poetry, and with the abstract properties of language in literature—often to the exclusion of anything else. Thus it is the encaustic surface, not the image, that generates excitement in the paintings of Jasper Johns; the aleatory or chance factors in the music of John Cage; the aspirate rather than the syllable, as a measure of line in poetry of Robert Creeley—all of these as expressions of the self, rather than formal explorations of the limits and nature of the medium itself.

Modernism has, beyond dispute, been responsible for one of the great surges of creativity in Western culture. The period from 1850 to 1930 probably saw more varied experiments in literature, poetry, music, and painting—if not more great masterpieces—than any previous period we have known. Much of this arose out of the creative tension of culture, with its adversary stance, against the bourgeois social structure. Yet there has been a price. One cost has been the loss of coherence in culture, particularly in the spread of an antinomian attitude to moral norms and even to the idea of cultural judgment itself. The greater price was exacted when the distinction between art and life became blurred so that what was once permitted

---

[8] Clearly not all Modernist writers are "anti-bourgeois" in any overt sense. T. S. Eliot was a High-Church Anglican and William Faulkner a traditionalist in his Southern politics. Yet both men were great "experimenters" in poetry and in the novel. Despite their specific political or cultural *beliefs*, one of the effects of their "modernist styles" was to disrupt the "rational cosmology" which underlay the bourgeois world view of an ordered relationship of space and time. (See pp. 108–119.)

in the *imagination* (the novels of murder, lust, perversity) has often passed over into *fantasy*, and is acted out by individuals who want to make their "lives" a work of art, and when, with the "democratization" of criticism, the touchstone of judgment is no longer some consensual agreement on standards, but each "self's" judgment as to how art enhances that "self."

Changes in culture interact with a social structure in complicated ways. Where there is a patronage system, the patron—be it prince, or church, or state—commissions a work of art, and the cultural needs of the institution, such as the Church, or the tastes of the prince, or the demands for glorification by the State, will shape the regnant style of the time. But where art is bought and sold, the market is where culture and social structure cross. One would expect that where culture has become a "commodity" the bourgeois taste would prevail. But in extraordinary historical fact, this has not been the case.

The phrase "cultural hegemony"—identified with the Italian Marxist Antonio Gramsci—signifies the dominance of a single group in shaping the prevailing world view which gives a people an interpretation of the age. There have been many times where a single world view, growing out of and serving a dominant class, has prevailed. In the twelfth century—the "Age of Faith" symbolized by Innocent III —we see the apotheosis of Church control over society not in the uniformity of devotion, but, as Bryan Wilson has put it, "because the imprint of faith and order demanded by ecclesiastical authority dominated the social framework." The closest analogue today—in the regulation of daily life, the heavy-handed control of production and distribution, and the restraint of impulse and the glorification of authority—is the Soviet world, where the Party exercises complete cultural hegemony. It is an ideologicaly prescribed social order.

Marxists have assumed that under capitalism there has also been a single cultural hegemony—the ideas of the "ruling class." Yet the astonishing fact is that in the last hundred years, if there has been a dominant influence—in the high culture at least—it has been the avowed enemy of that class, Modernism.

At the start, the capitalist economic impulse and the cultural drive of modernity shared a common source, the ideas of liberty and liberation, whose embodiments were "rugged individualism" in economic affairs and the "unrestrained self" in culture. Though the two had a common origin in the repudiation of tradition and the authority of the past, an adversary relation between them quickly developed. One can say, as Freud would, that the discipline required by work was threatened by the libidinal energies diverted to culture. This may perhaps be true, but it is abstract. What would seem to be the more likely historical explanation is that the bourgeois attitudes of calculation and methodical restraint came into conflict with the impulsive searchings for sensation and excitement that one found in Romanticism, and which passed over into Modernism. The antagonism deepened as the organization of work and production became bureaucratized and individuals were reduced to roles, so that the norms of the workplace were increasingly at variance with the emphasis on self-exploration and self-gratification. The thread connecting Blake to Byron to Baudelaire—who is the avatar of Modernism—may not be literal, but it is a figurative symbolic lineage.

So long as work and wealth had a religious sanction, they possessed a transcendental justification. But when that ethic eroded, there was a loss of legitimation, for the pursuit of wealth alone is not a calling that justifies itself. As Schumpeter once shrewdly remarked: The stock exchange is a poor substitute for the Holy Grail.

The central point is that—at first, for the advanced social groups, the intelligentsia and the educated social classes, and later for the middle class itself—*the legitimations of social behavior passed from religion to modernist culture.* And with it here was a shift in emphasis from "character," which is the unity of moral codes and disciplined purpose, to an emphasis on "personality," which is the enhancement of self through the compulsive search for individual differentiation. In brief, not work but the "life style" became the source of satisfaction and criterion for desirable behavior in the society.

Yet paradoxically, the life style that became the imago of the free self was not that of the businessman, expressing himself through his "dynamic drive," but that of the artist defying the conventions of the society. And, as I have tried to show (see pp. 38–41), increasingly, it is the artist who begins to dominate the audience, and to impose his judgment as to what is to be desired and bought. The paradox is completed when the bourgeois ethic, having collapsed in the society, finds few defenders in the culture (do any writers defend *any* institutions?) and Modernism as an attack on orthodoxy, has triumphed and become the regnant orthodoxy of the day.

V

Any tension creates its own dialectic. Since the market is where social structure and culture cross, what has happened is that in the last fifty years the economy has been geared to producing the life styles paraded by the culture. Thus, not only has there been a contradiction *between* the realms, but that tension has produced a further contradiction *within* the economic realm itself. In the world of capitalist enterprise, the nominal ethos in the spheres of production and organization is still one of work, delayed gratification, career orientation, devotion to the enterprise. Yet, on the marketing side, the sale of goods, packaged in the glossy images of glamour and sex, promotes a hedonistic way of life whose promise is the voluptuous gratification of the lineaments of desire. The consequence of this contradiction, as I put it in these pages, is that a corporation finds its people being straight by day and swingers by night.

What has happened in society in the last fifty years—as a result of the erosion of the religious ethic and the increase in discretionary income—*is that the culture has taken the initiative in promoting change*, and the economy has been geared to meeting these new wants.

In this respect, there has been a significant reversal in the historical pattern of social change. During the rise of capitalism—in the "modernization" of any traditional society—one could more readily change the economic structure of a society: by forcing people off the land into factories, by imposing a new rhythm and discipline of work, by using brutal means or incentives (e.g., the theory of interest as the reward for "abstinence" from consumption) to raise capital. But the "superstructure"—the patterns of family life, the attachments to religion and authority, the received ideas that shaped people's perceptions of a social reality—was more stubbornly resistant to change.

Today, by contrast, it is the economic structure that is the more difficult to change. Within the enterprise, the heavy bureaucratic layers reduce flexible adaptation, while union rules inhibit the power of management to control the assignment of jobs. In the society, the economic enterprise is subject to the challenges of various veto groups (e.g., on the location of plants or the use of the environment) and subject more and more to regulation by government.

But in the culture, fantasy reigns almost unconstrained. The media are geared to feeding new images to people, to unsettling traditional conventions, and the highlighting of aberrant and quirky behavior which becomes imagos for other to imitate. The traditional is stodgy, and the "orthodox" institutions such as family and church are on the defensive about their inability to change.

Yet if capitalism has been routinized, Modernism has been trivialized. After all, how often can it continue to shock, if there is nothing shocking left? If experiment is the norm, how original can anything new be? And like all bad history, Modernism has repeated its end, once in the popgun outbursts of Futurism and Dadaism, the second time in the phosphorescent parodies of Pop paintings and the mindless minimalism of conceptual art. The exclamation points that end each sentence of the Manifestoes have simply become four dots that trail away in the tedium of endless repetition. And what is there in the end. As Beckett summed it up in his sad dialogue: [9]

Vladimir: Say you are, even if it's not true.
Estragon: What am I to say?
Vladimir: Say, I am happy.
Estragon: I am happy.
Vladimir: So am I.
Estragon: So am I.
Vladimir: We are happy.
Estragon: We are happy. (Silence.) What do we do now, now that we are happy.
Vladimir: Wait for Godot.

In the revelation of wisdom, the Owl of Minerva flies at dusk because life had become gray on gray. In the victorious apocalypse of Modernism, the dawn is a series of gaudy colors whirling in strobismic light. Today, Modernism has become not the work of serious artists but the property of the *culturati*, the "cultural mass" (see p. 20), the distribution sector of cultural production, for whom the shock of the old has become the chic of the new. The *culturati* have carried over, in rhetoric, the adversary stance against bourgeois orderliness and sobriety, yet they impose a conformity of their own on those who deviate from its guarded canons.

In the 1960s, one beheld the "new" phenomenon of the counter-culture. Yet the very name was a conceit. The "adversary culture" was concerned with art, the use of the imagination to transfigure recalcitrant memory or intractible materials into a *work* that could, in its power, transcend its time. It existed in the realm of culture. The so-called counter-culture was a children's crusade that sought to

[9] Samuel Beckett, *Waiting for Godot* (New York: Grove Press, 1954) p. 39. Reprinted by permission.

eliminate the line between fantasy and reality and act out in life its impulses under a banner of liberation. It claimed to mock bourgeois prudishness, when it was only flaunting the closet behavior of its liberal parents. It claimed to be new and daring when it was only repeating in more raucous form—its rock noise amplified in the electronic echo-chamber of the mass media—the youthful japes of a Greenwich Village bohemia of a half century before. It was less a counter-culture than a counterfeit culture.

In this double contradiction of capitalism, what has been established in the last thirty years has been the tawdry rule of fad and fashion: of "multiples" for the *culturati*, hedonism for the middle classes, and pornotopia for the masses. And in the very nature of fashion, it has trivialized the culture.

VI

Has Modernism been "co-opted," as Herbert Marcuse suggests? In one dimension, yes. It has been converted into a commodity for promotion and profit. But in the deeper transformations of structure, that process can only undermine the foundations of capitalism itself. The sociological truism is that a societal order is shored up by its legitimations, which provide the defenses against its despisers. But the legitimation of the culture, as I have argued, is the quest for self-gratification and the expression of "personality." It attacks established orthodoxy in the name of personal autonomy and heterodoxy. Yet what modern culture has failed to understand is that Orthodoxy is not the guardian of an existent order, but is itself a judgment on the adequacy and moral character of beliefs, from the standpoint of "right reason." The paradox is that "heterodoxy" itself has become conformist in liberal circles, and exercises that conformity under the banner of an antinomian flag. It is a prescription, in its confusions, for the dissolution of a shared moral order.

Does power still lie in the economic realm, and largely in the hands of the giant corporations? To a considerable extent this is still so in Western society, yet such an argument misreads the nature of societal change today. A capitalist order had historical strength when it fused property with power through a set of ruling families to maintain the continuity of the system. The first deep, internal structural change in capitalism was the divorce of family and property from managerial power and the loss of continuity through the chain of elites. Economic power today lies in *institutions* whose chiefs cannot pass along their power to their heirs and who, increasingly—since property is not private (but corporate), and technical skill, not property, is the basis of managerial positions—-no longer have the traditional natural rights, justifications, and legitimacy in the exercise of that power, and feel it keenly.[10] The larger fact is that a modern society multiplies the number of constituencies and, given the increasing interdependence of economic and social effects, the political order becomes the place where power is wielded in order to manage the *systemic* problems arising out of that interdependence and the increasing competition of other, state-directed economies. The major consequence, as I argue in the section on "The Public Household" (p. 227 et seq.), is the expansion of State power, and the fact that the State budget, not the division of profits within the enterprise, becomes the major arbiter of economic decisions (including the formation of capital), and that competition not between capitalist and workers, but between the multiple constituencies (where corporations still exercise a large degree of influence) is the mode of allocating power in the society.

VII

A final word on religion, which for me is the fulcrum of the book. I do not (*pace* Durkheim) see religion as a "functional necessity" for society, or that without religion a society will dissolve. I do not believe in religion as a patch for the unraveled seams of society. Nor do societies "dissolve," though in periods of extreme crises (like times of war) the loss of legitimation may sap the will to resist. Religions cannot be manufactured. Worse, if they were, the results would be spurious and soon vanish in the next whirl of fashion.

As Max Weber bitingly observed more than a half century ago:

The need of literary, academic, or cafe-society intellectuals to include religious feelings in the inventory of their sources of impressions and sensations, and among the topics for discussion, has never yet given rise to a new religion. Nor can a religious renascence be generated by the need of authors to compose books, or by the far more effective need of clever publishers to sell such books. No matter how much the appearance of a widespread religious interest may be stimulated, no religion has ever re-

---

[10] For an extended discussion of that change, see my essay, "The Break-up of Family Capitalism," in my book, *The End of Ideology* (Glencoe, Il.: The Free Press, 1960).

sulted from the needs of intellectuals or from their chatter. The whirlgig of fashion will presently remove this subject of conversation and journalism, which fashion has made popular.[11]

Religions grow out of the deepest needs of individuals sharing a common awakening, and are not created by "engineers of the soul."

My concern with religion goes back to what I assume is the constitutive character of culture: the wheel of questions that brings one back to the existential predicaments, the awareness in men of their finiteness and the inexorable limits to their power (the transgression of which is *hamartia*), and the consequent effort to find a coherent answer to reconcile them to the human condition. Since that awareness touches the deepest springs of consciousness, I believe that a culture which has become aware of the limits in exploring the mundane will turn, at some point, to the effort to recover the sacred.[12]

We stand, I believe, with a clearing ahead of us. The exhaustion of Modernism, the aridity of Communist life, the tedium of the unrestrained self, and the meaninglessness of the monolithic political chants, all indicate that a long era is coming to a slow close. The impulse of Modernism was to leap beyond: beyond nature, beyond culture, beyond tragedy—to explore the *apeiron*, the boundless, driven by the self-infinitizing spirit of the radical self.

We are groping for a new vocabulary whose keyword seems to be limits: a limit to growth, a limit to the spoliation of the environment, a limit to arms, a limit to the tampering with biological nature. Yet if we seek to establish a set of limits in the economy and technology, will we also set a limit to the exploration of those cultural experiences which go beyond moral norms and embrace the demonic in the delusion that all experience is "creative"? Can we set a limit to *hubris*? The answer to that question could resolve the *cultural* contradiction of capitalism and its deceptive double, *semblable et frère*, the culture of modernity. It would leave only the economic and political mundane to be tamed.

DANIEL BELL
January, 1978
Cambridge, Massachusetts

[11] *The Sociology of Religion*, translated by Ephraim Fischoff (Boston: Beacon Press, 1963), p. 137.

[12] This is the theme of my Hobhouse Lecture, given at the London School of Economics, May 19, 1977, as "The Return of the Sacred: the Argument on the Future of Religion," and printed in the *British Journal of Sociology*, December 1977.

Preface

THIS BOOK stands in a dialectical relation to my previous book, *The Coming of Post-Industrial Society*. In that volume, I sought to show how technology (including intellectual technology) and the codification of theoretical knowledge as a new principle for innovation and policy were reshaping the techno-economic order, and with it, the stratification system of the society as well. In these essays, I deal with culture, especially the idea of modernity, and with the problems of managing a complex polity when the values of the society stress unrestrained appetite. The contradictions I see in contemporary capitalism derive from the unraveling of the threads which had once held the culture and the economy together, and from the influence of the hedonism which has become the prevailing value in our society.

As in the previous volume, I also have a more formal theoretical intention. Almost all of contemporary social science thinks of society as some unified "system," organized around some single major principle (for Marx, it is property relations; for Talcott Parsons, it is a dominant value, such as achievement) which seeks to "reproduce" itself through the dominant institutions. It is my belief, on the other hand, that one can best analyze modern society by thinking of it as an uneasy amalgam of three distinct realms: the social structure (principally the techno-economic order), the polity, and the culture. The idea of post-industrialism, I argued, is limited specifically to changes in the techno-economic order. But changes in the social structure do not *determine* either the polity or the culture. If anything, in most instances in the contemporary world, it is the political order which has become the true control system of the society.

The argument elaborated in this book is that the three realms— the economy, the polity, and the culture—are ruled by contrary axial principles: for the economy, efficiency; for the polity, equality; and for the culture, self-realization (or self-gratification). The resulting disjunctions have framed the tensions and social conflicts of Western society in the past 150 years.

The chapters in this book were drawn originally from a larger manuscript whose very size and detail made the argument unwieldy and cumbersome. Though published at different times, they have been drawn from a common fount, and have been rewritten now to make a coherent statement on the interrelated economic and cultural crises of bourgeois society and the exhaustion of cultural modernism.

This volume sets the general ground of the argument. In the next years, I hope to publish a number of other volumes developing the themes and sketching a more formal theoretical structure.

Any book—mine at least—is a dialogue, or sometimes a debate, with one's friends. This is especially true of the present volume. My preoccupation with modernism as the central feature of cultural life took shape in a sometimes sustained, sometimes intermittent, yet continuing, dialogue and debate with Steven Marcus. For a number of years we taught a seminar together at Columbia College on literature and society, each year exploring a different aspect of modernity. In those seminars, and in the discussions which spilled over from them, I learned a great deal from Marcus. The fact that he would probably reject my formulations about culture, and the conservative conclusions to be drawn from them, does not reduce my intellectual and personal debt to him. The themes that are elaborated in the last essay, "The Public Household," which is an effort to affirm liberalism as a political philosophy, derive in equal measure from a continuing dialogue and debate with my friend Irving Kristol. The fact that he would reject, if not my formulations, my liberal conclusions on social policy, in no way qualifies my thanks to him.

One profits from a milieu, and I have been fortunate in the responses of friends with whom I have taken up some of these issues: Diana Trilling, for her observations on the liberal culture; Irving Howe, for many exchanges on modernism; S. M. Lipset, for his thoughts on intellectuals; Robert Heilbroner, for our summer talks on technology; Robert M. Solow, for his lucid pedagogy on economic questions. Needless to say, none of them bears responsibility for the way I have used their responses.

I am grateful to Midge Decter, my editor at Basic Books, who sharpened the argument by her close reading of the text.

My original institutional debt is to the Russell Sage Foundation. In a sabbatical year there, as a Visiting Fellow in 1969–1970, I began the large manuscript from which much of this material has been drawn. This book, like my previous one, represents a discharge of that debt. I also wish to thank the Aspen Institute for Humanistic Studies for its hospitality in July 1974 when, as a scholar-in-residence at Aspen, I was able to write the essay, "The Public Household." The National Endowment for the Humanities has given S. M. Lipset and myself a grant to begin a comparative study of intellectuals in four countries; I have drawn on the working papers prepared for that study to reformulate some of the conceptions in the essays in Part One of this book. I also give thanks for the help, under enormous pressure, of my secretary, Mrs. Sara Hazel, in typing the larger portions of this manuscript.

What pleases me most is that I have a book—its themes not only intellectual but also personal, its emphasis not only sociological but also humanistic—that I can give to my wife, Pearl. Her gifted literary criticism strikes a note of sanity in a discordant world and sets a standard I have tried to meet.

Acknowledgments

THE CHAPTERS in this book have been rewritten from earlier drafts to provide a continuity of theme and argument.

The first essay, "The Cultural Contradictions of Capitalism," was drawn from a larger manuscript written in the winter of 1969–1970. A section of that draft, using that title, appeared in *The Public Interest*, Fall 1970. Another section, which is incorporated in the present chapter, was read at an Arden House conference of the Columbia University School of Business and the Institute of Life Insurance, and published, in part, as "American Culture and the Concept of Change," in the small book *Change or Revolution* (1971), edited by Edward Sullivan.

The second essay, "The Disjunctions of Cultural Discourse," draws freely from three inter-related essays, with additional material: "The Eclipse of Distance," *Encounter*, May 1963; "Modernity and Mass Society," in *Studies in Public Communication*, University of Chicago, Summer 1961; and "The Disjunction of Culture and Social Structure," *Daedalus*, Winter 1965.

The third essay, "The Sensibility of the Sixties," was drawn from the larger manuscript written in 1969–1970, and appeared under the title "Sensibility in the Sixties," in *Commentary*, June 1971.

"Toward the Great Instauration: Religion and Culture in a Post-Industrial Age" was given as the keynote lecture of a symposium on ethics and technology, celebrating the fiftieth anniversary of the Haifa Technicon, in Haifa, Israel, December 1974. It was published in *Social Research*, Fall 1975. The present chapter is a revised version of that lecture.

The first section of the fifth essay, "Unstable America: Transitory and Permanent Factors in a National Crisis," was published under the title "Unstable America" in *Encounter*, June 1970; the second part is drawn from a larger paper, "The Next Twenty-five Years," written in the spring of 1974 for a conference of the CIBA Foundation in London.

"The Public Household," in a somewhat shorter form, initially appeared in *The Public Interest*, Fall 1974.

THE
CULTURAL
CONTRADICTIONS
OF
CAPITALISM

Introduction /
The Disjunction
of Realms:
A Statement of Themes

IN THE SPRING of 1888, Friedrich Nietzsche sketched the Preface of his last book, *The Will to Power*, which he planned to be his magnum opus, as follows:

> What I relate is the history of the next two centuries. I describe what is coming, what can no longer come differently: *the advent of nihilism*. This history can be related even now; for necessity itself is at work here. This future speaks even now in a hundred signs. . . . For some time now our whole European culture has been moving as toward a catastrophe, with a tortured tension that is growing from decade to decade: restlessly, violently, headlong, like a river that wants to reach the end, that no longer reflects, that is afraid to reflect.[1]

The source of this nihilism for Nietzsche was rationalism and calculation, a temper of life whose intention was to destroy "unreflective spontaneity." If there was a single symbol for him which summed up the force of nihilism, it was modern science.[2]

[1] Friedrich Nietzsche, *The Will to Power*, ed. Walter Kaufmann (New York: Random House, 1967), p. 3. Italics in the original.

[2] This is the theme, too, but in a positive sense, of Bazarov, the character of Turgenev's who proclaimed himself the first nihilist. The source of nihilism for him was the "skeptical conscience of modern Science . . . whose watchword is *Reality*, and not negation." The characterization is Edward Garnett's, in his 1895 introduction to *Fathers and Children*. Garnett writes: "What, then, is Bazarov? . . . Representing the creed which has produced the militant type of Revolutionist in every capital of Europe, *he is the bare mind of Science first applied to Politics*. His own

For Nietzsche, what had happened was that tradition, the unwitting, unquestioning "means for obtaining homogeneous, enduring characters for long generations," had been destroyed. Instead, "we have [now] reached the opposite point; indeed, we wanted to reach it: the most extreme consciousness, man's ability to see through himself and history." The organic ties to the soil, "the inalienability of property," had been ruptured, and in their place had come a commercial civilization. Nietzsche speaks of the disorganizing principles of the time: "newspapers (in place of daily prayers), the railway, the telegraph, the centralization of a tremendous number of different interests in a single soul, which for that reason must be very strong and protean."[3]

This theme is foreshadowed in Nietzsche's first book, *The Birth of Tragedy*, written in 1870–1871, when he was 26 years old. His great demon, that monster of consciousness, is Socrates, the "despotic logician," whose "great Cyclops eye" never "glowed with the artists's divine frenzy," whose "voice always spoke to *dissuade*." Socrates begins the devitalization of culture by introducing distance and questioning, the skepticism of knowledge that is gained by intoxication and dream. Socrates is "the great exemplar of . . . *theoretical man*," who has "the insatiable zest for knowledge" and who "finds his highest satisfaction in the unveiling process itself, which proves to him his own power."[4]

Nihilism, then, is the end process of rationalism. It is man's self-conscious will to destroy his past and control his future. It is modernity at its *extreme*. Although at bottom it is a metaphysical condition, nihilism pervades all of society, and in the end must destroy itself.[5]

---

immediate origin is German Science interpreted by that spirit of logical intensity, Russian fanaticism, or devotion to the Idea, which is perhaps the distinguishing genius of the Slav. . . . Inasmuch as the early work of the pure scientific spirit, knowing itself to be fettered by the superstitions, the confusions, the sentimentalities of the Past, was necessarily destructive, Bazarov's primary duty was to Destroy." See *Fathers and Children* (London: Heinemann, 1951), p. 10.

[3] Op. cit., p. 44.

[4] *The Birth of Tragedy*, trans. Francis Golffing (Garden City, N.Y.: Doubleday Anchor, 1956). The phrases quoted here occur on pp. 84, 92, 95. All italics in the original.

[5] Compare, however, the change of mood between the two books in envisaging the end of science and modernity. In *The Birth of Tragedy*, Nietzsche writes: "The fact that the dialectical drive toward knowledge and scientific optimism has succeeded in turning tragedy from its course suggests that there may be an eternal conflict between the theoretical and the tragic world view, in which case tragedy could be reborn only when science had at last been pushed to its limits and, faced with those

There is a second, very different view of nihilism which one finds in historic Western religion, and which is expressed in contemporary literature by Joseph Conrad, who began writing at the time Nietzsche went mad. It is the idea that civilization is a thin coating of protection against the anarchic impulses and atavistic roots of life which lurk just below the surface of existence and which constantly press to burst out. For Nietzsche, it is the will to power which is the road to salvation; for Conrad, it is the will to power which threatens civilization.

"In Conrad's view," writes Hillis Miller, "civilization is the metamorphosis of darkness into light. It is a process of transforming everything unknown, irrational, or indistinct into clear forms, named and ordered, given a meaning and use by man." Civilization has two dimensions. "To be safe, civilized man must have a blind devotion to immediate practical tasks, a devotion which recalls the Victorian cult of work. For Conrad as for Carlyle work is protection against unwholesome doubt or neurotic paralysis of will." And second is the idea of fidelity, a necessary trust in others. Civilization, for Conrad, "is at once a social ideal and an ideal of personal life. The ideal society is imagined in the relation among men on board a well-ordered ship: a hierarchical structure, with those at the bottom owing obedience to those above, and the whole forming a perfect organism."[6]

The controlling fact for Conrad, however, is that society is not natural but a construct, with an arbitrary set of rules to regulate social relations lest the thin crust of civility give way. In this contrivance, society is interconnected from social top to bottom, from political right to left, in a secret but unspoken complicity to maintain these rules so that all its members, from the Great Personages and police officials to the radicals who plot the overthrow of the system, can assume their postures, go through the motions, and

---

limits, been forced to renounce its claim to universal validity" (p. 104). But in *The Will to Power*, in a note written in 1884, Nietzsche says: "I exult in the progressive militarization of Europe and in its inner anarchy . . . . the day of sneaking hypocrisy (with mandarins at the top, as Comte dreamed) is over. The barbarian and wild beast in each of us is affirmed. Precisely for that reason philosophy will get a move on. One day Kant will be regarded as a scarecrow." See no. 127 in the Kaufmann edition, p. 78; I have reworked Kaufmann's translation of Nietzsche's rough notes, to emphasize the thrust of the passage.

6 J. Hillis Miller, *Poets of Reality* (Cambridge: Harvard University Press, 1965), pp. 14, 16. It is striking that the image of the ship—and that of the orchestra as well —was also used by Saint-Simon to describe a harmonious society ordered by function.

mouth their parts in the play-act of convention. Society is thus a form of mystification.

This is the theme of Conrad's powerful novel about nihilism, *The Secret Agent*, which was prompted by anarchist activities at the turn of the century — the bombings and the random murders of "bourgeois-looking" people in the streets. It is the novel that adumbrates the more widespread terrorism by radicals in the 1960s.

Because society is so fragile, a single act, an exploded bomb, can tear the fabric to shreds, destroy all the roles, and leave men bare to their impulses. This was always the rationale of the anarchist conception of *die Tat* (the deed), the romantic act which in a flash would transform society. But the fuller ramifications of this idea are spelled out in Conrad's novel by the reactionary First Secretary of the Russian Embassy, who initiates the action that sets the plot moving. There must be, he remarks to Verloc, a destructive act that will "make it clear that you are perfectly determined to make a clean sweep of the whole social creation." But to do so, one must direct one's blows "at something outside the ordinary passions of humanity." An ordinary bombing could be dismissed as "mere class hate." But what is one to say, he continues,

to an act of destructive ferocity so absurd as to be incomprehensible, inexplicable, almost unthinkable; in fact, mad? Madness alone is truly terrifying, inasmuch as you cannot placate it either by threats, persuasion, or bribes.

And thus develops *die Tat*. "I am a civilized man," continues the First Secretary. "I would never dream of directing you to organize a mere butchery [and] I wouldn't expect from a butchery the result I want. Murder is always with us. It is almost an institution. The demonstration must be against learning—science. But not every science will do. The attack must have all the shocking senselessness of gratuitous blasphemy." And the act is to blow up the Greenwich Observatory, the First Meridian, the demarcation of time zones—the destruction of time and, symbolically, of history as well.

What happens, of course, is that the young man carrying the bomb, the unwitting messenger of the deed, dallies, and destroys himself in the explosion. But we see thus through Conrad, on the personal and the symbolic level, the essential terror of nihilism: the *acte gratuit*, the senseless act—madness.[7] This is his fear, if not his prophecy, for the future.

Is this our fate—nihilism as the logic of technological rationality or nihilism as the end product of the cultural impulses to strike down all conventions? The visions are there before us, as are many of the signs which had been foretold. Yet I wish to reject these seductive, and simple, formulations, and propose instead a more complex and empirically testable sociological argument.

I believe we are coming to a watershed in Western society: we are witnessing the end of the bourgeois idea—that view of human action and of social relations, particularly of economic exchange—which has molded the modern era for the last 200 years. And I believe that we have reached the end of the creative impulse and ideological sway of modernism, which, as a cultural movement, has dominated all the arts, and shaped our symbolic expressions, for the past 125 years. In developing this argument there is a great temptation to start from these powerful literary conceptions—powerful because they dramatize the issues—or others in the same vein, such as those of Burckhardt and Spengler, who have been hailed as prophets of the new times. Yet I choose not to do so, not because they are false, but because they are misleading.

Nietzsche and Conrad, each in his own way a different side of a double mirror, highlight the recurrent possibilities of disintegration in every society, particularly since they draw their ideas and imagery from the realm of culture. But this is misleading as history and as sociology. Their view of the world, and of social change, is apocalyptic, a tradition going back to the Revelation of John, the notion of "last days," and given force by Augustine's reflections on the downfall of Rome.

Despite our preoccupation with revelation, and later with revolution, the structures of a society—modes of life, social relations, norms and values—are not reversed overnight. The structures of power may change quickly: new men arrive, new routes of social ascent are opened, new bases of command created. Yet such dramatic overturns are largely a circulation of elites. Societal structures change much more slowly, especially habits, customs, and

---

[7] Joseph Conrad, *The Secret Agent* (Garden City, N.Y.: Doubleday Anchor, 1953). See pp. 39–40 for the speech of the First Secretary.

established, traditional ways. Our fascination with the apocalypse blinds us to the mundane: the relations of exchange, economic and social; the character of work and occupations; the nature of family life; and the traditional modes of conduct which regulate everyday life. Even when a political order is toppled by war or revolution, the task of building a new societal structure is a long and difficult one, and must necessarily use the bricks of the old order. If the intention of any science is to show us the structures of reality underlying appearances, then we have to understand that the time-dimensions of social change are much slower, and the processes more complex, than the dramaturgic mode of the apocalyptic vision, religious or revolutionary, would have us believe.

If the first difficulty is with the distortion of historical time, the second is with the monolithic view of society. Central to the imagination of the nineteenth century was the view of society as a web (and in the literary hallucinations, a spider web). Or in the more abstract philosophical vein, as elaborated by Hegel, each culture, each "period" of history, and correspondingly each society, was a structurally interrelated whole, unified by some inner principle. For Hegel, it was the *Geist*, or inner spirit. For Marx it was the mode of production, which determined all other social relations. Thus historical or social change was defined as a succession of fundamentally different unified cultures—the Greek world, the Roman world, the Christian world—each with its qualitatively different "moment" of consciousness, or different mode of production—slavery, feudalism, and capitalism—and each resting on different kinds of social relations and forces of production. In this view, history is dialectical, the new mode negating the previous one and preparing the way for the next to come, the underlying tow being the *telos* of rationality.[8]

[8] The Hegelian-Marxist conception assumes that history has a meaning: a progressive movement of consciousness or the control by man over nature and himself to escape the constraints of necessity. Can one say, today, that history has such a *telos*?

Spengler's *Decline of the West* is a different order of prophecy. He uses a biological metaphor: "For everything organic the notions of birth, death, youth, age, lifetime are fundamentals. . . ." And culture, for him, has morphologies: ". . . between the Differential Calculus and the dynastic principles of politics in the age of Louis XIV, between the Classical city-state and the Euclidean geometry, between the space-perspective of Western oil-painting and the conquest of space by railroad, telephone and long-range weapon, between contrapuntal music and credit economics . . . are deep uniformities." Thus Spengler is able to invoke the idea of the "destiny" or fated trajectory of a culture.

The difficulty with this argument is that while seemingly dissimilar modes, such

Within each period, every phase of a culture, from its morals and art, through its political form, to its philosophy, is shaped by this single *Geist* (leading to the idea, in cultural history, of the "style" of a period); or every aspect of a society is determined, directly or indirectly, by the prevailing economic mode, whether the hierarchical relation of feudal baron and serf, or the formally free commodity exchanges between individuals whose relations are mediated by the monetary sale of everything, from goods to culture.

This view of interconnectedness, of a web, becomes a powerful image in nineteenth-century fiction, particularly in the great novels of social realism which sought to depict all strata of society. In Dickens's *Bleak House*, as Richard Locke has pointed out, the action is resolved when "Inspector Bucket of the London police brings the questing heroine to the symbolic center of England—a dark graveyard in a London slum from which a smallpox epidemic and a network of deadlocked legal and sexual claims have spread out like ripples in a filthy well until they touch all of British society." And as Steven Marcus points out, "the notion of the web is to be found almost everywhere. It is prominently there in the later Dickens, it is all over the place in George Eliot, particularly in *Middlemarch*, and it figures centrally for Darwin in the *Origin of Species*. It forms as it were the underlying structural conception of sociology, which regards society as a web of relations."[9]

Whatever truth there may once have been in this view, I do not think it holds any longer. It may well be that at some points of

---

as contrapuntal music and credit economics, may have a common *origin* in a conception, say, of abstract relations, they are not necessarily linked in their subsequent development. A socialist economy might forgo credit yet retain contrapuntal music, for as I try to show below, elements embedded in the economic and cultural systems follow different "rules" of development and usage. Economic items are subject to the rule of *utility*, and one decides to use them or not on the basis of efficiency; but innovations in culture become part of the permanent repertoire of mankind, to be drawn upon by artists of different cultures and used as part of a recombination of forms. In short, I think it is quite false to think of culture or society as an organism.

See *The Decline of the West* (New York: Alfred A. Knopf, 1939), pp. 5, 7.

[9] Steven Marcus, *Engels, Manchester and the Working Class* (New York: Random House, 1974), pp. 57–58. Mr. Locke's remarks occur in his review of John le Carré's *Tinker, Tailor, Soldier, Spy* (*New York Times Book Review*, June 30, 1974). It is no accident, perhaps, that the view of society as a web figures most prominently, in contemporary literature, in novels about the police or espionage: the police are supposed to watch everybody, and thus form the link among all levels of society, and espionage deals with secrecy, or the hidden ties of societal networks.

Western history—the Christian Middle Ages, the rise of bourgeois civilization—there may have been unified social and cultural modes. Religion and its idea of hierarchy were reflected in the social structure of the feudal world, and religious passions infused the symbolism of the time. With the rise of the bourgeoisie, there may have been a single societal mode threaded through all realms from economic relations to moral conduct to cultural conceptions to character structure. And at the time one could see history as a progressive advance in man's power over nature and himself.

None of this holds today. History is not dialectical. Socialism has not succeeded capitalism, and those states that call themselves socialist have appeared almost entirely in pre-capitalist or agrarian-dominated societies, rather than in the advanced industrial societies. And society, I would say, is not integral, but disjunctive; the different realms respond to different norms, have different rhythms of change, and are regulated by different, even contrary, axial principles. If one is to understand my argument about the vicissitudes of bourgeois life and modernist culture which come to a head in the cultural contradictions of capitalism, one has to follow, first, my propositions about the way to think about society.

Against the holistic view of society, I find it more useful to think of *contemporary* society (I leave aside the question of whether this can be applied generally to the inherent character of society) as three distinct realms, each of which is obedient to a different axial principle. I divide society, analytically, into the *techno-economic* structure, the *polity*, and the *culture*. These are not congruent with one another and have different rhythms of change; they follow different norms which legitimate different, and even contrasting, types of behavior. It is the discordances between these realms which are responsible for the various contradictions within society.[10]

[10] This methodological premise is at variance with the two regnant paradigms in contemporary sociology, namely Marxism and functionalism. Even though the two schemas differ sharply in other respects, both have a common premise: that society is a structurally interrelated system and that one can understand any social action only in relation to that unified system. For Marxists, economics and culture are part of a "totality" defined through the process of commodity production and exchange. For functionalists, from Durkheim to Parsons, society is integrated through a common value system which legitimates, and so controls, all the ramified behavior in the society. I spell out my differences more fully in an essay in *Theories of Social Change*, which I edited for the Russell Sage Foundation (New York: Basic Books, forthcoming).

The techno-economic order is concerned with the organization of production and the allocation of goods and services. It frames the occupation and stratification system of the society and involves the use of technology for instrumental ends. In modern society, the axial principle is *functional rationality*, and the regulative mode is *economizing*. Essentially, economizing means efficiency, least cost, greatest return, maximization, optimization, and similar measures of judgment about the employment and mix of resources. The contrast is one of costs and benefits, and these are usually expressed in monetary terms. The axial structure is bureaucracy and hierarchy, since these derive from the specialization and segmentation of functions and the need to coordinate activities. There is a simple measure of value, namely utility. And there is a simple principle of change, namely the ability to substitute products or processes because they are more efficient and yield higher return at lesser cost, the principle of productivity. The social structure is a reified world because it is a structure of roles, not persons, and this is laid out in the organizational charts that specify the relationships of hierarchy and function. Authority inheres in the position, not in the individual, and social exchange (in the tasks that have to be dovetailed) is a relation between roles. A person becomes an object or a "thing," not because the enterprise is inhumane, but because the performance of a task is subordinated to the organization's ends. Since the tasks are functional and instrumental, the management of enterprise is primarily technocratic in character.

The polity is the arena of social justice and power: the control of the legitimate use of force and the regulation of conflict (in libertarian societies within the rule of law), in order to achieve the particular conceptions of justice embodied in a society's traditions or in its constitution, written or unwritten. The axial principle of the polity is legitimacy, and in a democratic polity it is the principle that power can be held and governance exercised only with the consent of the governed. The implicit condition is the idea of equality, that all men are to have an equal voice in this consensus. But the idea of citizenship which embodies this conception has in the past 100 years been expanded to include equality not only in the public sphere, but in all other dimensions of social life as well—equality before the law, equality of civil rights, equality of opportunity, even equality of results—so that a person is able to participate fully, as a citizen, in the society. Much of this may be formal, but it is always the source to which aggrieved groups have recourse when seeking justice in the society. The axial structure is that of representation or participation: the existence of political parties and/or social groups to express the interests of particular segments in the society, to be a vehicle of representation or a means of participating in decisions. The administrative aspects of the polity may be technocratic, and as problems become more technical there is a tendency for technocratic modes to spread. But since political action, fundamentally, seeks to reconcile conflicting and often incompatible interests, or seeks the authority of a covering statute or constitutional mode as the ground of judgment, political decisions are made by bargaining or by law, not by technocratic rationality.

By culture, my third realm, I mean less than an anthropologist's definition of culture as the artifacts and patterned ways of life of a group, and more than the genteel notions of, say, Matthew Arnold, for whom culture is the achievement of perfection in the individual. I mean by culture—and here I follow Ernst Cassirer—the realm of symbolic forms and, in the context of the argument in this book, more narrowly the arena of *expressive symbolism*: those efforts, in painting, poetry, and fiction, or within the religious forms of litany, liturgy, and ritual, which seek to explore and express the meanings of human existence in some imaginative form.[11] The *modalities* of culture are few, and they derive from the existential situations which confront all human beings, through all times, in the nature of consciousness: how one meets death, the nature of tragedy and the character of heroism, the definition of loyalty and obligation, the redemption of the soul, the meaning of love and of sacrifice, the understanding of compassion, the tension between an animal and a human nature, the claims of instinct and restraint. Historically, therefore, culture has been fused with religion.

One can see, thus, that there are different "rhythms" of social change and that there are no simple, determinate relations among the three realms.[12] The nature of change in the techno-economic

---

[11] I leave out here the question of the cognitive modes, philosophy and science, which surely belong within the realm of culture. I am not sketching here a complete sociological grammar. I do try to deal with this and other conceptual questions in the essay, previously cited, for the Russell Sage Foundation book.

[12] There is another, more complex question: Does human nature change over historical time, in response to changes in modes of production or some other historicist turn, or is human nature invariant? If human nature remains the same,

order is linear in that the principles of utility and efficiency provide clear rules for innovation, displacement, and substitution. A machine or a process that is more efficient or more productive replaces one that is less efficient. This is one meaning of progress. But in culture there is always a *ricorso*, a return to the concerns and questions that are the existential agonies of human beings. Though the answers may change, the forms they take may derive from the other changes in society. In different times, the answers may vary, or they may be recast in new aesthetic forms. But there is no unambiguous "principle" of change. Boulez does not replace Bach. The new music or the new painting or the new poetry becomes part of an enlarged repertoire of mankind, a permanent depository from which individuals can draw, in renewable fashion, to remold an aesthetic experience.

In a conceptual sense, one can specify divergent organizational principles of change. In the social structure, particularly in the techno-economic order, change follows a path first defined by Émile Durkheim. The enlargement of a social sphere leads to greater interaction, and this interaction in turn leads to specialization, complementary relations, and structural differentiation. The most obvious model is an economic enterprise, in which specialization and structural differentiation are responses to the change in scale. But in culture the increase in interaction, owing to the breakdown of segmented societies or of parochial cultures, leads to *syncretism* —the mingling of strange gods, as in the time of Constantine, or the mélange of cultural artifacts in modern art (or even in the living rooms of middle-class professional families). Syncretism is the jumbling of styles in modern art, which absorbs African masks or Japanese prints into its modes of depicting spatial perceptions; or the merging of Oriental and Western religions, detached from their histories, in a modern meditative consciousness.

Modern culture is defined by this extraordinary freedom to ransack the world storehouse and to engorge any and every style it comes upon. Such freedom comes from the fact that the axial principle of modern culture is the expression and remaking of the "self" in order to achieve self-realization and self-fulfillment. And in its

---

how can we speak of a growth of "consciousness"? But if human nature changes, how do we understand the past? These questions are taken up in my essay, "Technology, Nature, and Society," in *The Frontiers of Knowledge*, The Frank Nelson Doubleday Lectures, 1st series (Garden City, N.Y.: Doubleday, 1975).

search, there is a denial of any limits or boundaries to experience. It is a reaching out for all experience; nothing is forbidden, all is to be explored.

Within this framework, one can discern the structural sources of tension in the society: between a social structure (primarily techno-economic) which is bureaucratic and hierarchical, and a polity which believes, formally, in equality and participation; between a social structure that is organized fundamentally in terms of roles and specialization, and a culture which is concerned with the enhancement and fulfillment of the self and the "whole" person. In these contradictions, one perceives many of the latent social conflicts that have been expressed ideologically as alienation, depersonalization, the attack on authority, and the like. In these adversary relations, one sees the disjunction of realms.

This notion of the disjunction of realms is a general, theoretical approach to the analysis of modern society. At this point, it might be useful to define the particular terms that differentiate sociotechnical, socio-economic and socio-political systems.

Industrialism is the application of energy and machinery for the mass production of goods. Both the United States and the Soviet Union, though differing markedly in other respects, are both technical and industrial societies. The phase of post-industrialism represents a shift in the kinds of work people do, from manufacturing to services (especially human and professional services) and a new centrality of theoretical knowledge in economic innovation and policy. For similar reasons, both the United States and the Soviet Union could become post-industrial societies.

Capitalism is an economic-cultural system, organized economically around the institution of property and the production of commodities and based culturally in the fact that exchange relations, that of buying and selling, have permeated most of the society. Democracy is a socio-political system in which legitimacy lies in the consent of the governed, where the political arena is available to various contending groups, and where fundamental liberties are safeguarded.

Though capitalism and democracy historically have arisen together, and have been commonly justified by philosophical liberalism, there is nothing which makes it either theoretically or practically necessary for the two to be yoked. In modern society, the political order increasingly becomes autonomous, and the management of the techno-economic order, or the democratic planning, or the management of the economy, becomes ever more independent of capitalism.

Soviet communism, which should more correctly be called bureaucratic collectivism, is a state-directed society which has sought to fuse all realms into a single monolith and to impose a common direction, from economics to politics to culture, through a single institution, the Party. Whether the Party can maintain such monolithic control in a society that becomes increasingly differentiated, without broadening the arena of elite participation in decision making, is increasingly open to question.

These distinctions are necessary for two reasons. First, they point out the fact that the question of the movement from industrial to post-industrial society and the question of the movement from capitalism to socialism or bureaucratic collectivism are two distinctive questions with respect to developments along two very different axes. The post-industrial society centers on the technology, the kind of *work* people do (though there are political implications in the relative decline of the working class), and the organization of *knowledge*. The questions of whether a system is capitalist or socialist, or capitalist or bureaucratic collectivist, are questions about the management of the *economy* and the *ethos* of the society. Second, the contradictions of capitalism of which I speak in these pages, have to do with the disjunction between the kind of organization and the norms demanded in the economic realm, and the norms of self-realization that are now central in the culture. The two realms which had historically been joined to produce a single character structure—that of the Puritan and of his calling—have now become unjoined. The principles of the economic realm and those of the culture now lead people in contrary directions. These contradictions have arisen primarily in American and other Western societies. It is not at all clear that the Communist world, with its drive for efficiency and its promise of self-realization, is immune to these contradictions. We shall have to wait and see when (or if) a consumer society is achieved in the Soviet Union. So far as Maoist China is concerned, the Russians are already the damned.

If we turn from our analytical distinctions to sociological history, we can trace this disjunction between social structure and culture in an extraordinary contrast of changing moral tempers.

The fundamental assumption of modernity, the thread that has run through Western civilization since the sixteenth century, is that the social unit of society is not the group, the guild, the tribe, or the city, but the person. The Western ideal was the autonomous man who, in becoming self-determining, would achieve freedom. With this "new man" there was a repudiation of institutions (the striking result of the Reformation, which installed individual conscience as the source of judgment); the opening of new geographical and social frontiers; the desire, and the growing ability, to master nature and to make of oneself what one can, and even, in discarding old roots, to remake oneself altogether. What began to count was not the past but the future.

This is expressed in a twofold development. In the economy, there arises the bourgeois entrepreneur. Freed from the ascriptive ties of the traditional world, with its fixed status and checks on acquisition, he seeks his fortune by remaking the economic world. Free movement of goods and money and individual economic and social mobility become the ideal. At its extreme, laissez-faire becomes "rampant individualism." In the culture, we have the rise of the independent artist, released from church and princely patron, writing and painting what pleases him rather than his sponsor; the market will make him free.[13] In the development of culture, this search for independence, the will to be free not only of patron but of all conventions, finds its expression in modernism and, in its extreme form, in the idea of the untrammeled self.

The impulse driving both the entrepreneur and the artist is a restlessness to search out the new, to rework nature, and to refashion consciousness. As Marx wrote, in an almost hyperbolic paean to the bourgeoisie in *The Communist Manifesto*:

The bourgeoisie, during its rule of scarce one hundred years, has created more massive and more colossal productive forces than have all

---

[13] In the eighteenth century, the growth of publishing and the creation of a market made the writer not only independent but in some cases, such as Alexander Pope, quite wealthy. As Oliver Goldsmith wrote in 1762: "At present the few poets of England no longer depend on the Great for subsistence, they have now no other patrons but the public, and the public, collectively considered, is a good and generous master. . . . Every polite member of the community, by buying what a man of letters writes, contributes to reward him. The ridicule therefore of living in a garret, might have been wit in the last age, but continues such no longer, because no longer true." Quoted in Alexander Beljame, *Men of Letters and the English Public in the XVIIIth Century* (London: Kegan Paul, 1948), p. 385; the first French edition appeared in 1881. For the figures on Pope's wealth from the sale of his books, see pp. 366–370.

preceding generations together. Subjection of nature's forces to man, machinery, application of chemistry to industry and agriculture, steam navigation, railways, electric telegraphs, clearing of whole continents for cultivation, canalization of rivers, whole populations conjured out of the ground—what earlier century had even a presentiment that such productive forces slumbered in the lap of social labour? . . .

The bourgeoisie cannot exist without constantly revolutionizing the instruments of production, and thereby the relations of production, and with them the whole relations of society. . . . All fixed, fast, frozen relations, with their train of ancient and venerable prejudices and opinions, are swept away, all new-formed ones become antiquated before they can ossify. All that is solid melts into air, all that is holy is profaned, and man is at last compelled to face with his sober senses his real conditions of life and his relations with his kind.[14]

For the artist, the restless vanity of the untrammeled self is best expressed by Byron, whose impetuous romanticism imprinted itself on an age:

The great object of life is Sensation—to feel that we exist—even though in pain—it is this 'craving void' which drives us to Gaming—to Battle—to Travel—to intemperate but keenly felt pursuits of every description whose principal attraction is the agitation inseparable from their accomplishment.[15]

Both impulses, historically, were aspects of the same sociological surge of modernity. Together they opened up the Western world in a radical way. Yet the extraordinary paradox is that each impulse then became highly conscious of the other, feared the other, and sought to destroy it. Radical in economics, the bourgeoisie became conservative in morals and cultural taste. The bourgeois economic impulse was organized into a highly restrictive character structure whose energies were channeled into the production of goods and into a set of attitudes toward work that feared instinct, spontaneity, and vagrant impulse. In the extreme Puritanism of America, laws were passed to constrain intemperate behavior, while in painting and literature bourgeois taste ran to the heroic and banal.

The cultural impulse—I take Baudelaire as its exemplary figure —thus turned into rage against bourgeois values. "To be a useful man has always appeared to me as something quite hideous," Baudelaire declared. Utility, rationalism, and materialism were barren, and the bourgeois had no spiritual life and no excesses. The

14 Karl Marx, *Selected Works* (Moscow: 1935), vol. 1, pp. 210, 208–209.
15 *Byron's Letters and Journals*, ed. Leslie A. Marchand (Cambridge: Harvard University Press, Belknap, 1974), vol. 3, p. 109.

"cruel implacable regularity" of industry was what the modern business house had created: "Mechanization will have . . . Americanized us, Progress will have well atrophied us, our entire spiritual part. . . ."[16]

What is striking is that while bourgeois society introduced a radical individualism in economics, and a willingness to tear up all traditional social relations in the process, the bourgeois class feared the radical experimental individualism of modernism in the culture. Conversely, the radical experimentalists in the culture, from Baudelaire to Rimbaud to Alfred Jarry, were willing to explore all dimensions of experience, yet fiercely hated bourgeois life. The history of this sociological puzzle, how this antagonism came about, is still to be written.[17]

In the history of bourgeois society, a number of sociological "crossovers" took place which radically transformed both the cultural and economic realms. In the culture there was a radical change in the meaning of the individual from a being to a self. Of equal import, there was a shift from the hold of restraint to the acceptance of impulse. In the economy, there was a crucial change in the character of the motivations which lead a man to work and to relate himself positively and negatively to work.

Classical philosophy had a metaphysical theology, as Lovejoy

[16] See César Graña, "Bourgeois Enterprise and Modern Life," in *Bohemian versus Bourgeois* (New York: Basic Books, 1964), especially pp. 95–98; and Joseph D. Bennett, *Baudelaire: A Criticism* (Princeton: Princeton University Press, 1944), especially chaps. 2 and 3 for Baudelaire's conception of evil, which relates to the discussion that follows.

[17] Is there a parallel with the Communist world? The Russian Revolution released an unprecedented burst of vitality and experimentation in all the arts. Hundreds of artists and writers took up the revolution with enthusiasm. "Cubism and futurism were the revolutionary forms in art foreshadowing the revolution in the political and economic life of 1917," declared Malevich. Constructivism was proclaimed the new aesthetic of Communist society. In design, painting, and sculpture there were the innovations of Tatlin, Lissitsky, Gabo, and Pevsner, as well as the abstractions of Kandinsky and Malevich. In the theater there were the stylistic experiments of Meyerhold, Tairov, and Vakhtangov. In poetry there were the triumphant futurists, such as Mayakovsky ("the streets are our brushes, the squares our palette"), and the symbolists, such as Blok and Bely (who interpreted the revolution as a religious epiphany). In fiction there was the writing of Babel and Pilnyak, Zamyatin and Bulgakov; in the cinema the films of Eisenstein and Pudovkin.

By the 1930s, it was finished. All that was left was the cold pudding of a Party-defined "socialist realism." Those who had created the feverish experiments were prisoners, suicides, silent, or abroad. Clearly there was a question whether, in a society so single-mindedly focused on mobilizing a populace for industrialization, the independence or the vagrant impulses of artists and writers would not be a "diversion" from the creation of the "new man" and the channeling of economic energies which the Party sought to direct.

puts it, which thought of *beings* that had a nature, and therefore a common quality. As Plato wrote in the *Timaeus*, "a 'good' being must be free from 'envy,' that that which is more perfect necessarily engenders, or overflows into, that which is less perfect, and cannot 'remain within itself.'" There was a hierarchy of virtue, in which the lower derived from the higher. But in the modern consciousness, there is not a common being but a *self*, and the concern of this self is with its individual *authenticity*, its unique, irreducible character free of the contrivances and conventions, the masks and hypocrisies, the distortions of the self by society. This concern with the authentic self makes the motive and not the action—the impact on the self, not the moral consequence to society—the source of ethical and aesthetic judgments.[18]

But the larger context was the crossover from religion to secular culture in the way expressive conduct is handled in modern society. In the history of society, particularly of Western society, there has always been a dialectic of release and restraint. We find in the great historical religions a fear of the demonic, of human nature unchecked. And these religions have been religions of restraint. The shift to release occurs with the breakup of religious authority in the mid-nineteenth century. In effect, the culture—particularly modernist culture—took over the relation with the demonic. But instead of taming it, as religion tried to do, the secular culture (art and literature) began to accept it, explore it, and revel in it, coming to see it as a source of creativity. In the cry for the autonomy of the aesthetic, there arose the idea that experience in and of itself was the supreme value, that everything was to be explored, anything was to be permitted—at least to the imagination, if not acted out in life. In the legitimation of action, the pendulum had swung to the side of release, away from restraint.[19]

Modernism has thus been the seducer. Its power derived from the idolatry of the self. Its appeal stemmed from the idea that life itself

[18] For two books which, together, provide a complete picture of this transformation, see Arthur O. Lovejoy, *The Great Chain of Being* (Cambridge: Harvard University Press, 1936), especially chap. 2, on Greek philosophy, and chap. 10, on Romanticism (the quotation from the *Timaeus*, above, is on pp. 315–316); and Lionel Trilling, *Sincerity and Authenticity* (Cambridge: Harvard University Press, 1972).

[19] The argument is elaborated in my essay on religion and culture, pp. 157. For an extraordinary discussion of the role of the demonic in its relation to theology and art, see the section "The Demonic" in Paul Tillich, *The Interpretation of History* (New York: Charles Scribner's Sons, 1936), pp. 77–115. The essay appeared originally in German in 1926.

should be a work of art, and that art could only express itself against the conventions of society, particularly bourgeois society. When tied to politics, as it has sometimes been, modernism became subversive of contemporary society, whether in the rage of men of the right, such as Wyndham Lewis, or the japes of men of the left, such as Breton and the surrealists.

Today modernism is exhausted. There is no tension. The creative impulses have gone slack. It has become an empty vessel.[20] The impulse to rebellion has been institutionalized by the "cultural mass"[21] and its experimental forms have become the syntax and semiotics of advertising and haute couture. As a cultural style, it exists as radical chic, which allows the cultural mass the luxury of "freer" life-styles while holding comfortable jobs within an economic system that has itself been transformed in its motivations.

If one turns to the economic impulse, the problem of virtue arose because of the dual, and necessarily contradictory, role of the individual as both *citoyen* and *bourgeois*. As the first, he had obliga-

---

[20] As a veteran modernist poet, Octavio Paz, has written: "Today . . . modern art is beginning to lose its powers of negation. For some years now its rejections have been ritual repetitions: rebellion has turned into Procedure, criticism into rhetoric, transgression into ceremony. Negation is no longer creative. I am not saying that we are living the end of art: we are living the end of the *idea of modern art*." Mr. Paz has written a subtle discussion of the idea of the modern, particularly of the somewhat different form it took in Hispanic culture. My only quarrel would be with the word "today." I believe that modernism lost its power 50 years ago. See Octavio Paz, *Children of the Mire: Modern Poetry from Romanticism to the Avant-Garde* (Cambridge: Harvard University Press, 1974). The quotation is on p. 149.

For an earlier view, from a more hostile source, see Renato Poggioli, *The Theory of the Avant-Garde* (Cambridge: Harvard University Press, 1968), especially pp. 209–231, for the very cogent discussion of modernity and modernism.

[21] By "cultural mass" I mean, in the first instance, an audience large enough to sustain a world of cultural production on its own. In an occupational sense, this cultural mass would consist primarily of those persons in the knowledge and communications industries who, with their families, would number several million persons.

Sociologically, this cultural mass has three components. It comprises not the creators of culture but the *transmitters*: those working in higher education, publishing, magazines, broadcast media, theater, and museums, who process and influence the reception of serious cultural products. It is in itself large enough to be a *market* for culture, purchasing books, prints, and serious music recordings. And it is also the group which, as writers, magazine editors, movie-makers, musicians, and so forth, produces the popular materials for the wider mass-culture audience.

But this covers only the cultural mass in the large. Inevitably, there are smaller circles—those that Tom Wolfe calls the culturati—which seek to set a more cultural tone, those who seek to be "mod," or "with it," or "trendy." The Germans have a term for this—*Tendenz*, to turn with the cultural winds. What fashion is to couture, and fads to a youth culture, *Tendenz* or *Tendenz vending* is to the culturati.

tions to the polity of which he was a part; as the second, he had private concerns which he pursued for his own self-interest. Jeremy Bentham had denied there was such an entity as a community. It was, he said, a fictitious body. But there is a real distinction between a social decision and the sum total of individual decisions: A society might decide that, to redress its balance-of-payments deficit, it should conserve oil, but each man, following his own needs, may increase his purchases. It is equally clear that what an individual often wants for himself (such as an open highway) in the aggregate becomes a nightmare. So the balance of private appetite and public responsibility is a real one. How is it maintained?

In the early development of capitalism, the unrestrained economic impulse was held in check by Puritan restraint and the Protestant ethic. One worked because of one's obligation to one's calling, or to fulfill the covenant of the community. But the Protestant ethic was undermined not by modernism but by capitalism itself. The greatest single engine in the destruction of the Protestant ethic was the invention of the installment plan, or instant credit. Previously one had to save in order to buy. But with credit cards one could indulge in instant gratification. The system was transformed by mass production and mass consumption, by the creation of new wants and new means of gratifying those wants.

The Protestant ethic had served to limit sumptuary (though not capital) accumulation. When the Protestant ethic was sundered from bourgeois society, only the hedonism remained, and the capitalist system lost its transcendental ethic. There remains the argument that capitalism serves as the basis for freedom, and for a rising standard of living and the defeat of poverty. Yet even if these arguments were true—for it is clear that freedom depends more upon the historical traditions of a particular society than upon the system of capitalism itself; and even the ability of the system to provide for economic growth is now questioned—the lack of a transcendental tie, the sense that a society fails to provide some set of "ultimate meanings" in its character structure, work, and culture, becomes unsettling to a system.[22]

The cultural, if not moral, justification of capitalism has become

[22] For an elaboration of this argument, see Irving Kristol, "When Virtue Loses All Her Loveliness'—Some Reflections on Capitalism and 'The Free Society,'" in *The Public Interest*, no. 21 (Fall 1970), reprinted in *Capitalism Today*, ed. Daniel Bell and Irving Kristol (New York: Basic Books, 1971).

hedonism, the idea of pleasure as a way of life. And in the liberal ethos that now prevails, the model for a cultural imago has become the modernist impulse, with its ideological rationale of the impulse quest as a mode of conduct. It is this which is the cultural contradiction of capitalism. It is this which has resulted in the double bind of modernity.

The word "economics" comes from the Greek, *oikos*, a household, but the ancient world did not know an economy, a system of interdependent markets regulated by price, as we do; nor did they think in "economic" terms, that is by the idea of calculation. Production was for the household and was geared to needs. These needs were biologically derived—sufficient food, adequate shelter, efficient sanitation. As Aristotle said, "There is a bound fixed [for the property needed for the art of household management]."

What defines bourgeois society is not needs, but wants. Wants are psychological, not biological, and are by their nature unlimited. Society is seen not as a natural association of men—the polis or the family—ruled by a common purpose, but as a composite of atomistic individuals who pursue only their own gratification. Man's psychology, as pictured by Hobbes in the first book of the *Leviathan*, is an appetitive drive which reverses the Platonic hierarchy of the rational spirit, and these appetites drive him ferociously to achieve his desires. In a modern society, the engine of appetite is the increased standard of living and the diversity of products that make up so much of the splendid color of life. But it is also, in its emphasis on display, a reckless squandering of resources. The psychological origin of inequality, as Rousseau brilliantly sketched it in the *Second Discourse*, comes when "solitary" man begins to assemble and finds that the strongest, the handsomest, the best dancer and the best singer get an undue share of the goods. Envy begins to show its face. In order to be like the handsomest or the most artful, the others begin to dissemble, cosmetics are used to mask the rough and the ugly, appearances begin to count for more than reality. If consumption represents the psychological competition for status, then one can say that bourgeois society is the institutionalization of envy.[23]

---

[23] It is surprising how little the idea of envy has been utilized in sociological literature as the source of status competition. A neglected writer, in this respect, is Adam Smith, who, in his *Theory of Moral Sentiments*, declared that if people were

Where resources are prodigal, or individuals accept a high degree of inequality as normal or just, this consumption can be accommodated. But when everyone in society joins in the demand for more, expecting this as a matter of right, and resources are limited (more by cost than by quantity), then one begins to see the basis for the tension between the demands in the polity and the limitations set by the economy. We see here a crossover whereby "unrestrained appetite" has moved from the economic realm to the polity. Looking at the Western polity in the second half of the twentieth century, we see five elements that together are structurally transforming the old market system.

First, we find institutionalized expectations of economic growth and a rising standard of living; these have been converted, in the current change of values, into a sense of *entitlements*. What we have, today, is a revolution of rising entitlements.

Second, we realize the incompatibility of various wants and, more important, of diverse values. The philosophers of the Enlightenment assumed that to any single question there was a single answer. These answers, when put together coherently, formed a rational solution to social problems. The fundamental need was to be "objective" in the formulation of answers: to reduce the "biases" that derived from parochial upbringing, to eliminate prejudice and superstition, to forgo tradition and self-interest, and the like. To become objective one had to "purify" ideas (this was the original meaning of that quixotic term *ideology*), and to be ethically rational one had to "universalize" one's conduct as a categorical imperative. Yet we come to understand that there are inherent incompatibilities between such values as liberty and equality, efficiency and spontaneity, knowledge and happiness. And we know, empirically, that if we add up the costs of all the social goals decided on by a society (as governmental bodies have sought to do, beginning with the Eisenhower Commission on National Goals in 1959), we find that we do not have sufficient resources to achieve them simultaneously. The problems of choice are inescapable.

Third, we recognize that there are enormous "spillover" effects from economic growth. It is obvious that the increase in the number

---

ruled by economic motives alone, there would be little stimulus to increase production above necessities or needs. It is because men are driven by an impulse for status that economic "development" began. This is the theme elaborated as well by Thorstein Veblen in his famous, but now neglected, *Theory of the Leisure Class*.

of automobiles creates a stifling smog over the cities; that is relatively easy to deal with. More vexing is the fact that increased use of chemical fertilizers to increase food yields (which has made American agriculture the most efficient in the world) also results in the runoff of nitrates into the rivers and lakes, and the pollution of these waters. How does one make the trade-off between food and pollution or, in an analogous case, between strip-mining for coal and the large-scale scarring of countryside?

The simultaneous convergence of increasing demand, the lag in capacity (particularly primary processing capacity, as in steel), and the rising cost of resources (let alone the political manipulation of oil prices) has led, fourth, to a worldwide inflation. But inflation, as we begin to see, is not a transient element but a structural component of a modern economy, the largely inescapable consequence of a commitment to economic growth and full employment. The question, however, is whether such inflation can be "controlled" at a manageable rate.

And fifth, we have begun to center the crucial decisions about the economy and the society in the political cockpit, rather than in the diffused, aggregated market. This is a consequence not of any ideological conversion (if anything, there has been resistance even on the part of those who, despite their ideology, have maintained and extended the system of political controls, such as Eisenhower and Nixon) but of the structural transformations of the Western polity.

The fundamental political fact in the second half of the twentieth century has been the extension of *state-directed economies*. These developed first because of the need to rescue the system from depression, later because of the demands of a war economy and the enlargement of military commitments, and finally because of the strategic role of fiscal policy in affecting levels of spending and patterns of investment. In the last quarter of the twentieth century, we now move to *state-managed societies*. And these emerge because of the increase in the large-scale social demands (health, education, welfare, social services) which have become entitlements for the population.

The new "class struggles" of the post-industrial society are less a matter of conflict between management and worker in the economic enterprise than the pull and tug of various organized segments to influence the state budget. Where state expenditure approximates 40 percent of Gross National Product, as it almost does in the

United States, or more than 50 percent, as in the Scandinavian countries, the chief political issues become the allocation of monies and the incidence of taxation. This is what I mean by the emergence of "fiscal sociology" (the term is Schumpeter's) as the central feature of modern political economy.

The question of "state-society" relationships, of the public interest and private appetite, is clearly the salient problem for the polity in the coming decades. The institutions of law, economics, and politics in bourgeois society have been oriented to individuals and the regulation of exchanges between them—in the ideas of formal rationality and the rule of law as primarily procedural rather than substantive. The nature of "public law," dealing with the substantive claims of the community as prior to those of individuals, will be one of the major problems for legal theory.

Sociologically, there is a question of the weight of state influence. A system of state capitalism could easily be transformed into a corporate state, that of state socialism into one so burdened with the competing demands of social groups as to limit the economy's growth capability and to overload the political system with multiple claims. Yet it is also likely that in the United States a state-directed economy and a state-managed society will please no one. The business corporations resent government regulation, even though it may sustain profits, for the degree of interference with managerial authority is real. Radicals are becoming increasingly suspicious of government and planning (as benefiting only the planners and bureaucrats), even though their first reaction to any issue is to call for more "government," as if the abstraction itself were coterminous with the public good. And the state management that will emerge will be a cumbersome, bureaucratic monstrosity, wrenched in all directions by the clamor for subsidies and entitlements by various corporate and communal groups, yet gorging itself on increased governmental appropriations to become a Leviathan in its own right.

The major difficulty is twofold: Western society lacks both *civitas*, the spontaneous willingness to make sacrifices for some public good, and a political philosophy that justifies the normative rules of priorities and allocations in the society.

Liberal economics assumed that the market was a sufficient arbiter of the public weal; there, the differential utilities of individuals and the scarcity of different goods would come to an equilibrium that harmonized the intensity of desires and the willingness to pay the asking price. Classical Marxism had an entirely different answer to the problem of relative justice in society. It assumed that competition, envy, and evil all resulted from scarcity, and that the abundance of goods would make such conflicts unnecessary. But what we have come to realize is that, the question of resources aside, we will never overcome scarcity. In the post-industrial society (as I pointed out in my previous book) there would be new scarcities which nineteenth-century utopians could never envision—scarcities of information, which would arise from the growth of technical knowledge and the increasing need for popularization, and from the rising costs of "time" as a result of increased participation by individuals and the need to coordinate these activities in the political process.

Economics is the art of allocating scarce goods among competing demands. The conceit of Marxism was the thought that in Communism, economics would be "abolished"; this was why one did not have to think about the questions of relative privilege and social justice. But the point is that we still have to think in terms of economics, and probably always will. The question, then, is whether we can arrive at a set of normative rules which seek to protect liberty, reward achievement, and enhance the social good, within the constraints of "economics."

In these essays, I propose the idea of a *public household*—not a third sector alongside the domestic household and the market economy, but one which embraces the two and seeks to utilize market mechanisms where possible, yet within the explicit framework of social goals. It is a liberal conception because of the belief that the individual should be the primary unit of civil society, and that individual achievement should have a just reward. But what I seek to do is to detach political liberalism from bourgeois society. Historically, the two are associated in origin, yet the one is not dependent on the other. In fact, political liberalism as a philosophy has suffered because it has been used to justify the unrestrained claims of private economic appetite. The problem for the Public Household is how to adjudicate the claims of group versus group, where the problem is clearly right versus right, rather than right or wrong; of weighing the claims of group memberships against individual rights; of balancing liberty and equality, equity and efficiency. The starting point, I believe, has to be a recognition of the public character of resources and needs (not wants), and the principle of *relevant differences* in deciding the justice of various claims. These are the intentions of the major essay in the section on the polity.

The last quarter of the twentieth century will see significant shifts in economic and political power, but these will largely be shifts in the power of national states, rather than ones arising out of the competition of social systems such as capitalism and socialism.[24] The economic power of advanced industrial society rests in its high technology, its ability to mobilize capital, and the strength of its managerial competences. It was responsible, one almost forgets, for one of the great booms of economic history, one which lasted over a quarter of a century. World industrial production increased an extraordinary three and a half times between 1948 and 1973, an average rate of increase of 5 percent a year. (Japan's growth rate was double that of the world's average, Britain's was half—both capitalist societies.) For an entire generation, as the *Economist* has pointed out, all industrial countries prospered.[25] It was this investment boom, in fact, that laid the structural basis for the worldwide inflation in the advanced capitalist societies in the early 1970s.

The energy issue exposed the vulnerability of the Western industrial societies, because of their dependence on oil, a situation which arose out of its cheapness. (Was the Soviet Union exempt because it was Communist, or because it had a full supply of oil and natural gas?) And the shift of capital, because of oil revenues, has illustrated the weakness of a world economy that had been hitched almost entirely to the dollar.

[24] In his apocalyptic book *The Human Prospect*, Robert Heilbroner raises the question of whether different national societies or the different social systems, capitalism and socialism, can cope with the large ecological resources, and population crises he envisages by the end of the century. He then proceeds to discuss the capability of "capitalism" or "socialism" to deal with these crises. But *capability* is a political question, and the effective units of political action, necessarily, are the different national societies, not the abstract social systems. I do not mean to minimize the character of a social system in shaping the patterns of income and power distributions within a society, and thus creating effective points of influence, but I do not believe that such distributions are the way—and the effective reasons why—a society responds to crises. Sweden and the United States, the Soviet Union and Yugoslavia might all respond differently, less because of their "social systems" than because of the political will which is embodied in national tradition and a sense of *civitas*. Or, to put it more formally, the social "actor" is not the "system" but the political society.

[25] "Who Will Survive the Slump?," *Economist*, December 28, 1974, pp. 40–42.

Yet it is all too soon to write off Western economic power. By the end of the decade, the dependence of the Western countries on Middle East oil may be largely reduced; there will be new and different sources and kinds of energy. For a period of time, there may be a large-scale shift of capital to the Middle East countries, but the basic economic lead of the West is in high technology and management, and this is bound to reassert itself. What the international economic events of the 1970s revealed was a failure of political will to match economic urgencies, and this is a different and more disturbing aspect of the instability of the international order.

But I write not of the events of the decade but of the deeper cultural crises which beset bourgeois societies and which, in the longer run, devitalize a country, confuse the motivations of individuals, instill a sense of *carpe diem*, and undercut its civic will. The problems are less those of the adequacy of institutions than of the kinds of meanings that sustain a society.

Bourgeois society, Irving Kristol has written, is morally and intellectually unprepared for calamity. On the one hand, there is the liberal temper, which redefines all existential questions into "problems" and looks for "solutions" to problems. (Again, it is the rationalist idea that to any single question there is a single answer.) On the other, hand, there is the utopian assumption of limitless ends achievable through the marvelous engine of economic, if not technological, efficiency. Yet calamity has struck, and will strike again and again.

In the past, human societies have been prepared for calamity by the anchorages that were rooted in experience yet provided some transtemporal conception of reality. Traditionally, this anchorage was religion, for religion, as Clifford Geertz has noted, "tunes human actions to an envisaged cosmic order and projects images of cosmic order onto the plane of human experience."[26] Modern societies have substituted utopia for religion—utopia not as a transcendental ideal, but one to be realized through history (progress, rationality, science) with the nutrients of technology and the midwifery of revolution.

The real problem of *modernity* is the problem of belief. To use an unfashionable term, it is a spiritual crisis, since the new anchorages have proved illusory and the old ones have become submerged. It is a situation which brings us back to nihilism; lacking a past or a

[26] Clifford Geertz, *The Interpretation of Cultures* (New York: Basic Books, 1973), p. 90.

future, there is only a void. Nihilism was once a heady philosophy, as it was for Bazarov, when there was something to destroy and something to put in its place. But today what is there left in the past to destroy, and who has the hope for a future to come?

The effort to find excitement and meaning in literature and art as a substitute for religion led to modernism as a cultural mode. Yet modernism is exhausted and the various kinds of post-modernism (in the psychedelic effort to expand consciousness without boundaries) are simply the decomposition of the self in an effort to erase individual ego. The idea of revolution still mesmerizes some,[27] but the real problems arise the "day after the revolution," when the mundane world again intrudes upon consciousness, and one finds that the moral ideas are abstract against the intractable desire for material incentives or to pass privileges on to one's children. Thus one finds a revolutionary society itself becoming bureaucratic or being enmeshed ceaselessly in the turmoil of permanent revolution.[28]

What holds one to reality, if one's secular system of meanings proves to be an illusion? I will risk an unfashionable answer—the return in Western society of some conception of religion. In his *Lettre du voyant*, Rimbaud remarked, "Je sais qu'il faut être voyant, se faire voyant." To be a *voyant* means to discern, on the far side of art and history, realities which the eyes of others have yet failed to see, to "inspector l'invisible et entendre l'inouï."[29]

If it is true that what the poet says hearkens toward the future, then in that country where contemporary poetry has had the

[27] Nadezhda Mandelstam has written of the Russian experience: "My brother Evgeni Yakovlevich used to say that the decisive part in the subjugation of the intelligentsia was played not by terror and bribery (though, God knows, there was enough of both), but by the word 'Revolution,' which none of them could bear to give up. It is a word to which whole nations have succumbed, and its force was such that one wonders why our rulers still needed prisons and capital punishment." *Hope Against Hope* (New York: Atheneum, 1970), p. 126.

[28] One of the most amusing and revealing episodes of the Chinese cultural revolution was the fact that when hundreds of thousands of inspired youths flooded Peking in 1966, they found that each contingent wore button badges announcing its city, but some badges were scarcer and thus rarer than others. Immediately and spontaneously a market arose in which different badges were traded at discount. Youths proudly showed off the scarce badges they were able to get by trade—as they demonstrated against the restoration of capitalism and for the cultural revolution. See *Red Guard: The Political Biography of Dai Msiau-ai*, ed. Gordon A. Bennett and Ronald N. Montaperto (Garden City, N.Y.: Doubleday Anchor, 1972), p. 99.

[29] See Poggioli, op. cit., p. 215. The full text of the *Lettre du voyant* is translated, awkwardly, as "The Poet as Visionary," in Edgell Rickword, *Rimbaud: The Boy and the Poet* (London: Background Books, 1963), pp. 153-155.

strongest voice, and expressed the most human anguish—in Soviet Russia—religion would have the strongest flowering in the culture, if the political shackles of the regime were undone. In the invisible writing that is soundlessly heard, the recurrent underground theme is the salvation of man through the resurrection of traditional faith.[30]

What religion can restore is the continuity of generations, returning us to the existential predicaments which are the ground of humility and care for others. Yet such a continuity cannot be manufactured, nor a cultural revolution engineered. That thread is woven out of those experiences which give one a tragic sense of life, a life that is lived on the knife-edge of finitude and freedom.

[30] This is the thread which runs through the poems of *Doctor Zhivago*. In the final poem, "Garden of Gethsemane," Pasternak writes:

> But now the book of life has reached a page
> Which is more precious than are all the holies.
> That which was written now must be fulfilled.
> Fulfilled be it, then. Amen.
>
> • • •
>
> I shall descend into my grave. And on the third day rise again.
> And, even as rafts float down a river,
> So shall the centuries drift, trailing like a caravan,
> Coming for judgment, out of the dark, to me.

And that thread is picked up by Joseph Brodsky a decade later:

> The total of all today's embraces
> gives far less of love than the outstretched arms of
> Christ on the cross. This lame poet's finding
> looms before me in Holy Week, sixty-seven,
> blocking my leap to the nineteen-nineties.

"The poems of Yurii Zhivago," trans. Bernard Guilbert Guerney, in *Doctor Zhivago* (New York: Pantheon, 1958), pp. 558–559; Joseph Brodsky, "Adieu, Mademoiselle Véronique," in *Selected Poems*, trans. George Kline (New York: Harper & Row, 1973), p. 136. The "lame poet," as the translator notes, is a direct reference to Pasternak, who walked with a slight limp.

PART ONE

THE DOUBLE BIND
OF MODERNITY

The Cultural Contradictions of Capitalism

THE RELATIONSHIP between a civilization's socio-economic structure and its culture is perhaps the most complicated of all problems for the sociologist. A nineteenth-century tradition, one deeply impregnated with Marxist conceptions, held that changes in social structure determined man's imaginative reach. An earlier vision of man—as *homo pictor*, the symbol-producing animal, rather than as *homo faber*, the tool-making animal—saw him as a creature uniquely able to prefigure what he would later "objectify" or construct in reality. It thus ascribed to the realm of culture the initiative for change. Whatever the truth of these older arguments about the past, today culture has clearly become supreme; what is played out in the imagination of the artist foreshadows, however dimly, the social reality of tomorrow.

Culture has become supreme for two complementary reasons. First, culture has become the most dynamic component of our civilization, outreaching the dynamism of technology itself. There is now in art—as there has increasingly been for the past 100 years—a dominant impulse toward the new and original, a self-conscious search for future forms and sensations, so that the idea of change and novelty overshadows the dimensions of actual change. And, second, there has come about, in the last 50 years or so, a legitimation of this cultural impulse. Society now accepts this role for the imagination, rather than seeing culture, as in the past, as setting a norm and affirming a moral-philosophic tradition against which the new could be measured and (more often than not) censured. Indeed, society has done more than passively accept innovation; it has provided a market which eagerly gobbles up the new, because it believes it to be superior in value to all older forms. Thus, our culture has an unprecedented mission: it is an official, ceaseless search for a new sensibility.

It is true, of course, that the idea of change dominates the modern economy and modern technology as well. But changes in the economy and technology are constrained by available resources and financial cost. In politics, too, innovation is limited by existing institutional structures, by the veto power of contending groups, and to some extent by tradition. But the changes in expressive symbols and forms, difficult as it may be for the mass of people to absorb them readily, meet no resistance in the realm of culture itself.

What is singular about this "tradition of the new" (as Harold Rosenberg has called it) is that it allows art to be unfettered, to break down all genres and to explore all modes of experience and sensation. Fantasy today has few costs (is *anything* deemed bizarre or unspeakable today?) other than the risk of individual madness. And even madness, in the writings of such social theorists as Michel Foucault and R. D. Laing, is now conceived to be a superior form of truth! The new sensibilities, and the new styles of behavior associated with them, are created by small coteries which are devoted to exploring the new; because the new has value in and of itself, and meets with so little resistance, the new sensibility and its behavior-styles diffuse rapidly, transforming the thinking and actions of, the cultural mass (if not the larger masses of people), that new, large stratum of the intelligentsia in the society's knowledge and communications industries.

Along with this emphasis on the new has come the ideology, self-consciously accepted by the artist, that art will lead the way, will serve as the avant-garde. Now the very idea of an avant-garde—an advance assault team—indicates that modern art or culture would never permit itself to serve as a "reflection" of an underlying social structure but, rather, would open the way to something radically new. In fact, as we shall see, the very idea of an avant-garde, once its legitimacy is accepted, serves to institutionalize the primacy of culture in the fields of manners, morals, and, ultimately, politics.

34

The first major formulation of this conception of the avant-garde was made by the man who, ironically, has come to serve as the very symbol of technocratic rule, Henri de Saint-Simon. For all his vision of the engineer as the driving force of the new society, Saint-Simon knew that men were in want of inspiration, that Christianity itself was worn out, and that a new cult was needed. He found this new cult in the cult of art itself. The artist would reveal to society the glorious future, exciting men with the prospect of a new civilization. In a dialogue between an artist and a scientist, Saint-Simon gave the term "avant-garde" its modern cultural (rather than its earlier, military) meaning:

It is we, artists, who will serve you as avant-garde: the power of the arts is in fact most immediate and most rapid: when we wish to spread new ideas among men, we inscribe them on marble or on canvas; ... and in that way above all we exert an electric and victorious influence. We address ourselves to the imagination and to the sentiments of mankind, we should therefore always exercise the liveliest and the most decisive action. ...
What a most beautiful destiny for the arts, that of exercising over society a positive power, a true priestly function, and of marching forcefully in the van of all the intellectual faculties in the epoch of their greatest development! This is the duty of artists, this their mission. . . .[1]

The commonplace observation that today there is no longer a significant avant-garde—that there is no longer a radical tension between new art which shocks and a society that is shocked—merely signifies that the avant-garde has won its victory. A society given over entirely to innovation, in the joyful acceptance of change, has in fact institutionalized the avant-garde and charged it, perhaps to its own eventual dismay, with constantly turning up something new. In effect, "culture" has been given a blank check, and its primacy in generating social change has been firmly acknowledged.

[1] From *Opinions littéraires, philosophiques, et industrielles*, quoted by Donald Egbert, "The Idea of 'Avant-Garde' in Art and Politics," *American Historical Review* 73 (December 1967): 343.

I

THE MEANING OF CULTURE

Culture, for a society, a group, or a person, is a continual process of sustaining an identity through the coherence gained by a consistent aesthetic point of view, a moral conception of self, and a style of life which exhibits those conceptions in the objects that adorn one's home and oneself and in the taste which expresses those points of view. Culture is thus the realm of sensibility, of emotion and moral temper, and of the intelligence, which seeks to order these feelings.

Historically, most cultures and social structures have exhibited unity, although there have always been small groups expressing esoteric, deviant, usually libertine values. Classical culture expressed its unity through the fusion of reason and will in the pursuit of virtue. Christian culture exhibited consistency in the replication of the ordered ranks of society and the ordered ranks of the church with the hierarchies of heaven and hell, in the quest for salvation both in its social and aesthetic representations. In early modern times, bourgeois culture and bourgeois social structure fused a distinct unity with a specific character structure around the theme of order and work.

Classical social theory (I use the word "classical" here to denote the nineteenth- and early twentieth-century masters) also saw culture as unified with the social structure. Marx, as I have said, argued that the mode of production shaped all the other dimensions of a society. Culture as ideology reflected a substructure and could not have an autonomy of its own. Moreover, in bourgeois society, culture was tied to the economy because culture, too, had become a commodity, to be evaluated by the market and bought and sold through the exchange process. Max Weber argued that thought, conduct, and societal structure were highly integrated, in that all its branches—science, economy, law, and culture—were predominantly rationalistic. Even the modes of art were predominantly rationalistic. For Weber, this was true in a double sense: the cosmological aspects of Western thought and culture were characterized by the elimination of magic (in Schiller's phrase, the "disenchantment of the world"); and the structure and formal organization, the stylistics of the arts, were rational. Weber's particular example was Western harmonic chordal music, which rested on a scale that permitted a maximum of ordered relations, unlike primitive and non-Western music.[2] Finally Pitirim Sorokin, in his *Social and Cultural Dynamics*, argued that cultures were integrated by mentalities ("the central principle, 'the reason'"), which unite thought and meaning and permeate all aspects of a society. Contemporary society is sensate, in that it is empirical, materialistic, extraverted, oriented to technique, and hedonistic.

Against these views, what I find striking today is the radical disjunction between the social structure (the techno-economic order) and the culture. The former is ruled by an economic principle defined in terms of efficiency and functional rationality, the organization of production through the ordering of things, including men as things. The latter is prodigal, promiscuous, dominated by an anti-rational, anti-intellectual temper in which the self is taken as the touchstone of cultural judgments, and the effect on the self is the measure of the aesthetic worth of experience. The character structure inherited from the nineteenth century, with its emphasis on self-discipline, delayed gratification, and restraint, is still relevant to the demands of the techno-economic structure; but it clashes sharply with the culture, where such bourgeois values have been completely rejected—in part, paradoxically, because of the workings of the capitalist economic system itself.

DISCRETIONARY SOCIAL BEHAVIOR

As a discipline, sociology is based on the assumption that variations in the behavior of persons or groups in the society are attributable to their class or other strategic position in the social structure, and that individuals so differentially placed will vary systematically in their interests, attitudes, and conduct on the basis of distinct social attributes: common age, sex, occupation, religion, urban-rural location, and so forth. The presumption is that these attributes cluster in specific ways—usually identified in social-class terms—so that voting behavior, buying habits, child-rearing, and the like vary systematically on a class or status basis and are predictable.

[2] See Max Weber, *The Rational and Social Foundations of Music*, ed. Don Martindale et al. (Carbondale, Ill.: Southern Illinois University Press, 1958).

For the majority of the society, and for many aspects of social life (e.g., voting), this general proposition may still hold true. But it is increasingly evident that for a significant proportion of the population the relation of social position to cultural style—particularly if one thinks in such gross dimensions as working class, middle class, and upper class—no longer holds. The question of who will use drugs, engage in orgies and wife-swapping, become an open homosexual, use obscenity as a political style, or enjoy "happenings" and underground movies is not easily related to the "standard variables" of sociological discourse. Age and education may be more relevant discriminators; but given the expansion of mass higher education, even education alone is no longer an easy predictor of behavior. One finds many children of upper-middle-class families who joyfully embrace what they think is the "freedom" of working-class or black, lower-class life-styles, and others who do not. There is a significant leveling of patterns of child-training, which was one of the major indicators of different class styles in the past.

Just as in the economy the growth of what economists call *discretionary income*—income above that necessary for the fulfillment of basic needs—allowed individuals to choose many varied items to exemplify different consumption styles (swimming pools, boats, travel), so the expansion of higher education and the extension of a permissive social atmosphere has widened the scope of *discretionary social behavior*. The more idiosyncratic aspects of personal experience and life history—personality attributes, or somatic body-type constitution, positive or negative experience with parents, experience with peers—become increasingly more important than patterned social attributes in shaping a person's life-style. As the traditional social class structure dissolves, more and more individuals want to be identified not by their occupational base (in the Marxist sense), but by their cultural tastes and life-styles.

THE ARTIST MAKES THE AUDIENCE

A change has been taking place, as well, in the relation of artist to public. The familiar image, a product of nineteenth-century Romanticism, was that of a coterie of artists, engaged in difficult experimental work to which the smug middle-class audience responded with scorn and outrage. This was the fate of the Impressionist painters, who appeared first in the *Salon des Refusés* (1863) to emphasize their own disgust with the regnant taste, and who had to wait 20 years for the *Salon des Indépendants* for the same freedom to exhibit. The avant-garde artist identified this rejection with freedom, and he depended on such tension with the audience to articulate his own work. This well-known pattern came to be regarded as a congenital condition of modern art. But as James Ackerman writes, "within the last decade [this pattern] was broken by one of history's most abrupt and radical changes in the relationship of art and its public . . . the new era became recognizable first in the ultimate reception of the work of the New York School of artists in the mid- and late 1950s." Jackson Pollock, Willem de Kooning, Franz Kline, Mark Rothko, Barnett Newman, Robert Motherwell, David Smith, the men responsible for what Clement Greenberg called "abstract expressionism" (and Harold Rosenberg "action painting"), were preoccupied with problems of structure and medium—breaking away from the easel, using paint itself as a subject for art, involving the artist's own person in the painting—of a special and esoteric nature outside the experience of the layman. Professor Ackerman observes that "their art was so difficult to approach that even the majority of approving professional critics missed the mark and praised it for irrelevant reasons." In fact, the immediate response of an incredulous public was to call it a sham. But within half a decade the major figures in the school had been acclaimed, and their paintings dominated the museums and the galleries. Their conceptions of art now set the taste for the public.[3]

Perhaps the change in this case is not so abrupt as Professor Ackerman makes it seem. There had been earlier and similar changes in the role of "difficult" art in Paris decades earlier, when Picasso and Matisse began to shape public taste. But the general point stands. The middle-class audience, the wealthy buyer, no longer controls art. In painting, in film (perhaps less so in advanced music), the artist, and usually the avant-garde artist, now dominates the cultural scene. It is he who swiftly shapes the audience and the market, rather than being shaped by them.

This change is related, I believe, to the dissociation of social location and cultural style. Ackerman also writes:

[3] James Ackerman, "The Demise of the *Avant Garde*: Notes on the Sociology of Recent American Art," *Comparative Studies in Society and History* 2 (October 1969): 371–384, esp. 378.

If one's position in society implies no determinate base of judgment in areas outside one's competence, one has a choice between having no opinion or accepting the opinion of the expert, and the most available expert is the professional manufacturer of opinion. The altered response to the arts is, I believe, a product of public deference to museums, commercial galleries, and the news media.

Whether there is now a general habit of "trusting the experts" is debatable. In politics, there has been a notable populist reaction against the expert or technocrat. But the situation in art is different. Here we see, not the victory of the expert, but of "culture" itself—or more specifically of its predominant current, modernism. The culture of the past 100 years, that of the "modern movement," has triumphed over a society that in its social structure (economics, technology, and occupational bases) remains bourgeois. The culture has become detached and self-determining. Yet with all that, the culture (as exemplified in the modern movement) feels itself under attack—does not understand or accept its victory—and remains, as Lionel Trilling has called it, an "adversary culture."

"Any historian of the literature of the modern age," Trilling writes, "will take virtually for granted the adversary intention, the actually subversive intention, that characterizes modern writing—he will perceive its clear purpose of detaching the reader from the habits of thought and feeling that the larger culture imposes, of giving him a ground and a vantage point from which to judge and condemn, and perhaps revise, the culture that has produced him."[4]

The legend of modernism is that of the free creative spirit at war with the bourgeoisie. Whatever the truth of such a view when, say, Whistler was accused of having "flung a pot of paint in the public's face," in our time the idea is a caricature. Who in the world today, especially in the world of culture, defends the bourgeoisie? Yet in the domain of those who think themselves serious about culture, and of their widespread and trailing *epigoni*, the legend of the free creative spirit now at war, no longer merely with bourgeois society but with "civilization" or "repressive tolerance" or some other agency that curtails "freedom," still sustains an adversary culture.

The adversary culture has come to dominate the cultural order, and this is why the hierophants of the culture—the painters, the writers, the filmmakers—now dominate the audience, rather than vice versa. Indeed, the subscribers to this adversary culture are

[4] Lionel Trilling, *Beyond Culture* (New York: Viking, 1965), pp. xii–xiii.

sufficiently numerous to form a distinct cultural class. Compared to the society as a whole, the membership in this class is not large. No statistical estimates are possible, and the figure could vary from a few hundred thousand to a couple of million. But size alone is meaningless, for, compared to the past, three extraordinary changes are evident.

First, there has been an evident change in scale. Even though tiny by comparison with the numbers of the total society, the present cultural class is numerous enough for these individuals no longer to be outcasts, or a bohemian enclave, in the society. They function institutionally as a group, bound by a consciousness of kind.

Second, while minority life-styles and cultures have often conflicted with those of the majority, what is striking today is that the majority has no intellectually respectable culture of its own—no major figures in literature, painting, or poetry—to counterpose to the adversary culture. In this sense, bourgeois culture has been shattered.

Third, and perhaps most important, the protagonists of the adversary culture, because of the historic subversive effect on traditional bourgeois values, substantially influence, if not dominate, the cultural establishments today: the publishing houses, museums, and galleries; the major news, picture, and cultural weeklies and monthlies; the theater, the cinema, and the universities.

Today, each new generation, starting off at the benchmarks attained by the adversary culture of its cultural parents, declares in sweeping fashion that the status quo represents backward conservatism or repression, so that, in a widening gyre, new and fresh assaults on the social structure are mounted.

The historic process I have been sketching has deep roots in the past. It has remarkable cultural drive and continuity. Much of that drive was obscured in the 1950s, essentially a decade of political conservatism and cultural bewilderment. Politically, this was a period of disillusionment. It witnessed the final rupture of the intellectuals from Stalinism, a shattering of the belief that the Soviet Union was "progressive" merely because it called itself socialist. A number of sociologists—Raymond Aron, Edward Shils, S. M. Lipset, and myself—thus came to view the 1950s as characterized by an "end of ideology." By this we meant that the older political ideas of the radical movement had become exhausted and no longer had the power to compel allegiance or passion among the intelligentsia.[5]

Although there was a widespread disillusionment with the chiliastic promises of political radicalism, there was almost no positive viewpoint to take its place. The welfare state and the mixed economy were not the sort of goals that could capture the passions of the intelligentsia. Moreover, even if radical political hopes were momentarily shattered, the basic cultural stance remained the same: the rejection of bourgeois values. Indeed, the continuity of radicalism in the 1950s was possible not through politics but through the culture.

The experience of the 1940s had traumatized the intelligentsia of the 1950s, and the reflections on that experience determined its cultural concerns. The pervasive cultural theme of the era was the depersonalization of the individual and the atomization of society. World War II was horrible, of course. But war, even the mass bombing of cities, had been prefigured in the imagination, and, curiously, once something has been imagined, it loses some of its capacity to arouse complete indignation or fear. But concentration camps enfolding tens of millions, and death camps that processed millions of people like cattle through a slaughterhouse, had never been imagined.[6]

---

[5] I should point out that the analysis of the "end of ideology" did not assume that all social conflict had ended and that the intelligentsia would forswear the search for new ideologies. In fact, as I wrote in 1959, "The young intellectual is unhappy because the 'middle way' is for the middle-aged, not for him; it is without passion and is deadening. . . . In the search for a 'cause' there is a deep, desperate, almost pathetic anger." The argument was also made that new ideologies would arise as a source of radicalism and that these would be third-world ideologies, not the humanistic ones of nineteenth-century Western society. See *The End of Ideology* (Glencoe, Ill.: Free Press, 1960), pp. 373 et seq.

[6] The culture of the 1950s—the writers who were read and studied as exemplars of the contemporary spirit—reflected that incomprehension of totalitarian terror. The primary literary figure was Franz Kafka, whose novels and stories, written 30 years before, were found to have anticipated that dense bureaucratic world where justice could not be located and where the torture machine inflicted a horrible death on its victims. The writings of Kierkegaard were "discovered," perhaps because he counseled that no rational belief in ultimate meanings was possible, only the leap of faith. The neo-orthodox theology of Barth and Niebuhr was pessimistic about man's ability to transcend the sinfulness inherent in human pride. Simone Weil's essays dealt with the desperate search for grace. Camus scrutinized the moral paradoxes of political action. In the "theater of the absurd," Ionesco wrote plays like *The Chairs*, in which objects came to have a life of their own, as if the reified things of the world had actually drawn the spirit out of man and taken over his will. In the theater of silence, exemplified by Beckett's *Waiting for Godot*, the confusions of time and self were played out in a minimal rectangle of reality.

The point is relevant because there is a tendency to assume that because political conservatism dominated the period the serious culture was sterile. It was not.

The sociology of the 1950s was similarly concerned with the theory of the "mass society" and the rediscovery of "alienation." The theory of the mass society saw in the modern world the shattering of the traditional primary-group ties of family and local community; it saw traditional orders replaced by the "mass," in which each person lived in atomistic or anomic fashion. The rediscovery of alienation—and it was a *re*discovery, for though it has been associated with Marxism, the first generation of Marxist writers (Kautsky, Plekhanov, Lenin) had never used the term—became the primary theme of sociology. It had not been discussed before this time.[7]

On a more mundane level, the most popular book of sociology in the 1950s was David Riesman's *The Lonely Crowd*, which described a major change in character structure in contemporary society—from an individual who was self-disciplined and self-motivated (in short, the historic bourgeois man) to one who was responsive primarily to his peer group and the pressure of "others." The very title of the book conveyed a judgment about the quality of the change. Similarly, the prototypical book of the emerging youth culture in the 1950s was J. D. Salinger's *The Catcher in the Rye*, whose narrator, Holden Caulfield, epitomized a new kind of person, almost autistic in his inability to establish real connections in the world around him. The "beats," led by Allen Ginsberg and Jack Kerouac, harbingers of the youth movement of the 1960s, had already "dropped out" of the society.

In short, though political ideas had become exhausted—and political life was dominated by the threat of a foreign Communist foe—the cultural intelligentsia brooded on themes of despair, anomie, and alienation, themes which were to achieve a political incarnation in the 1960s.

[7] The contemporary rediscovery of alienation had a double source. On the one hand, it was associated, principally through the writings of Max Weber, with the sense of powerlessness that individuals felt in the society. Marx's emphasis on the worker "separated" from the means of production became, in Weber's perspective, one special case of a universal trend in which the modern soldier is separated from the means of violence, the scientist from the means of inquiry, and the civil servant from the means of administration. On the other hand, it was a theme put forward by Marxist revisionists, principally of the post-Stalinist generation, who hoped to find the sources of a new humanism in Marx's early writings, mainly the *Economic-Philosophical Manuscripts*. In both instances, the theory of mass society and the theme of alienation, what was involved were critical cultural judgments on the quality of life in modern society.

THE MIDDLEBROWS OF THE 1950S

The affluence of middle-class America in the 1950s had its counterpart in a widespread "middlebrow" culture. The term itself reflected the new style of cultural criticism. In effect, culture, as it came to be conceived in the mass middle-class magazines, was not a discussion of serious works of art but a style of life that was organized and "consumed." Following suit, cultural criticism became a snob's game, played by advertising men, magazine illustrators, home decorators, women's magazine editors, and East Side homosexuals as one more fashionable amusement. The game of high-low-and-middle became *démodé* once the middlebrows caught on, to be quickly replaced by the new game of in-and-out. To be "in" meant to be well ahead of the crowd in fashion, or, perversely, to like what the vulgar masses liked (the New York *Daily News*, fast-paced, grade-B movie thrillers, popular songs) rather than what the pretentious middle classes liked. When in-and-out was replaced by "camp," the game was the same, except that fashion had become low fashion.

But even though cultural criticism became a game, it was also a serious problem for the intellectual, who was now invited to play a role in a culture he had always mocked. The writers for *Partisan Review* now came to dominate the *New Yorker*, a magazine that had been scorned in the 1930s and 1940s. Writers for *Commentary* were invited to write in the *New York Times Sunday Magazine* section. Even the *Saturday Evening Post* began running articles in its "Adventures of the Mind" series by such writers and critics as Randall Jarrell and Clement Greenberg. Many of the radical writers felt that the mass media courted them in order to provide prestige for the mass magazines; and an even more sinister motive, the "taming" of radical criticism altogether, was suspected. What was not realized was that society itself had lost its cultural moorings.

The relationship of the serious critic and intellectual to the burgeoning mass culture of the 1950s became a discrete problem in itself and the source of many a lengthy essay and symposium. The fundamental response of the radical intellectual was a wide-ranging attack on middle-class culture. For the serious critic, the real enemy, the worst kitsch, was not the vast sea of trash but middlebrow culture; or, as Dwight Macdonald labeled it, "Midcult." In "Masscult," Macdonald wrote, "The trick is plain—to please the crowd by any means. But Midcult has it both ways: it pretends to respect the standards of High Culture while in fact it waters them down and vulgarizes them."[8]

Hannah Arendt, a thoughtful and disquieting social critic, took the classical argument one step further and blended with it a historical-Marxist analysis. She argued that bourgeois "society"—she here means the relatively homogeneous community of educated and cultivated persons—had always treated culture as a commodity and had gained snob values from its exchange; there had always existed a certain tension between culture (i.e., the producers of art) and society (which consumed it).[9] But for her there were two crucial differences between the past and the present. In the old days, individualism flourished or was made possible through an escape *from* society, often into rebel or bohemian worlds. ("A good part of the despair of individuals under conditions of mass society is due to the fact that these avenues of escape are, of course, closed as soon as society has incorporated all the strata of the population.") Moreover, though "society" in the past coveted culture largely for its snob appeal, it did not *consume* culture, even if it abused or devalued it and turned "cultural things into social commodities." Mass society, "on the contrary, wants not culture, but entertainment, and the wares offered by the entertainment industry are indeed consumed by society just as are any other consumer goods."

In sum, though in the 1950s there was a burning out of the radical political will, this radical will—the distancing of self from the society—was maintained in the culture and through cultural criticism. When new political impulses arose in the 1960s, radicalism found the values of the adversary culture—the attack on society through such themes as mass society, anomie, alienation—as the Ariadne's thread which allowed it to emerge into a new radical period.

[8] Macdonald's idiom itself needs explaining. In the early 1930s, the "tough" phase of American radicalism, a Bolshevik habit of compressing words—*politburo* for the political bureau of the Party, or *orgburo* for the organization bureau—caught on. Thus, the vogue of proletarian literature was known as *proletcult*. Macdonald adopted this jargon for his own sardonic style; see *Masscult & Midcult*, Partisan Review Series, no. 4, 1961.

[9] Hannah Arendt, "Society and Culture," in *Culture for the Millions?*, ed. Norman Jacobs (Princeton: Van Nostrand, 1961), pp. 43-53. The argument is elaborated in *Between Past and Future* (New York: Viking, 1961), pp. 197-226.

ENTER MODERNISM

We come to an extraordinary sociological puzzle. A single cultural temper, mood, movement—its very amorphousness or protean nature precludes a single encapsulating term—has persisted for more than a century and a quarter, providing renewed and sustained attacks on the social structure. The most inclusive term for this cultural temper is *modernism*: the self-willed effort of a style and sensibility to remain in the forefront of "advancing consciousness." What is the nature, then, of this sentiment that, antedating even Marxism, has been attacking bourgeois society and, without the kind of sustained organization a political movement possesses, has been able to sustain such a program? Why did it so capture the artistic imagination that it could preserve itself through generations and have fresh appeal for each new cohort of the intelligentsia?

Modernism pervades all the arts. Yet if one looks at particular examples, there seems to be no single unifying principle. It includes the new syntax of Mallarmé, the dislocation of forms in cubism, the stream of consciousness in Virginia Woolf and Joyce, the atonality of Berg. Each of these, as it first appeared, was "difficult" to understand. In fact, as a number of writers have suggested, original difficulty is a sign of modernism. It is willfully opaque, works with unfamiliar forms, is self-consciously experimental, and seeks deliberately to disturb the audience—to shock it, shake it up, even to transform it as if in a religious conversion. This very difficulty is clearly one source of its appeal to initiates, for esoteric knowledge, like the special formula of the magi or the hermeticism of ancient priests, gives one an enhanced sense of power over the vulgar and the unenlightened.

Irving Howe has suggested that the modern must be defined in terms of what it is not, as an "inclusive negative." Modernity, he writes, "consists in a revolt against the prevalent style, *an unyielding rage against* the official order." But this very condition, as Howe points out, creates a dilemma: "Modernism must always struggle but never quite triumph, and then, after a time, must struggle in order not to triumph."[10] This is true, I think, and explains its continuing adversary stance. But it does not explain the "unyielding

[10] Irving Howe, ed., *The Idea of the Modern in Literature and the Arts* (New York: Horizon Press, 1967), p. 13. My italics.

rage," or the need to negate every prevalent style including, in the end, its own.

Modernism, seen as a whole, exhibits a striking parallel to a common assumption of the social science of the late nineteenth century. For Marx, Freud, and Pareto, the irrationality of the substructures of reality belied the surface rationality of appearances. For Marx, beneath the exchange process was the anarchy of the market; for Freud, beneath the tight reins of ego was the limitless unconscious, driven by instinct; for Pareto, under the forms of logic were the residues of irrational sentiment and emotion. Modernism, too, insists on the meaninglessness of appearance and seeks to uncover the substructure of the imagination. This expresses itself in two ways. One, stylistically, is an attempt to eclipse "distance"—psychic distance, social distance, and aesthetic distance—and insist on the absolute presentness, the simultaneity and immediacy, of experience. The other, thematically, is the insistence on the absolute imperiousness of the self, of man as the "self-infinitizing" creature who is impelled to search for the beyond.

Modernism is a response to two social changes in the nineteenth century, one on the level of sense perception of the social environment, the other of consciousness about the self. In the everyday world of sense impressions, there was a disorientation of the sense of space and time, derived from the new awareness of motion and speed, light, and sound that came from the revolution in communication and transport. The crisis in self-consciousness arose from the loss of religious certitude, of belief in an afterlife, in heaven or hell, and from the new consciousness of an immutable boundary beyond life and the nothingness of death. In effect, these were two new ways of experiencing the world, and often the artist himself was never wholly aware of the disorientation in the social environment which had shaken up the world and made it seem as if there were only pieces. Yet he had to reassemble these pieces in a new way.

MODERNISM: SYNTAX AND FORM

For the second half of the nineteenth century, then, an ordered world was a chimera. What was suddenly real, in molding the sense perception of an environment, was movement and flux. A radical change in the nature of aesthetic perception had suddenly occurred. If one asks, in aesthetic terms, how modern man differs from the Greeks in experiencing sensations or emotions, the answer would have to do not with the basic human feelings, such as friendship, love, fear, cruelty, and aggression, which are common to all ages, but with the temporal-spatial dislocation of motion and height. In the nineteenth century, for the first time in history, men could travel faster than by foot or on an animal, and gain a different sense of changing landscape, a succession of images, the blur of motion, which he had never before experienced. Or one could, first in a balloon and later in a plane, rise thousands of feet in the sky and see from the air topographical patterns that the ancients had never known.

What was true of the physical world was equally true of the social. With the growth of numbers and density in the cities, there was greater interaction among people, a syncretism of experience that provided a sudden openness to new styles of life and to a geographical and social mobility that had never been available before. In the canvases of art, the subjects were no longer the mythological creatures of the past, or the stillness of nature, but the promenade and the *plage*, the bustle of city life, and the brilliance of night life in an urban environment transformed by electric light. It is this response to movement, space, and change which provided the new syntax of art and the dislocation of traditional forms.

In the classical pre-modern view, art was essentially contemplative; the viewer or spectator held "power" over the experience by keeping his aesthetic distance from it. In modernism, the intention is to "overwhelm" the spectator so that the art product itself— through the foreshortening of perspective in painting, or the "sprung rhythm" of a Gerard Manley Hopkins in poetry—imposes itself on the spectator in its own terms. In modernism, genre becomes an archaic conception whose distinctions are ignored in the flux of experience.

It is this modernist effort to capture the flux which gives meaning, I think, to Virginia Woolf's gnomic remark, "On or about December 1910, human nature changed." As Irving Howe comments, in this hyperbole there is a "frightening discontinuity between the traditional past and the shaken present . . . the line of history has been bent, perhaps broken."

In making this break, in the emphasis on the absolute present, both artist and spectator are forced to make and remake themselves anew each moment. With the repudiation of unbroken continuity, and the belief that the future is in the present, one loses the classical sense of wholeness or completeness. The fragment or the part replaces the whole. One finds a new aesthetic in the broken torso, the isolated hand, the primitive grimace, the figure cut by the frame, rather than in the bounded whole. And in the mingling and jostling of styles, the very idea of genre and boundary, of principles appropriate to a genre, is abandoned. One might say, in fact, that aesthetic disaster itself becomes an aesthetic.

MODERNISM: NOTHINGNESS AND SELF

The sense of movement and change—the upheaval in the mode of confronting the world—established vivid new conventions and forms by which people judged their sense perceptions and experience. But more subtly, the awareness of change prompted a deeper crisis in the human spirit, the fear of nothingness. The decline of religion, and especially of belief in an immortal soul, provoked a momentous break with the centuries-old conception of an unbridgeable chasm between the human and the divine. Men now sought to cross that gulf and, as Faust, the first modern, put it, attain "godlike knowledge," to "prove in man the stature of a god" or else confess his "kinship with the worm."

As a consequence of this superhuman effort, in the nineteenth century the sense of the self came to the fore. The individual was considered unique, with singular aspirations, and life assumed a greater sanctity and preciousness. The enhancement of the single life became a value for its own sake. Economic meliorism, antislavery sentiment, women's rights, and the end of child labor and cruel punishments became the social issues of the day. But in a deeper metaphysical sense, this spiritual enterprise became the basis of the idea that men could go beyond necessity, that they would no longer be constrained by nature but could arrive, in Hegel's phrase, at the end of history, in the kingdom of perfect freedom. The "unhappy consciousness" of which Hegel wrote is the realization of a divine power and status that man must strive to achieve. The deepest nature of modern man, the secret of his soul as revealed by the modern metaphysic, is that he seeks to reach out beyond himself; knowing that negativity—death—is finite, he refuses to accept it. Behind the chiliasm of modern man is the megalomania of self-infinitization. In consequence, the modern hubris is the refusal to accept limits, the insistence on continually reaching out; and the modern world proposes a destiny that is always *beyond*: beyond morality, beyond tragedy, beyond culture.[11]

THE TRIUMPH OF THE WILL

In Western consciousness there has always been tension between the rational and the nonrational, between reason and will, between reason and instinct, as the driving forces of man. Whatever the specific distinctions, rational judgment was traditionally thought to be superior in the hierarchy, and this order dominated Western culture for almost two millennia.

Modernism dirempts this hierarchy. It is the triumph of the spirited, of the will. In Hobbes and Rousseau, intelligence is a slave to appetite and the passions. In Hegel, the will is the necessary component of knowing. In Nietzsche, the will is fused with the aesthetic mode, in which knowledge derives most directly ("apprehended, not ascertained," as he says in the first line of *The Birth of Tragedy*) from intoxication and dream. And if the aesthetic experience alone is to justify life, then morality is suspended and desire has no limit. Anything is possible in this quest of the self to explore its relation to sensibility.

The emphasis of modernism is on the present or on the future, but never on the past. Yet when one is cut off from the past, one cannot escape the final sense of nothingness that the future then holds. Faith is no longer possible, and art or nature or impulse can erase the self only momentarily in the intoxication or frenzy of the Dionysian act. But intoxication always passes, and there is the cold morning after, which arrives inexorably with the break of day. This

[11] Compare these powerful statements by two contemporary writers. In Malraux's *Man's Fate* (New York: Vintage Books, 1961), p. 228, Old Gisors describes to Ferral man and his desires: "To be more than a man in a world of men. To escape man's fate. [To be] not powerful: all powerful. The visionary disease, of which the will to power is only the intellectual justification, is the will to godhead: every man dreams of being god."

In Saul Bellow's *Mr. Sammler's Planet* (New York: Viking, 1970), pp. 33–34, old Sammler reflects: "You wondered whether . . . the worst enemies of civilization might not prove to be its petted intellectuals who attacked it at its weakest moments —attacked it in the name of reason and in the name of irrationality, in the name of visceral depth, in the name of sex, in the name of perfect and instant freedom. For what it amounted to was limitless demand—insatiability, refusal of the doomed creature (death being sure and final) to go away from this world unsatisfied. A full bill of demand and complaint was therefore presented by each individual. Non-negotiable. Recognizing no scarcity in any human department."

inescapable eschatological anxiety leads inevitably to the feeling—the black thread of modernist thought—that each person's own life is at the end of time. The sense of an ending, the feeling that one is living in an apocalyptic age, is, as Frank Kermode has observed, "as endemic to what we call modernism as apocalyptic utopianism is to political revolution. . . . Its recurrence is a feature of our cultural tradition."[12]

In discussing modernism, the categories of "left" and "right" make little sense. Modernism, as Thomas Mann phrased it, cultivates "a sympathy for the abyss." Nietzsche, Yeats, Pound, and Wyndham Lewis were politically to the right. Gide was a pagan, Malraux a revolutionist. But whatever the political stripe, the modern movement has been united by rage against the social order as the first cause, and a belief in the apocalypse as the final cause. It is this trajectory which provides the permanent appeal and the permanent radicalism of that movement.

Traditional modernism sought to substitute for religion or morality an aesthetic justification of life; to create a work of art, to be a work of art—this alone provided meaning in man's effort to transcend himself. But in going back to art, as is evident in Nietzsche, the very search for the roots of self moves the quest of modernism from art to psychology: from the product to the producer, from the object to the psyche.

In the 1960s a powerful current of post-modernism developed which carried the logic of modernism to its farthest reaches. In the theoretical writings of Norman O. Brown and Michel Foucault, in the novels of William Burroughs, Jean Genet and, up to a point, Norman Mailer, and in the porno-pop culture that is now all about us, one sees a logical culmination of modernist intentions. They are, as Diana Trilling put it, "the adventurers beyond consciousness."

There are several dimensions to the post-modernist mood. Thus, against the aesthetic justification for life, post-modernism has completely substituted the instinctual. Impulse and pleasure alone are real and life-affirming; all else is neurosis and death. Moreover, traditional modernism, no matter how daring, played out its impulses in the imagination, within the constraints of art. Whether demonic or murderous, the fantasies were expressed through the ordering principle of aesthetic form. Art, therefore, even though

[12] Frank Kermode, *The Sense of an Ending* (New York: Oxford University Press, 1967), p. 98.

subversive of society, still ranged itself on the side of order and, implicitly, of a rationality of form, if not of content. Post-modernism overflows the vessels of art. It tears down the boundaries and insists that *acting out*, rather than making distinctions, is the way to gain knowledge. The "happening" and the "environment," the "street" and the "scene," are the proper arena not for art but for life.

Extraordinarily, none of this is in itself completely new. There has always been an esoteric tradition within all Western religion which has sanctioned participation in secret rites of release, debauch, and total freedom for those, the "gnostics," who have been initiated into secret sects through secret knowledge. Gnosticism, in its intellectual formulations, has provided the justification for the attacks on the restraints that every society has imposed on its members. Yet in the past this knowledge was kept hermetic, its members were secretive. What is most striking about post-modernism is that what was once maintained as esoteric is now proclaimed as ideology, and what was once the property of an aristocracy of the spirit is now turned into the democratic property of the mass. The gnostic mode has always beat against the historic, psychological taboos of civilization. That assault has now been made the platform of a widespread cultural movement.

The post-modern temper, looked at as a set of loosely associated doctrines, itself goes in two directions. One is philosophical, a kind of negative Hegelianism. Michel Foucault sees man as a short-lived historical incarnation, "a trace on the sand," to be washed away by the waves. The "ruined and pest-ridden cities of man called 'soul' and 'being' will be de-constructed." It is no longer the decline of the West, but the end of all civilization. Much of this is modish, a play of words pushing a thought to an absurd logicality. Like the angry playfulness of Dada or surrealism, it will probably be remembered, if at all, as a footnote to cultural history.

But the post-modern temper, moving in another direction, does carry a much more significant implication. It provides the psychological spearhead for an onslaught on the values and motivational patterns of "ordinary" behavior, in the name of liberation, eroticism, freedom of impulse, and the like. It is this, dressed up in more popular form, which is the importance of the post-modernist doctrine. For it means that a crisis of middle-class values is at hand.

DEATH OF THE BOURGEOIS WORLD-VIEW

The bourgeois world-view—rationalistic, matter-of-fact, pragmatic—had by the mid-nineteenth century come to dominate not only the techno-economic structure but also the culture, especially the religious order and the educational system which instilled "appropriate" motivation in the child. It reigned triumphant everywhere, opposed only in the realm of culture by those who disdained its unheroic and anti-tragic mood, as well as its orderly attitude toward time.

As we have seen, the last 100 years have witnessed an effort by anti-bourgeois culture to achieve autonomy from the social structure, first by denying bourgeois values in the realm of art, and second by carving out enclaves where the bohemian and the avant-gardist could live a contrary style of life. By the turn of the century the avant-garde had succeeded in establishing a "life-space" of its own, and by 1910–1930 it was on the offensive against traditional culture.

In both doctrine and life-style, the anti-bourgeois won out. This triumph meant that in the culture antinomianism and anti-institutionalism ruled. In the realm of art, on the level of aesthetic doctrine, few opposed the idea of boundless experiment, of unfettered freedom, of unconstrained sensibility, of impulse being superior to order, of the imagination being immune to merely rational criticism. There is no longer an avant-garde, because no one in our postmodern culture is on the side of order or tradition. There exists only a desire for the new—or boredom with the old and the new.

The traditional bourgeois organization of life—its rationalism and sobriety—now has few defenders in the culture, nor does it have any established system of cultural meanings or stylistic forms with any intellectual or cultural respectability. To assume, as some social critics do, that the technocratic mentality dominates the cultural order is to fly in the face of every bit of evidence at hand. What we have today is a radical disjunction of culture and social structure, and it is such disjunctions which historically have paved the way for more direct social revolutions.

In two fundamental ways that new revolution has already begun. First, the autonomy of culture, achieved in art, now begins to pass over into the arena of life. The post-modernist temper demands that what was previously played out in fantasy and imagination must be acted out in life as well. There is no distinction between art and life. Anything permitted in art is permitted in life as well.

Second, the life-style once practiced by a small *cénacle*, whether the cool life mask of a Baudelaire or the hallucinatory rage of a Rimbaud, is now copied by the "many" (a minority in the society, to be sure, but nonetheless large in number) and dominates the cultural scene. This change of scale gave the culture of the 1960s its special surge, coupled with the fact that a bohemian life-style once limited to a tiny elite is now acted out on the giant screen of the mass media.

The combination of these two changes adds up to the renewal of the onslaught by the "culture" against the "social structure." When such attacks were launched before—say, André Breton's surrealist proposal in the early 1930s that the towers of Notre Dame be replaced by an enormous glass cruet, one of the bottles filled with blood, the other with sperm, the church itself becoming a sexual school for virgins—they were understood as heavy-handed japes, perpetrated by the licensed "fools" of society. But the rise of a hip-drug-rock culture on the popular level (and the "new sensibility" of black-mass humor and violence in the arena of culture) undermines the social structure itself by striking at the motivational and psychic-reward system which has sustained it. In this sense, the culture of the 1960s had a new and perhaps distinctive historic meaning, as an end, and as a beginning.

II

FROM THE PROTESTANT ETHIC TO THE PSYCHEDELIC BAZAAR

Changes in cultural ideas have an immanence and autonomy because they develop from an internal logic at work within a cultural tradition. In this sense, new ideas and forms derive from a kind of dialogue with, or rebellion against, previous ideas and forms. But changes in cultural practices and life-styles necessarily interact with social structure, since works of art, decoration, records, films, and plays are bought and sold in the market. The market is where social structure and culture cross. Changes in culture as a whole, particularly the emergence of new life-styles, are made possible not only by changes in sensibility, but also by shifts in the social structure itself. One can see this most readily, in American society, in the development of new buying habits in a high consumption economy and the resultant erosion of the Protestant ethic and the Puritan temper, the two codes which sustained the traditional value system of American bourgeois society. It is the breakup of this ethic and temper, owing as much to changes in social structure as to changes in the culture, that has undercut the beliefs and legitimations that sanctioned work and reward in American society. It is this transformation and the lack of any rooted new ethic that are responsible, in good part, for the sense of disorientation and dismay that marks the public mood today. What I propose to do here is to take my general argument about modernism and bourgeois society and trace out the effects more specifically in American society, which has been the exemplar of the bourgeois mode.

THE SMALL-TOWN LIFE

The Protestant ethic and the Puritan temper were codes that emphasized work, sobriety, frugality, sexual restraint, and a forbidding attitude toward life. They defined the nature of moral conduct and social respectability. The post-modernist culture of the 1960s has been interpreted, because it calls itself a "counter-culture," as defying the Protestant ethic, heralding the end of Puritanism, and mounting a final attack on bourgeois values. This is too facile. The Protestant ethic and the Puritan temper, as social facts, were eroded long ago, and they linger on as pale ideologies, used more by moralists to admonish and by sociologists to mythologize than as behavioral realities. The breakup of the traditional bourgeois value system, in fact, was brought about by the bourgeois economic system—by the free market, to be precise. This is the source of the contradiction of capitalism in American life.

The Protestant ethic and the Puritan temper in the United States were the world-view of an agrarian, small-town, mercantile and artisan way of life. In the United States, as Page Smith reminds us, "if we except the family and the church, the basic form of social organization up to the early decades of the twentieth century was the small town."[13] The life and character of American society were shaped by the small town, and its religions. They were necessary to enforce strong codes of community sanctions in a hostile environment; they provided meaning and justification for work and restraint in subsistence economies.

If the core values of American society are summed up by the terms "Puritan temper" and "Protestant ethic," they are represented by the two men who stand as exemplars of the early American spirit, Jonathan Edwards as the Puritan and Benjamin Franklin as the Protestant. The thought and homiletics of these two men laid down the specific virtues and maxims of the American character. As Van Wyck Brooks wrote in *America's Coming-of-Age*:

> For three generations the prevailing American character was compact in one type, the man of action who was also the man of God. Not until the eighteenth century did the rift appear and with it the essential distinction between "Highbrow" and "Lowbrow." It appeared in the two philosophers, Jonathan Edwards and Benjamin Franklin, who shared the eighteenth century between them. In their singular purity of type and in the apparent incompatibility of their aims they determined the American character as a racial fact, and after them the Revolution became inevitable. Channing, Lincoln, Emerson, Whitman, Grant, Webster, Garrison, Edison, Rockefeller, Mrs. Eddy, Woodrow Wilson are all, in one way or another, permutations and combinations of these two grand progenitors of the American mind.[14]

Without doubt, as Brooks and, following him, Perry Miller have insisted, the thought of the Puritan theocracy is the great influential fact in the history of the American mind. In the mid-eighteenth century, America's leading intellectuals were clergymen and their thoughts were about theology. For more than 100 years, their thought dominated all speculative philosophy in America. And even when the theology was gone, the deep sense of guilt, especially about sexual conduct, which had been instilled in the American character lay imprinted and almost ineradicable for another century.

"It is notorious," George Santayana observed more than 50 years ago, "how metaphysical was the passion that drove the Puritans to these shores; they went there in the hope of living more perfectly in

13 Page Smith, *As a City upon a Hill* (New York: Alfred A. Knopf, 1960), p.vii.
14 Van Wyck Brooks, *America's Coming-of-Age* (Garden City, N.Y.: Doubleday Anchor, 1958; orig. ed., 1915), p. 5.

the spirit."[15] The core of the Puritan belief was hostility to civilization. The society of the time was corrupt, and one had to return to the primitive simplicity of the original church, which drew its will directly from God rather than from man-made institutions.

The Puritans had signed a covenant which committed each man to an exemplary life. But no person—or doctrine—can live at a fever pitch of intensity for prolonged periods, especially when it means maintaining a life of stern discipline over the springs of impulse. Calvinism, even in the early American colonies, was constantly being nibbled away as new doctrines, such as Arminianism (the basis of Wesley's Methodism), tried to replace absolute predestination with conditional election. What Jonathan Edwards did was to provide a renewal of the Absolute and a psychological mechanism whereby the individual could scrutinize himself and hold himself to account. In *The Great Christian Doctrine of Original Sin Defended* (1758), Edwards attacked those who would relax Calvinism. He argued that depravity is inevitable because the identity of consciousness makes all men one with Adam. He believed in a privileged elect, not of those bearing the outward sign of work but of those who experienced saving grace by some inner illumination, by a transforming experience.

If Jonathan Edwards was the aesthetic and intuitive Puritan, Benjamin Franklin was the pragmatic and utilitarian Protestant. He was a practical man who looked at the world with an unblinking eye, intent mainly on "getting ahead" by frugality, industry, and native shrewdness. Franklin's life exemplified that fundamental American characteristic, self-improvement. Trying to imitate the manner of Addison's *Spectator*, Franklin wrote his own paragraphs, compared them with his mentor, and rewrote them, thus acquiring a vocabulary and fashioning a style of his own. Doggedly, he taught himself French, Italian, Spanish, and Latin. To relieve the "itch" of youthful passions, he entered into a common-law union with his landlady's daughter and had two children by her.

The key word in Franklin's vocabulary was "useful." His one book, the *Autobiography*, was begun as something that might be useful to his son; that purpose served, the book was never finished. He invented a stove, founded a hospital, paved the streets, estab-

[15] George Santayana, *Character and Opinion in the United States* (New York: Braziller, 1955; orig. ed., 1920), p. 7.

lished a city police force, for all these were useful projects. He believed it was useful to believe in God, for God rewards virtue and punishes vice. In *Poor Richard's Almanack* (1732–1757), Franklin pilfered the world's store of aphorisms and adapted them as homilies for the poor. "As Poor Richard says" became a phrase that gave weight to all the right virtues. There were, Franklin said, 13 useful virtues: temperance, silence, order, resolution, frugality, industry, sincerity, justice, moderation, cleanliness, tranquillity, chastity, and humility. There is perhaps no better inventory of the American creed. Franklin wrote that he gave to each a week's strict attention, setting down in a notebook the measure of daily success achieved in its practice. And thus he went through "a course complete in thirteen weeks and four courses a year."[16]

Yet all this was partly cunning, and perhaps even deceit. While Franklin was thrifty and industrious, his success, like that of many a good Yankee, came from his capacity to make influential friends, an uncanny ability to advertise himself, and the charm and wit reflected in his person and his writing. (Even the "itch" proved renewable, for he sired two more illegitimate children.) He amassed a modest fortune, retired to pursue his interest in natural philosophy and electricity, and for six years Franklin used his leisure for disinterested study before being drawn into public life.

Two images have come down to us as the essence of the American character: the piety and torment of Jonathan Edwards, obsessed with human depravity, and the practicality and expedience of Benjamin Franklin, oriented to a world of possibility and gain. Again, it is Van Wyck Brooks who best portrayed this dualism, writing almost 60 years ago:

So it is that from the beginning we find two main currents in the American mind running side by side but rarely mingling—a current of overtones and a current of undertones—and both equally unsocial: on the one hand, the transcendental current, originating in the piety of the Puritans, becoming a philosophy in Jonathan Edwards, passing through

---

[16] In his magisterial work, *The Protestant Ethic and the Spirit of Capitalism*, Max Weber sees Franklin as the embodiment of both. He cites his "sermons," as he calls them (". . . Time is money . . . Remember that credit is money. If a man lets his money lie in my hands after it is done, he gives me the interest . . ."), as marking the characteristic ethos of the "new man." Interestingly, Weber cites Franklin more often than he cites Luther, Calvin, Baxter, Bailey, or any of the other Puritan divines to describe the lineaments of the new ethic. See Max Weber, *The Protestant Ethic and the Spirit of Capitalism*, trans. Talcott Parsons (London: G. Allen & Unwin, 1930).

Emerson, producing the fastidious refinement and aloofness of the chief American writers, and resulting in the final unreality of most contemporary American culture; and on the other hand, the current of catchpenny opportunism, originating in the practical shifts of Puritan life, becoming a philosophy in Franklin, passing through the American humorists and resulting in the atmosphere of our contemporary business life. . . .[17]

Whatever the irrational mystery at the foundation of Puritan theology, the community itself was ruled by a rational morality in which the moral law was a cold and righteous necessity. The core of Puritanism, once the theological husks are stripped away, was an intense moral zeal for the regulation of everyday conduct, not because the Puritans were harsh or prurient, but because they had founded their community as a covenant in which all individuals were in compact with each other. Given the external dangers and psychological strains of living in a closed world, the individual had to be concerned not only with his own behavior but with the community. One's own sins imperiled not just oneself but the group; by failing to observe the demands of the covenant, one could bring down God's wrath on the community.

The terms of the covenant committed each person to an exemplary life. But the very explicitness of the covenant—and the intimacy of village life—made everyone aware of the sins of temptation and the temptations of the flesh.[18] This made the members more self-scourging, and after being sinners—for there was a considerable amount of illicit sexual activity and a bucolic realism about sex—they were also great repenters. The ritual of confession was at the heart of Puritanism both in New England and, later, in the Midwestern revivalist communities which carried the moral scourging, if not the theology of Puritanism, across the country.

[17] Brooks, op. cit., p. 10.

[18] Perhaps the most powerful literary illustration of these illicit impulses is Hawthorne's short story "Young Goodman Brown," an oneiromantic vision of a black mass in the woods of Salem. In the story, Young Goodman Brown leaves his wife to go into the woods with the devil (who bears a serpent rod = phallus) to be baptized into the mysteries of sin. To his surprise and horror, he recognizes all the "good" people of the town joyfully moving toward the initiation ceremony, and recognizes, as well, his own young wife Faith. The ceremony and the music have the form of a religious liturgy, but the content is the flowers of evil. In the end it is never clear whether this was, for Goodman Brown, an actual event or a dream in which he was struggling with his own sinful impulses. But his life from then on was miserable. ("On the Sabbath day, when the congregation were singing a holy psalm he could not listen because an anthem of sin rushed loudly upon his ear . . .") He led a cankered and shriveled existence, and his dying hour was gloom. See "Young Goodman Brown," in *The Novels and Tales of Nathaniel Hawthorne* (New York: Modern Library, 1937), pp. 1033–1042.

The towns that were established, first in the wilderness and then in the prairies, faced the problem of maintaining some social order among a population that often had a high proportion of social misfits and ne'er-do-wells. A town of a few hundred families could not jail those who deviated from its code, or drive them all out. A system of social control by gossip or shaming, by public confession and repentance, became the means of preventing large-scale breakdown in many communities. The idea of respectability—the distrust of lightheartedness, pleasure, drink—became so deeply ingrained that it persisted long after the initial material necessity was gone. If, in the beginning, work and riches were the signs of election, in the next century they became the badges of respectability.

PURITANISM AS AN IDEOLOGY

A value system is often diffuse and inchoate. When it is organized into a specific code and formulated as a set of religious dogmas, an explicit covenant, or an ideology, it becomes a means of mobilizing a community, of enforcing discipline or a set of social controls. Why an ideology lingers on and grows even stronger, long after its initial congruence with a social movement has disappeared, is a complicated instance of the sociology of domination: witness the hold of Mormon theology, which grew out of the antinomian doctrine of progressive revelation yet today functions as a source of conservatism; or the ideology of egalitarian Communism in the Soviet Union, half a century after the revolution, to justify the rise of a new class. In such situations, the ideology carries with it the authority and sanctity of the past; it has been instilled into the child and becomes the only conceptual map of the world as well as of the moral norms of conduct. Often, though the original rhetoric and symbols remain, the content has been subtly redefined, over time, to justify the established social codes and social controls that buttress the social power of the predominant class.

This is the *functional* component of an ideology. But there is a cognitive or intellectual component as well. It is in the character of ideologies not only to reflect or justify an underlying reality but, once launched, to take on a life of their own. A truly powerful ideology opens up a new vision of life to the imagination; once formulated, it remains part of the moral repertoire to be drawn upon by intellectuals, theologians, or moralists as part of the range of possibilities open to mankind. Unlike economies or outmoded technologies, they do not disappear. These "moments of consciousness," as Hegel termed them, are renewable; they can be called upon and reformulated throughout the history of a civilization. Thus an ideology gnawed at, worried to the bone, argued about, dissected, and restated by an army of essayists, moralists, and intellectuals becomes a force in its own right.

This was the fate of Puritanism. Long after the harsh environment that fostered the initial ideology had been mitigated, the force of the belief remained. As Van Wyck Brooks once noted so pungently: "When the wine of the Puritans spilled, the aroma became transcendentalism, and the wine itself commercialism."

As an idea system, Puritanism underwent a transfiguration over a period of 200 years, from rigorous Calvinist predestination, through Edwards' aesthetic illuminations, into the transcendentalism of Emerson, and it finally dissolved into the "genteel tradition" after the Civil War. As a set of social practices, it was transmogrified into the social Darwinist justifications of rampant individualism and money-making (as Edmund Morgan has observed, Benjamin Franklin earned his own money; John D. Rockefeller thought his came from God) and the constricting codes of small-town life.

THE NEW LIBERATION

The major intellectual attack on Puritanism came in the first decade and a half of the twentieth century from the realm of culture and from the Young Intellectuals, a Harvard College group that included Walter Lippmann, Van Wyck Brooks, John Reed, and Harold Stearns.[19] *America's Coming-of-Age*, as Van Wyck Brooks entitled his book of 1915, meant that the culture had to confront the new reality and plunge into "actuality." American literature, Brooks argued, had stood remote from life, achieving its salvation by avoiding contact with actuality. Puritanism, he said, had become "a dry old Yankee stalk."

There were several facets to the attack on Puritanism. First, there was the desire, expressed principally by Brooks, for a more inclusive

[19] For a discussion of the Young Intellectuals, see Henry F. May, *The End of American Innocence*, pt. 3 (New York: Alfred A. Knopf, 1959). For a characteristic voice, see Harold Stearns, *America and the Young Intellectual* (New York: Doran, 1921).

culture reflecting the America of the immigrant, the Negro, and the urban scene. If America was to come of age, its culture had to be more cosmopolitan and reflect the vitality of the society. And second was the demand for sexual freedom. "A Puritan," Harold Stearns wrote, "was a sexually inadequate person who, unable to enjoy himself, derived his only satisfaction from interfering with the enjoyment of others." The children of the upper middle class flocked into Greenwich Village to create a new Bohemia. "They had read Nietzsche and Marx and Freud and Krafft-Ebing," Brooks wrote in retrospect. "Many of them wished to try out new ideas of sex, which had hitherto been kept in the cellars of young people's minds. . . ."[20]

The exuberance of life was summed up in a series of catchwords. One of them was "New." There was the New Democracy, the New Nationalism, the New Freedom, the New Poetry, and even the *New Republic* (which was started in 1914). A second was *sex*. Even to use the word openly sent a *frisson* through the readers of the press. Margaret Sanger, in 1913, coined the term "birth control." Ellen Key, the Swedish feminist, argued that marriage should not be a matter of legal or economic compulsion. Emma Goldman, the anarchist, lectured on homosexuality, the "intermediate sex." Floyd Dell celebrated free love, and many of the Young Intellectuals lived in ostentatious unmarried monogamy. And a third catchword was *liberation*. Liberation, as the movement self-consciously called itself, was the wind blowing from Europe, a wind of modernism come to the American shore. In art it was the Fauves and cubism, shown principally in the Armory Show of 1913. In the theater it meant symbolism, suggestion and atmosphere, the acceptance of the non-realist influence of Maeterlinck, Dunsany, and Synge. In literature there was a vogue for Shaw, Conrad, and Lawrence. But the greatest influence was in "philosophy," where the currents of irrationalism, vitalism, and instinct, refracted through Bergson and Freud, spread rapidly in vulgarized form.

The "favorite doctrine of the Rebellion," as Henry May has written, was that happiness would follow complete instinctual self-expression. A simpleminded Freudianism declared that most of the Puritan evil in the world was due to self-control, and the way to

---

[20] Van Wyck Brooks, *The Confident Years: 1885-1915* (New York: Dutton, 1952), p. 487. The phrase "cellars of young people's minds" came from Ernest Poole's novel *The Harbor*, describing Princeton life in the early 1900s.

freedom lay in the release of repressed sexual impulses. Henri Bergson's doctrine of vitalism, presented in a poetic prose (in two years, his *Creative Evolution* sold as many copies in America as it did in France in 15), became the basis for a popularized doctrine of the life force, a biological, purposive spirit which reanimated the universe. Syndicalism, which had become fashionable among left-wing intellectuals, was associated with the vitalism of Bergson through Georges Sorel, who was acclaimed as his philosophical disciple. Francis Grierson, whose work consisted of mystical and aphoristic essays ("a mixture of Carlyle and Elbert Hubbard"), was taken as a prophet of the age.[21]

The Young Intellectuals, in their very attack on Puritanism and a crabbed way of life, preached an ethic of hedonism, of pleasure and play—in short, a consumption ethic; yet, ironically—or is it not the trajectory of such "rebellion"—the consumption ethic was to be realized less than a decade later by a capitalism that, without self-consciousness, called itself (was it in faint echo of the "rebellion") the "new capitalism."

If the intellectual justifications of Puritanism had evaporated, its social practices gained new strength in the small towns precisely because of the fear of change. Change in this instance meant the rise of a new way of life—the life of the big cities, turbulent, cosmopolitan, and sinful. A definition of respectability was at stake, and this found its symbol in the idea of Temperance.

A style of life is justified by a set of values, regulated by institutions (church, school, family), and embodied in character structure. Where this style is expressed by a homogeneous set of persons, there exists what sociologists call a "status group." The style of life symbolized by the Temperance movement, though it developed later than Puritanism, had its source in the Protestant doctrines of industry, thrift, discipline, and sobriety; its institutional foundation in the Fundamentalist churches; and its character emphasis in the idea of restraint.

The norm of abstinence had become part of the public morality

---

[21] Grierson is forgotten today, but he was greatly admired by Mallarmé in France and hailed by Floyd Dell and Francis Hackett in the United States. Edwin Bjorkman's *Voices of Tomorrow* (New York: Mitchell Kennerly, 1913), a rhapsodic account of the new ideas, placed Grierson along with Bergson and Maeterlinck as representative of the period's main tendency. A sketch of Grierson can be found in Brooks, *The Confident Years*, pp. 267–270.

of American society. It was a device for assimilating the immigrant, the poor, and the deviant into middle-class status, if not into middle-class economic fact. But by the end of the nineteenth century it was no longer voluntary; instead, it was the coercive weapon of a social group whose own style of life was no longer ascendant. For if the new urban groups would not willingly accept temperance as a way of life, then it would have to be imposed by law and made a matter of ceremonial deference to the values of the traditional middle class.

With the development of the Anti-Saloon League in 1896, the Temperance movement found a concentrated symbol for the cultural struggle of the traditional rural Protestant society against the emerging urban and industrial social system. The attack on the saloon allowed the Prohibition movement to bring together many diverse elements under one political banner. For the small-town native American Protestant, the saloon epitomized the social habits of the immigrant population. For the Progressive, the saloon was the source of the corruption he felt to be the bane of political life. For the Populist, it became the root of his antipathy to the debilitating effects of urban life.

In familiar pattern, morality turned into moralizing, and righteousness became self-righteousness. The affirmation and confidence of nineteenth-century life had soured into a constricted and crabbed fear of the future. As Richard Hofstadter has written: "Prohibition could be made an outlet for the troubles of every cramped libido. In an earlier day, anti-Catholicism had served as the pornography of the Puritan: the inhibited mind had wallowed in tales of errant priests and nuns. During the Prohibition movement, both prurience and fear were exploited by those who dwelt on the linkage of alcohol and sexual excess, or on the fear of insanity and racial degeneracy, even of the racial self-assertion of the Negro." If one could not convert the sinner, one could stamp out the sin—and the sinner as well. Prohibition was more than a matter of alcohol. It was the crux of character and a turning point in a way of life.

But something else was going on, and this was the transformation of the American social structure, and the end of small-town dominance of American life as a social fact. There was, first, the continuing demographic change, which resulted in the growth of urban centers and the shift in political weight. But more broadly, a consumption society was emerging, with its emphasis on spending and material possessions, and it was undermining the traditional value system, with its emphasis on thrift, frugality, self-control, and impulse renunciation. Integral to both social changes was a technological revolution which, through the automobile, the motion picture, and the radio, broke down rural isolation and for the first time fused the country into a common culture and a national society. This social transformation was responsible for the end of Puritanism as a set of practices that could support the traditional value system.

If we retrace the social process, we can see that 200 years earlier, in the early eighteenth century, the social structure had been fused with a culture that sustained it. Gradually, that culture became attenuated, and by the beginning of the twentieth century, small-town Protestantism no longer had any effective cultural symbols or cultural modes that could provide a set of effective symbolic meanings, or defenses against attacks. An emerging new cultural system, based as it was on an urban middle class and new radical groups, was able in short order to launch so effective a criticism of the older culture that almost no one would try to defend it. To maintain its legitimacy, the status group embodying the traditional values resorted to political means of reaffirming its domination. But a status group can do this effectively only if its social base is congruent with the social structure. And the base of the Temperance groups, the old social foundation—rural small-town life based on agrarian values—was undermined by the new industrial transformations of the early twentieth century. Having staked their fate on enacting the old middle-class virtues into the law of the land, the Temperance groups found at the time of repeal that such norms had been repudiated as socially valid modes of behavior, and to that extent had lost much of their legitimacy. Thus, a change had first been effected in the culture, but it could only become effective when it was confirmed within the social structure itself.

THE TRANSPARENT LIFE

The cultural transformation of modern society is due, singularly, to the rise of mass consumption, or the diffusion of what were once considered luxuries to the middle and lower classes in society. In this process, past luxuries are constantly redefined as necessities, so that it eventually seems incredible that an ordinary object could ever have been considered out of the reach of an ordinary man. For example, because of problems of temperature, homogeneity, and transparency, large windowpanes were once expensive luxuries and rare; yet after 1902, when the Frenchman Fourcault introduced a workable industrial means for manufacturing window glass by extrusion, they became commonplace items in city storefronts or country homes, creating a new range of display and vista.[22]

Mass consumption, which began in the 1920s, was made possible by revolutions in technology, principally the application of electrical energy to household tasks (washing machines, refrigerators, vacuum cleaners, and the like), and by three social inventions: mass production on an assembly line, which made a cheap automobile possible; the development of marketing, which rationalized the art of identifying different kinds of buying groups and whetting consumer appetites; and the spread of installment buying, which, more than any other social device, broke down the old Protestant fear of debt. The concomitant revolutions in transportation and communications laid the basis for a national society and the beginnings of a common culture. Taken all together, mass consumption meant the acceptance, in the crucial area of life-style, of the idea of social change and personal transformation, and it gave legitimacy to those who would innovate and lead the way, in culture as well as in production.

The symbol of mass consumption—and the prime example of the way technology has revolutionized social habits—is, of course, the automobile. Frederick Lewis Allen has observed how hard it is for us today to realize how separate and distant communities were when they depended wholly on the railroad and horse-and-wagon for transportation. A town not near a railroad was really remote. For a farmer who lived five miles out of the county seat it was an event to take the family to town for a Saturday afternoon; a trip to a friend ten miles away was likely to be an all-day expedition, since the horse had to be rested and fed. Each small town, each farm, was dependent mainly on its own resources for amusement and company. Horizons were close, and individuals lived among familiar people and familiar things.

The automobile swept away many sanctions of the closed small-

[22] The illustration is taken from Jean Fourastie, *The Causes of Wealth* (Glencoe, Ill.: Free Press, 1959), p. 127. Professor Fourastie's book, like Siegfried Giedeon's *Mechanization Takes Command* (New York: Oxford University Press, 1948), is a fascinating miscellany of examples of this process.

town society. The repressive threats of nineteenth-century morality, as Andrew Sinclair has observed, relied in large measure on the impossibility of escaping from the place, and consequences, of misbehavior. By the middle of the 1920s, as the Lynds observed in Middletown, boys and girls thought nothing of driving 20 miles to dance at a roadhouse, safe from the prying eyes of neighbors. The closed car became the *cabinet particulier* of the middle class, the place where adventurous young people shed their sexual inhibitions and broke the old taboos.[23]

The second major instrument of change in the closed small-town society was the motion picture. Movies are many things—a window on the world, a set of ready-made daydreams, fantasy and projection, escapism and omnipotence—and their emotional power is enormous. It is as a window on the world that the movies have served, in the first instance, to transform the culture. "Sex is one of the things Middletown has long been taught to fear," the Lynds observed when they revisited Middletown ten years later, and "its institutions . . . operate to keep the subject out of sight and out of mind as much as possible." Except in the movies, to which the youngsters flocked.

Adolescents not only enjoyed the movies but went to school there. They modeled themselves after movie stars, repeated movie jokes and gestures, learned the subtleties of behavior between the sexes, and thus developed a veneer of sophistication. And in their efforts to act out this sophistication, to resolve their baffled uncertainties and perplexities by outwardly confident action, the pattern was "not so much . . . the lives of their own cautious parents as . . . the alternative other worlds about them." Films glorified the cult of youth (girls wore bobbed hair and short skirts), and middle-aged men and women were advised "to make hay while the sun shines." The idea of "freedom" was exemplified by the legitimacy of the

[23] The Lynds quoted one Middle Western observer: "Why on earth do you need to study what's changing this country? . . . I can tell you what's happening in just four letters: A–U–T–O!" Robert S. Lynd and Helen Merrell Lynd, *Middletown* (New York: Harcourt, Brace, 1929), p. 251. In 1890 a pony was the wildest dream of a Middletown boy. By 1923, "the 'horse culture' of Middletown had almost disappeared." The first automobile appeared there in 1900. By 1906 there were "probably 200 in the city and county." At the end of 1923 there were more than 6,200 cars, one for every six persons, or roughly two for every three families. As the Lynds observed: "Group-sanctioned values are disturbed by the inroads of the automobile upon the family budget. A case in point is the not uncommon practice of mortgaging a home to buy an automobile" (p. 254).

speakeasy and one's readiness to cut loose at wild parties. "The mockery of ethics, of the old 'inner goodness' of the film heroes and heroines," writes Lewis Jacobs, "was paralleled by the new regard for material things."

The automobile, the motion picture, and radio are technological in origin: advertising, planned obsolescence, and credit are all sociological innovations. David M. Potter has commented that it is as hopeless to understand a modern popular writer without understanding advertising as it would be to understand a medieval troubadour without understanding the cult of chivalry, or a nineteenth-century revivalist without understanding evangelical religion.

The extraordinary thing about advertising is its pervasiveness. What marks a great city if not its lighted signs? Passing over in an airplane one sees, through the refractions of the night sky, the clusters of red, orange, blue, and white signs shimmering like highly polished stones. In the centers of the great cities—Time Square, Piccadilly, the Champs-Elysées, the Ginza—people gather in the streets under the blinking neon signs to share in the vibrancy of the milling crowd. If one thinks about the social impact of advertising, its most immediate, yet usually unnoticed, consequence has been to transform the physical center of the city. In redoing the physical topography, replacing the old *duomos* or municipal halls or palace towers, advertising has placed a "burning brand" on the crest of our civilization. It is the mark of material goods, the exemplar of new styles of life, the herald of new values. As in fashion, advertising has emphasized glamour. A car becomes the sign of the "good life" well lived, and the appeal of glamour becomes pervasive. A consumption economy, one might say, finds its reality in appearances. What one displays, what one shows, is a sign of achievement. Getting ahead is no longer a matter of rising up a social ladder, as it was in the late nineteenth century, but of adopting a specific style of life—country club, artiness, travel, hobbies—which marks one as a member of a consumption community.

In a complex, multi-group, socially mobile society, advertising also takes on a number of new "mediating" functions. The United States was probably the first large-scale society in history to build cultural change into the society, and many status problems arose simply because of the bewildering rapidity of such change. Few societies, in fact, can absorb quick change. The major social institutions—family, church, educational system—were set up to transmit established habits of the society. A society in rapid change inevitably produces confusions about appropriate modes of behavior, taste, and dress. A socially mobile person has no ready guide for acquiring new knowledge on how to live "better" than before, and his guides become the movies, television, and advertising. In this respect, advertising begins to play a more subtle role in changing habits than merely stimulating wants. The advertising in the women's magazines, the house-and-home periodicals, and sophisticated journals like the *New Yorker* was to teach people how to dress, furnish a home, buy the right wines—in short, the styles of life appropriate to the new statuses. Though at first the changes were primarily in manners, dress, taste, and food habits, sooner or later they began to affect more basic patterns: the structure of authority in the family, the role of children and young adults as independent consumers in the society, the pattern of morals, and the different meanings of achievement in the society.

All of this came about by gearing the society to change and the acceptance of cultural change, once mass consumption and a high standard of living were seen as the legitimate purpose of economic organization. Selling became the most striking activity of contemporary America. Against frugality, selling emphasized prodigality; against asceticism, the lavish display.

None of this would have been possible without that revolution in moral habit, the idea of installment selling. Although it had been practiced fitfully in the United States before World War I, installment selling had two stigmas. First, most installment sales were to the poor, who could not afford major expenditures; they paid weekly sums to a peddler who both sold the goods and made the weekly collection; installment selling was thus a sign of financial instability. Second, installment selling meant debt to the middle class, and going into debt was wrong and dangerous. As Micawber would say, it was a sign of living beyond one's means, and the result would be misery. Being moral meant being industrious and thrifty. If one wanted to buy something, one should save for it. The trick of installment selling was to avoid the word "debt" and emphasize the word "credit." Monthly charges were billed by mail, and the transactions were thus handled on a businesslike basis.

Saving—or abstinence—is the heart of the Protestant ethic. With Adam Smith's idea of parsimony or frugality, and Nassau Senior's idea of abstinence, it was firmly established that saving multiplied future products and earned its own reward by interest. The denouement was the change in banking habits. For years, such was the grim specter of middle-class morality that people were afraid to be overdrawn at the bank, lest a check bounce. By the end of the 1960s, the banks were strenuously advertising the services of cash reserves that would allow a depositor to overdraw up to several thousand dollars (to be paid back in monthly installments). No one need be deterred from gratifying his impulse at an auction or a sale. The seduction of the consumer had become total.

Van Wyck Brooks once remarked about morality in Catholic countries that as long as heavenly virtues are upheld, mundane behavior may change as it will. In America, the old Protestant heavenly virtues are largely gone, and the mundane rewards have begun to run riot. The basic American value pattern emphasized the virtue of achievement, defined as doing and making, and a man displayed his character in the quality of his work. By the 1950s, the pattern of achievement remained, but it had been redefined to emphasize status and taste. The culture was no longer concerned with how to work and achieve, but with how to spend and enjoy. Despite some continuing use of the language of the Protestant ethic, the fact was that by the 1950s American culture had become primarily hedonistic, concerned with play, fun, display, and pleasure—and, typical of things in America, in a compulsive way.

The world of hedonism is the world of fashion, photography, advertising, television, travel. It is a world of make-believe in which one lives for expectations, for what will come rather than what is. And it must come without effort. It is no accident that the successful new magazine of the previous decade was called *Playboy* and that its success—a circulation of 6 million by 1970—is due largely to the fact that it encourages fantasies of male sexual prowess. If, as Max Lerner once wrote, sex is the last frontier in American life, then the achievement motive in a go-go society finds its acme in sex. In the 1950s and the 1960s, the cult of the Orgasm succeeded the cult of Mammon as the basic passion of American life.

Nothing epitomized the hedonism of the United States better than the State of California. A cover story in *Time*, called "California: A State of Excitement," opened:

California is virtually a nation unto itself, but it holds a strange hope, a sense of excitement—and some terror—for Americans. As most of them see it, the good, godless, gregarious pursuit of pleasure is what California is all about. The citizens of lotusland seem forever to be lolling around swimming pools, sautéing in the sun, packing across the Sierra, frolicking nude on the beaches, getting taller each year, plucking money off the trees, romping around topless, tramping through the redwoods and—when they stop to catch their breath—preening themselves on-camera before the rest of an envious world. "I have seen the future," says the newly returned visitor from California, "and it plays."[24]

Fun morality, in consequence, displaces "goodness morality," which stressed interference with impulses. Not having fun is an occasion for self-examination: "What is wrong with me?" As Dr. Wolfenstein observes: "Whereas gratification of forbidden impulses traditionally aroused guilt, failure to have fun now lowers one's self-esteem."[25]

Fun morality centers, in most instances, on sex. And here the seduction of the consumer has become almost total. The most tell-tale illustration, I believe, was a double-page advertisement by Eastern Airlines in the *New York Times*, in 1973, saying: "Take the Bob and Carol, Ted and Alice, Phil and Anne Vacation." The blatant theme was a takeoff on *Bob and Carol and Ted and Alice*, a sniggering film about the fumbling attempts of two friendly couples to engage in wife-swapping. Here was Eastern Airlines saying, in effect: "We will fly you down to the Caribbean. We will rent you a cabana. Fly now, pay later." Eastern does not tell you *what* you pay, but you can postpone the money (and forget the guilt) and take the Bob and Carol, Ted and Alice, and for further titillation another couple is added) Phil and Anne vacation. Compare this with Franklin's 13 useful virtues, which included temperance, frugality, tranquillity, and chastity. At the turn of the century, a church in the Midwest might have property on which a brothel was located. And one could then at least say: "Well, we are losing bodies, but we are earning money to save souls." Today, when one sells bodies, one is no longer also saving souls.

What this abandonment of Puritanism and the Protestant ethic does, of course, is to leave capitalism with no moral or transcendental ethic. It also emphasizes not only the disjunction between the norms of the culture and the norms of the social structure, but also an extraordinary contradiction within the social structure itself. On the one hand, the business corporation wants an individual to work hard, pursue a career, accept delayed gratification—to be, in the

[24] *Time*, November 7, 1969, p. 60.
[25] Martha Wolfenstein, "The Emergence of Fun Morality," in *Mass Leisure*, ed. Eric Larrabee and Rolf Meyersohn (Glencoe, Ill.: Free Press, 1958), p. 86.

crude sense, an organization man. And yet, in its products and its advertisements, the corporation promotes pleasure, instant joy, relaxing and letting go. One is to be "straight" by day and a "swinger" by night. This is self-fulfillment and self-realization!

POP HEDONISM

What happened in the United States was that traditional morality was replaced by psychology, guilt by anxiety. A hedonistic age has its appropriate psychotherapies as well. If psychoanalysis emerged just before World War I to deal with the repressions of Puritanism, the hedonistic age has its counterpart in sensitivity training, encounter groups, "joy therapy," and similar techniques that have two characteristics essentially derived from a hedonistic mood: they are conducted almost exclusively in groups; and they try to "unblock" the individual by physical contact, by groping, touching, fondling, manipulating. Where the earlier intention of psychoanalysis was to enable the patient to achieve self-insight and thereby redirect his life—an aim inseparable from a moral context—the newer therapies are entirely instrumental and psychologistic; their aim is to "free" the person from inhibitions and restraints so that he or she can more easily express his impulses and feelings.

A hedonistic age also has its appropriate cultural style—pop. Pop art, according to the critic Lawrence Alloway, who gave the style its name, reflects the aesthetics of plenty. The iconography of pop art comes from the everyday world: household objects, images from the movies and the mass media (comic strips and billboards), food (hamburgers and Coca-Cola bottles), and clothing. The point about pop is that there is no tension in the paintings—only parody. In pop art one finds Alex Hay's five-foot enlargement of an ordinary mailing label, Roy Lichtenstein's giant composition notebook, Claes Oldenburg's large hamburger in vinyl; parodies of the objects, but always in good-natured fun. The aesthetics of pop, as Suzi Gablik writes, presupposes "the erosion of a previous established hierarchy of subject matter (Mondrian and Mickey Mouse are now equally relevant) and the expansion of art's frame of reference to include elements considered until now as outside its range, such as technology, kitsch, and humor...."[26]

[26] "The Long Front of Culture," in *Pop Art Redefined*, ed. John Russell and Suzi Gablik (London: Thames and Hudson, 1969), p. 14. A capital document of the

And finally, a hedonistic age had its own appropriate prophet—Marshall McLuhan. A hedonistic age is a marketing age, defined by the fact that knowledge becomes coded in messages organized as formulas, slogans, and binary distinctions. By grasping the code, a person feels comfortable in understanding the complex world about him. McLuhan is the writer who not only has defined the hedonistic age in terms of such coding devices, but also has topped the trick by exemplifying in his own style the device of coding that age's own thoughts in a set of formulas appropriate to the time. The idea that the medium is the message (so that ideas are secondary or do not count); that some media are "hot," like radio (it excludes people), while others are "cool," like television (it requires involvement to complete the participation); that print culture is linear, while visual culture is simultaneous—all these distinctions are not meant to be used analytically, or tested by some empirical means; they are litanies to assuage a person's anxieties and enhance his sense of well-being within the new modes of communication. They are Turkish baths of the mind. All in all, Marshall McLuhan was an advertising man's dream, in more ways than one.

In the 1960s a new cultural style appeared. Call it psychedelic, or call it, as its own protagonists have, a "counter-culture." It announced a strident opposition to bourgeois values and to the traditional codes of American life. " 'The bourgeoisie,' " we were told, " 'is obsessed by greed; its sex life is insipid and prudish; its family patterns are debased; its slavish conformities of dress and grooming are degrading; its mercenary routinization of life is intolerable. . . .' "[27]

What is funny about such pronouncements is their polemical and ideological caricature of a set of codes that had been trampled long ago, beginning 60 years earlier, with the Young Intellectuals. Yet such a caricature was necessary to make the new counter-culture seem more daring and revolutionary than it was. The assault was an act of bravado, in order to emphasize a distinction that was not there. For while the new movement was extreme, it was neither

---

movement, we are told, is Richard Hamilton's letter of January 16, 1957, in which he wrote that pop art was "Popular (designed for a mass ·audience), Transient (short-term solution), Expendable (easily forgotten), Low-cost, Mass-produced, Young (aimed at Youth), Witty, Sexy, Gimmicky, Glamourous, Big Business. . . ."

[27] Theodore Roszak, *The Making of a Counter Culture* (Garden City, N.Y.: Doubleday, 1969), p. 35.

daring nor revolutionary. In fact, is was simply an extension of the hedonism of the 1950s, and a democratization of the libertinism that had already been achieved by sections of the advanced upper classes long before. Just as the political radicalism of the 1960s followed the failure of political liberalism the decade before, so the psychedelic extremes—in sexuality, nudity, perversions, pot, and rock—and the counter-culture followed on the forced hedonism of the 1950s.

We are now in a position to sum up the process. The erosion of traditional American values took place on two levels. In the realm of culture and ideas, the withering attack on small-town life as constricting and banal was first organized in the 1910s by the Young Intellectuals as a self-consciously defined group, and this attack was sustained in the next decade in the journalistic criticism of H. L. Mencken and in the sketches and novels of Sherwood Anderson and Sinclair Lewis.

But a more fundamental transformation was occurring in the social structure itself: the change in the motivations and rewards of the economic system. The rising wealth of the plutocracy, becoming evident in the Gilded Age, meant that work and accumulation were no longer ends in themselves (though they were still crucial to a John D. Rockefeller or an Andrew Carnegie), but means to consumption and display. Status and its badges, not work and the election of God, became the mark of success.

This is a familiar process of social history with the rise of new classes, though in the past it was military predators whose scions went from spartan to sybaritic living. Yet such parvenu classes could distance themselves from the rest of society, and such social transformations often developed independently of changes in the lives of the classes below. But the real social revolution in modern society came in the 1920s, when the rise of mass production and high consumption began to transform the life of the middle class itself. In effect the Protestant ethic as a social reality and a life-style for the middle class was replaced by a materialistic hedonism, and the Puritan temper by a psychological eudaemonism. But bourgeois society, justified and propelled as it had been in its earliest energies by these older ethics, could not easily admit to the change. It promoted a hedonistic way of life furiously—one has only to look at the transformation of advertising in the 1920s—but could not justify it. It lacked a new religion or value system to replace the old, and the result was disjunction.

In one respect what we see here is an extraordinary historic change in human society. For thousands of years, the function of economics was to provide the daily necessities—the subsistence—of life. For various upper-class groups, economics has been the basis of status and a sumptuary style. But now, on a mass scale, economics had become geared to the demands of culture. Here, too, culture, not as expressive symbolism or moral meanings but as life-style, came to reign supreme.

The "new capitalism" (the phrase was first used in the 1920s) continued to demand a Protestant ethic in the area of production—that is, in the realm of work—but to stimulate a demand for pleasure and play in the area of consumption. The disjunction was bound to widen. The spread of urban life, with its variety of distractions and multiple stimuli; the new roles of women, created by the expansion of office jobs and the freer social and sexual contacts; the rise of a national culture through motion pictures and radio—all contributed to a loss of social authority on the part of the older value system.

The Puritan temper might be described most simply by the term "delayed gratification," and by restraint in gratification. It is, of course, the Malthusian injunction for prudence in a world of scarcity. But the claim of the American economic system was that it had introduced abundance, and the nature of abundance is to encourage prodigality rather than prudence. A higher standard of living, not work as an end in itself, then becomes the engine of change. The glorification of plenty, rather than the bending to niggardly nature, becomes the justification of the system. But all of this was highly incongruent with the theological and sociological foundations of nineteenth-century Protestantism, which was in turn the foundation of the American value system.

In the 1920s, and in the 1950s and 1960s, these incongruities were eschewed with the blithe assurance that there was a consensus in the society on the moral verity of material abundance. There was a vulgar effort in the crude boosterism of the 1920s (e.g., Bruce Barton's assertion that Jesus was the greatest salesman of all time.[28])

---

[28] Barton, an advertising man, was a founder of the agency popularly known as BBD&O (Batten, Barton, Durstine, and Osborn). His theme was expressed in the book *The Man Nobody Knows*, which was published in 1924 and became an

to create a moral apologia. And in the 1950s there was the sophisticated rhetoric in the Luce magazines about the secret of productivity and the "permanent revolution" of change that was the contribution of the American economic system to the coming prosperity of the world. The singular fact is that *Time*, like the *Reader's Digest*, was founded in the 1920s, and both magazines were the vehicles for the transformation of values (the one of the urban middle class, the other of the small-town lower middle class) into the life-styles of mid-twentieth-century America. The genius of Henry Luce—and it is the sociological quiddity that the *Ausländer* Luce, raised in China, not the United States, celebrates native values more than the native himself—was to take the traditional American values, the belief in God, in work, in achievement, and to translate these, through the idiom of the coming urban civilization, into the creed of American destiny ("the American century") on a world scale. He did this by fusing the nervous rhythms of the new expressive journalism, the language reflecting the new appearances, with the pace of urban life and the new hedonism. In this context, it is no accident that Luce's own magazine, his singular creation, was *Fortune*. (The impetus for *Time* had come from Luce's journalist colleague at Yale, Britton Hadden, the idea for *Life* from Daniel Longwell and other editors at *Time*.) American business was the dynamic agency tearing up small-town life and catapulting America into world economic dominance; and it was doing so within the language and cover of the Protestant ethic. The fact of transition is evident. The overt contradictions in the language and ideology—the lack of any coherent moral or philosophical doctrine—have only become manifest today.[29]

---

immediate best-seller. As Frederick J. Hoffman portrays it: "The 'real Jesus' whom Mr. Barton purported to have uncovered from the biblical text had proved his skill as a business organizer by having brought twelve obscure men from their inefficient pasts and 'welded them' into the greatest organization of all time. Jesus had known and followed 'every one of the principles of modern salesmanship,' Barton averred. The parables were among the most powerful advertisements of all time. And as for Jesus having been the founder of modern business, Barton pointed simply to the words of the master himself: 'Wist ye not that I must be about my father's *business*?'" See *The Twenties* (New York: Viking, 1955), p. 326.

[29] For a brilliant exploration of this question, see Kristol, "When Virtue Loses All Her Loveliness," in *Capitalism Today*.

THE ABDICATION OF THE CORPORATE CLASS

The ultimate support for any social system is the acceptance by the population of a moral justification of authority. The older justifications of bourgeois society lay in the defense of private property, which itself was justified on the ground, elaborated by Locke, that one infused one's own labor into property. But the "new capitalism" of the twentieth century has lacked such moral grounding, and in periods of crisis it has either fallen back on the traditional value assertions, which have been increasingly incongruent with social reality, or it has been ideologically impotent.

It is in this context that one can see the weakness of American corporate capitalism in trying to deal with some of the major dilemmas of the century. Political (and value) conflicts in the United States can be looked at from two different perspectives. From one, there have been economic and class issues which divided farmer and banker, worker and employer, and led to functional and interest-group conflicts that were especially sharp in the 1930s. Along a different sociological axis, one can see the politics of the 1920s, and to some extent that of the 1950s, within the framework of "tradition" versus "modernity," with the rural, small-town Protestant intent on defending his historic values against the cosmopolitan liberal interested in reform and social welfare. The issues here are not primarily economic but socio-cultural. The traditionalist defends fundamentalist religion, censorship, stricter divorce and anti-abortion laws; the modernist is for secular rationality, freer personal relations, tolerance of sexual deviance, and the like. These represent the political side of cultural issues, and to the extent that culture is the symbolic expression and justification of experience, this is the realm of symbolic or expressive politics.

In this respect, the great symbolic issue of American cultural politics was Prohibition. It was the major—and almost the last—effort by small-town and traditionalist forces to impose a specific value, the prohibition of liquor, on the rest of the society; and initially, of course, the traditionalists won. In a somewhat different sense, McCarthyism in the 1950s represented an effort by some traditionalist forces to impose a uniform political morality on the society through conformity to one ideology of Americanism and a virulent form of anti-Communism. And, in a contrary fashion, the McGovern campaign of 1972 was fueled largely by a "new politics"

77

which represented the furthest tendencies of the modernists—the women's libbers, sexual nonconformists, and cultural radicals, allied for the moment, with blacks and other minority groups.

Now, the curious fact is that the "new capitalism" of abundance, which emerged in the 1920s, has never been able to define its view of these cultural-political issues, as it had of the economic-political conflicts. Given its split character, it could not do so. Its values derive from the traditionalist past, and its language is the archaism of the Protestant ethic. Its technology and dynamism, however, derive from the spirit of modernity—the spirit of perpetual innovation and of the creation of new "needs" on the installment plan. The one thing that would utterly destroy the new capitalism is the serious practice of deferred gratification.

When members of the corporate class have taken a stand on cultural-political issues, they have often divided on geographical lines. Midwesterners or Texans or those coming from small-town backgrounds display traditionalist attitudes; Easterners or products of Ivy League schools are more liberal. More recently, the division has been based on education and age rather than region. But the singular fact remains. The new capitalism was primarily responsible for transforming the society, and in the process undermined the Puritan temper, but it was never able to develop successfully a new ideology congruent with the change, and it used—and often was trapped by—the older language of Protestant values.

The forces of modernity, which took the lead against the traditionalists on these social and cultural issues, were a mélange of intellectuals, professors, and welfare- and reform-minded individuals (though, paradoxically, the Prohibition movement at its inception was allied with the reformers against the evils of industrialism and city life), joined, for political reasons, by labor leaders and ethnic politicians who represented urban forces.[30] The dominant philosophy was liberalism, which included a critique of the inequalities and social costs generated by capitalism. The fact that the

---

[30] In an analogous sense, in the organized labor movement the AFL-CIO finds itself on its own cleft stick. In economic matters, it is liberal or left, but it stridently rejects cultural radicalism as alien to its beliefs. This is because the labor movement is truly an American movement and has shared the dominant values of the capitalist order. Trade unionism, as George Bernard Shaw once said, is the capitalism of the proletariat, at least when the economic order is expanding and affluent.

corporate economy had no unified value system of its own, or still mouthed a flaccid version of Protestant virtues, meant that liberalism could go ideologically unchallenged. In the realm of culture, and of cultural-social issues—of political philosophy, in short—the corporate class had abdicated. The important consideration is that, *as an ideology*, liberalism had become dominant in the culture during these past decades.

From a *cultural* point of view, the politics of the 1920s to 1960s was a struggle between tradition and modernity. In the 1960s the new cultural style denounced bourgeois values and the traditional codes of American life. But, as I have tried to show, bourgeois culture vanished long ago. What the counter-culture embodied was an extension of the tendencies initiated 60 years ago by political liberalism and modernist culture, and represents, in effect, a split in the camp of modernism. For it sought to take the preachments of personal freedom, extreme experience ("kicks" and "highs"), and sexual experimentation to a point in *life-style* that the liberal mentality—which would approve of such ideas in *art and imagination*— is not prepared to go. Yet liberalism finds itself uneasy in trying to say why. It approves a basic permissiveness, but cannot with any certainty define the bounds. And this is its dilemma. In culture, as well as in politics, liberalism is now up against the wall.

Liberalism also finds itself in disarray in an arena where it had sought to reform capitalism—the economy. The economic philosophy of American liberalism had been rooted in the idea of growth. One forgets that in the late 1940s and 1950s Walter Reuther, Leon Keyserling, and other liberals had attacked the steel companies and much of American industry for being unwilling to expand capacity, and had urged the government to set target growth figures. Cartelization, monopoly, and the restriction of production had been historic tendencies of capitalism. The Eisenhower administration consciously chose price stability over growth. It was the liberal economists who instilled in the society the policy of the conscious planning of growth through government inducements (e.g., investment credits, which industry at first did not want) and government investment. The idea of potential GNP and the concept of "shortfall" —posting a mark of what the economy at full utilization of resources could achieve, compared to the actual figure—was introduced in the Council of Economic Advisers by the liberals. The idea of growth has been so fully absorbed as an economic ideology that one no longer realizes, as I have said, how much of a liberal innovation it was.

The liberal answer to social problems such as poverty was that growth would provide the resources to raise the incomes of the poor.[31] The thesis that growth was necessary to finance public services was the crux of John Kenneth Galbraith's *The Affluent Society*. And yet, paradoxically, it is the very idea of economic growth that is now coming under attack—and by liberals. Affluence is no longer seen as an answer. Growth is held responsible for the spoliation of the environment, the voracious use of natural resources, the crowding in recreation areas, the density in the cities, and the like. One finds, startlingly, the idea of zero economic growth—or John Stuart Mill's idea of the "stationary state"—now proposed as a serious goal of government policy. Just as the new politics rejected the traditional problem-solving pragmatism of American politics, it now also rejects the newer, liberal policy of economic growth as a positive goal for the society. But without a commitment to economic growth, what is the *raison d'être* of capitalism?[32]

THE HINGE OF HISTORY

In historical retrospect, bourgeois society had a double source, and a double fate. The one current was a Puritan, Whig capitalism, in which the emphasis was not just on economic activity but on the formation of *character* (sobriety, probity, work as a calling). The other was a secular Hobbesianism, a radical individualism which saw man as unlimited in his appetite, which was restrained in politics by a sovereign but ran fully free in economics and culture. The two impulses had always lived in uneasy tandem. Over time, those

[31] More technically, it was based on the welfare economics theorem of Pareto optimality—namely, that one should seek a condition where some people will be better off without anyone being worse off. The direct redistribution of income is politically difficult, if not impossible. However, from new or added national income, a higher proportion of the gains can be used to finance social welfare programs; and this, as Otto Eckstein pointed out in "The Economics of the Sixties," *The Public Interest*, no. 19 (Spring 1970), pp. 86–97, was precisely what Congress was willing to do when economic growth was resumed in the Kennedy administration.

[32] The discussion of these questions is continued in Part Two of this book.

relations dissolved. As we have seen, in the United States the Puritan emphasis degenerated into a crabbed, small-town mentality, emphasizing only the idea of respectability. The secular Hobbesianism fed the mainsprings of modernity, the ravenous hunger for unlimited experience. The Whig view of history as open and progressive has faltered, if not disappeared, under the appearance of new bureaucratic apparatuses which have eclipsed the liberal view of societal self-management. The faiths which sustained all these beliefs have been shattered.

The cultural impulses of the 1960s, like the political radicalism which paralleled it, are, for the while, largely spent. The counterculture proved to be a conceit. It was an effort, largely a product of the youth movement, to transform a liberal life-style into a world of immediate gratification and exhibitionistic display. In the end, it produced little culture and countered nothing. Modernist culture, which has had deeper and more enduring roots, has been an effort to transform the imagination. But the experiments in style and form, the rage and effort to shock, all of which produced an effulgent explosion in the arts, are now exhausted. They are reproduced mechanically by the cultural mass, that stratum which itself is not creative but which distributes and denatures culture, in a process of absorption that robs art of the tension which is a necessary source of creativity and dialectic with the past. The society has become preoccupied with the more nagging and threatening questions of shortages, scarcities, inflation, and structural imbalances of income and wealth within and between nations; and for these reasons the questions of culture have now receded.

Yet the questions of culture remain, at bottom, the fundamental ones. As Irving Kristol and I wrote in the Introduction to *Capitalism Today*): "One cannot understand the important changes that have been taking place, and are taking place, in modern society without taking full account of capitalism's uneasy self-consciousness. This self-consciousness is no mere ideological superstructure. It is one of the most fateful and fundamental realities of the system itself." These changes are fateful and fundamental because they involve the nature of will and the character of a people, and the legitimacy and moral justifications of the system—the very elements that sustain a society.

What is striking about the rise and fall of civilizations—and it was the basis of the philosophy of history of the talented Arabic thinker Ibn Khaldun—is that societies pass through specific phases whose transformations signal decline. These are the transformations from simplicity to luxury (what Plato, who wrote about this in Book 2 of *The Republic*, called the change from the healthy city to the fevered city), from asceticism to hedonism.

It is striking that every new, rising social force—be it a new religion, new military force, or new revolutionary movement—begins as an ascetic movement. Asceticism emphasizes non-material values, renunciation of physical pleasures, simplicity and self-denial, and arduous, purposeful discipline. That discipline is necessary for the mobilization of psychic and physical energies for tasks outside the self, for the conquest and subordination of the self in order to conquer others. As Max Weber remarked: "Discipline acquired during wars of religion was the source of the unconquerableness of both the Islamic and Cromwellian cavalries. Similarly, inner-worldly asceticism and the disciplined quest for salvation in a vocation pleasing to God were the sources of the virtuosity in acquisitiveness characteristic of the Puritans."[33]

The discipline of the old religious "warriors of God" was channeled into military organization and battle. What was historically unique about the Puritan temper was the devotion of this-worldly asceticism to an occupational calling and to work and accumulation. Yet the end of the Puritan's being was not primarily wealth. As Weber remarked, the Puritan got nothing out of his wealth for himself but the proof of his own salvation.[34] And it was this furious energy that built an industrial civilization.

For the Puritan, "the most urgent task" was to destroy spontaneous, impulsive behavior and bring order into the conduct of life. Today one finds asceticism primarily in revolutionary movements and revolutionary regimes. Puritanism, in the psychological and sociological sense, is to be found in Communist China and in the regimes which fuse revolutionary sentiment with Koranic purposes, as in Algeria and Libya.

In the scheme of Khaldun, reflecting in the fourteenth century the vicissitudes of Berber and Arabic civilizations, the sequences of transformation went from the Bedouin to the sedentary to the hedonistic life, and from there, in three generations, to the decline

[33] Max Weber, *The Sociology of Religion*, trans. Ephraim Fischoffs, (Boston: Beacon Press, 1963), p. 203.
[34] Weber, *Protestant Ethic*, p. 71.

82

of the society. In the hedonistic life, there is a loss of will and fortitude. More importantly, men become competitive with one another for luxuries, and lose the ability to share and sacrifice. There then follows, says Khaldun, the loss of *asabîyah*, that sense of solidarity which makes men feel as brothers to one another, that "group feeling which means (mutual) affection and willingness to fight and die for each other."[35]

The basis for *asabîyah* is not only the sense of shared sacrifice and shared danger—the elements which hold platoons of fighting men or underground revolutionary cadres together—but also some moral purpose, a *telos* which provides the moral justifications for the society. At the start, the United States was held together by an implicit covenant, the sense that this was the continent where God's design would be unfolded, a belief which underlay the deism of Jefferson. As this belief receded, what held the society together was a unique polity, an open, adaptive, egalitarian, and democratic system which was responsive to the many claimants that sought inclusion in the society and which respected the principles of law as embodied in the Constitution and abided by the decisions of the Supreme Court. Yet this responsiveness itself was possible largely because of the expansiveness of the economy, and the promise of material wealth as a solvent for social strains. Today the economy is troubled and the political system is burdened with issues that it has never before had to confront. One problem—and it is the theme of my concluding essay, "The Public Household"—is whether the system itself can manage the huge overload of issues. This depends, in part, on "technical" economic answers and equally on the stability of the world system. But the deeper and more difficult questions are the legitimations of the society as expressed in the motivations of individuals and the moral purposes of the nation. And it is here that the cultural contradictions—the discordances of character structure and the disjunction of realms—become central.

Changes in culture and moral temper—the fusion of imagination and life-styles—are not amenable to "social engineering" or political control. They derive from the value and moral traditions of the society, and these cannot be "designed" by precept. The ultimate sources are the religious conceptions which undergird a society; the

[35] Ibn Khaldun, *The Muqaddimah: An Introduction to History*, trans. Franz Rosenthal (New York: Pantheon Books, 1958). The crucial section is in vol. 1, chap. 3; the quotation above is from p. 313.

proximate sources are the reward systems and motivations (and their legitimations) which derive from the arena of work.

American capitalism, as I have tried to show, has lost its traditional legitimacy, which was based on a moral system of reward rooted in the Protestant sanctification of work. It has substituted a hedonism which promises material ease and luxury, yet shies away from all the historic implications of a "voluptuary system," with all its social permissiveness and libertinism. The culture has been dominated (in the serious realm) by a principle of modernism that has been subversive of bourgeois life, and the middle-class life-styles by a hedonism that has undercut the Protestant ethic which provided the moral foundation for the society. The interplay of modernism as a mode developed by serious artists, the institutionalization of those played-out forms by the "cultural mass," and the hedonism as a way of life promoted by the marketing system of business, constitutes the cultural contradiction of capitalism. The modernism is exhausted, and no longer threatening. The hedonism apes its sterile japes. But the social order lacks either a culture that is a symbolic expression of any vitality or a moral impulse that is a motivational or binding force. What, then, can hold the society together?

This is joined to a more pervasive problem derived from the nature of modern society. The characteristic style of industrialism is based on the principles of economics and economizing: on efficiency, least cost, maximization, optimization, and functional rationality. Yet it is this very style that is in conflict with the advanced cultural trends of the Western world, for modernist culture emphasizes anti-cognitive and anti-intellectual modes which look longingly toward a return to instinctual sources of expression. The one emphasizes functional rationality, technocratic decision making, and meritocratic rewards; the other, apocalyptic moods and anti-rational modes of behavior. It is this disjunction which is the historic cultural crisis of all Western bourgeois society. This cultural contradiction is, in the longer run, the most fateful division in the society.

The Disjunctions of Cultural Discourse

IN THE PREVIOUS CHAPTER, I tried to show that the disjunction between culture and social structure creates a pervasive set of tensions which the society (as well as the individual) finds difficult to manage. But there remains another, central issue: the coherence of culture itself in modern society, and the question of whether culture, rather than religion, can provide a comprehensive or transcendental set of ultimate meanings, or even satisfactions, in daily life.

The question of the coherence of culture was set forth by Wordsworth, in his "Preface to the Lyrical Ballads" (1800), when he deplored "the craving for extraordinary incident" and the thirst for "outrageous stimulation" created by the rapid spread of communication and the quickening pace of life, so that "the works of Shakspeare [sic] and Milton, are driven into neglect by frantic novels, sickly and stupid German Tragedies, and deluges of idle and extravagant stories in verse. . . ." Almost 150 years later, when T. S. Eliot reflected on the problem, he pointed out that culture had come to have different meanings when related to the whole society or to a group or class, and he concluded: "As a society develops towards functional complexity and differentiation, we may expect the emergence of several cultural levels: in short, the culture of the class or group will present itself."[1]

---

[1] See William Wordsworth, *Selected Poems and Prefaces* (Boston: Houghton Mifflin, 1965), p. 449; and T. S. Eliot, *Notes Towards the Definition of Culture* (London: Faber and Faber, 1948), p. 25.

Both these developments have been exacerbated in contemporary times, and both have been taken to be the central sociological problems of culture—even though they have been presented, strikingly, by eminent literary figures. The extension of vulgarity has threatened to overwhelm the serious culture; the growth of highly vocal sub-cultures has offered modes of self-absorption to significant segments of the society (*vide* the youth culture of recent years).

But the underlying problem, I submit, is less these overt sociological developments than a breakup in the very discourses—the languages, and the ability of the languages to express an experience —which give culture its present incoherence. Much of this is due to the ambiguity of the term "modernity" and what it expresses. More is due to the breakup of underlying syntactical structures of cultural styles. At root, there is the fact—or, I should say, my argument—that a unified cosmology, which since the Renaissance had organized the perception of space and time in a specifically "rational" way, has itself been broken up by centrifugal aesthetic forces and by a fundamental shift in the relation of the artist to both the aesthetic experience and the spectator (what I call the eclipse of distance), and that, in consequence, modernity itself produces an incoherence in culture.

In the forefront of consciousness, the pervasive sense of disorientation which has spread through the culture (and which is a source of the crisis of modernity) is attributable to the lack of language that can adequately relate one to transcendental conceptions—a philosophy of first causes or an eschatology of final things. The religious terminology which pervaded our modes of comprehension has become threadbare, and the symbols which soaked our poetic and rhetorical modes (compare the King James Version to the New English Bible) have become attenuated. The poverty of emotive language in our time reflects the impoverishment of a life without litany or ritual.

In one sense, none of this is new. Man, seemingly, has had the recurrent feeling—call it alienation, forlornness, or existential despair—of being lost, or cast out of the world. In Christian sensibility there is the agonized theme of the separateness of man from God. In the aesthetic humanism of Schiller there is the lament that the "zoon condition" of Greek life, where man was a perfect whole, has given way to the differentiation of function, resulting in an estrangement of the intuitive and speculative minds and the dissociation of sensibility. In Hegel, there is the cosmic drama of the movement of the world from a pre-existent primordial unity through the dualities of nature and history, thought and experience, man and spirit, to the re-unification of the Absolute in the "realization" of philosophy. For Marx, in a more naturalistic mode, it was the division of labor (mental and physical, town and country) which was generally responsible for alienation in work, plus the specific fact that in a commodity-exchange society a man becomes "reified" in his labor, so that his personality is dissolved in his function.

Contemporary experience, in its effort to articulate its own disorientation, draws from all these speculative and philosophical reflections. But at times excessively so, for musings about "the human conditon" only blur the distinctiveness of modern times and the distinctive ways in which some of these larger truths are expressed in concrete fashion. Yet modes of experience do vary radically in time and place. Lucien Febvre once pointed out that the age of Rabelais had little *visual* sense, that hearing in particular seemed to precede and remain more important than sight, a primacy which was reflected in the imagery of the prose and poetry of the time. Marcel Granet attempted to show how particular conceptions of number (but not quantity), space, and time played a distinct role in the formulation of classical Chinese political philosophy and classical Chinese art.

Contemporary social science, however, has tended to eschew this form of analysis. It deals with formal organizations or social processes (such as industrialization), but rarely with the contradictory modes of experience themselves, modes which mediate between social structure and culture. The following observations, an exploration in sociological analysis, seek to illustrate the ways in which social perceptions are shaped, often unconsciously, by contradictory modes of experience, and the way a discordant culture expresses the root perplexities of a time.

THE REVOLUTION IN SENSIBILITY

Our technical civilization has not only been a revolution in production (and in communication); it has been a revolution in sensibility as well. The distinctiveness of this civilization—call it "mass society" or "industrial society"—can be understood in a number of ways; I choose to define it (not exhaustively) within these dimensions: number, interaction, self-consciousness, and future-time orientation. In effect, the way in which we confront the world is conditioned by these elements.

Number. In 1789, when George Washington was inaugurated as the first president of the United States (and the Constitution had just been ratified), American society consisted of fewer than 4 million people, of whom 750,000 were blacks. Few people lived in cities; New York, then the capital, had a population of 33,000. In all, 200,000 individuals lived in what were then defined as "urban areas," places with more than 2,500 inhabitants. It was a young population: the median age was 16, and there were only 800,000 males above that age.

Because the United States was a small country, members of the political elite knew each other, as did the thin stratum of leading families. But for most persons, living in isolated clumps or in sparsely inhabited areas, life was vastly different. People rarely traveled great distances; a visitor from afar was a rarity. News meant local gossip, and the few news sheets concentrated on parochial events. The ordinary person's image of the world and its politics was extremely circumscribed.

Today, the United States numbers well over 210 million people, more than 140 million of whom live in metropolitan areas (that is, within a county containing at least one city of 50,000 residents). Less than 10 million people live on farms. The median age is about 30, and 140 million people are over 17 years of age. Few persons live or work in social isolation. Even those who work on the farms are tied to the national society by the mass media and the popular culture.

In the way in which we perceive the world today, as against 1789, two aspects are striking: the difference in the number of persons each of us *knows*, and the number each of us *knows of.* On the job, in school, in the neighborhood, in a profession, in a social mi-

88

lieu, an individual today knows literally hundreds if not thousands of other persons; and with the multiplication of the mass media—with the enlargement of the political world, and the enormous proliferation of entertainment figures and public personalities—the number of persons one *knows of* accelerates steeply. Simply, then, the number of encounters each of us has, and the range of names, events, and knowledge we have to master—this is the most obvious fact about the world which today confronts us as a given.

Interaction. The "mass society," however, is not composed of numbers alone. Czarist Russia and Imperial China were large land-mass societies, with huge numbers of people. But these societies were essentially segmented, each village largely recapitulating the features of the other. It was Émile Durkheim who, in his *Division of Labor*, gave us the clue to what is distinctive about the mass society. New social forms emerge when segmentation breaks down and people interact with each other, when ensuing competition leads not necessarily to conflict but to more complex divisions of labor, complementary relationships, and increased structural differentiation.

What is distinctive, then, about contemporary society is not only its size and number, but the increased interaction—both physical (through travel, larger work units, and greater housing densities) and psychic (through the mass media)—which ties us to so many other persons, directly and symbolically. Increased interaction leads not only to social differentiations but, as a mode of experience, to psychic differentiation as well—to the desire for change and novelty, to the search for sensation, and to the syncretism of culture, all of which mark so distinctively the rhythm of contemporary life.

Self-consciousness. To the classic question of identity "Who are you?" a traditional man would say, "I am the son of my father."[2] A person today says, "I am I, I come out of myself, and in choice and action I make myself." This change of identity is the hallmark of our own modernity. For us experience, rather than tradition, authority, revealed utterance, or even reason, has become the source of understanding and identity. Experience is the great source of self-consciousness, the confrontation of self with diverse others.

---

[2] One sees this, of course, in the traditional Russian patronymic, or in the usual Arab form of naming, such as Ali ben Ahmed, or in the residues of old English names, such as John/son, Thom/son, and the like.

Insofar as one makes one's *own* experience the touchstone of truth, one seeks out those with whom one has common experience in order to find common meanings. To this extent, the rise of generations, and the sense of generation, is the distinct focus of modern identity.[3] But this change is, also, the source of an "identity crisis."

The idea of reality, sociologically, is a fairly simple one. Reality is a confirmation by "significant others." Traditionally, the bar mitzvah is a confirmation by the Jewish community, the marking out of a new status (the acceptance of responsibility for the covenant) in a ceremonial act. Graduation from school is a confirmation in a new role and a new status. When a person is confirmed by others, there has to be some sign of recognition.

Reality breaks down when the confirming "others" have lost their meaning for the person seeking to locate himself or find a place in the society. The sociological problem of reality in our time—in terms of social location and identity—arises because individuals have left old anchorages, no longer follow inherited ways, are constantly faced with the problems of choice (the ability to choose careers, life-styles, friends, or political representatives is, for the mass of people, something new in social history), and no longer find authoritative standards or critics to guide them. The change from family and class to generation as the "structural" source of confirmation thus creates new strains in identity.

Time-orientation. Ours is a society that has become "future-oriented" in all its dimensions: a government has to plan for future growth; a corporation has to plan for future needs (capital sources, market and product changes, etc.); the individual has to think in terms of a career. In effect, society no longer goes on in crescive fashion; it becomes mobilized for specific ends.

The greatest pressures today devolve upon the young person. At an early age he is under pressure to make firm choices: to get good

---

[3] In traditional Western society, or in the early phases of contemporary society, *social class* was usually the main source of identity. The rise and fall of social classes, as Schumpeter noted, was the rise and fall of families. In the earlier quest for position and power in society one sought to rise with one's class, or, as more open mobility became possible, to rise out of one's class (cf. Stendhal's "Young Man from the Provinces"). Social class is still today a potent shaper of identity, but it decreases in importance with the rise of education as the chief route to "place" in society. Both in the literary sphere (where the process has a long history) and now in the political realm, the generation assumes great importance. For the immigrant worlds, and America has been a land of many such worlds, the generation has been the chief source of psychic identity for the intellectual.

grades in school, to enter a good college, to choose a vocation. At all stages he is rated, and the performance ratings now become a card of identity that he carries throughout his life. The failure to provide adequate mechanisms during the transitional period (that is, school guidance, vocational counseling) leads to obvious strains and invites opting out of the system. In this respect, the "beat" fad of the 1950s parallels the behavior of the early industrial worker when the machine harness was slipped over him as he came off the farm. In both instances one finds wild outbursts (the machine-breaking of the early Industrial Revolution is matched, perhaps, by dropout rates in high schools and colleges), the pastoral romance (which in the case of the beats became slum romance), and similar forms of unorganized class struggle.

The new emphasis on the future in terms of social as well as individual planning—and the resistance to this emphasis because of the new kinds of pressures which such an emphasis entails—is a new dimension of our experience in American society.

These four elements shape the way in which individuals respond to the world. Two of them, number and interaction, are features of the social environment which structure our responses, unconsciously, in the way the balancing of mass and size of type on the front page of a newspaper tends to direct our eye in a determinate sequence. They are responsible, primarily, for the emphasis in modern sensibility of *immediacy, impact, sensation,* and *simultaneity.* These rhythms also tend to shape the technical forms of painting, music, and literature. The emergence of self-consciousness (or the "cult of experience") and the pressures of a mobilized society, particularly where the social mechanisms have been inadequate to handle the problems of innovation and adaptation, have led to more open and conscious modes of ideological response to the society— rebellion, alienation, retreatism, apathy, or conformity—which are sharply etched on the surface of the culture. Thus the other two, self-consciousness and mobilized time, become modes of experience in themselves.

THE DIREMPTION OF CULTURE

These modes of experience (together with some more formal aspects of industrial society, principally functional specialization, and the requirements of the new "intellectual technology") are reflected not only in disjunctions between the social structure and the culture but also between the modes of cognitive and emotive expression.

I single out for illustration three realms in which these disjunctions have occurred: (1) The disjunction of *role* and *person*; (2) functional specialization, or the disjunction between *role* and *symbolic expression*; and (3) the change in vocabulary from metaphor to mathematics.

THE DISJUNCTION OF ROLE AND PERSON

In contemporary sociology, as in the intellectual world as a whole, there has been a debate as to whether modern society is one of increasing depersonalization or of increasing freedom. It seems strange that views so diametrically opposite are held by intellectually responsible persons with little effort to mediate, reconcile, or even establish the terms in which the debate is conducted.

In a theoretical sense, the roots of the two positions (as expressed in modern sociology) go back to Max Weber and Émile Durkheim. For Weber, the drift of society was one of increasing bureaucratization (or functional rationality), in which greater specialization of function meant increasing separation of the individual from control over the enterprises of which he was a part. Regulated by the norms of efficiency, calculability, and specialization, man is, in this view, an appendage to "the clattering process of the bureaucratic machinery."

Durkheim had a contrary perspective. In the way he dichotomized social change, the shift from "mechanical solidarity" to "organic solidarity" was a movement from homogeneity to heterogeneity, from uniformity to diversity. Societies of the first kind had little division of labor; the collective spirit was so strong that violations of rules were dealt with in a retributive way. Societies of the second type featured a complex division of labor, a separation of sacred from secular elements, a greater choice of occupation, and a loyalty to one's profession, rather than to the parochial group, as the source of identity or belonging. Sharing some elements of nineteenth-century evolutionary beliefs, though not the unilinearity of a Henry Maine or a Herbert Spencer, Durkheim saw social development as inherently "progressive" in its unfolding, though precipitating new kinds of problems. (In one sense, the emphasis of a Weber is on *rationalization*, of a Durkheim on the *rational*.)

This bifurcation continued in contemporary sociology and in intellectual life generally. Those adhering to the Marxist or existentialist positions point to the depersonalization inherent in modern bureaucratic life: *vide* Marcuse, Fromm, Tillich. Others, such as Talcott Parsons or Edward Shils, have stressed the way in which modern society allows for greater variety of choice—its emphasis on achievement, upgrading of occupations, and greater individualism.

How does one thread one's way through this debate? As William James once said, whenever you meet a contradiction, make a distinction, for people often use the same words to mean two different things. In a curious way, both theories are correct, largely because each is talking about a different dimension. If one makes the distinction between *roles* and *persons*, one can perhaps see the way each theory talks past the other.

I think it is quite evident, following Weber, that modern society increasingly forces a narrow specialization of roles. Broad aspects of life which were once centered in the family (namely work, play, education, welfare, health) are increasingly taken over by specialized institutions (enterprises, schools, trade unions, social clubs, the state). Role definitions (the many different hats we wear) become sharper, and in the crucial area of work, where in the nineteenth-century *mythos* a man found his identity, tasks and roles become minutely specialized. (*The Dictionary of Occupational Titles* lists over 20,000 different specialized jobs in its analysis of vocational opportunities. We even see this in intellectual tasks. *The National Register of Scientific and Specialized Personnel*, in compiling lists of intellectual talents in the country, cites about 900 fields in the sciences.)

Within organizations, the creation of hierarchies, job specifications, minutely defined responsibilities, rating systems, escalator promotions, and the like give emphasis to this sense of the fragmentation of self, as it is defined through the *role*. At the same time it is also clear that, as a *person*, one now has a wider range and variety of choices than ever before. There are many more different kinds of jobs and professions. One can travel to many different places and live in different cities. In the area of consumption (and using culture as a form of consumption), there is a wider provenance for creating a personal, or a chosen, style of life. All of this is summed up in the term "social mobility," a term distinctive in its modern application.

Modern life creates a bifurcation of role and person which for a sentient individual becomes a strain.[4]

FUNCTIONAL SPECIALIZATION: THE DISJUNCTION OF ROLE AND SYMBOLIC EXPRESSION

A characteristic of science, as of almost all organized human activity, is the increasing segmentation, differentiation, and specialization (subdivision and subspecialization) of each field of knowedge. Natural philosophy, which was an inclusive term in the seventeenth century, then subdivided into the natural sciences of physics, chemistry, botany, zoology, and so forth. Speculative philosophy of the nineteenth century gave rise to sociology, psychology, mathematical logic, symbolic logic, analytical philosophy, and so forth. In any of the fields today, new problems give rise to further specializations: chemistry, which was once divided into analytical, organic, inorganic, and physical, is in one accounting subdivided into carbohydrate, steroid, silicone, nuclear, petroleum, and solid state.

One sees this process not only in the fields of knowledge but also in the character of organizations, as new problems give rise to new functions and to new specializations for dealing with them. Thus a business corporation which once had a simple staff-and-line organization now finds itself confounded with the problems of coordinating a dozen broad functions, such as research, marketing, advertising, quality control, personnel, public relations, design, finance, and production, let alone the dozens of subspecializations

[4] This distinction between role and person is somewhat different from the distinction between office and person. Any society, in order to enforce authority, emphasizes a distinction (most notably in an army) between a rank and the person bearing the rank. One obeys the rank, not the person. One respects an office (e.g., a judge) not necessarily the individual. But a role is a segmented aspect of an individual's daily activity. It is not a formally defined set of responsibilities (as is a rank or office) but a set of prescriptive behavior patterns defined by social usage.

within each of the functions (so that personnel, for example, would include labor relations, internal communications, job training, plant security, safety, time records, welfare and medical benefits, and the like). And one finds similar divisions in *every* formal organization, whether it be a business enterprise, a university, a hospital, or a governmental agency.

The point of all this is that the high degree of specialization—both in the fields of knowledge and in the structures of organizations—inevitably creates an almost unbearable strain between the culture and the social structure. In fact, it becomes quite difficult to speak even of "the" culture, for not only do specializations create "sub-cultures" or private worlds—in the anthropological sense—but these in turn create private languages and private signs and symbols which often (the case of the jazz musician is the most obvious) infiltrate the "public" world of culture.

Today, the culture can hardly, if at all, reflect the society in which people live. The system of social relations is so complex and differentiated, and experiences are so specialized, complicated, or incomprehensible, that it is difficult to find common symbols to relate one experience to another.

In the nineteenth century, the "agency" of expression was the novel. The function of fiction, paradoxically, was to report fact. When social classes began to confront each other in the nineteenth century in the comedy of manners and morals, there was great curiosity about how each class lived, or how individuals who moved up the social ladder took on, or failed to take on, new class styles and modes. There was equally great interest in the nature of work.

The extraordinarily differentiated social structure which has come into being today makes it difficult for a novelist—or even a sociologist—to probe the nature of the worlds of work. Thus fiction, like social criticism, tends to deal with consumption styles or reflect in the themes of alienation and bureaucratization the writer's animosity against the honeycomb complexity of social structure, but rarely to deal with the experience of work. (In Joseph Heller's recent novel *Something Happened* the setting is work, but we never find out what the protagonist does or what the company makes. It is one long monologue about the self.)

Insofar as experiences in the society can no longer be generalized into the culture, culture itself becomes private, and the individual arts either technical or hermetic. At the turn of the century, the function of the critic was to mediate between the creative new experiments being conducted in painting and music, and to find a common aesthetic to explain them. Today there is no critic who can assimilate music to painting or painting to music—and it is probably not the fault of the critic. Even the arts have become highly technical: the New Criticism in literature as a parallel to the technical innovations of the great masters of the novel; the complex intentions of abstract expressionist painting, with its new emphasis on surface and space.

The real difficulties in the appreciation of the "modern" (both in literature and painting) have been masked by the fact that they have become modish and, through their popularizers and imitators, common coin for the consumption culture. The only genuine avant-garde movement today is in music, and it remains so because the new electronic music, post-Webern tonalities, and new mathematics of serial music are so technical that even a critic finds it difficult to act as intermediary to other arts, let alone the general public.

The rise of pop art, the introduction of chance elements in music, the appreciation of "junk" as aesthetic, and the vogue for "happenings" in which paint, sculpture (posture), music, and dance are fused into one—all reflect the reaction against the technical and hermetic elements in art. These trends not only represent new ways to shock even a blasé public but also pose a new kind of threat to the traditional (and formal) conceptions of genre. If John Dewey could say that "art is experience," what these practitioners are saying is that all experience is art. In effect, they deny specialization by insisting on the fusion of all arts into one. Theirs is an erasure of all boundaries between the arts, and between art and experience.

THE DISJUNCTION OF VOCABULARY: FROM METAPHOR TO MATHEMATICS

Reality is always inferential (who has seen custom?), and we employ concepts to describe reality. In the history of culture, one or another mode of experience has always been dominant as the source of concepts. It is the change in language—the expansion of the abstract mode of thought—which exacerbates the disjunction of our experience.

In the primitive world-view—and in such sophisticated primitivism as Zen Buddhism—the world was presented in its immediacy and concreteness. Greek cosmogony gave us a vocabulary of first-level abstraction. The pre-Socratics introduced metaphor; Plato, with the idea of the Demiurge, the symbol; and Aristotle, the idea of analogy. (Our traditional modes of thought employ all three. Imagery can be visual, aural, or tactile, but it employs the techniques of metaphor, symbol, or analogy in "picturing" the world.)

Theological speech, as derived from Christian thought, is deeply soaked in symbols—the Cross, the Messiah, the Epiphanies, the Sacraments—and the language emphasizes mystery and personality: grace, charisma, *kairos*, passion or suffering, ritual. The breakdown of theological beliefs and the rise of a scientific world-view, leading to the enthronement of physics and the natural sciences, gave us in the eighteenth and nineteenth centuries a mechanical cosmology—the image of the world as a machine, or as a celestial clock. This ordered world reached its apogee in two images: the beauty and precision of Laplace's *Mécanique céleste*, in which the universe functioned as a jewel; and the idea of the "great chain of being," in which all creatures were united in one perfect strand. In Alexander Pope's words:

> Vast chain of Being! which from God began,
> Natures ethereal, human, angel, man,
> Beast, bird, fish, insect, what no eye can see,
> No glass can reach; from Infinite to thee . . .

The language of analysis, once derived from theology, was now wrested from the early physical sciences. (Poetry, driven, as Whitehead put it, from the world of fact by science, resorted to ambiguity as its mode of expression, while modern existentialist theology finds its mode in paradox.) In the social sciences the key terms were Force, Motion, Energy, Power (and while these terms have specific referents in physics, they have few operational specificities in social analysis). But as the natural sciences progressed, the social sciences added new biological analogies to the metaphors derived from physics: evolution, growth, organic structure and function, and these terms, until very recently, were the language of sociology.

Even when, in the nineteenth century, social science sought to find a language of its own—"economic man," "psychological man," "capitalism," and so forth—this led to a conceptual realism or what Whitehead called "the fallacy of misplaced concreteness." The search for "a language of one's own" in order to avoid the trap of reification has led (as exemplified in Talcott Parsons' *Structure of Social Action*) to "analytical abstraction." Thus, theory construction in sociology, for one, has become a highly deductive system derived from a few basic axioms or really analytical concepts, such as the patterned variables in the action schema of Parsons, in which the empirical referents no longer stand for concrete entities—the individual, society, and the like.

But in the more general sweep of knowledge, the dominant mode of intellectual language today is mathematical, and especially in our new "intellectual technology" (linear programming, decision theory, simulation) we have the "new" language of variables, parameters, models, stochastic processes, algorithms, heuristics, minimax, and other terms which are being adopted by the social sciences. Yet the type of mathematics that is influential here is not the deterministic calculus of classical mechanics, but a calculus of probabilities. Life is a "game"—a game against nature, a game of man against man—and one follows rational strategies that can provide maximum payoffs at maximum risks, minimax payoffs at minimax risks, and that most lovely of terms in utility preference theory, a payoff that is provided by a "criterion of regret."

But all of this leads to a paradox: the modern vocabulary is purely rational, with no referent other than its self-contained mathematical formulas. In a modern cosmology (as in physics, and now in the other sciences as well), pictures have gone, words have gone, and what remain—apart from elegance, but even here it is the elegance of formal ingenuity—are abstract formulas. And underneath these formulas there is no law of nature as we knew it before, eternal, universal, immutable, and readily discernible. Underneath are uncertainty and the breakup of temporal and spatial sequence.[5]

Thus our vocabulary reinforces the emergence of an abstract, if not mystical, world conception. And this is the penultimate disjunction between the everyday world of fact and experience, and the world of concepts and matter.

---

[5] The world of particle physics, as I understand it, has itself fallen back on metaphor—"the eightfold way," "charmed quarks"—in its own bewilderment at catching this will-o'-the-wisp. The history of physics has been the search for the ultimate unit of matter; but in the end it may turn out that there is no such entity, but only a set of relationships which change with the position of the observer, or with the different rates of decay of the particles themselves, as a function of their changing relationships. We may, then, end, as Anaximander did, only with the "boundless," not the bounded.

THE ECLIPSE OF DISTANCE

Every culture, we have tended to assume, hangs together in some fashion, and this we have called its style. A religious culture has a greater unity than most because all the elements of the culture are directed toward some common end: to emphasize mystery, to create awe, to exalt, to transcend. This unity, emphasized in mood, runs like a thread through its architecture, its music, its painting, and its literature—in its spires, liturgies, litanies, spatial representation of figures, and sacred text. Secular cultures rarely have this conscious design. Yet they, too, have a common style, expressed in rhythms and moods. We talk, for instance, of baroque, rococo, or mannerist styles. And these are translated into techniques which are responses to underlying elements in the civilization; they are perceived, but not often consciously expressed. Such elements pervade all aspects of a culture, even though they are expressed in varied ways. It is usual among contemporary critics to contrast high culture (or serious culture) with mass culture (entertainment culture) and to see the latter as a perversion or denaturing of the former. But both are assumed to be part of a *common* culture, and in some way they must express common underlying rhythms or moods.

Yet to think of cultures in this way may be deceptive if we assume that there is some holistic principle at any single time which uniquely defines that "world"—in the way, for example, that Hegel could talk of a Greek world, or a Roman world, or a Christian civilization. Let us leave aside the historical question of whether it is fruitful to think of past cultures in terms of single unifying themes—we almost have to, since this has become the given of our language of discourse. Can one, however, find a single principle which defines modernity—other than the tantalizing search for the elusive principle itself? I do not think we can, and I submit four arguments to support my contention.

THE VARIETIES OF CULTURAL EXPERIENCE

The most striking aspect of mass society is that, while it incorporates the broad mass into society, it creates greater diversity and variety and a sharpened hunger for experience, as more and more aspects of the world—geographical, political, and cultural—come within the purview of ordinary men and women. This very enlargement of horizon, this syncretic mingling of the arts, this search for the new, whether as a voyage of discovery or as a snobbish effort to differentiate oneself from others, is itself the creation of a new style, of a kind of modernity.

At the heart of the problem is the meaning of the idea of culture. When one speaks of a "classical culture" or a "Catholic culture" (almost in the sense of a bacterial culture—a breeding of distinctly identifiable strains), one thinks of a long-linked set of beliefs, traditions, rituals, and injunctions which in the course of its history has achieved something of a homogeneous style. But modernity is, distinctively, a break with the past *as* past, catapulting it into the present. De Tocqueville said that aristocracy made a chain of all members of the community from king to peasant; democracy breaks the chain, severing every one of its links. As a result, de Tocqueville went on, democracy "makes every man forget his ancestors"—an attractive idea to men like Whitman, who declared that the "enemy" was the word "Culture," and a literature "smelling of prince's favors . . . and built entirely [upon] the idea of caste." For de Tocqueville, the characteristic aspect of modernity was the fact that "the woof of time is every instant broken, and the track of generations effaced."

Modernity has been defined as "the tradition of the new." Under such conditions, not even an avant-garde is possible, for an avant-garde is by its very nature a rejection of some particular tradition. The characteristic avant-garde tactic is scandal. In modern culture, scandal is eagerly pursued only as yet another sensation. Modernity castrates the avant-garde by quickly accepting it, just as it accepts, with equal equanimity, elements from the Western past, the Byzantine past, the Oriental past (and present) in its *omnium-gatherum* of cultures. The old concept of culture is based on continuity, the modern on variety; the old values tradition, the contemporary ideal is syncretism.

Little more than 100 years ago, the Anglo-American world of cultivated discourse was bounded by the classical writers, Latin poets, Greek and Renaissance art, the French *philosophes* (Voltaire and Rousseau), and some German literature, introduced mostly through the translations of Carlyle.[6] Today the boundaries of the

[6] "In the eighteenth century," Whitehead wrote in *Science and the Modern World*, "every well-educated man read Lucretius, and entertained ideas about atoms."

world, geographically speaking, have been broken, and the range of the arts within the traditional frames of literature, painting, sculpture, and music, as well as outside those frames, is almost limitless. It is not only that, for example, the art market has become international, so that Polish painters show in Paris, and American painting is bought in England; or that the theater now ignores national frontiers (so that Chekhov, Strindberg, Brecht, O'Neill, Tennessee Williams, Giraudoux, Anouilh, Ionesco, Genet, and Beckett are performed simultaneously in Paris, London, New York, Berlin, Frankfurt, Stockholm, Warsaw, and a hundred other cities on several continents). Even more, the range of culture is so diffuse, the "topics" of interest so proliferated, that it is almost impossible to find a center of gravity that can truly define the "cultivated" man. In the Great Exhibition Hall of the contemporary arts, the display open to any man who seeks to apprise himself of the world's culture is staggering.[7]

What, then, is culture? Who, then, is the well-educated person? What is the community of discourse? It is in the nature of modernity to deny that such questions have any single answer.

And when Ralph Waldo Emerson made his first trip abroad to meet contemporary European intellectuals, the range of their discourse still had a common frame. With Wordsworth: "The conversation turned on books. Lucretius he esteems a far higher poet than Virgil. . . . He proceeded to abuse Goethe's *Wilhelm Meister*. It was full of all manner of fornication." With Carlyle: "Plato he does not read, and he disparaged Socrates. . . . Gibbon he called the 'splendid bridge from the old world to the new.' . . . *Tristram Shandy* was one of his first books after Robinson Crusoe." See *English Traits* (Boston: Houghton Mifflin, 1876), pp. 14–24.

[7] "The invention of tape-recording and long-playing records," Stanley Edgar Hyman pointed out years ago, "with their booming production and sales, may turn out to be an even greater cultural revolution than paperbacks, and they certainly have done more for poetry than any form of publishing. Here literally hundreds of companies, some no larger than a label, produce countless thousands of records, making a wide variety of music available everywhere, and stimulating a growing demand for live music outside its familiar centers. Technically, in high-fidelity and stereophonic sound, the reproduced sound is of a quality and range unimaginable two decades ago. A single company, Folkways, has issued several hundred records of folk music, some of it as exotic and unlikely as *Eskimo Music of Alaska and the Hudson Bay* or *Temiar Dream Songs from Malaya*, and it is possible for anyone with the price to have a collection that could not have been matched by any of the world's great archives a generation ago. Not long ago, a lucky world traveler with an interest could hear that many folksongs in a busy lifetime." In *Culture for the Millions?*, ed. Norman Jacobs (Princeton: Van Nostrand, 1961), p. 126.

THE LACK OF A CENTER

It is not only the bewildering variety of cultural demesnes (and the vast multiplication of practitioners, serious, semi-skilled, or amateur) that creates a sense of diffuseness, but the lack of a *center*, geographical or spiritual, to provide both authority and a place where leading painters, musicians, and novelists can meet and get to know one another. In the past almost all societies with a "high culture" had some center—the agora, or piazza, or marketplace—where, in the concentration, exchange, competition, and jousting, artists stimulated each other, creating and deriving a sense of vitality from the interchange. Paris, in the early decades of the twentieth century ("the banquet years," as Roger Shattuck has called them) and later, in the 1920s, was such a center, in which all the arts stimulated one another and were somehow interinvolved. A ballet by Fokine might have decor by Chagall or Picasso and music by Stravinsky or Satie. Through its public schools and the tight triangle of Oxford, Cambridge, and London, England has had an elite whose members could count on direct literary and social acquaintance with each other. "What has astonished me, and what astonishes any American," Irving Kristol wrote in *Encounter* (October 1955), "is the extent to which almost *all* British intellectuals are cousins—not literally, of course, but in a metaphorical sense that is more than empty rhetoric. . . . they went to the same public school (the number of people who seem to have known George Orwell at Eton is only matched by the number of people who are writing books about him); or one's father was a contributor to someone else's father's magazine; and so on and on. A tight little island, indeed."

The United States has always lacked such a center. In the middle of the nineteenth century, Boston provided a unifying ground and, through the mingling of church, wealth, and culture, created a style of sorts. But its very unity was "self-defeating" in that it was a New England style, and could never dominate the country as a whole. Toward the end of the century, New York became a center for aspiring and parvenu Society, and to some extent a cultural center as well, but it could never encompass the different American regional cultures—the Midwest, the border states, the South, and the Southwest—that had begun to manifest themselves. Even in the years shortly before World War I and after it, with the burgeoning of Greenwich Village as topography and symbol, New York caught but one element of American culture, the avant-garde, and that only for a while, since it turned out to serve mostly as a way station on the road to Paris.

Given the sheer size of the country and the heterogeneity of ethnic and religious groups, American intellectuals, as Kristol has put it, "Meet one another in the dark, so to speak." The men who edit the large magazines usually lack the opportunity to meet anyone of distinction in politics, drama, or music. The political people are in Washington, the publishing and theater people in New York, the movie people in Los Angeles, and the professoriat is scattered across the country in the large universities. The universities have become the dominant force in the American cultural world today: many novelists, composers, painters, and critics find their havens in the far-flung universities, and many of the major literary and cultural quarterlies are edited there.

Even when, as in New York, there does exist an acknowledged, large center for publishing, theater, music, and painting, the enormous numbers who congregate there, plus the great stress on professionalism, make for a compartmentalization that isolates serious artists from one another. Few painters know theater people or musicians or writers. Composers talk to composers, painters to painters, writers to writers. In the past a distinct minority, who thought of themselves as forming an avant-garde, consciously sought out others who were experimenting in the same field. They were drawn together either by a common mood of rebellion or by a common aesthetic (sometimes, as in the case of Italian futurism, by both). Today, a voracious audience of sophisticates quickly snaps up and adopts any avant-garde before it even has a chance to proclaim its rebellion, and the increasingly technical nature of experimentation in the arts, whether it be serial composition in music or minimalism in painting, seems to deny the possibility of a common aesthetic. In the past, such technical considerations were bridged by the existence of a class of *hommes des lettres* or by critics, such as Apollinaire and Karl Kraus, who could move about with ease in a number of fields and provide common links between them. But today even the critics are specialists, and the compartmentalization grows more hermetic.

In the 1930s, the politicalization of culture through Marxism made, for the moment, for a single aesthetic with specific touch-stones to explain the different arts (and for critics who mechanically applied those criteria in the interest of a unified idea of culture), while that radical world provided a common milieu for artists, writers, and musicians. Today that politically unified world has vanished, and except for professional ties or, occasionally, academic ones, no common milieu exists.

What is most striking is the insularity of national cultures. In the 1920s and 1950s, intellectuals and writers were highly aware of each other, and there was a considerable degree of international contact. T. S. Eliot's *Criterion* in the 1920s and *Partisan Review* in the 1950s would run long articles or "letters" from different cities, reporting on new themes in the arts and in culture. Today the lack of contact is dispiriting. To some extent, writers and intellectuals may be more caught up in the politics of their own societies. Or perhaps the arts have become more technical and professionalized. But the larger reason, I would submit, is the exhaustion of modernism itself. What modernism did, at its apogee, was to throw up new revolutionary movements (and, with each, a manifesto): futurism, imagism, vorticism, cubism, Dadaism, constructivism, surrealism, and so forth. Modernism was new and news. It proclaimed new aesthetics, new forms, new styles. But these *isms* are now passé (or as one wit has put it, all "isms" are now "wasms"). And there is no center; there are only peripheries.

A culture thrives where there is a center and where the intensity of interaction among persons creates a concentration of effects that vivifies the efforts of those involved. The lack of a center for modernist culture, both nationally and internationaly, and the fragmentation of culture into compartmentalized segments inevitably tend to break up the discourse which sustains a culture for the entire society.

THE VISUAL CULTURE

One of the most important ways in which modernity confronts high culture is to deny the idea of a single hierarchy of the arts, or of the unity of culture (e.g., Periclean Greece, the city-states of the Italian Renaissance, Elizabethan England). This unity is no longer possible in the modern world and was perhaps not so true of earlier periods as one tends to assume.[8] Thus Meyer Schapiro writes:

> We look in vain in England for a style of painting that corresponds to Elizabethan poetry and drama; just as in Russia in the nineteenth century there was no true parallel in painting to the great movement of literature. In these instances, we recognize that the various arts have different roles in the culture and social life of a time and express in their content as well as style different interests and values. The dominant outlook of a time— if it can be isolated—does not affect all the arts in the same degree, nor are all the arts equally capable of expressing the same outlook.[9]

H. Stuart Hughes has recalled Henry Adams' observation that in 1800 the United States possessed a cultural equipment that was almost exclusively restricted to theology, literature, and oratory; the realm of the visual arts, and of sensuous consumption, was practically nonexistent.[10]

Today, the "dominant outlook" is visual. Sound and sight, and particularly the latter, organize the aesthetic and command the audience. It could almost not be otherwise in a mass society.[11]

Mass entertainments (circuses, spectacles, theaters) have always been visual, but there are two distinct aspects of contemporary life that necessarily emphasize the visual element. First, the modern

[8] Western culture, beginning with the Greeks, has always made the distinction— paralleling the one between leisure and work—between the creative and the utilitarian arts. Even the Church, which was charged with ennobling the humble artisan, accepted this distinction, perhaps because Catholic culture was at its height in a historical period when leisure and work were sharply separated. Literature and music, as contemplative arts, have always been in the pantheon; painting and sculpture, whose craft status is more ambiguous, were included, however, in part because these arts served to reinforce religious authority, in part because their products were acquisitions that could aggrandize the status of their collectors.

In traditional China, interestingly enough, the shadings were drawn somewhat differently. The sublime arts were poetry, calligraphy, and painting, the ones practiced by the literati for their own enjoyment, and which would be understood only by their peers. The other forms of artistic expression—sculpture, bronzes, household and funerary ceramics—the Chinese considered merely the products of artisans. On the latter point, see Mario Prodan, *Chinese Art* (New York: Pantheon, 1958), pp. 24–26.

[9] Meyer Schapiro, "Style," in *Anthropology Today*, ed. Sol Tax (Chicago: University of Chicago Press, 1953), p. 295.

[10] H. Stuart Hughes, "Mass Culture and Social Criticism," in *Culture for the Millions?*, p. 143.

[11] In the history of sensibility—an extraordinarily neglected field—it is striking to find that the imagery of the French poets in the sixteenth century emphasizes smell, taste, and hearing, and seems unable to "picture" or visualize an individual or a place in order to make these "real" to a reader. There is no imagery of vista or landscape or seascape. Reality derived more from smell and sound than from sight.

world is an urban world. Life in the great city and the way stimuli and sociability are defined provide a preponderance of occasions for people to *see*, and *want* to see (rather than read and hear) things. Second is the nature of the contemporary temper, with its hunger for action (as against contemplation), its search for novelty, and its lust for sensation. And it is the visual element in the arts which best appeases these compulsions.

A city is not only a place but a state of mind, a symbol of a distinctive style of life whose major attributes are variety and excitement; a city also presents a sense of scale that dwarfs any single effort to encompass its meaning. To "know" a city, one must walk its streets; but to "see" a city, one must stand outside in order to perceive it whole.[12] From a distance, the skyline "stands for" the city. Its massed density is the shock of cognition, its silhouette the enduring mark of recognition. This visual element is its symbolic representation.

The cityscape, man-made, is etched in its architecture and its bridges. The key materials of an industrial civilization, steel and concrete, find their distinctive use in these structures. The use of steel, replacing masonry, allowed architects to erect a simple frame on which to "drape" a building, and to push that frame high into the sky. The use of reinforced concrete allowed the architect to create "sculptured" shapes that have a free-flowing life of their own. In these new forms one finds a powerful new comprehension and organization of space.

In the new conceptions of space, there is an inherent eclipse of distance. Not only is physical distance compressed by the newer modes of modern transportation, creating a new emphasis on travel and the visual pleasure of seeing so many different places, but the very techniques of the new arts, principally cinema and modern painting, act to eclipse the psychic and aesthetic distance between the viewer and the visual experience. The emphases in cubism on simultaneity and in abstract expressionism on impact are efforts to intensify the immediacy of the emotion, to pull the spectator into the action rather than allow him to contemplate the experience. Such is the underlying principle, as well, of the cinema, which, in its use of montage, goes further than any other contemporary art in

[12] For an imaginative discussion of this point, see R. Richard Wohl and Anselm L. Strauss, "Symbolic Representation and the Urban Milieu," *American Journal of Sociology* 64 (March 1958): 523-532.

the direction of "regulating" emotion, by selecting the images, the angles of vision, the length of a single scene, and the "synapse" of composition. This central aspect of modernity—the organization of social and aesthetic responses in terms of novelty, sensation, simultaneity, and impact—finds its major expression in the visual arts.

So predominantly has the modern aesthetic become a visual one that dams, bridges, silos, and road patterns—the ecological relationships of structures to environment—all become matters of aesthetic concern.[13] The organization of space, whether it be in modern painting, architecture, or sculpture, has become the primary aesthetic problem of mid-twentieth-century culture, as the problem of time (in Bergson, Proust, and Joyce) was the primary aesthetic concern of the first decades of this century. In this preoccupation with space and form, the vitality of modern culture has been expressed best in its architecture, painting, and cinema. In the middle of the twentieth century, these have been the significant arts, and their outlook the significant one of our time. Insofar as the debate about the effects of mass society on high culture has neglected this understanding—for the debate has been shaped by humanists whose conceptions of high culture were formulated mainly about literature—it has failed to confront the most important aspect of the nature of mass culture, the glaring fact that it is a visual culture.

It is quite true, I believe, that contemporary culture is becoming a visual culture rather than a print culture. The sources of this change are less motion pictures and television, as media, than the new sense of geographical and social mobility that people began to experience in the middle of the nineteenth century, and the new aesthetic which arose in response. The closed spaces of village and house began to give way to travel, to the excitement of speed (created by the railroad), and to the pleasures of the promenade, the *plage*, the plazas, and similar experiences of everyday life which figure so prominently in the work of Renoir, Manet, Seurat, and other impressionist and post-impressionist painters.

Marshall McLuhan's distinctions between "hot" and "cool" media, and his notion of the television-created "global village," seem to me to be without much meaning, except on a trivial level. (If any-

---

[13] See, for example, the suggestive book by Erich Gutkind, *Our World from the Air* (Garden City, N.Y.: Doubleday, 1952), and the exhibit on roads organized by Bernard Rudofsky for the Museum of Modern Art, September 1961.

thing, the spread of wider communication nets tends to bring about the disintegration of larger societies into fragmentary ethnic and primordial units.) But there are real consequences for the coherence of a culture in the relative weights of print and the visual in the formation of knowledge. The print media allow for self-pacing and dialogue in comprehending an argument or in reflecting on an image. Print not only emphasizes the cognitive and the symbolic but is also, most importantly, the necessary mode for conceptual thought. The visual media—I mean here film and television—impose their pace on the viewer and, in emphasizing images rather than words, invite not conceptualization but dramatization. In the emphasis television news places on disasters and human tragedies, it invites not purgation or understanding but sentimentality and pity, emotions that are quickly exhausted, and a pseudo-ritual of pseudo-participation in the events. And, as the mode is inevitably one of overdramatization, the responses soon become either stilted or bored. Theater art and painting have likewise gone on to further expressions of shock and to the exploration of extreme situations, and, more recently, as audiences have differentiated, so has the cinema. Television, as the most "public" of media, has its limits. Yet the visual culture as a whole, because it lends itself more readily than print to those impulses of modernism that are taken up by the cultural mass, itself becomes more rapidly depleted in the cultural sense.

THE BREAKUP OF THE RATIONAL COSMOS

The Western aesthetic intention, from the mid-sixteenth to the mid-nineteenth century, was to establish certain formal principles of art around the rational organization of space and time. The aesthetic ideal of congruity operated as a regulative principle in which the focus was on a relational whole and a unity of form. The painting of the Renaissance, in the principles laid down by Alberti, was "rational" not only in that it applied formal mathematical principles to the depiction of a scene (e.g., the role of proportion and perspective), but also in that it sought to translate into art a rational cosmography of space as depth, and time as sequence. In music, the introduction of harmonic chords, a unique feature of the West, brought an ordered structure of sound intervals that unified rhythm and melody into a structural harmony and balanced "foreground" melody with "background" chords.

The fundamental intention of the neo-classical critics, such as Lessing in his *Laocoön*, was to set forth "laws" of aesthetic perception: Poetry and painting, working through different sensuous media, differ in the fundamental principles governing their creation, since painting can only concentrate a single moment of action in space, whereas poetry deals with successive actions in time.[14] Each genre has its own relevant sphere, and these cannot be mixed. Underneath all this was a fundamental cosmological picture of the world: depth, the projection of a three-dimensional space, created an "interior distance" which provided a simulation of the real world; narrative, with the idea of a beginning, a middle, and an end, gave a chronological chain to sequence, providing a sense of progression and conclusion.

The origins go back to the spatial conceptions of the Renaissance but are rooted in the Newtonian world-view of an ordered universe. As Joan Gadol has written:

The basic features of European art were shaped by this Euclidean spatial conception down through the nineteenth century. In perspective, in the ideal of organic form, and in the classical orders, the spatial logic of proportionality persisted long after the aesthetic theory of *concinnitas* was abandoned. After the rise of empiricism in philosophy, regular proportions could no longer be looked upon as "objective" per se, as the harmonious relations by which Nature binds the elements of the phenomenal world. Yet artistic space continued to remain geometrically lawful and uniform. It remained rational, governed by "rule" through all the modifications of the Renaissance style, from Mannerism through Impressionism, and this was so because the spatial intuition which ordered the new artistic image of the world gave rise to a theoretical world picture as well. A new cosmology came to support the artistic image, taking the place of its earlier, aesthetic-metaphysical basis. What ultimately justified modern Europe's artistic faith in the homogeneity of the universe and its systematic, rational order was the scientific cosmology that had its inception in the Copernican system of the world.[15]

[14] "The rule is this: succession in time is the province of the poet, co-existence in space that of the artist. To bring together into one and the same picture two points of time necessarily remote . . . is an encroachment of the painter on the domain of the poet, which good taste can never sanction." G. E. Lessing, *Laocoön* (New York: Noonday Press, 1965), p. 109.

[15] Joan Gadol, *Leon Battista Alberti, Universal Man of the Early Renaissance* (Chicago: University of Chicago Press, 1969), p. 151.

The magisterial work that sketches the emergence and the transformation of the modern world-view of space and time, as related from mathematics to art, is

The second classical principle that regulated the aesthetic intentions of most Western art and literature was the idea of *mimesis*, or the interpretation of reality through imitation. Art was a mirror of nature, a representation of life. Knowledge was a reflection of what was "out there," known through a *Spiegelbild*, a copy of what was seen, as perceived through the senses. Judgment was essentially contemplation, a beholding of reality, and its *mimesis* was a reflection of its worth. Contemplation allowed the spectator to create *theoria* (which meant, originally, looking), and *theoria* meant a distancing of oneself—usually an aesthetic distance—from an object or an experience, in order to establish the necessary time and space to absorb it and judge it.

Modernism is the disruption of *mimesis*. It denies the primacy of an outside reality, as given. It seeks either to rearrange that reality, or to retreat to the self's interior, to private experience as the source of its concerns and aesthetic preoccupations. The origins of this change lie in philosophy, primarily in Descartes and in the codifications of the new principles by Kant. There is an emphasis on the self as the touchstone of understanding and on the activity of the knower rather than the character of the object as the source of knowledge. In the Kantian revolution (he called it a Copernican revolution), mind is the active agent, scanning and selecting experience from the maelstrom of the world, though still within the fixed coordinates of space and time as the given axes of perception. Yet the breach was made. Activity—making and doing—becomes the source of knowledge. *Praxis* and consequence are substituted for *theoria* and first causes.

In art and literature, the activity theory of knowledge becomes

---

Ernst Cassirer's "The Individual and the Cosmos," in *Renaissance Philosophy*, ed. Ernst Cassirer et al. (New York: Barnes and Noble, 1963).

Cassirer's ideas were related in extraordinary fashion to the theory of optics and to the painter's visualization of space by Erwin Panofsky. Speaking of Alberti, Panofsky writes: ". . . to compare a painting to a window is to ascribe to, or to demand of, the artist a direct visual approach to reality. . . . The painter is no longer believed to work 'from the ideal image in his soul,' as had been stated by Aristotle and maintained by Thomas Aquinas and Meister Eckhart, but from the optical image in his eye. . . . In short, the space presupposed and presented in Hellenistic and Roman painting lacks the two qualities which characterize the space presupposed and presented in 'modern' art up to the advent of Picasso: continuity (hence measurability) and infinity." See Erwin Panofsky, *Renaissance and Renascences in Western Art* (Stockholm: Almqvist and Wiksell, 1960), pp. 120, 122, et seq.

the agency for the transformation of the older modes of *mimesis* and given coordinates of space and time. And instead of contemplation, we find substituted *sensation, simultaneity, immediacy*, and *impact*. These new intentions provide a common, formal syntax for all the arts from the mid-nineteenth to the mid-twentieth century.

Alberti considered a painting to be a means of looking out onto the visible world; this was the basis of the contemplative element and of the "distance" between the spectator and the experience. Modern painting has a completely different conception. For Cézanne there was the denial of nature as *mimesis*. In his aesthetics, he made the famous dictum that all the structures of the real world are variations on the three basic solids, the cube, the sphere, and the cone. And his pictorial space was organized in planes to emphasize one or another of these forms. With Turner we get the Cartesian turn from depicting *objects* as we know them to capturing *sensations* of perception. In his "Rain, Steam and Speed," the painting of a train crossing a bridge over the Thames, we get the effort to catch motion in a way never before done.

These changes in the conception of space and motion are worked out logically in the various movements that bring modernism to its apogee—in post-impressionism, futurism, expressionism, and cubism. And the techniques are developed to express these new intentions. In the paintings of Vuillard, the patterning on the dresses of the figures in the fore repeat the patternings of the paper on the wall, so that figure and ground almost merge as one. In the paintings of Munch, the "interior distance" of the painting is foreshortened so that, as in the picture of the young girl sitting at the edge of the bed, there is little distinction between foreground and background, and the picture "leaps up" at one. It was Maurice Denis, the theoretician of post-impressionism, who established the credo of the new spirit, saying, "We must close the shutters." A painting was not to be an illusion of depth, of three dimensions in two, but a single surface in which the element of immediacy was dominant.

Kant had said that the categories of space and time were a synthetic a priori, the fixed categories of mind that allowed one to organize experience. But in the historicism of Dilthey the argument was made that even space and time, the fundamental modes of experiencing reality, were not fixed but changed with different cultural modes. Thus relativism and historical perspective replaced the fixed vantage point and the objective correlative of the spectator. In art this changing consciousness is exemplified in futurism and cubism.

For the futurists, distance, either of time or space, does not exist. In their "Technical Manifesto," they said their goal in organizing a painting was "to put the spectator in the center of the picture."[16] What they sought was an identity between object and emotion, an identity not through contemplation but through action. With equal justice, remarks Joshua Taylor, they might have said "we want to thrust the world into the mind of the spectator." In cubism we find an effort, in a half-muddled way, to approximate the conceptions of relativity. In relativity theory, writes C. H. Waddington, "we have been confronted with something not contemplated in classical physics —a multiplicity of frames of space, each one as good as any other." For the cubists the grasp of reality meant, then, the effort to look at things "from all sides at once," and to capture this sense of simultaneity by overlapping the multiple planes of different objects on the single plane of the flat surface of the painting. The one viewpoint is eclipsed by the multiple viewpoints that are slivered through the same plane simultaneously.

Thus one discerns the intentions of modern painting: on the syntactical level, to break up ordered space; in its aesthetic, to bridge the distance between object and spectator, to "thrust" itself on the viewer and establish itself immediately by impact. One does not interpret the scene; instead, one feels it as a sensation and is caught up by that emotion.

". . . Rature ta vague litterature," Mallarmé advised; scratch out all words with a too specific reference to brute reality and concentrate on the words themselves and their relationship within the phrase and the sentence. "Aesthetic form in modern poetry, then," Joseph Frank has written, "is based on a space-logic that demands a complete reorientation in the reader's attitude to language. Since the primary reference of any word group is to something inside the poem itself, language in modern poetry is really reflexive. The meaning-relationship is completed only by the simultaneous per-

[16] The "Technical Manifesto" can be found in *Futurism*, ed. Joshua Taylor (New York: Museum of Modern Art, 1961), pp. 125–127.

ception in space of word-groups that have no comprehensible relation to each other when read consecutively in time."[17]

Not only does sequence lose its role as a guide to meaning, but the very idea of a correspondence between a word and a single meaning is torn apart. In a famous letter to Paul Demeny, Rimbaud proclaimed that dictionary definitions, fixed rules of syntax and grammar, were only for fossils, for academicians. Each word is an idea—in Aldous Huxley's phrase, "a haunting enigma." As Roger Shattuck has observed: "True classical style in writing required that a word have one clear, logical meaning in each context. [For example, La Bruyère's dictum "Among all the different expressions which can render one of our ideas, there is only one which is the right one, the true one."] For the symbolists—Mallarmé above all—language was endowed with a mystery of meaning that increased with the number of different directions each word could point. Jarry held a similarly advanced theory of poetic meaning, maintaining that all meanings that can be discovered in a text are equally legitimate. There is no single true meaning, banishing other faulty ones."[18]

What literature toward the end of the nineteenth century was trying to grasp, within the convention of words and sentences, was the sense of life not as successive discrete entities but as a stream-of-consciousness. The phrase is William James's, and appears in a chapter in his *Principles of Psychology* of 1890; it became widely known through its central position in the popular *Psychology: The Briefer Course*, published in 1892. The notion of a stream-of-consciousness implies that even where there is a time gap, the consciousness after the elapsed time still overlaps with the consciousness before the interval, so that *experienced* time is not chronological but simultaneous. Of equal importance to our sense of meaning, when we experience time as a stream-of-consciousness, the transitive elements of that stream have as much meaning and impact as the substantive points which denote entities. As James writes in a striking passage: "We ought to say a feeling of *and*, a feeling of *if*, a feeling of *but*, and a feeling of *by*, quite as readily as we say a feeling of *blue* or a feel-

---

[17] Joseph Frank, "Spatial Form in Modern Literature," in *The Widening Gyre: Crisis and Mastery in Modern Literature* (New Brunswick, N.J.: Rutgers University Press, 1963), p. 13.

[18] Roger Shattuck, *The Banquet Years* (New York: Random House, 1968), p. 36.

ing of *cold*. Yet we do not: so inveterate has our habit become of recognizing the existence of the substantive parts alone, that language almost refuses to lend itself to any other use."

While conventional language held to a sense of ordered substantives bridged by the transitive prepositions, modernist literature has sought to emphasize these transitive elements as the synapses which carry the nerve impulses of feeling, to plunge one into the maelstrom of sensations. The effort is anticipated by Flaubert in *Madame Bovary*. In the scene at the country fair (I follow the exposition of Joseph Frank), on the street there is the surging, jostling mob, mingling with the livestock. Raised slightly above the street on a platform are the bombastic, speech-making officials. From a window in the inn overlooking the spectacle are the lovers Emma and Rodolphe, watching the proceedings and carrying on their conversation in stilted phrases. "Everything should sound simultaneously," Flaubert later wrote, in commenting on the scene; "one should hear the bellowing of cattle, the whispering of the lovers, and the rhetoric of the officials all at the same time." But since language proceeds in time, it is impossible to create this simultaneity of experience except by breaking up temporal sequence. And this is exactly what Flaubert does: he dissolves the sequence by cutting back and forth (the cinematographic analogy is quite deliberate), and in a final crescendo the two sequences—M. le Président citing Cincinnatus and Rodolphe describing the irresistibly magnetic attraction between lovers—are juxtaposed in a single sentence to reach a unified effect.

This spatialization of form (to use Joseph Frank's phrase) interrupts the time-flow of a narrative to fix attention on the interplay of relationships within an immobilized time area. It is one strategy to capture what James called the "perceptual flux." The other, which is at the heart of the experiments of Gertrude Stein, James Joyce, and Virginia Woolf, is to immerse the reader in the stream of time itself. In *Jacob's Room* (1922), Virginia Woolf creates a shift of sensibility through the interaction of images which dissolve into one another. In *Mrs. Dalloway* (1925), the story of one day in the life of a woman, the technique of flashbacks creates the stream-of-consciousness. In *The Waves* (1931), the novel has become entirely a series of interior monologues. Joyce's *Ulysses* (1922), in the most extraordinary display of virtuosity, exhibits all the techniques of the *assemblages* of time and emphasizes the idea of shifting perspectives, not only by juxtapositions and flashbacks but also by the adoption of a different style for each chapter, so as to emphasize the multiple ways a story can be told. And Gertrude Stein, in the earliest effort of all (*The Making of Americans*, published in 1925 but written 20 years before), seeks to exemplify her idea of "time-knowledge" (but not "narrative") by writing the total and repetitious history of a family (the book runs to 900 pages) almost entirely in the present tense. As she observed about the novel:

> . . . in *The Making of Americans* . . . I gradually and slowly found out there were two things I had to think about: the fact that knowledge is acquired, so to speak, by memory; but when you know anything, memory doesn't come in. At any moment that you are conscious of knowing anything, memory plays no part. When any of you feels anybody else, memory doesn't come into it. You have the sense of the immediate.

> . . . I was trying to get this present immediacy without trying to drag in anything else. I had to use present participles, new constructions of grammar. The grammar-constructions are correct, but they are changed, in order to get this immediacy. In short, from that time I have been trying in every possible way to get the sense of immediacy, and practically all the work I have done has been in that direction.[19]

In music one finds similar patterns of change. In the modernist canon there has been a growing obsession with sound—that is, with the foreground alone. The change from Wagner to Schoenberg indicates this transition. Schoenberg's early work showed the influence of Wagner, but subsequently Schoenberg denied the necessity of a structural harmonic background and applied the structural principle to the foreground alone. In the music following Schoenberg even this principle is surrendered, and temporal sequences are almost completely abandoned for aleatory elements, clang patterns, or, as in the bouffé innovations of John Cage, silence.

The period from 1890 to 1930 was the great period of modernism, in its brilliant explorations of style and its dazzling experiments of form. In the 45 years since, there has been almost no innovation that was not attempted in that period, with the exception of those efforts to fuse technology with music or technology with painting and sculpture (e.g., the "environments" created by Rauschenberg, in which the patterns of light and the arrangement of "sculpture" are changed randomly by the weight of the spectators on pressure

---

[19] Miss Stein's description is in "How Writing Is Written," a lecture at Oxford, reprinted in Somerset Maugham's *Introduction to Modern English and American Literature* (New York: New Home Library, 1943), pp. 1356–1365.

mats or the heat effects of a spectator's body on sensors), efforts that put the burden of art on memory (rather than on objects), yet which have left nothing memorable. If there has been a single aesthetic it has been the effort to destroy the idea of the object. This began with a changing conception of the "duration" of art. Tchelitchew once complained that the paintings of Picasso would not last more than 50 years because of the quality of the canvas, and Picasso shrugged. There were the experiments in art as self-destruction, in the machines of Tinguely; or as "instantaneous events," such as the "flashlight pictures" that Picasso "drew" for Clouzot (which are recorded on film). If there was a new aesthetic it was the effort, as analyzed by Harold Rosenberg, to define the meaning of painting in "action," arguing that the value of the painting lay not in the object produced, but in the action of the painter in producing it; and what the spectator had to learn to appreciate was not the image he saw, but the suggestion of kinesthetic activity behind it. For an art that was thus oriented to the "new," a remarkable burden was being placed on "memory" to sustain it.

The extraordinary point is that in all the arts—painting, poetry, fiction, music—the modernist impulse has a common syntax of expression underlying the diverse nature of the genres. It is, as I have said, the eclipse of distance between the spectator and the artist, between the aesthetic experience and the work of art. One sees this as the eclipse of psychic distance, social distance, and aesthetic distance.

The loss of psychic distance means the suspension of time. Freud has said that in the unconscious there is no sense of time: one experiences the events of the past not *as if* they were of the present, but with the immediacy, the *actualité*, of the present. This is why the unconscious, with its storehouse of the past, and especially of childhood terrors, remains so threatening and has to be held down. The meaning of maturity, for Freud, was the ability to interpose the necessary distance, a sense of past and present, in order to make the necessary distinctions between what was past, as past, and what derived from the present. But the thrust of modernist culture is to disrupt or break up that sense of past and present. In Proust's *Remembrance of Things Past*, sensory experience awakens involuntary memory, showing how deeply the past remains within us and how it can overcome the present. In *The Sound and the Fury* (1929),

Faulkner begins *in medias res*. Someone is talking, we do not know who; only gradually do we realize that it is an idiot child named Benjy, which, to our confusion, is also the name of another character. And as the novel unfolds, we have to sort out a set of sequences from the confusions of memory. In the loss of psychic distance, there is a loss of temporality and the direction which time's arrow has usually pointed. One may gain a degree of spontaneity, as Natalie Sarraute has argued, by plunging, without warning or preparation, into the heart of the "tropisms" or movements that form her novels, but what one also loses is the sense of climax, of achievement, which has been the struggling effort of the individual in focusing his consciousness from polymorphous perversity to maturity.

The breakup of aesthetic distance means that one has lost control over the experience—the ability to step back and conduct one's "dialogue" with the art. In the experimental theater of the Russian director Tairov in the 1920s, there was no distinction between stage and audience, no formal barrier of proscenium or arch. The action began and took place in and around the spectator, enveloping him in the action and involving him in the events. (Mark Rothko, who produced powerful monochromatic canvases which could be as large as 8 feet wide and 12 feet high, once suggested that the viewer stand 18 *inches* away.) Perhaps the starkest illustration of the loss of aesthetic distance is the cinema, the only new art form developed in the last 2,500 years. In the technical nature of cinema, the event—the distance (close-up or long shot), the duration of the "clip," the concentration on one character rather than another, the pace and rhythm of the images—is "imposed" on the spectator as he sits enveloped (and this is literally the case in the cinema of Abel Gance in the 1930s or in the later Cinerama and multi-screen roundhouse movies) in the darkness of the movie house. And the influence of the cinematic technique—the rapid cutting, the flashback, the interweaving of themes and breakup of sequence—has become so pervasive as to overwhelm the novel, provide a model for multi-media light shows, and shape the presentation of advertisements and all the multi-sensory stimuli that assault us daily in the world we find ourselves thrown into.[20]

[20] I leave aside here the question of the loss of social distance, the reasons for which lie less in aesthetic than in sociological considerations. Yet the effects are as important as well. The loss of social distance means the loss of manners and the erosion of civility, which has made contact between persons manageable and allowed individuals to have a "walking space" of their own. In the leveling that ensues,

All of this, inevitably, creates a distortion of commonsense perception in the total range of human experience. The effect of immediacy, impact, simultaneity, and sensation as the mode of aesthetic —and psychological—experience is to *dramatize* each moment, to increase our tensions to a fever pitch, and yet to leave us without a resolution, reconciliation, or transforming moment, which is the catharsis of a ritual. This is necessarily the case, since the effects that are created derive not from *content* (some transcendental call, a transfiguration, or a purgation through tragedy or suffering) but almost entirely from *technique*. There is constant stimulation and disorientation, yet there is also emptiness after the psychedelic moment has passed. One is enveloped and thrown about, given a psychic "high" or the thrill of the edge of madness; yet beyond the involvement in the whirlwind of the senses, there are the dull routines of everyday life. In the theater the curtain falls, the play ends. In life one has to go home, go to bed, awaken the next morning, brush one's teeth, wash one's face, shave, defecate, and go to work. Everyday time, necessarily, is different from psychedelic time; and how far can this disjunction be stretched?

The search for the modern was a search for the heightening of experience in all dimensions, and the attempt to make those experiences immediate to the sensibility of people. Yet there is every indication that we have come to the end of that phase, at least in the element of high culture (if such a conception is still possible), especially as these searches have passed over into the vulgarizations of the cultural mass. The literature of modernity—the literature of Yeats, Lawrence, Joyce, and Kafka—was a literature which, as Lionel Trilling put it, took "to itself the dark power which certain aspects of religion once exercised over the human mind." It was, in its private way, concerned with spiritual salvation. But its successors seem to have lost concern with salvation itself. In this sense, present-day art has become post-modern and post-Christian.

At the other, curving end of the trajectory, then, is the overturn

---

distinctions of speech, taste, and style become erased, so that any one usage, or grammar, is as good as any other. In the personal sense, loss of social distance means an invasion of privacy, the increasing inability to maintain formal relations with others where desirable, to escape the crowd, or to define one's task and work as one's own. In mobilized societies, the individual is submerged in the Party, the group, or the commune. In the hedonistic societies of the West, there is an emphasis on surface relationships and on quick exchanges between individuals that are mediated by personality and appearances.

of the "rational cosmology" which shaped Western thought from the fifteenth century on: the sequence of time (beginning, middle, end), the interior distance of space (foreground and background, figure and ground), and the sense of proportion and measure that united both in a single conception of order. The eclipse of distance, as an aesthetic, sociological, and psychic fact, means that for human beings, and for the organization of thought, there are no boundaries, no ordering principles of experience and judgment. Time and space no longer form the coordinates of a home for modern men. Our ancestors had a religious anchorage which gave them roots, no matter how far they might seek to wander. The deracinated individual can only be a cultural wanderer, without a home to return to. The problem, then, is whether culture can regain a coherence, a coherence of sustenance and experience and not only of form.[21]

[21] The theme of an "eclipse of distance" was first sketched in a short essay in *Encounter* (May 1963), and this section draws substantially on that essay, with much elaboration. The evidence for the argument involves a large variety of sources. In addition to the citations in previous footnotes, I have drawn largely on the following: Erich Auerbach, *Mimesis: The Representation of Reality in Western Literature* (Princeton: Princeton University Press, 1953); Joseph Frank, *The Widening Gyre* (New Brunswick, N.J.: Rutgers University Press, 1963), which includes the brilliant essay "Spatial Form in Modern Literature," originally published in a shorter version in the *Sewanee Review* in 1945; Aldous Huxley, *Literature and Science* (New York: Harper & Row, 1963); Roger Shattuck, *The Banquet Years* (New York: Random House, 1968); Joshua Taylor, *Futurism* (New York: Museum of Modern Art, 1961); C. H. Waddington, *Behind Appearance: A Study of the Relations Between Painting and the Natural Sciences in this Century* (Cambridge: M.I.T. Press, 1970). William James's discussion of the stream-of-consciousness is in *Psychology: The Briefer Course*, ed. Gordon Allport (New York: Harper Torchbook, repr. 1961).

The Sensibility
of the Sixties

EACH DECADE—we think now of decades or generations as the units of social time—has its hallmarks. That of the 1960s was a political and cultural radicalism. The two were yoked by a common impulse to rebellion, but political radicalism, *au fond*, is not merely rebellious but revolutionary, and seeks to install a new social order in place of the previous one. Cultural radicalism, apart from the formal revolutions in style and syntax, is largely rebellious only, since its impulses derive from rage; for that reason, one can see in the sensibility of the sixties, the exhaustion of a crucial aspect of cultural modernism. I take that decade, therefore, as a case study for my general argument.

In defining the sensibility of the 1960s, one can see it in two ways: as a reaction to the sensibility of the 1950s, and as a reversion to, yet also an extension of, an earlier sensibility which had reached its apogee in the modernism of the years before World War I.

The sensibility of the 1950s was largely a literary one. In the writings of such representative critics of the period as Lionel Trilling, Yvor Winters, and John Crowe Ransom, the emphasis was on complexity, irony, ambiguity, and paradox. These are properties peculiar to the mind. They foster a critical attitude, a detachment and distance which guard one against any overwhelming involvement, absorption, immolation in a creed or an experience. At worst a form of quietism, at best a mode of self-consciousness, this attitude is essentially moderate in tone. The sensibility of the 1960s rejected that mood in savage, even mindless fashion. In its fury with the times, the new sensibility was loud, imprecatory, prone to obscenity, and given to posing every issue, political or otherwise, in disjunctive correlatives.

The more enduring mood, however, derives from the earlier impulses. The modernist innovations that flared so effulgently between 1895 and 1914 wrought two extraordinary changes in the culture. First, there was the set of *formal* revolutions in the arts I have discussed in the previous chapter—the breakup of poetic syntax, the stream-of-consciousness in fiction, the multiplicity of the picture plane on the canvas, the rise of atonality in music, the loss of sequence in temporal representation and of foreground and background in spatial pictorialization. And second, there was a new presentation of the self, which Roger Shattuck (in *The Banquet Years*) has characterized in terms of four traits—the cult of childhood; the delight in the absurd; the reversal of values so as to celebrate the baser rather than the higher impulses; and a concern with hallucination.

We shall leave aside, for the moment, the questions about aesthetic innovations. What was most striking about the 1960s was that the earlier preoccupations with the self were now repeated, albeit in a shriller and harsher form. The stress on the pain of childhood was replaced, in the "confessional" poetry of Robert Lowell, Anne Sexton, and Sylvia Plath, by the revelation of the most private experiences—even psychotic seizures—of the poet, though the sense of innocence remained intact in the work of poets like Allen Ginsberg, with its visionary emphasis derived from Whitman, Blake, and the Indian Vedas. The sense of absurdity was extended so that—as in the plays of Ionesco—objects began to take on a life of their own. The reversal of values became virtually complete, though this time all joy and prankishness had been drained out of the celebration of the base. Hallucination, of course, was enthroned in the drug and psychedelic experience.

Yet to all this, the sensibility of the 1960s added something distinctly its own: a concern with violence and cruelty; a preoccupation with the sexually perverse; a desire to make noise; an anticognitive and anti-intellectual mood; an effort once and for all to erase the boundary between "art" and "life"; and a fusion of art and politics.

To take each of these traits briefly, in turn:

The violence and cruelty that one saw splashed on film was not meant to effect catharsis, but sought instead to shock, to maul, to sicken. Films, happenings, paintings vied with each other in presenting gory detail. One was told that such violence and cruelty simply reflected the world around us, but the 1940s, a gorier and far more brutal decade, did not produce the lingering on sanguinary detail one found in films of the 1960s like *Bonnie and Clyde* and *M*A*S*H*.

The sexually perverse is as old as Sodom and Gomorrah, at least in recorded time, but rarely has it been flaunted as openly and directly as in the 1960s. In such films as Andy Warhol's *The Chelsea Girls* and the Swedish *I Am Curious (Yellow)*, in such plays as *Futz* and *Ché*, one found an obsessive preoccupation with homosexuality, transvestism, buggery, and, most pervasive of all, publicly displayed oral-genital intercourse. What this obsession seemed to represent was a flight from heterosexual life, perhaps in response to the release of aggressive female sexuality which was becoming evident at the end of the decade.

The 1950s, one could almost say of its sensibility, had been a period of silence. The plays of Samuel Beckett tried to achieve a sense of silence, and the music of John Cage even attempted an aesthetic of silence. But the 1960s was preeminently a period of noise. Beginning with the "new sound" of the Beatles in 1964, rock reached such soaring crescendos that it was impossible to hear oneself think, and that may indeed have been its intention.

The anti-cognitive, anti-intellectual mood was summed up in the attack on "content" and interpretation, in the emphasis on form and style, in the turn to "cooler" media like film and dance—a sensibility, in Susan Sontag's words, "based on indiscriminateness, without ideas [and] beyond negation."

Erasing the boundary between art and life was a further aspect of the breakup of genre, the conversion of a painting into a happening, the taking of art out of the museum into the environment, the turning of all experience into art, whether it had form or not. By celebrating life, this process tended to destroy art.

Art and politics were probably more intensely fused in the 1960s than at any time in modern history. During the 1930s, art had served politics, but in a heavy-handed ideological way. In the 1960s the emphasis was not on ideological content, but on temper and mood. Guerrilla theater and demonstration art had little content except anger. One would have to go back to the anarchism of the 1890s, when art was also suffused with politics, to find a comparable tone; but what was most evident in the 1960s was the scale and intensity of feeling that was not only anti-government, but almost entirely anti-institution and ultimately antinomian as well.

And yet what is striking about the 1960s is that with all the turbulence, there was not one noteworthy revolution in aesthetic form. The preoccupation with machines and technology only served to recall the Bauhaus and Moholy-Nagy; the theater echoed the practices of Alfred Jarry and the theories of Antonin Artaud; the japes in art repeated Dada or drew rhetorically from surrealism. Only in the novel, perhaps, in the linguistic brilliance of Nabokov, the spatial dislocations of Burroughs, and some elements of the *nouveau roman* in France, did any interesting innovations appear. It was a decade, despite all the talk of form and style, empty of originality in both. But in sensibility, there was an exacerbation of tone and temper, the fruits of an anger, political in origin, which spilled over into art as well. What remains important for cultural history was a mood which turned against art, and an effort by a cultural mass to adopt and act out the life-style which hitherto had been the property of a small and talented elite.

THE DISSOLUTION OF "ART"

The arbiters of culture in the 1950s prided themselves on holding out against the indiscriminate, the meretricious, and the trashy, which were pouring from the mass media; and the pretentious and the arty, which were the stamp of what was then universally known as "middlebrowism." They sought to do this by insisting on a classic conception of culture and by setting forth a trans-historical and transcendental criterion for the judgment of art.

Perhaps the most incisive formulation of this point of view was Hannah Arendt's. "Works of art," she wrote, "are made for the sole purpose of appearance. The proper criterion by which to judge appearance is beauty . . . in order to become aware of appearances we must first be *free to establish a certain distance* between ourselves and the object. . . ."

We have here a Greek view of art in which culture is essentially contemplative. Art is not life, but in a sense something contrary to life, since life is transient and changing, while art is permanent. To this Miss Arendt adds the Hegelian concept of *objectification*. A work of art is the projection by the creative person of an idea or an emotion into an object outside himself: ". . . What is at stake here," Miss Arendt wrote, "is much more than the psychological state of the artist; it is the objective status of the cultural world which insofar as it contains tangible things—books and paintings, statues, buildings, and music—comprehends, and gives testimony to, the entire recorded past of countries, nations, and ultimately of mankind. As such the only nonsocial and authentic criterion for judging these specifically cultural things is their relative permanence and even eventual immortalily. Only what will last through the centuries can ultimately claim to be a cultural object."[1]

The paradox is that this view—which in the 1960s came to seem so archaic—was undercut not by the lowbrows or middlebrows but by the highbrows, the very prelectors of modern culture themselves. For in seeking to define what was distinctive about the new sensibility, they denied precisely the terms set forth by Miss Arendt. The locus of art and culture, they argued, had moved from the independent work to the personality of the artist, from the permanent object to the transient process. It was Harold Rosenberg, explicating the work of Jackson Pollock, Willem de Kooning, Franz Kline, and other "action painters," as he called them, who first stated the concept forcefully. "At a certain moment," Rosenberg wrote, "the canvas began to appear to one American painter after another as an arena in which to act—rather than as a space in which to reproduce, re-design, analyze, or 'express' an object, actual or imagined. *What was to go on the canvas was not a picture but an event.* . . . In this gesturing with materials the aesthetic, too, has been subordinated. Form, color, composition, drawing . . . can be dispensed with. What matters always is the revelation contained in the act."

If painting is an action, there is no difference between the preliminary sketch and the finished object. The second cannot be "better" or more complete than the first. There are no preliminaries or hierarchies in art, and each act is an event by itself. In effect, the work

---

[1] Hannah Arendt, "The Crisis in Culture," in *Between Past and Future: Eight Exercises in Political Thought*, ed. Hannah Arendt (New York: Viking, 1961), p. 202.

qua work is dissolved in the act, and so is the critic. "The new painting," Mr. Rosenberg concluded, "has broken down every distinction between art and life. It follows that anything is relevant to it. Anything that has to do with action—psychology, philosophy, history, mythology, hero-worship. Anything but art criticism. The painter gets away from art through his act of painting; the critic can't get away from it. The critic who goes on judging in terms of schools, styles, form—as if the painter was still concerned with producing a certain kind of object (the work of art) instead of living on the canvas—is bound to seem a stranger."[2]

Mr. Rosenberg proved a formidably accurate prophet. The entire movement of art in the 1960s sought to dissolve the work of art as a "cultural object," and to erase the distinction between subject and object and between art and life. Nowhere was this more apparent than in sculpture, or in the fusion of sculpture and painting and the dissolution of both into spaces, environments, motions, media-mixes, happenings, and "man-machine" interaction systems.

Sculpture classically dealt preeminently with objects. It concerned itself with mass as solid form, and was anchored in three-dimensional space. It was placed on a base or plinth that removed it spatially from the mundane ground or wall. In the 1960s all this went. The base was removed so that the sculpture fused with its surroundings. Mass dissolved into space and space turned into motion. Thus the "minimal sculpture" (of Donald Judd, Robert Morris, Dan Flavin) abandoned imagery altogether. It sought to be nothing other than what it set forth: boxes, shapes, relations which were neither organic nor figurative nor emblematic nor anthropomorphic. They were literally *Dinge an sich.* Similarly, one saw this in a show organized by the Whitney Museum in the summer of 1968, and labeled "Anti-Illusion: Procedures and Materials." The materi-

[2] Harold Rosenberg, *The Tradition of the New* (New York: Horizon Press, 1959) p. 25 et seq. The essay "American Action Painters" first appeared in 1952. In a footnote to his article, "Hans Hofmann: Nature into Action," in *Art News*, May 1957, Mr. Rosenberg provided an additional thought: "In turning to action, abstract art abandons its alliance with architecture, as painting had earlier broken with music and with the novel, and offers its hand to pantomine and dance. . . . In painting the primary agency of physical motion (as distinct from illusionary representation of motion as with the Futurists) is the line conceived not only as the thinnest of planes, nor as edge, contour, or connective, but as stroke or figure (in the sense of 'figure skating'). In its passage on the canvas, *each such line can establish the actual movement of the artist's body as an esthetic statement.*" My italics.

als were hay, grease, dirt, dog food, etc. The catalogue notes by James Monte opened with this observation: "The radical nature of many works in this exhibition depends less on the fact that new materials are being used by the artists than on the fact that the acts of conceiving and placing the pieces take precedence over the object quality of the works." The sculptures "each exist in either a deobjectified or scattered or dislocated state and in some instances the three conditions simultaneously."[3] Lynda Benglis' works of latex were poured onto the floor and allowed to develop their own form. Barry La Va used combinations of bulk chalk and mineral oil in conjunction with paper or cloth; when these were mixed, different forms emerged, depending on the degree of dryness or dampness, absorption or saturation. "La Va is able to use time as a substantial element in the recent pieces; he can project the sequential development of the work in a way analogous to that in which a biologist estimates the growth of micro-organisms developed in a laboratory." The air sculpture of Michael Asher was literally a curtain of air defining the height, width, and depth of a transit area from one gallery to the next. One felt the "space" by pressure on the body when passing through. "The disembodied literalism of the piece neatly alludes to a slab form without carpentry. Feeling and therefore knowing replaces the cycle of seeing and hence knowing the sculptural presence."

In 1968, too, Robert Morris declared before a notary public that he was "withdraw[ing]" from a construction he had made "all aesthetic quality and content." Commenting on this extreme development of the "anti-form" movement, Harold Rosenberg wrote:

Aesthetic withdrawal . . . legitimizes "process" art—in which chemical, biological, physical or seasonal forces affect the original materials and either change their form or destroy them, as in works incorporating growing grass and bacteria or inviting rust—and random art, whose form and content are decided by chance. Ultimately, the repudiation of the aesthetic suggests the total elimination of the art object and its replacement by an idea for a work or by the rumor that one has been consummated—as in conceptual art. Despite the stress on the actuality of the materials used, the principle common to all classes of de-aestheticized art is that the finished product, if any, is of less significance than the procedures that brought the work into being and of which it is the trace.[4]

[3] James Monte and Marcia Tucker, *Anti-Illusion: Procedures/Materials* (New York: Whitney Museum, 1969).

[4] Harold Rosenberg, "De-aestheticization," *New Yorker*, January 24, 1970, p. 62. Reprinted in *The De-definition of Art* (New York: Horizon Press, 1972), pp. 28–38.

A decade and a half after his initial—and, at the time, approving—anticipation of "gestural" or "process" art, Rosenberg was now clearly a shade unhappy at the strident stage which this tendency had reached. He was now at pains to remind the younger artists that "aesthetic qualities inhere in things whether or not they are works of art. The aesthetic is not an element that exists separately, to be banished at the will of the artist. Morris could no more withdraw aesthetic content from his construction than he could inject it where it was missing."[5]

Painting followed a similar trajectory. From its origins in the distant past, painting always based itself on two elements: a symmetrical, geometric field and a flat surface. The first cave painter who put a line around the image he drew on the wall separated the picture from the environment; painting then became a symbol, rather than a magical manipulation, of reality.

In the last decades, we have witnessed the final break with field and surface, the traditional arena of painting. Pasted matter, as in collage, breaks up the surface; shaped canvases break up the geometrical field. Assemblages come off the wall. Environments surround the individual. In these two milieus, as Allan Kaprow, a leader of the movement, points out, the illusion of space in the painting becomes the literal distance between all the solids in the work.

In 1969 the Museum of Modern Art gave its imprimatur to the new movement with the show "Spaces," organized by Jennifer Licht. Here the eclipse of distance was complete: the picture was reversed and the spectator stood within rather than without. In the catalogue for the show, Miss Licht wrote:

In the past, space was merely an attribute of a work of art, rendered by illusionistic conventions in painting or by displacement of volume in sculpture, and the space that separated viewer and object was ignored as just distance. This invisible dimension is now being considered as an active ingredient, not simply to be represented but to be shaped and characterized by the artist, and capable of involving and merging viewer and art in a situation of greater scope and scale. In effect, one now enters the interior space of the work of art—an area formerly experienced only visually from without, approached, but not encroached upon—and is presented with a set of conditions rather than a finite object.

[5] Ibid.

The show consisted of six rooms, or spaces, one of which was filled with large constructions of yellow and green fluorescent light tubes. Another room had white acoustical panels. A third, of vacuum-coated glass, was almost entirely black. In a fourth, a gymnasium-like room, one could lie on mats or be wrapped in canvas shrouds and the like. In the garden a light, sound, and heat environment was organized by the Pulse group to provide a mixed-media response.

Environmental art erases the boundary between the space and the person. Happenings erase the distance between the situation, or event, and the spectator. In happenings, not just color and space but also heat, smell, taste, and motion become aspects of the work. As Allan Kaprow puts it: "Fundamentally, Environments and Happenings are similar. They are passive and active sides of a single coin whose principle is *extension*."

A happening is a pastiche that combines an environment as art-setting with a theatrical performance. It was originally a painters' theater, in which one saw the manipulation of objects and materials that made up the field of painting taken down from the wall and put into the open. It brings the spectator into the process of "creation" itself.

In a happening, as Jan Kott has observed, "all the signs are literal: a pyramid of chairs is only a pile of chairs placed one on top of the other; a stream of water which drenches the audience is merely a stream of water which drenches the viewers. In reality, there is not even a partition between the viewer and actors. . . ."

In this, the mimetic and symbolic functions of theater, to use Kott's language, are eliminated. The expressive content becomes dissolved in the literal, and meanings as metaphor or emblems disappear. Even the idea of the evocative loses meaning because the event does not represent or picture something—it *is*. The emphasis on the literal is part of the attack on metaphysical expression. In Zen, for example, a philosophy which during the 1960s attracted many painters and poets, one does not use words like "hard" or "soft," for these are attributes or qualities of a substance; and qualities and substance are metaphysical terms. One has to be exactly literal, and if comparisons are made they must refer to specific tactile experiences denoted by stone, wood, water, etc.

THE DEMOCRATIZATION OF GENIUS

The notion of a hierarchy in the arts and of a cultural division of the audience (e.g., highbrows, middlebrows, and lowbrows), which was the hallmark of such representative cultural interpreters of the 1950s as Hannah Arendt and Dwight Macdonald, necessarily implied the idea of standards and a vocation which guarded and defined those standards; namely, criticism. The 1940s and the 1950s have in fact been called the age of the critic and of the critical schools: the New Criticism of John Crowe Ransom, the textual criticism of R. P. Blackmur, the moral criticism of Lionel Trilling, the socio-historical criticism of Edmund Wilson, the dramaturgical stance of Kenneth Burke, the linguistic analysis of I. A. Richards, the mythopoeic criticism of Northrop Frye.

The theme of the 1960s, in contrast, was a distrust of criticism. Susan Sontag, a leading theurgist of the new sensibility, declared in *Against Interpretation* (1966), whose title summed up this sensibility: "Today . . . the project of interpretation is largely reactionary. Like the fumes of the automobile and of heavy industry which befoul the urban atmosphere, the effusion of interpretations of art today poisons our sensibilities. . . . Interpretation is the revenge of the intellect upon art. Even more. It is the revenge of the intellect upon the world."

It was not only criticism but literature, with its "heavy burden of 'content,'" which drugged the senses. The "model arts of our time," she wrote, "are actually those with much less content, and a much cooler mode of moral judgment—like music, films, dance, architecture, painting, sculpture."

Inevitably, the distinction between high and low (or mass or popular) culture came in for special scorn. As Miss Sontag saw it, this was merely a distinction between "unique and mass-produced objects." In an era of mass technological reproduction, the work of the serious artist was deemed to have a special value because it bore an individual, personal signature. "But in the light of contemporary practice in the arts, this distinction appears extremely shallow. Many of the serious works of art of recent decades have a decidedly impersonal character . . . rather than . . . 'individual personal expression.'"

The new sensibility was a redemption of the senses from the

mind. "Sensations, feelings, the abstract forms and styles of sensibility count. It is to these that contemporary art addresses itself . . . we are what we are able to see (hear, taste, smell, feel) even more powerfully and profoundly than we are what furniture of ideas we have stocked in our heads."

Moreover, "if art is understood as . . . a programming of sensations, then the feeling (or sensation) given off by a Rauschenberg painting might be like that of a song by the Supremes." Thus, further distinctions were erased, and sophisticated painting and popular music became equally valid for the "reorganization of consciousness" (or of the "sensorium"), which was now proclaimed as the function of art. In all this there was a "democratization" of culture in which nothing could be considered high or low, a syncretism of styles in which all sensations mingled equally, and a world of sensibility which was accessible to all.

If there was a democratization of culture in which a radical egalitarianism of feeling superseded the older hierarchy of mind, there was also, by the end of the 1960s, a democratization of "genius." The idea of the artist as genius, as a being apart who (in the description of Edward Shils) "need not regard the laws of society and its authorities" and who aims "only to be guided by the inner necessities of the expansion of the self—to embrace new experiences," goes back to the early 19th century. The artist, it was thought, looked at the world from a special point of view. Whistler proclaimed that artists were a class apart whose standards and aspirations stood outside the comprehension of the vulgar. If there was "a conflict between a genius and his public," Hegel declared in a sentence which (as Irving Howe has noted) thousands of critics, writers, and publicists have echoed through the years, "it must be the public that is to blame . . . the only obligation the artist can have is to follow truth and his genius."

In France, where the "man of letters," as Tocqueville observed, had long taken the lead in "shaping the national temperament and the outlook on life," this tradition took particularly deep hold. Not only were artists different, by virtue of their genius, from other mortals; they were also intended to be, as Victor Hugo put it, the "sacred leaders" of the nation. Indeed, with the decline of religion, the writer was more and more invested with the prerogatives of the priest, for he was seen as a man endowed with supernatural vision.

In a constricted world, the writer alone was the unadaptable man, the wanderer—like Rimbaud—in perpetual flight from the mundane. Joyce in Trieste, Pound in London, Hemingway in Paris, Lawrence in Taos, Allen Ginsberg in India—these are the very prototypes of this artist-hero type in the twentieth century. The pilgrimage to places far from the bourgeois home had become a necessary step in attaining independence of vision. Underlying all of this is the belief that art tells a truth which is higher than that perceived via the ordinary cognitive mode, that the "language" of art, in the words of Herbert Marcuse, "must communicate a truth, an objectivity which is not accessible to ordinary language and ordinary experience."[6]

But what if, as Lionel Trilling has wryly observed (in a view which even "rather surprises" himself), ". . . art does not always tell the truth or the best kind of truth and does not always point out the right way"? What if art "can even generate falsehood and habituate us to it, and . . . on frequent occasions . . . might well be subject, in the interests of autonomy, to the scrutiny of the rational intellect"? This question is perhaps too large to be gone into here. But the exaltation of the artistic vision above all others also raises another, more pressing question: If the language of art is not accessible to ordinary language and ordinary experience, how can it be accessible to ordinary people? One solution of the 1960s was to make each man his own artist-hero. In May 1968 the students at the École des Beaux Arts in Paris called for a development of consciousness which would guide the "creative activity immanent in every individual," so that the "work of art" and "the artist" would become "mere moments in this activity." And a 1969 catalogue of revolutionary art at the Moderna Muséet in Stockholm carried this injunction further by declaring that "Revolution is Poetry. There is poetry in all those acts which break the system of organization." But such activist pronouncements—and the 1960s were not lacking in them—do not solve the problem of modernism, they only evade it.

At the heart of the problem is the relationship of culture to tradition. When one speaks of a classical culture or a Catholic culture, for example, one thinks of a long-linked set of beliefs, traditions, and

[6] Herbert Marcuse, *An Essay on Liberation* (Boston: Beacon Press, 1969), p. 40.

rituals which over the course of history have achieved a distinctive style. The style results not only from an internally cohesive set of commonsense perceptions or formal conventions, but also from some notion of an ordered universe and of man's place in it. By its very nature, modernity breaks with the past, *as* past, and erases it in favor of the present or the future. Men are enjoined to make themselves anew rather than to extend the great chain of being.

Where culture is related to the past, accessibility to culture is shaped by tradition and expressed in ritual. Personal experiences and feelings are seen as idiosyncrasies, irrelevant to the great chain of continuity. But when culture is concerned with the individual personality of the artist, rather than with institutions and laws, then singularity of experience becomes the chief test of what is desirable, and novelty of sensation becomes the main engine of change.

Modernist culture is a culture of the self par excellence. Its center is the "I" and its boundaries are defined by identity. The cult of singularity begins, as so much in modernity does, with Rousseau, who declares in the opening lines of his *Confessions*: "I am commencing an undertaking, hitherto without precedent. . . . Myself alone! I know the feelings of my heart." And indeed, this pronouncement *is* completely without precedent in literature in its assertion of absolute singularity ("I am not made like any of those in existence") and its dedication to absolute frankness ("I have neither omitted anything bad nor interpolated anything good").

Yet it would be a mistake to confuse the "I" which begins every sentence of the first page of that book with simple narcissism (though that too is there); or to view the studied effort to shock the reader with dismaying detail (". . . in agonies of death she broke wind loudly") as nothing more than a form of exhibitionism. What Rousseau was attempting in the *Confessions* was to exemplify, as ruthlessly as seemed necessary, his dictum that truth is grasped through sentiment or feeling, rather than through rational judgment or abstract reasoning. "I feel, therefore I exist." Thus Rousseau's Vicar revises the axiom of Descartes and at one stroke overturns the classical definition of authenticity as well as the definition of artistic creation which flows from it.

How can one know whether an experience is "authentic"—i.e., whether it is true and therefore valid for all men? The classical tradition had always identified authenticity with authority, with mastery of craft, with knowledge of form, and with the search for perfection, whether aesthetic or moral. Such perfection could be achieved, in Santayana's words, only through "purification," though a purging away of all accidental elements—the sentimental, the pathetic, the comic, the grotesque—in the quest for that essence which signifies completeness of form. Even where art is identified with experience, as in the theories of John Dewey, the emphasis remains on completeness as a criterion of aesthetic satisfaction. For Dewey, art was a process of shaping which involved an interaction between the "directive intent" of the artist and the refractory nature of experience. The work of art was complete when the artist had achieved "internal integration and fulfillment." Art, in other words, remained a matter of pattern and structure, and the relationships among its separate elements had to be perceivable for a work of art to have meaning.

But the new sensibility that emerged in the 1960s scorned such definitions completely. Authenticity in a work of art was defined almost exclusively in terms of the quality of immediacy, both the immediacy of the artist's intention and the immediacy of his effect upon the viewer. In the theater, for example, spontaneity was all; the text was virtually eliminated and the reigning form became improvisation—exalting the "natural" over the contrived, sincerity over judgment, spontaneity over reflection. When Judith Malina, the director of the Living Theatre, said, "I don't want to be Antigone [onstage], I am and want to be Judith Malina," she aimed to do away with illusion in the theater, as the painters have eliminated it in art.

But to forgo the "representation" of another, in this instance, is not merely to forgo a text; it is to deny the commonality of human experience and to insist on a false uniqueness of personality. Antigone is a symbol—traditionally acted out on a stage spatially separated from the audience—which restates certain perennially recurrent human problems: the demands of civil obedience, the faithfulness of vows, the nature of justice. To eliminate Antigone, or deny her corporeality, is to repudiate memory and to discard the past.

Similarly, writing in the 1960s was judged by its genuineness of feeling, by its success in projecting "the unvarnished imaginative impulse," and by its assertion that thought should not mediate spontaneity. Allen Ginsberg has said that he writes "to let my imagination go [to] scribble magic lines from my real mind." Two of his best-known poems, we were told over and over, were written without forethought or revision: the long first part of *Howl* was typed off in one afternoon; *Sunflower Sutra* was completed in twenty minutes, "me at my desk scribbling, Kerouac at cottage door waiting for me to finish." And in the same improvisatory manner, Jack Kerouac came to the point of typing his novels nonstop onto enormous rolls of paper—six feet per day—with never a revision.

Most of these reports from the artist's workbench were approving, for the critics of the new sensibility were hardly less personal in tone than the artists. Faced with a play, a book, or a film, their purpose seemed less to evaluate it in traditional aesthetic terms than to express themselves about it: the work served mainly as an occasion for a personal statement. Thus did each work of art, whether painting, novel, or film, become a pretext for "another" work of "art"—the critic's declaration of his *feelings* about the original work. "Action" art thus brought "action" response, and every man became his own artist. But in the process, all notion of objective judgment went by the board.

The democratization of genius is made possible by the fact that while one can quarrel with judgments, one cannot quarrel with feelings. The emotions generated by a work either appeal to you or they don't, and no man's feelings have more authority than another man's. With the expansion of higher education, and the growth of a semi-skilled intelligentsia, moreover, a significant change has taken place in the scale of all this. Large numbers of people who might previously have been oblivious to the matter now insist on the right to participate in the artistic enterprise—not in order to cultivate their minds or sensibilities, but to "fulfill" their personalities. Both in the character of art itself and in the nature of the response to it, the concern with self takes precedence over any objective standards.

This development has not been unforeseen. Thirty years ago Karl Mannheim warned that:

> . . . the open character of democratic mass society, together with its growth in size and the tendency toward general public participation, not only produces far too many elites but also deprives these elites of the exclusiveness which they need for the sublimation of impulse. If this minimum of exclusiveness is lost, then the deliberate formulation of taste, of a guiding principle of style, becomes impossible. The new impulses,

intuitions and fresh approaches to the world, if they have no time to mature in small groups, will be apprehended by the masses as mere stimuli. . . .[7]

Other theorists of mass society like Ortega y Gasset, Karl Jaspers, Paul Tillich, Emil Lederer, and Hannah Arendt, whose writings were so influential in the 1950s, were also concerned with the social consequences of the loss of authority, the breakup of institutions, and the erosion of tradition; but their emphasis was political rather than cultural. They saw mass society as highly unstable and a prelude to the onset of totalitarianism. But while their theory about the relation of the "masses" to society seems in retrospect overly simple in its judgments about social structure and crude in its analysis of the nature of politics, it did prove startlingly relevant to one segment of society—the contemporary world of culture. What these theorists called "massification"—to use one of their clumsier terms —is now taking place in the world of the arts. Style has become synonymous with fashion, and "new" styles in art displace one another in constant and bewildering succession. The cultural institutions do not work in opposition to the present, thereby providing the necessary tension for testing the claims of the new, but surrender without struggle to the passing tides.

High art, as Hilton Kramer has observed, "has always been elitist, even if the elite was only an elite of sensibility, rather than of social position. High art requires exceptional talent, exceptional vision, exceptional training and dedication—it requires exceptional individuals. . . ."[8] Such a requirement is of course repugnant to any kind of populist ideology—including the populist ideology which holds sway in present-day American culture. Hence the haste with which so many critics have rushed to align themselves on the side of popular culture.[9]

For the serious critic the situation poses a real dilemma. "The

[7] Karl Mannheim, *Man and Society in an Age of Reconstruction* (New York: Harcourt, Brace and Company, 1941), pp. 86–87.

[8] Hilton Kramer, "High Art and Social Chaos," *New York Times*, December 28, 1969; see also Kramer's *The Age of the Avant Garde* (New York: Farrar, Straus and Giroux, 1973), particularly his fine essay "Art and Politics: Incursions and Conversations," pp. 522–529.

[9] "Ours is the first cultural epoch," Lionel Trilling has written, "in which many men aspire to high achievement in the arts and, in their frustration, form a dispossessd class which cuts across the conventional class lines, making a proletariat of the spirit." "On the Modern Element in Modern Literature," in *The Idea of the Modern in Literature and the Arts*, ed. Irving Howe (New York: Horizon Press, 1967).

profession of criticism," as Hilton Kramer points out, "made its historical debut at the very moment when high art needed to be defended against a large, ignorant public for the first time." But that situation has long since changed. High art itself is in disarray, if not "decadent" (though that term has never been adequately defined); the "public" is now so culturally voracious that the avant-garde, far from needing defenders among the critics, is in the public domain. The serious critic, then, must either turn against high art itself, thereby pleasing its political enemies, or, in John Gross's phrase, "resign himself to being the doorman at the discothèque." This is the trajectory of the democratization of cultural genius.

THE LOSS OF SELF

The situation is most grave, perhaps, in the area of literature. The novel came into being some 200 years ago, created by the sense of a world in upheaval. It was a means of reporting on the world of fact through the imagination, and the touchstone of the novel was involvement with experience—in all its variety and immediacy—refracted through the emotions and disciplined by the intellect. A novelist is, so to speak, a sample of one whose personal experiences are a kind of *ur*-experience. When he goes back into his own unconscious to scrape the burns of his psyche, he is in touch—if he is a good novelist—with a collective unconscious as well.

For the first 100 years or so of the novel's existence, the task of the novelist was to elucidate society. But that task was eventually to prove impossible. As Diana Trilling has written, in seeking to define the contemporary burden of the novelist: "For the advanced writer of our time, the self is his supreme, even sole referent. Society has no texture or business worth bothering about; it exists because it weighs upon us and because it conditions us so absolutely. . . . [The] present-day novelist undertakes only to help us define the self in relation to the world that surrounds us and threatens to overwhelm it."[10]

This is a brilliantly accurate statement about the first half of the

---

[10] Diana Trilling, "The Moral Radicalism of Norman Mailer," in *Claremont Essays* (New York: Harcourt Brace and World, 1964), pp. 177–178.

century; by the time we reached the 1960s, however, the novelist had lost even the self as referent, as the boundaries between the self and the world grew increasingly blurred. Mary McCarthy has said that a new kind of novel, "based on statelessness," was beginning to be written at this time, and she cites as evidence the writings of Vladimir Nabokov and William Burroughs. I think this is to some extent true. In any event, writing in the mid-1960s became increasingly autistic, and the voice of the novelist grew more and more disembodied.

In reading the novelists who have touched the nerve of the age, one finds that the major preoccupation of the 1960s was *madness*. When the social life has been left behind, and the self, as a bounded subject, has been dissolved, the only theme left is the theme of dissociation, and every important writer of the decade was in one way or another involved with this theme. The novels are hallucinatory in mode; many of their protagonists are schizoid; insanity, rather than normalcy, has become the touchstone of reality. Despite all the social turmoil of the decade, not one novel by these writers was political; none (with the exception of Bellow's *Mr. Sammler's Planet*) dealt with radicalism, youth, or social movements—yet all were anagogical in one way or another. What all this adds up to in the sensibility of these writers is an apocalyptic tremor—like the swallows before a storm—that seems to warn of some impending holocaust.[11]

The obvious writers were the "black humorists"—Joseph Heller, J. P. Donleavy, Bruce J. Friedman, Thomas Pynchon, and, for a more "pop" audience, Terry Southern. They dealt with absurd and nihilistic situations, the plots are nutty and mischievous, the style cool, farcical, zany, and slapstick. In all of the situations the individual is a kind of shuttlecock, batted back and forth by the inanities of huge and impersonal institutions. In *Catch-22*—one of the most popular novels of the 1960s—the protagonist cannot escape from the Air Force because by invoking a rule to show that he is mad, he proves he is really sane. It is the classical theme of folly.

[11] This reading, I know, completely ignores many prominent novelists of the decade—such as Updike, Salinger, Cheever, J. F. Powers, Styron, Roth, Malamud, and Baldwin. I can only say that these men have busied themselves with the more traditional concerns of the novelist—which is to report the doings of man in a social framework, though Malamud, to be sure, has often gone off into the exploration of fantasy. Given my own sociological reading of the apocalyptic temper of the times, I feel that the novelists I have chosen are the ones making the more distinctive statements about the sensibility of the decade.

In the science fiction and futurism of Anthony Burgess, Kurt Vonnegut, and William Burroughs the absurdities are heightened as the characters undergo actual changes in their physical form. The emphasis is on the gratuitousness of events and on the blurring of good and evil. In John Barth's *Giles Goat-Boy* the world is fought over by two giant computers. In Thomas Pynchon's *The Crying of Lot 49* the "plot" centers on a worldwide conspiracy—a theme that also occurs in Burroughs—and we await the end of America in an onrush of doomsday saturnalia.

Schizoid themes were made explicit in Ken Kesey's *One Flew over the Cuckoo's Nest*, Barth's *The End of the Road*, and Mailer's *An American Dream*. In Kesey's book, parts of it written under the influence of peyote and LSD, a character fakes insanity to escape a jail term but ends up being lobotomized, while a schizoid Indian giant who has been a patient in the same hospital breaks out and "goes sane." In Mailer's *An American Dream*—with its obviously symbolic title—the protagonist Stephen Rojack acts out a variety of omnipotence fantasies—including confrontation with the CIA and other mysterious forces—and ends up by celebrating the power of thought waves to reach out to the beyond.

In the other major novelists of the period—Nabokov, Bellow, Burroughs, and Genet—the themes of fantasy predominate. Nabokov's *Pale Fire* is a kind of fantastic detective story (as well as a melodramatic, labyrinthine conceit about power, love, and learning) consisting of an elaborate commentary on a long poem by a protagonist who may be a spy or the deposed king of an imaginary country resembling Russia—the confusion of identity is crucial. *Ada* (or *Ardor*, or many other versions) is an equally complex fantasy about love, which deliberately plays with anachronism to obliterate all distinctions between past and future time.

Saul Bellow—the only writer who is in the end anti-apocalyptic —raises the question: "Was it the time . . . to blow this great, blue, white, green planet, or to be blown from it?" *Mr. Sammler's Planet* revolves, in large part, around the plan of an Indian physicist to colonize the moon as an escape from the overcrowding of the earth. Interwoven with Dr. Lal's plan is a purported memoir of the life of one of the pioneering futurists, H. G. Wells. And Mr. Sammler himself—the novel's beautifully rendered protagonist—is stateless, as though to emphasize the dissolution of all past structures.

Nabokov and Bellow are by temperament observers of the world, but with Burroughs and Genet the apocalypse is upon us. The world is literally and symbolically dismembered. In Burroughs the excremental vision becomes tactile. Though *Naked Lunch* is ostensibly about the author's battle with drug addiction, the theme of feculence runs like an open sewer through the book: there is a great preoccupation with anality, with bodily discharges of all kinds, with a horror of the female genitalia, and a lingering upon such images as the reflexive ejaculation of a hanged man during his execution. People are turned into crabs, or huge centipedes, or carnivores. Burroughs has said that the "novelistic form is probably outmoded," and writers will have to develop more precise techniques "producing the same effect on the reader as lurid action photos." His novels—*Naked Lunch*, and the trilogy including *The Soft Machine*, *Nova Express*, and *The Ticket that Exploded*—are "cut-up" books: "You can cut into *Naked Lunch* at any intersection." It is a "continuous showing," for *Naked Lunch* has no use for history. The other novels are written in strips and pasted up arbitrarily. Reality has no reality, for there are no more dimensions and no more boundaries.

Similar preoccupations run through the work of Jean Genet, but his writing is above all a celebration of the underclass. As Susan Sontag has written, "Crime, sexual and social degradation, above all murder, are understood by Genet as occasions for glory." Genet sees the world of thieves, rapists, and murderers as the only honest world, for here the profoundest and most forbidden human impulses are expressed in direct, primitive terms. For Genet, fantasies of cannibalism and bodily incorporation represent the deepest truth about human desires.[12]

THE DIONYSIAC PACK

Nowhere was the apocalyptic mood acted out more tirelessly than in that movement which called itself the "Dionysiac theater," and which regarded the acting troupe as a kind of Dionysiac pack.

[12] It may seem strange to include Genet in an "American" group, and to label him a writer of the 1960s. Yet though his major writing was done in the 1940s and 1950s, the books which won Genet an American following—*Our Lady of the Flowers*, *The Thief's Journal*, and *Funeral Rites*—did not appear in translation until the 1960s. Burroughs, too, was writing in the 1950s, but both men emerged fully in the American consciousness only in the 1960s.

Its main emphasis was on spontaneity, on orgiastic release, on sensory communication, on Eastern mysticism and ritual; its intention, unlike that of the older radical theater, was not to change the ideas of the audience so much as to reconstruct the psyches of both audience and actors through joint participation in ceremonies of liberation. The movement fostered a school of theater which was anti-discipline and anti-craft, on the ground that any shaping of performers or text, any form of artifice or calculation, was "non-creative and anti-life."

In the traditional theater of the well-wrought play, there are no loose ends, no moral ambiguities, no unused bits of plot; there is always an underlying logic that guides the action to its conclusion, for the playwright wants to make a point. But the "new theater" distrusted what was orderly and condemned it as arbitrary and selective. Necessarily such a theater was not one of playwrights, for a written play is to some extent circumscribed and bounded, while the new theater wanted to break open the action, to erase the distinction between spectator and stage, between audience and actor. Distrusting thought, it sought to recapture in the theater a sense of primitive ritual.

The prototype of the new sensibility in the drama was the Living Theatre, organized by Julian Beck and Judith Malina. After traveling in Europe for several years, the troupe evolved a new style of random action and preached a form of revolutionary anarchism. Their new credo was that "the theater must be set free" and "taken out into the street." In words reminiscent of Marinetti's Futuristic Manifesto, Beck launched an attack on the theater of the past:

> All forms of the theater of lies will go. . . . We don't need Shakespeare's objective wisdom, his sense of tragedy reserved only for the experience of the high-born. His ignorance of collective joy makes him useless to our time. It is important not to be seduced by the poetry. That is why Artaud says, "Burn the Texts."
> In fact the whole theater of the intellect will go. The theater of our century, and centuries past, is a theater whose presentation and appeal is intellectual. One leaves the theater of our time and goes and thinks. But our thinking, conditioned by our already conditioned minds, is so corrupt that it is not to be trusted. . . .

Accordingly, in *Paradise Now*, the star piece of the Living Theatre, audiences were invited to cross the footlights and join the actors onstage, while other performers wandered all through the house smoking marijuana and engaging members of the audience in conversation. Now and then one or another actor would return to the stage, strip down to a loincloth, and encourage the audience to follow his lead. The intention (seldom achieved) was to organize some sort of mass saturnalia. Finally everyone was exhorted to leave the theater, convert the police to anarchism, storm the jails, free the prisoners, stop the war, and take over the cities in the name of "the people."

If there was a single avatar of the new sensibility in the theater, it was the French writer and critic Antonin Artaud, who died in 1948. Trained originally as an actor, Artaud in 1928, together with Robert Aron, founded the Théâtre Alfred Jarry, where, in the spirit of Jarry, he proceeded to exorcise the audience. Artaud believed that one had "to put an end" to the subjugation of theater to text, and to recover the notation of a kind of unique language halfway between gesture and thought. While he did not advocate cruelty or sadism in daily life, Artaud believed that the ritualized violence of his theater could serve a therapeutic function by providing the audience with a sense of release. In this respect, he is part of the large stream of post-modernists who have attacked rationality and sought to return to the primitive roots of impulse.

In the United States of the 1960s, where the children of the affluent played, sometimes fatally, at revolution, and toyed, sometimes fatally, with hallucination, it was inevitable that theories like those behind Artaud's "Theater of Cruelty" would become fashionable without ever being really understood. For in all the talk which went on during this period about the theater as ritual, there was a curious sense of emptiness, lack of conviction, and sheer theatricality.[13]

Ritual, as Émile Durkheim has pointed out, depends first of all upon a clear distinction between the sacred and the profane, agreed upon by all participants in the culture. Ritual guards the portals of the sacred, and one of its functions is to preserve those taboos essential to an ongoing society through the sense of awe that ritual invokes; ritual, in other words, is a dramatized representation of sacred power. In a society which does not, however, start with this fundamental distinction between two realms of being, and which

---

[13] The "poor theater" of the Polish director Jerzy Grotowski, with its elimination of costumes, lighting, and sets, and its emphasis on suffering and death, enjoyed a similar vogue during this period, though its creator—an austere and isolated figure with a religious sense of calling—has since repudiated much of his following.

denies all notions of a hierarchy of ordered values, how can there be anything like meaningful ritual?

What the new theater called ritual devolved inevitably upon some celebration of violence. At first the violence remained within the confines of the work itself—as in the rite of exorcism in *The Blacks*, in which the murder of a white man by a black is symbolically reenacted. Later, however, when the hunger for sensation had escalated into a demand for something more lifelike, happenings gradually came to replace written plays as the chief arena for the enactment of violence. The theater only simulates life, after all, but in a happening real blood could—and did—flow. In the "Destruction in Art" symposium held in the Judson Church in New York in 1968, one of the participants suspended a live white chicken from the ceiling, swung it back and forth, and then snipped off its head with a pair of hedge clippers. He then placed the severed head between his legs, inside his unzipped fly, and proceeded to hammer the insides of a piano with the carcass. At the Cinémathèque in 1968, the German artist Herman Nitsch disemboweled a sheep onstage, poured the entrails and blood over a young girl, and nailed the carcass of the animal to a cross. At this happening, performers of the Orgy-Mystery Theater hurled quantities of blood and animal intestines over each other, presumably reenacting the taurobolium rite of Rome, where a sacrificial bull was slaughtered over the head of a man in a pit as part of his initiation into the Phrygian mysteries. Both these events were reported, with pictures, in the magazine *Art in America*. Another event presided over by Mr. Nitsch, involving the ritual slaughter of an animal, was featured in a front-page picture in the *Village Voice*.

Traditionally, violence has been repugnant to the intellectual as a confession of failure. In discourse, individuals resorted to force only when they had lost the power of persuasion by means of reason. So, too, in art the resort to force—in the sense of a literal reenactment of violence on the canvas, on the stage, or on the written page— signified that the artist, lacking the artistic power to suggest the emotion, was reduced to invoking the shock of it directly. But in the 1960s violence was justified not only as therapy but as a necessary accompaniment to social change. Watching the children of the French upper bourgeoisie mouth the phrases of violence and chant from Mao's Little Red Book in Jean-Luc Godard's *La Chinoise*, one realized that a corrupt romanticism was covering some dreadful drive to murder. Similarly, in Godard's *Weekend*, where a real slaughter of live animals takes place, one realized that the roots of a sinister blood-lust were being touched, not for catharsis but for kicks.

What the rhetoric of revolution permits—both in the new sensibility and the new politics—is the eradication of the line between playacting and reality, so that life (and such "revolutionary" actions as demonstrations) is played out as theater, while the craving for violence, first in the theater and then in the street demonstrations, becomes a necessary psychological drug, a form of addiction.

IN PLACE OF REASON

By the end of the 1960s, the new sensibility had been given a name (the counter-culture) and an ideology to go with it. The main tendency of that ideology—though it appeared in the guise of an attack on the "technocratic society"—was an attack on reason itself.[14]

In place of reason, we were told to give ourselves over to one form or other of pre-rational spontaneity—whether under the heading of Charles Reich's "Consciousness III," the "shamanistic vision" of Theodore Roszak, or the like. "Nothing less is required," said Mr. Roszak, one of the movement's most articulate spokesmen, "than the subversion of the scientific world view with its entrenched commitment to an egocentric and cerebral mode of consciousness. In its place, there must be a new culture in which the non-intellective capacities of personality—those capacities that take fire from visionary splendor and the experience of human communion—become the arbiters of the true, the good, and the beautiful."

Revolutionary change, we heard over and over, must embrace psyche as well as society. But when one sought clues as to what this

[14] It would be a mistake and a distortion to see this attack as coterminous with all radicalism. In fact, there is an older radical tradition which detests irrationalism, and a number of its adherents—Philip Rahv, Robert Brustein, Lionel Abel, Irving Howe—did in differnt essays attack aspects of the new sensibility. The difficulty with many of their arguments is that intellectually and aesthetically they are all allied with modernism and accepts its premises. Yet what the new sensibility did was to carry the premises of modernism through to their logical conclusions.

might mean in real terms—what form this new, presumably post-revolutionary, culture might take—one was given only further exhortations to cast off the deadening weight of cognition, and further celebrations of "the shaman's rhapsodic babbling."

Do these exhortations add up to anything more than a longing for the lost gratifications of an idealized childhood? This has been the recurrent yearning of all utopian movements. What was new, however, about the Arcadian fantasy of the 1960s other than its being dressed up in the language of psychology and anthropology—was that while in the past such longings were largely rhetorical (regard only the "eupsychia" of Fourier), in the 1960s one found the fantasies and sexual demands of childhood acted out during adolescence on a mass scale unprecedented in cultural history. For what else was the demand for negation and indiscriminateness than a denial of those necessary distinctions—between sexes and among ideas—which are the mark of adulthood? What else was the youth culture of the Aquarian Age, the rock-drug dance of springtime, than the desperate search for Dionysus? Yet how could that be possible when there was neither nature nor religion to celebrate or ritualize? All that there was, was the pathetic celebration of the self—a self that had been emptied of content and which masqueraded as being vital through the playacting of Revolution.

A CODA

In the 1970s—we are trapped by the mark of decades—the cultural radicalism itself has become exhausted. In painting there is a return to figure and representation, in sculpture a preoccupation with technology, materials, or a "conceptual statement" through communication devices. The theater has gone stale, and the novel has become more inwardly preoccupied with madness and technology, as exemplified in Pynchon's *Gravity's Rainbow*. For the cultural mass there is now "pornotopia" (to use Steven Marcus' term), the tedious reveling in pornography and kinky sex. Does this mark the end not only of a decade but of a cultural mode as well?

The "untrammeled self," as I pointed out earlier, was a product of bourgeois society, with its glorification of rampant individualism.

Though bourgeois society approved of rampant individualism in economics, it feared the excesses of self in culture, and sought to inhibit them. For a variety of complex historical reasons, the "cultural self" became anti-bourgeois, and sections of that movement allied themselves with political radicalism. Yet the impulses of the "cultural self" were not really radical, but rebellious. It sought to "express" itself by denying restraint and seeking release. What has occurred today is that restraint has gone slack, and the impulses to release find no tension—or creativity. More to the point, the search for release has become legitimated in a liberal culture and exploited (as in the music industry) by commercial entrepreneurs who affect a "mod" life-style of their own.

The rebellious impulses of cultural modernism now run smack up against a paradox. The radicalism of the non-Western world—that of China, Algeria, or Cuba—is a Puritanical one, while the Marxism of the Soviet Union is culturally repressive. Cultural modernism, though it still calls itself subversive, finds a home largely in bourgeois, capitalist society. That society, lacking a culture derived from its empty beliefs and desiccated religions, in turn, adopts as its norm the life-style of a cultural mass that wants to be "emancipated" or "liberated," yet lacks any sure moral or cultural guides as to what worthwhile experiences may be. Is cultural modernism exhausted, or will there be one more turn in the widening gyre, one more turn of the screw in which further inhibitions (against incest, against pederasty, against androgyny) are leveled? At this point, the question is really irrelevant. For the singular fact is that as a creative cultural force—creative in aesthetic form or content— modernism is finished. The climacteric was reached 50 years ago. The sensibility of the 1960s is relevant simply as evidence that the aesthetics of shock and sensation had only become trivial and tedious; and to the extent that it had become the property of the cultural mass, one more indication of the cultural contradictions of capitalism.

Toward the Great Instauration: Religion and Culture in a Post-Industrial Age

EVERY SOCIETY seeks to establish a set of meanings through which people can relate themselves to the world. These meanings specify a set of purposes or, like myth and ritual, explain the character of shared experiences, or deal with the transformations of nature through human powers of magic or *techne*. These meanings are embodied in religion, in culture, and in work. The loss of meanings in these areas creates a set of incomprehensions which people cannot stand and which prompt, urgently, their search for new meanings, lest all that remain be a sense of nihilism or the void. This essay, in the light of the previous chapters on the incoherence of culture, explores the relation of culture to work and to religion, and the possible direction of new meanings.[1]

Much of the character of men and the pattern of their social relations is shaped by the kind of work they do. If we take work as a

---

[1] This essay can also be read as a counterpart to another one, "Technology, Nature and Society: The Vicissitudes of Three World-Views and the Confusion of Realms," given at the Smithsonian Institution in December 1972 and included in the Frank N. Doubleday series, *Technology and the Frontiers of Knowledge* (Garden City, N.Y.: Doubleday, 1975), with a foreword by Daniel Boorstin. I have not included that essay here, for its focus is more on the emergence of philosophical world-views in relation to society than on the distinctive problems of culture, yet the two can be seen as complementary.

In the opening section of this chapter, I have repeated some formulations from my book *The Coming of Post-Industrial Society* to establish the framework of the discussion of religion and culture.

principle that divides the modalities of character, we can speak of pre-industrial, industrial, and post-industrial work. We can see this principle synchronically, when these elements co-exist within the same society, or we can see these as sequences through which societies pass. Depending upon one's purposes, each approach—since these are analytical constructs—is valid. But the distinction itself remains as a ground for understanding the meanings that derive from work.

Life in pre-industrial societies—still the condition of most of the world today—is primarily a *game against nature*. The labor force is overwhelmingly in the extractive industries: agriculture, mining, fishing, forestry. One works with raw muscle power, in inherited ways, and one's sense of the world is conditioned by the vicissitudes of the elements—the seasons, the storms, the fertility of the soil, the amount of water, the depth of the mine seams, the droughts and the floods. The rhythms of life are shaped by these contingencies. The sense of time is one of *durée*, and the pace of work varies with the seasons and the weather.

Industrial societies, producing goods, play a *game against fabricated nature*. The world has become technical and rationalized. The machine predominates and the rhythms of life are mechanically paced; time is chronological, mechanical, evenly spaced by the divisions of the clock. Energy has replaced raw muscle and provides the basis for the large leaps in productivity, the mass output of standardized goods which characterizes an industrial society. Energy and machines transform the nature of work. Skills are broken down into simpler components, and the artisan of the past is replaced by two new figures: the engineer, who is responsible for the layout and flow of work, and the semi-skilled worker, who is the cog between machines, until the technical ingenuity of the engineer creates a new machine which replaces him as well. It is a world of scheduling and programming in which the components are brought together at exact moments for assembly. It is a world of coordination in which men, materials, and markets are dovetailed for the production and distribution of goods. It is a world of organization—of hierarchy and bureaucracy—in which men are treated as things because one can more easily coordinate things than men. Thus a necessary distinction is introduced between roles and persons, and this distinction becomes formalized in the manning tables and organization charts of the enterprises.

A post-industrial society, because it centers on services—human services, professional and technical services—is a *game between persons*. The organization of a research team, or the relation between doctor and patient, teacher and pupil, government official and petitioner—a world, in short, where the modalities are scientific knowledge, higher education, community organization, and the like—involves cooperation and reciprocity rather than coordination and hierarchy. The post-industrial society is thus also a *communal* society in which the social unit is the community organization rather than the individual, and decisions have to be reached through some polity—in collective negotiations between private organizations, as well as government—rather than the market. But cooperation between men is more difficult than the management of things. Participation is a condition of community; and when many different groups want too many different things and are not prepared to bargain, then increased conflict or deadlock results. There is either a politics of consensus or a politics of stymie.

Yet these changes in social organization may, in an intangible way, herald more—a change in consciousness and cosmology, the dark tinge of which has always been present at the edge of man's conception of himself and the world, and which may now move to the phenomenological center. In existentialist terminology, man is "thrown" into the world, confronting alien and hostile powers which he has sought to understand and master. The first confrontation was with nature, and for most of the thousands of years of human existence, life has been a game against nature, to find a strategy which keeps nature at bay: to find shelter from the elements, to ride the waters and the wind, to wrest food and sustenance from the soil, the waters, and other creatures. The coding of much of human behavior has been shaped by the need to adapt to these vicissitudes.

Man as *homo faber* sought to make things, and in making things he dreamt of reworking nature. To be dependent on nature was to bend to its caprices. To remake nature, through fabrication and replication, was to enhance man's powers. The industrial revolution was, at bottom, an effort to substitute a technical order for the natural order, an engineering conception of function and rationality for the haphazard ecological distributions of resources and climate.

The post-industrial order turns its back on both. In the salient experience of work, men live more and more outside nature, and less and less with machinery and things; they live with, and encounter only, one another. The problems of group life, of course, are among the oldest difficulties of human civilization, going back to the cave and the clan. But now the context has changed. The oldest forms of group life were within the context of nature, and the overcoming of nature gave an external, common purpose to the lives of men. The group life that was hitched to things gave men a huge sense of power as they created mechanical artifacts to transform the world. But in the post-industrial world, for the majority of persons the older contexts have disappeared from view. In the daily round of work, men no longer confront nature, either as alien or beneficent, and few handle artifacts and things.

In the larger historical context, in pre-industrial society the character of men and the traditions of the group are shaped by society. In Durkheim's sense, society is an external reality which exists *sui generis*, independent of the individual. The world is a found world. In industrial society, men make things, but these ready-mades are not convertible truths; they exist as reified entities with independent existences of their own, outside of man. In post-industrial society, men know only one another, and have to "love one another or die." Reality is not "out there," where man stands "alone and afraid in a world [he] never made." Reality is now itself problematic and to be remade.

Will this changing experience create a change in consciousness and sensibility? For most of human history, reality was nature, and in poetry and imagination men sought to relate themselves to the natural world. In the last 150 years reality has been technics, tools, and things made by men, yet with an independent existence, outside men, in a reified world. Now reality is becoming only the social world, excluding nature and things, and experienced primarily through the reciprocal consciousness of others, rather than some external reality. Society increasingly becomes a web of consciousness, a form of imagination to be realized as a social construction. But with what rules, and with what moral conceptions? More than ever, without nature or *techne* what can bind men to one another?

I have presented three settings—the natural world, the technical world, and the social world—and three modes of relation to these realities. For each of these there is also, symbolically, a cosmological principle.

THE NATURAL WORLD

For the natural world, this cosmological principle is the trajectory from *fate* to *chance*. I take as my exemplar Greek thought, which reflected so magnificently on its experiences, and sought to embody these in religion, myth, and philosophy.

The Homeric *Hymn to Demeter* presents time as a cycle in which each year there is a rebirth of the dead plant world, and this vision and this ritual are translated, at least in the Mystery and Orphic traditions, into the theme that man's destiny comes full circle when life and death are followed by resurrection and a new life. In the myth of Er, which closes Plato's *Republic*, this eschatology is joined to a moral order. The myth of Er is a vision of last things, reported by a slain warrior marvelously restored to life. But while the story is traditional—the fortunes of souls born and reborn—the chief point is that man's happiness or misery throughout eternity depends on his actions in *this* life. Thus, philosophical principles are joined with Orphic and popular mythology to show men how to escape from the cycle of generations.

In this revised conception, time is the present. Time is not subject to the domination of eternity, as in the sonnet of Petrarch, but to fate, or what the Greeks called *moira*. As is apparent already in *The Iliad*, *moira* means a "part" or an allocated portion—that which belongs to the gods, of heaven, sea, and the misty darkness. *Moira* thus turns out to be spatial, rather than temporal, of co-existing provinces, rather than past, present, and future.

The pessimistic mood of life which one finds so marked at the end of the fifth century B.C., and which deepened in the fourth as Greece, torn apart by incessant warfare, succumbed to the half-savage Macedonian king, finds its expression in the rise of the Goddess of Chance. In any scheme of things which is bound to necessity, fate is always yoked to chance—chance not as probability or risk, as we think of it, but as tychism, an objective reality ruled by unknown forces. Thus, as men become more despairing, as they lose their "allotted portion" yet lack the sustaining inward principle to change their fate, the direction of their lives loses meaning and fate gives way to chance.

In the Hellenistic period (as against the Homeric) Tyche, as deified fortune, becomes the great goddess of the ancient world. In

Oedipus at Thebes, the field of action is no longer bounded by fate but by chance. Since there is no sure knowledge and Tyche rules, argues Jocasta, it is best to live at random.

When life has grown arbitrary, one becomes obsessed with, and prays to, chance. "Such was the paradoxical ending," concludes Professor Bernard Knox. "The movement of more than a century of brilliant and searching thought is movement not forward but back to the starting point . . . from the Homeric Olympians to the goddess Chance. But the circular progress is not on one plane; the point of return is on a lower level. The movement is a descending spiral."[2]

Thus the trajectory—from an allotted portion to random action, from a spatial order to haphazard disorder. The question is whether such a movement is not invariable when the ground of moral principle is derived from the vicissitudes of nature. It is a question to which we will return.

THE TECHNICAL WORLD

The technical world is defined by rationality and progress. History, said Hegel, was the immanent process in which self-consciousness triumphed over the limiting blinders of subjectivity to the fusion of will and action into absolute knowledge. Marx naturalized this historic process by seeing man's growth in the development of his material and technical powers, in the expansion of his means of controlling nature. The common framework was the idea of the "escape from necessity," those constraints of nature which limited men's powers. History, not as a mere record of human events but as a philosophical *demiurgos*, was the agency by which men would move from the "kingdom of necessity" to the "kingdom of freedom." The "end of history," thus, would signal the triumph of man over all constraints and his achievement of the total mastery of nature and the self.

This is the source of the modern temper. As embedded in science, it is expressed by Bacon through the governor of Salomon's House, or the College of Six Days' Work, in the *New Atlantis*: "The end of our foundation is the knowledge of causes, and secret motion of things; and the enlarging of the bounds of human empire, to the effecting of all things possible." In the *Cours de philosophie posi-*

[2] Bernard M. W. Knox, *Oedipus at Thebes* (New Haven: Yale University Press, 1957), pp. 167–168.

tive, perhaps the last individual attempt to write a synoptic account of human knowledge (it was completed in 1842), August Comte held that the only things perhaps inherently unknowable were the chemical composition of the distant stars and the question of whether there were "organized beings living on their surface." Within two decades, the astronomer Gustav Kirchhoff had applied spectrum analysis to the stars and provided the first part of that very knowledge which Comte had thought to be unattainable. We ourselves may soon be in a position to ascertain the second.

This compulsion to map the trajectory of knowledge drives us all, as modern men. Perhaps the most poignant effort was that of the historian Henry Adams, scion of one of America's great families, and onetime president of the American Historical Association. Henry Adams sought to plot a "social physics," a grid of history as attraction and reaction, as motion and mass, as lines of force, as a movement from unity to multiplicity. In his search for the unit of measurement he had discovered the "dynamometer of history"—the fact that with the introduction of modern sources of energy, all phenomena were moving through "doubling rates" of an exponential character. He felt he had discovered the hidden thread of the philosophy of history, "the law of acceleration." But he needed to chart its exact trajectory. He found the answer, he thought, in "Equilibrium of Heterogeneous Substances," a paper by Willard Gibbs, that brilliant yet introverted scientist whose neglected work laid down the foundation for statistical mechanics. In his paper, Gibbs propounded what he called the "phase rule," or the means whereby a single substance—his example was the changes of ice, water, and water vapor—in changing its phase, changed the equilibrium.

Adams was intrigued by the word "phase." Turgot and Comte, in their grand historical sketches, had divided history into phases, and Adams felt that he now had the formula for the exact division of historical time and a means of extrapolating the future. The future historian, he said "must seek his education in the world of mathematical physics. Nothing further can be expected from further study on the old lines. A new generation must be taught to think by new methods. . . ."

In 1909, Adams wrote an essay, "The Rule of Phase Applied to History," in which he sought to apply the law of inverse squares to the periods of history. He assumed that a new, mechanical phase had begun in 1600 with the thought of Galileo, Bacon, and Descartes, and that this phase lasted 300 years until the next, the electric phase (symbolized by the invention of the dynamo). Applying the law of inverse squares, if the mechanical phase lasted 300 years, the electrical phase would have a life equal to $\sqrt{300}$, or about 17 years. Then, around 1917, it would pass into the ethereal phase, the phase of pure mathematics. And by the same law, given the constant rate of acceleration, the square root of 17.5 would be about four years, bringing thought to the ultimate limit of its possibilities by the year 1921. (And yet, since we could not be completely sure when the starting point of the acceleration began, if we extended back the origin of the mechanical phase to 1500, and applied our law of inverse squares, we would reach the limit of thought in the year 2025; so, perhaps we still have some time to think.)

Thus was the cosmic picture of social evolution sketched in these equations of social physics. According to the phase rule, society had lived for thousands of years in the grip of fetish forces, the hold of religion on men; it had passed through a mechanical age and then into an electrical phase without "fairly realizing what had happened except in social and political revolutions." Now society was achieving a consciousness of itself in terms of science. In the phase of pure mathematics, the world of meta-physics, there might be a subsidence of consciousness and a new "indefinitely long stationary period such as John Stuart Mill foresaw."

Yet beyond this was a longer vision. In the "Letter to American Historians," which Adams wrote in 1910, as a valedictory at the age of 72, he called attention to Lord Kelvin's paper "On a Universal Tendency in Nature to the Dissipation of Mechanical Energy." Adams pointed out that seven years after Kelvin, Darwin had published his *Origin of Species*, and "society naturally and instinctively adopted the view that Evolution must be upward." But if there was a social physics that ruled history as well, would not the ultimate fate of society be entropy, or random disorder? Was not the degradation of energy finding its counterpart—and here he drew his illustrations from Gustave Le Bon's *The Psychology of Crowds*—in the turbulence of the masses?

The technical age is the age of the clock. But if so, then the clockwork is running down. "The universe has been terribly narrowed by thermodynamics," Adams wrote. "Already History and Sociology gasp for breath." And that was the final idea that Henry

Adams sought to convey. The train of history, impelled by the acceleration of knowledge, would become derailed. Mankind would increasingly be unable to solve its proliferating problems, since the acceleration in the pace of change was bringing us closer to the final limit of energy, and we would be unable to respond creatively to the challenge of the future.[3] Thus in the technical world we begin with progress and end with stasis.

THE SOCIAL WORLD

If the natural world is ruled by fate and chance, and the technical world by rationality and entropy, the social world can only be characterized as living in "fear and trembling."

Every society (to paraphrase Rousseau) is held together by coercion—army, militia, police—or by a moral order, the willingness of individuals to respect each other and to respect the rules of common law. In a pervasive moral order, the justification of the rightness of those rules is rooted in a system of shared values. Historically, religion, as that mode of consciousness which is concerned with ultimate values, has been the ground of a shared moral order.

The force of religion does not derive from any utilitarian quality (of self-interest or individual need); religion is not a social contract, nor is it only a generalized system of cosmological meanings. The power of religion derives from the fact that, before ideologies or other modes of secular belief, it was the means of gathering together, in one overpowering vessel, the sense of the sacred—that which is set apart as the collective conscience of a people.

[3] "No student of history [Adams wrote] is so ignorant as not to know that fully fifty years before the chemists took up the study of Phases, August Comte laid down in sufficiently precise terms a law of phase for history which received the warm adhesion of two authorities—the most eminent of that day—Émile Littré and John Stuart Mill. Nearly a hundred and fifty years before Willard Gibbs announced his mathematical formulas of phase to the physicists and chemists, Turgot stated the Rule of Historical Phase as clearly as Franklin stated the law of electricity. As far as concerns theory, we are not much further advanced now than in 1750, and know little better what electricity or thought is, as substance, than Franklin and Turgot knew it; but this failure to penetrate the ultimate synthesis of nature is no excuse for professors of history to abandon the field which is theirs by prior right, and still less can they plead their ignorance of the training in mathematics and physics which it was their duty to seek." In a phrase which echoed Vico, Adams concluded: "The theory of history is a much easier study than the theory of light."

"The Rule of Phase Applied to History" and "Letter to American Historians" are collected in *The Degradation of the Democratic Dogma* (New York: Macmillan, 1919); see pp. 284–285, 252–253, 141–142.

The distinction between sacred and profane—which in modern times has been explored principally by Émile Durkheim—is the starting point for the discussion of the fate of the social world. How did man come to think of two radically different, heterogeneous realms, the sacred and the profane? Nature itself is a unified continuum in a great chain of being, from microcosm to macrocosm. Only man has created dualities: of spirit and matter, nature and history, the sacred and the mundane. For Durkheim, the shared sentiments and affective ties that bind men together are central to any social existence. Religion is thus the consciousness of society. And since social life in all its aspects is made possible only by a system of symbols, that consciousness becomes fixed upon some object which is to be considered sacred.

If Durkheim's conception is valid, one can see the "crisis of religion" in a different light than the conventional one. When philosophers, and now journalists, write about the decline of religion or the loss of faith, they usually mean that the sense of the supernatural—the images of heaven and hell, of punishment and redemption—have lost their force over men. But Durkheim argued that religion did not derive from a belief in the supernatural or in gods, but from the division of the *world* (things, times, persons) into the sacred and the profane. If religion is declining, it is because the worldly realm of the sacred has been shrinking, and because the shared sentiments and affective ties between men have become diffuse and weak. The primordial elements that provide men with common identification and affective reciprocity—family, synagogue and church, community—have become attenuated, and people have lost the capacity to maintain sustained relations with each other in both time and place. To say, then, that "God is dead" is, in effect, to say that the social bonds have snapped and that society is dead.

FROM THE SACRED TO THE PROFANE

With the three settings and the three cosmologies, there are also three modes of attachment or identity by which individuals seek to relate themselves to the world. These are religion, work, and culture.

The traditional mode, of course, has been religion as a transmundane means of understanding one's self, one's people, one's history, and one's place in the scheme of things. In the development and differentiation of modern society—we call the process *secularization*—the social world of religion shrank; more and more, religion became a personal belief to be accepted or rejected, not as fate but as a matter of will, rational or otherwise. We can see this process vividly in the writings of Matthew Arnold, who rejects theology and metaphysics, the "old God," the "non-natural and magnified man," and finds meaning in morality and emotional subjectivism, a fusion of Kant and Schleiermacher. When that occurs, the religious mode becomes ethical and aesthetic—and inevitably thin and attentuated. It is, to that extent, a reversal of the steps by which Kierkegaard found his way back to religion.

Work, when it is a calling or vocation, is a translation of religion into a this-worldly attachment, a proof, through personal effort, of one's own goodness and worth. This was not only Protestant but the view of men like Tolstoy or Aleph Daled Gordon (the theorist of the kibbutz) who feared the corruption of a sumptuary life. The Puritan or the kibbutznik wanted to work in a calling. We feel that we are working because we are forced to, or that work itself has become routinized and diminished. As Max Weber wrote in the melancholy last pages of *The Protestant Ethic and the Spirit of Capitalism*: "Where the fulfillment of the calling cannot directly be related to the highest spiritual and cultural values, or when, on the other hand, it need not be felt simply as an economic compulsion, the individual gradually abandons the attempt to justify it at all." The sumptuary impulses replace the ascetic, the hedonistic way of life submerges the calling.

For the modern, cosmopolitan man, culture has replaced both religion and work as a means of self-fulfillment or as a justification —an aesthetic justification—of life. But behind this change, essentially from religion to culture, lies the extraordinary crossover in consciousness, particularly in the meanings of expressive conduct in human society.

In the history of Western society, there has always been a dialectic of release and restraint. The idea of release goes back to the Dionysiac festivals, Bacchanalian revels, saturnalias, the Gnostic sects of the first and second centuries and the subterranean threads unraveled since; or to the examples in biblical legend and history of Sodom and Gomorrah or the Babylonian episodes.

The great historic religions of the West have been religions of restraint. We find in the Old Testament an emphasis on the law, and a fear of human nature unchecked: an association of release with lust, sexual competitiveness, violence, and murder. The fear is the fear of the demonic—the frenzied ecstasy (ex-stasis) of leaving one's body and crossing the boundaries of sin. Even the New Testament, which suspends the law and proclaims love, recoils from the mundane implications of the suspension of law and erects a barrier. As Paul says in the *Epistles to the Corinthians*, rebuking the Corinth church for some of its practices: No, he says, the love we bring, the communion we practice, is not the release and the love of the body, but the release and the love of the spirit (I Corinthians 5: 1–2; 6: 12–20; 14: 1–28).

In Western society, religion has had two functions. First, it has guarded the portals of the demonic, seeking to defuse it by expressing it in emblematic terms, whether it be the symbolic sacrifice acted out in the *Akedah* of Abraham and Isaac, or the ritual sacrifice of Jesus on the Cross, which becomes transubstantiated in the wafer and the wine as the flesh and blood of Christ. And, second, it has provided a continuity with the past. Prophecy, whose authority has always been located in the past, became the basis of denying the validity of antinomian progressive revelation. Culture, when it was fused with religion, judged the present on the basis of the past, and provided a continuity of both through tradition. In these two ways, religion undergirded almost all of historic Western culture.

The crossover I speak about—it is not located in any particular person or specific point in time, but is a general cultural phenomenon—occurred with the breakup of the theological authority of religion in the middle of the nineteenth century. The culture—particularly the emerging current we now call modernism—took over, in effect, the relation with the demonic. But instead of taming it, as religion sought to do, the modernist culture began to accept the demonic, to explore it, to revel in it, and to see it (correctly) as the source of a certain kind of creativity.

Now, religion always imposes moral norms on culture. It insists on limits, particularly the subordination of aesthetic impulses to moral conduct. Once culture began to take over dealing with the demonic, there arose the demand for the "autonomy of the aesthetic," the idea that experience, in and of itself, is of supreme value: Everything is to be explored, anything is to be permitted (at least to the imagination), including lust, murder, and other themes which have dominated the modernist sur-real. The second aspect, as we have seen in the previous chapters, was to root all authority, all justification, in the demands of the "I," of the "imperial self." By turning one's back on the past, one dirempts or shreds the ties which compel continuity; one makes the new and the novel the source of interest, and the curiosity of the self the touchstone of judgment. Thus modernism as a cultural movement trespassed religion and moved the center of authority from the sacred to the profane.

THE THREE FAUSTS

The profane itself leads only in two directions—to a life of novelty and hedonism (and eventually debauch), or to what Hegel called "the self-infinitizing spirit," the search which carries man toward the reach of absolute, God-like knowledge. Men have often sought to reach for both.

The symbol of the quest for human self-aggrandizement is, of course, Faust, the figure in which an entire age recognized its mind and soul, its unhappy and divided consciousness, if not its destiny. And it should be no surprise to know that within Goethe, who established the modern figure for us, there is not one Faust but three.[4]

There is, first, the *Urfaust*, an early version of Part One, which Goethe wrote in 1775 when he was 26 but which was not discovered until 1887, although a section, *Faust, A Fragment*, was published in 1790. In the *Urfaust* (before the story of Gretchen) the theme is entirely man's quest for the undreamt-of power over the material world through knowledge. But how? Nature, says the young Goethe, is no mere machine. Science is prosaic because it searches for regularities and laws to understand nature. Only a poetical art like magic can unveil the secrets of nature's soul. As Santayana writes: "The magic arts are the sacrament that will initiate Faust into his new religion, the religion of nature."

---

[4] For the text, I have followed primarily *Goethe's Faust*, trans. Walter Kaufmann (Garden City, N.Y.: Doubleday Anchor, 1963), but my reading has been influenced heavily by George Santayana's essay "Goethe's Faust," in *Three Philosophical Poets* (Doubleday Anchor, 1953; orig. ed., Cambridge: Harvard University Press, 1910).

Faust opens his book of magic at the sign of the macrocosm and sees revealed to him the mechanism of the world in its complex chain of being. He feels he has grasped the totality of the world until he realizes that he has achieved not the inward knowledge of existence, but only a theory. What still eludes him, and what he yearns for, is reality itself.

All experience tempts Faust. He shrinks from nothing, ready to undertake anything that any mortal may have experienced. He is insatiable. The Earth-Spirit, attracted by this tempestuous man, rises and holds before him the turbulent, heaving, boiling cauldron of life. But in his readiness to plunge in and gather it all to himself, he is confronted with two dismaying realizations: His *imagination* may give him a universal scope, but his *life* never can. And since mind is the instrument of understanding, it is possible that the life of reason, not the life of nature, is, after all, the best good for man. He cannot accept these truths, and when he hears from the departing Earth-Spirit the cry, *du gleichst dem Geist den du begreifst, nicht mir*, he collapses. Yet he will not accept so unwelcome and chastening a truth. The quest for the rest of his life—and this makes up the substance of Faust Two and Faust Three—is the effort to contravene that knowledge. And, at the end, we are still not sure that his long and tortuous search has ever convinced him of its truth.

The Tragedy of Faust, Part One, which the world largely knows, was published in 1808. The theme is familiar. Faust argues that the curse of man is the unceasing *Wissendrang* which never gives him rest. He is sick of thought and study. The wager he makes with Mephistopheles is that if, after tasting all of life's sensations, the plenitude of experience, he acknowledges an ultimate contentment, the renunciation of eternal striving, he will accept eternal damnation.

If the *Urfaust* is, in Hegel's terms, the first moment of consciousness, the self-realization by thought of its own dilemma, Part One is the second moment, its negation, the plunge into the debauch, "the giddy whirl of a perpetually self-creating disorder." There is the release of primitive impulse in Auerbach's cellar, the Witch's kitchen, the Dionysian festival of the *Walpurgisnacht*, and the seduction of Gretchen. The theme is a Christian theme of redemption by sacrifice, the death of Gretchen as a propitiation for sin. The purity of Gretchen is played against the pedantry of Wagner and the cynicism of Mephistopheles. In the end, Gretchen the sinner will be saved, yet this is no answer, since passion, as suffering, is a surrender to a savior, and this is not the way for Faust.

For 60 years, Goethe wrestled with a conclusion. In 1831, at age 82, he sealed a parcel that contained the manuscript of Part Two. This *Sorgenkind*, this problem child of his life, was not to be opened before his death (yet, vain as he was, he broke the seal once to read from the manuscript to his daughter-in-law), because, as he wrote in his diary two months before the end of his life, there were no solutions. It took 60 years for Goethe to come to this third Faust, yet in the end the conclusion is inconclusive, filled with piety, platitude, irony, and ambiguity.

In Part Two, which is rarely read, Faust moves from his private world to the wider human society. He explores empire, science (the creation of the artificial man, Homunculus), and the sensualism of Greece (the episode with Helen); in the end he decides to give his life to practical works, to reclaim land from the sea, to drain the marshlands and hold back the tides, to master nature—for man.

Yet, despite such pronouncements, evil arises from the impatience of impulse and the action of excess. Near the land Faust has ordered reclaimed there is a small chapel, and nearby a cottage where a sweet old couple, Philemon and Baucis, live. The old people will not sell the land, and Faust orders them evicted and transferred to a better dwelling somewhere else. In the roughness of the action, the old couple are consumed by the fire which burns down the houses. Faust shows scant regret; these are unfortunate consequences, he says, of the will that strives for the betterment of man.

At the end, he is a blind and deluded man. He stands undaunted, his thoughts on the work he has set in hand, and on the future. He hears some digging and orders the spirits on, thinking grandly that they are building the canals he envisions; but the digging he hears is the digging only of his own grave.

Faust has been called the modern Prometheus, and Goethe's tragedy the "bible of Prometheanism."[5] But is there tragedy, if by tragedy we mean the comprehension of self-pride and the final understanding of one's human limits? And is he Promethean? Faust will not surrender his will, his unceasing striving. As Erich Heller remarks: "What is Faust's sin? The restlessness of spirit. What is

[5] It might be noted that Marx, himself an admirer of the figure of Prometheus, read *Faust* in Promethean terms.

Faust's salvation? The restlessness of spirit." As the angels say in the last scene as they carry Faust's soul to heaven:

> Wer immer strebend sich bemuht,
> Den konnen wir erlosen.
> > (lines 11936–11937)
>
> Who ever strives with all his power,
> We are allowed to save.
> > (Kaufmann, p. 493)

Faust is modern precisely because he strives—but with no memory, no continuity with the past. In the beginning of Part Two, the opening theme (by Ariel, the spirit of nature) is to "bathe him in the dew of Lethe's spray." The spirits in chorus seem to say (as Santayana remarks) that "Pity and remorse . . . are evil and vain; failure is incidental; error is innocent. Nature has no memory; forgive yourself and you are forgiven."

Faust's first words (after 60 years) are:

> Enlivened once again, life's pulses waken
> To greet the kindly dawn's ethereal vision;
> You, earth, outlasted this night, too, unshaken . . .

He has not grown better or become more aware of the world. He simply starts afresh, seeking the new once again, but on a broader stage, that of history and civilization. "His old loves have blown over, like the storms of a bygone year, and with only a dreamlike memory of his past errors, he goes forth to meet a new day."

But without memory, there is no maturity. For a human being this romanticism, this endless life without fulfillment, is only a recipe for tragedy or black comedy. There is only the constant search for new interests, new pastimes, new sensations, new adventures, new revels, new revolutions, new joys, new terrors, new . . . .

This is not Prometheus but Proteus, and a Proteus who never stops long enough for us to know his true shape or his ultimate purposes. And since there is no exit, we know, in the end, that the life of Faust on earth, and of those like him, is only the reflection of the seven divisions of hell.

FIRST CAUSES AND FINAL THINGS

The search for meanings brings us back to root questions, and the starting point in trying to determine where men can find an Archimedean principle is a double-faceted question: Is there an unchanging human character; and, if there is not, how can philosophy (which is charged with formulating, if not resolving, the problem) separate what is "merely" historic from what is permanent, in order to see how men can understand if not judge, the value of their existence.[6] There are three grounds for any search: nature, history, or religion.

The first ground of the argument is nature. This is the point clearly established by Leo Strauss in his *Natural Right and History*, and the axis of all his consequent objections to historicist or religious grounds of meaning. "The discovery of nature is the work of the philosopher," Strauss writes. The Old Testament, whose premise is a rejection of philosophy, does not know "nature," and there is no assumption of natural right as such in the Old Testament. The ground of biblical religion is revelation, not nature, and the source of moral conduct is *Halakah* (the law, or "the way").

Nature, in Greek thought, is the exact order of things (*physis*), and therefore prior to convention or positive law (*nomos*). Nature is "hidden" and has to be discovered; law has to follow the guides of nature. "Nature," Strauss writes, "is older than any tradition; hence it is more venerable than tradition. . . . By uprooting the authority of the ancestral, philosophy recognizes that nature is *the* authority." The "natural" end is moral and intellectual perfection. If this is the basis of natural right, the principles of right are unchangeable. Thus, Strauss concludes, "the discovery of nature is identical with the actualization of a human possibility which, at least according to

---

[6] This is the theme of the profound and esoteric argument between Leo Strauss and Alexander Kojève in *On Tyranny* (New York: Free Press, 1963). I have deliberately eschewed the term "human nature," and used the more clumsy term "human character," for "human nature" implies that human beings have some fixed properties. Furthermore, it suffers from all the ambiguities of the word "nature," which can mean, variously, a physical environment, the laws of matter, nature as an active force (as in "nature shapes" or "nature creates"), and so forth. For a discussion of the problems raised by these ambiguities, as well as for a more extended discussion of the problems of historicism which are raised later in this section, see my essay "Technology, Nature and Society," in *Technology and the Frontiers of Knowledge*, Frank Nelson Doubleday Lectures, (Garden City, N.Y.: Doubleday, 1975).

its own interpretation, is trans-historical, trans-social, trans-moral and trans-religious." The grounds of nature, thus, are unchanging and permanent.

My difficulty with this argument is threefold. The idea of a "natural end" assumes that there is a *telos* (in the Aristotelian sense of a design given in the form itself, or in the Hegelian meaning of a "realization" of philosophy at the end of history) which inevitably draws man towards that "moral and intellectual perfection." Yet I doubt that such a doctrine of immanence can be sustained in the light of what we know of human history. Or, as I believe Strauss uses the terms, the "natural end" as an "ideal" that stands outside of man, and is used as a "yardstick" to judge human actuality; it is thus a classical utopia. Yet if this is so, what we have is either pantheism which substitutes the idea of nature for God, with little gain; or some fixed human ideal which is either formal (because it would have to be general and abstract) or constricting, if it specifies a determinate moral code. My third objection, to which I shall return, is that human beings, given the conditions of their biological and sociological nurturing, cannot find an adequate identity in some universal code but live, necessarily, in the tension between the particular and the universal. Any set of meanings to be actualized in daily life must take that human condition into account.

There is a different answer, one which seeks to take history into account, yet to find an unchanging pattern. This is the answer of Vico, with his theory of recurrence, a theory that is later echoed, in different form, by Nietzsche.

For Vico, the civilizing elements in any age are religion, marriage, and proper respect for the dead. Each age runs its course, and decay becomes evident when societies lose their sense of shame, so that anything goes—when customs and laws are no longer respected, when equality leads to license, and the mean-spirited and the envious replace the humane. There is, then, a breakdown from within, or a conquest from without, and a reversion to barbarism, followed by a new cycle of three ages.

Within human history, there have been two cycles, one ancient and one modern, each with a common entelechy, yet shaped by two different modes of consciousness. There is the poetic logic of the ancients, the pictorial *bricolage* of myth and images; and the rational logic of the moderns, the conjectural world of theoretical reason and abstraction. Two worlds and, within each, three stages of a cognate cycle.

In the first cycle, the first age is that of brutish men against bare nature, fearful of the gods who control their fate, understanding their destiny largely through religion. The second age is an age of clans, of alliances between houses, whose values are warfare, honor, and military prowess. The third is the age of the plebs, of equality and democracy, an age ruled by appetite rather than natural needs. For Vico, these were the ages of gods, or heroes, and of men.

In the second cycle of Western time, the "frightful religions" of the first age of the gods are paralleled by Christianity; the patrician alliances of the age of heroes are reflected in the feudal order of the Middle Ages; and, finally, the "natural law of the philosophers" heralds the third phase. Yet the mark of the beast is already visible in Vico's time—the first half of the eighteenth century—in the excessive skepticism and the overweening materialism, the emphasis on utility, the reliance (if Vico knew the word) on technology, the "servants of a science uninformed by conscience." Philosophy has replaced religion, and science has replaced philosophy; but science itself has become involved in the abstract pursuit of the design of nature, and not in the purposes of men, so that there are no directions for human conduct.

Is there no escape from this wheel of determinism? For Vico, the source of knowledge is the principle of *verum factum*—"the true (*verum*) and the made (*factum*) are convertible." Thus, the condition of knowing is that of making; one can understand only what one has created. The promise of escape from the cycle of fate, then, is the ability of men to *make* their own history. There cannot be an immanent unfolding of a telic design, a deceptive "cunning of reason," or a *marche générale* of a class, but the cooperative effort of men to consciously direct their lives. The escape from endless recurrence is the plunge into a new kind of history.

The thread leads us, inexorably, to Marx, who believed that men can make their own history, within the constraints of given historical possibilities. Marx begins with a double conception of human nature. There is, first, the natural or *generic* man, whose essence, or species-being, is biological: the need for food, clothing, shelter, procreation—the production and reproduction of the necessities of life. And there is also *historical* man, whose nature is *emergent*.

Through *techne*, man masters nature and, in the realization of this power, gains new needs, new wants, new powers in the growing consciousness of himself. History, thus, is open, and in leaping from the kingdom of necessity to the kingdom of freedom, man will become *superman*.[7]

In this historicist view, man is defined not by nature but by history, and history is the record of the successive plateaus of man's developing powers. The difficulty with this view is that it cannot account for our continuing appreciation of the past, nor for the renewed use we make of it. If one believes that a specific historical substructure shapes the culture of an age (and what is historical materialism without that belief?), then how does one account for the quality of Greek art and thought, compared to that of today, and the persistence of the poetry the Greeks wrote and the philosophical questions they asked as relevant modes today? To say, as Marx did, that such thought represents the precocious childhood of the human race which we seek to reproduce "on a higher plane" (in other words, that thought has "evolved") begs every question.

The historicist answer is a conceit. Antigone is no child, and her keening over the body of her dead brother is not an emotion of the childhood of the race. Nor is the contemporary tale of Nadezhda Mandelstam, searching for the body of her dead husband (the Russian poet Osip Mandelstam, who disappeared in Stalin's concentration camps) in order to bury him properly, a case of precocity "on a higher plane."

There is something wrong, then, with the Marxian distinction. Yet the facts of history and change, the emergence of new powers, are real. I would revise Marx's answer this way. Man's powers are enlarged by *techne*. We can make more and more things: we do change nature. There is in social structure (the techno-economic order) a principle of linear change and cumulation. It is reflected in the ideas of productivity, technical efficiency, and functional rationality—and these rules guide us in the employment of resources,

---

[7] As Trotsky grandiloquently concludes in *Literature and Revolution*: "Man will become immeasurably stronger, wiser and subtler; his body will become more harmonized, his movements more rhythmic, his voice more musical. The forms of life will become dynamically dramatic. The average human type will rise to the heights of an Aristotle, a Goethe, or a Marx. And above this ridge new peaks will rise." See Leon Trotsky, *Literature and Revolution* (New York: Russell and Russell, repr. ed., 1957), p. 256.

within the given value system of the society. To the extent that man becomes more and more independent of nature, he has the means to construct the kind of society he wants.

But in culture there is no cumulation, but rather a *ricorso* to the primordial questions which confront all men in all times and places and which derive from the finiteness of the human condition and the tensions generated by the aspiration, constantly, to reach *beyond*. These are the existential questions which confront all human beings in the consciousness of history: how one meets death, the nature of loyalty and obligation, the character of tragedy, the meaning of courage, and the redemptiveness of love or communion. The answers will differ, but the questions are always the same.[8]

The principle of culture is thus that of a constant returning—not in its forms, but in its concerns—to the essential modalities that derive from the finitude of human existence. As Reinhold Niebuhr remarked: "There is therefore progress in human history; but it is the progress of all human potencies, both for good and evil."

What, then, are the guides to human conduct? They cannot be in nature, for nature is only a set of physical constraints at one extreme and existential questions at the other, between which man threads his way without any maps. It cannot be history, for history has no *telos* but is only instrumental, the expansion of man's powers over nature. There is, then the unfashionable, traditional answer: religion, not as a social "projection" of man into an external emblem, but as a transcendental conception that is outside man, yet relates man to something beyond himself.

No known society, as Max Weber observed, exists without some conception of experience which we would call religious. Every society, in the words of Talcott Parsons, "possesses some conceptions of a supernatural order, or spirits, gods or impersonal forces which are different from and in some sense superior to those forces conceived as governing ordinary 'natural' events, and whose nature and activities somehow give meaning to the unusual, the frustrating and the rationally impenetrable aspects of experience. . . . Religion is as much a human universal as language. . . ."[9]

---

[8] To that extent, the questions are tragedy and the answers are comedy. As that wise philosopher Groucho Marx once observed, it is easier to do tragedy than comedy, for all men cry at the same things, but laugh at different ones.

[9] Max Weber, *The Sociology of Religion*, trans. Ephraim Fischoff (Boston: Beacon Press, 1963), pp. xxvii–xxviii.

In the last 100 years the force of religion has diminished. At the dawn of human consciousness, religion was the major prism of man's cosmology, his sole way. almost, of explaining the world. Through ritual, the mechanism for binding shared sentiments, religion was the means of achieving social solidarity. Thus religion, as idea and institution, enveloped the whole of one's life in traditional society. But in modern society that life space has shrunk enormously. Religion found its central anchorage, revelation, undermined by rationalism, and the central core of its beliefs "demythologized" into history. What remained valid in orthodox religion—its tough-minded view of human nature, its view of man as *homo duplex*, the creature of at once both murderous aggression and the search for harmony—is too bleak a view for the utopianism that has burnished modern culture.

There has been a double process of decay. On the institutional level there has been *secularization*, or the shrinking of the institutional authority and role of religion as a mode of community. On the cultural level there has been *profanation*, the attenuation of a theodicy as providing a set of meanings to explain man's relation to the beyond. For Durkheim, ". . . the idea of the sacred is always and everywhere separated from the idea of the profane in the thought of men, and since we picture a sort of logical chasm between the two, the mind irresistibly refuses to allow the corresponding things to be confounded, or even merely put in contact with each other."[10]

What is surprising about Durkheim's conception is how little it seems to apply to modern life, particularly in the cultural sphere. For if there is one central psychological fact about modernist culture, it resides in the phrase "nothing sacred." One can argue that an impulse to *transgress* itself establishes the existence of worlds apart, but while the idea of transgression may have seemed daring in the nineteenth century, there are today almost no taboos left to transgress.

We are now confronted, wrote the German philosopher Eduard Spranger, with the final religious question: "What happens when in the innermost heart of a man every value certainly is lacking. In this lies the complete renunciation of the religious attitude. . . . Anyone who can no longer call a God his own gives himself over to the devil. And his essence is not real value indifference but a value

---

[10] Émile Durkheim, *The Elementary Forms of Religious Life* (New York: Free Press, 1965), p. 55.

reversal. Only if someone could say: 'there exists no genuine value,' could irreligion have taken entire possession of him. But no such man exists."

Where religions fail, cults appear. This situation is the reverse of early Christian history, when the new coherent religion competed with the multiple cults and drove them out because it had the superior strength of a theology and an organization. But when theology erodes and organization crumbles, when the institutional framework of religion begins to break up, the search for a direct experience which people can feel to be religious facilitates the rise of cults.

A cult differs from a formal religion in many significant ways. It is in the nature of a cult to claim some esoteric knowledge which had been submerged (or repressed by orthodoxy) for a long time but has now suddenly been illuminated. There is often some heterodox figure, mocked or scorned by the orthodox, who presents these new teachings. There are communal rites which often permit or spur an individual to act out impulses that had hitherto been repressed. In the cult, one feels as though one were exploring novel or hitherto tabooed modes of conduct. What defines a cult, therefore, is its implicit emphasis on magic rather than theology, on the personal tie to a guru or to the group, rather than to an institution or a creed. Its hunger is a hunger for ritual, and myth.

Will all this lead to a "new reformation"? Analogies are always tempting but deceptive. The Reformation—if one follows Erikson in his psychological interpretation—was not only an effort to break up corrupt institutions, but also the search of the son for a direct relation to the father, without mediation of the Church. The new cultic religiosity makes a distinction between personal faith and a cumulative historical tradition. The emphasis of the "new reformation" is on personal experience and personal faith unrelated to the past. Yet can such experience and faith have meaning without some tie to others—fathers—who have gone through the same vicissitudes? Can a faith be simply, naively, created anew, without memory?

What is being sought today, in the phrase of Alexander Mitscherlich, is a "society without fathers." The rejection of authority has come to mean the rejection of any notion of parent other than the peer group itself. Yet one wonders whether such a society is theologically or even psychologically possible. Religious belief, as Clifford Geertz writes, "involves not a Baconian induction from everyday experience—for then we should all be agnostics—but rather a prior acceptance of authority which transforms that experience." If the peer group of the cult is substituted for the larger society, then we are once more enclosed in the Durkheimian circle, shrunken as it may now be, with its fatal enthronement of idolatry.

Despite the shambles of modern culture, some religious answer surely will be forthcoming, for religion is not (or no longer) a "property" of society in the Durkheimian sense. It is a constitutive part of man's consciousness: the cognitive search for the pattern of the "general order" of existence; the affective need to establish rituals and to make such conceptions sacred; the primordial need for relatedness to some others, or to a set of meanings which will establish a transcendent response to the self; and the existential need to confront the finalities of suffering and death.

As Max Scheler said: "Since the religious act is an essential endowment of the human mind and soul, there can be no question whether this or that man performs it. . . . This law stands: every finite spirit believes either in God or in idols." Max Weber, who agreed with these formulations, stated that the answer could only be a personal decision, at once arbitrary and unconditional. Given the nature of contemporary political religions, and the claims of "the possessed" for final truths, the real difficulty, I must add, is not the posing of the alternatives but the question of who is God and who is the Devil.

As Weber has shown, religion, at crucial junctures of history, is sometimes the most revolutionary of all forces. When traditions and institutions become rigidified and oppressive, or when the discordance of voices and the babble of contradictory beliefs become intolerable, men seek for new answers. And religion, because it seeks living meanings at the deepest level of being, becomes the most forward response. In these circumstances, we look for new prophets. Prophecy breaks down ritualistic conservatism when it has lost all meaning, and prophecy provides a new gestalt when there have been too many meanings. The prophet confronts both the priest, whose only claim is the authority of the past, and the mystagogue who derives his power from the manipulation of magic as a means of salvation.

And yet, we may be looking in the wrong direction for signs. For Weber, prophecy is charismatic, since it derives from the personal qualities of the prophet, who is able to draw upon sources of grace from the *aussertägliche* (extramundane) world. And such a revolutionary force necessarily had to be charismatic because the prophets, like Hegel's "world-historical figures," had to be strong enough in their own persons to break the sanctity of tradition, or the cake of custom which encrusted the past. But such a prophet today, to employ an old Russian proverb, would be knocking down an open door. Who today defends tradition? And where is the power of the past to hold back any tides of the new?

There well may be a double answer. If one of the sources of despair lies in the existential questions, we can face them perhaps not by looking forward but by looking back. Human culture is a creation of men, the construction of a world to maintain *continuity*, to maintain the "un-animal" life. Animals seeing others die do not imagine it of themselves; people alone know their fate, and create rituals not just to ward off mortality but to maintain a "consciousness of kind" which is a mediation of fate. In this sense, religion is the awareness of a moment of transcendence, the passage out of the past, from which one has to come (and to which one is bound), to a new conception of the self as a moral agent, freely accepting the past (rather than just being shaped by it), and returning to tradition in order to maintain the continuity of moral meanings.

In every society, there are rites of incorporation and rites of release. The problem in modern society is that release itself has gone so far as to be without bounds. The difficulty with the new cults is that while their impulses are religious, in that they seek for some new meaning of the sacred, their rites are still largely ones of release. What I think the deeper currents of meaning are calling for is some new rite of incorporation, signifying membership in a community that has links with the past as well as the future. Yet as Goethe once remarked, "Was du ererbt von deinen Vätern hat, erwirb es, um es zu besitzen." (If you are to possess what you inherited from your forefathers, you must first earn it.)[11]

To this extent, a religion of incorporation is a redemptive process whereby individuals seek to discharge their obligations that derive from the moral imperatives of their community: the debts incurred

---

[11] In the modernist canon, this came to read: If you are to possess what you inherited from your fathers, you must first destroy it. See, for example, "Futurist Manifesto," in *Futurism*, ed. Joshua Taylor (New York: Museum of Modern Art, 1961).

in being nurtured, the debts to the institutions that maintain moral awareness. Religion, then, necessarily involves the mutual redemption of fathers and sons. It involves the acknowledgment, in Yeats's phrase, of "the blessed who can bless," of the laying on of hands in the continuity of generations.

But such a religious commitment involves a challenge to the modern liberal temper. The answers which a liberal temper seeks are ethical ones. The difficulty of a commitment to ethics alone is that it dissolves the particular—the primordial ties of father and son, or of individual and tribe—into the universal. Given what we know about the nature of man, the dream of the Enlightenment to make mankind *one*—its dream of Reason—is futile; those who live in the continuity of generations necessarily must live in the parochial identities that sustain them. Yet to be parochial alone is to be sectarian, and to lose the ties to other men, other knowledge, other faiths; to be cosmopolitan alone is to be rootless. One, then, necessarily lives in the tension between the particular and the universal, and accepts that painful double bind of necessity.

And finally, we have to live along a different axis as well: to move from the temporal (the past, present, and future which so obsess us) to the spatial; to see the world as it should be, as a space of "allotted portions," as the separation of realms. To understand the transcendent, man requires a sense of the sacred. To remake nature, man can invade the profane. But if there is no separation of realms, if the sacred is destroyed, then we are left with the shambles of appetite and self-interest and the destruction of the moral circle which engirds mankind. Can we—must we not—reestablish that which is sacred and that which is profane?

PART TWO

THE DILEMMAS OF

THE POLITY

An Introductory Note:
From the Culture
to the Polity

IN THE DISJUNCTION of realms, there are not only different rhythms in the movement of culture, polity, and social structure, but different time-scales as well. Despite the evanescence of fads, changes in culture and religion—what we might, in contemporary terms, describe as changes in sensibility and moral temper—do work themselves out over long historical time-frames. These changes, as I have argued, are not subject to manipulation or social intervention, since they derive from shared experiences and become ritualized, or are expressed in symbolic terms which have strong compelling power and therefore take a long time to fade or to be replaced by new sentiments. It took almost 300 years for Christianity to become established in the Roman Empire, and as Gibbon remarked of the conversion of Constantine, Rome then passed into an intolerable phase of its history, a phase that lasted for 250 years.

The polity is another dimension entirely. If religion and culture seek to establish ultimate meanings, the polity has to grapple with the mundane problems of everyday life. It must establish the norms of justice, and enforce claims and rights. It sets forth the rules of exchange and provides for the day-to-day security of its citizens. Inevitably, it is both an arena for contending parties and an independent force—the control system of the society in its management of foreign policy, its stabilization of the monetary system, and, increasingly, its direction of the economy as a whole.

It is these new, enlarged functions that give rise to a set of "contradictions" within the society that are different from the cultural ones. The political contradictions derive from the fact that liberal society was originally set up—in its ethos, laws, and reward systems —to promote *individual ends*, yet has now become an interdependent economy that must stipulate *collective goals*. This situation is complicated by the fact that sometimes these collectivities are subgroups of the society, and sometimes the collectivity is the entire society itself. In more mundane terms, the society must devote itself more and more to the production of public goods at the expense of private goods, and to the nurturing of a public rather than a private sector. In the crucial area of equality, the society increasingly must pay heed to group (rather than individual) rights and redress.

How these new tasks are met—if they can be met—affects everyone's immediate life. If the society is unmanageable and if the institutions are inflexible and unresponsive, then the disintegrative tendencies—polarization in some conditions, fragmentation in others—become intensified. If the society can respond, through a new public philosophy that commands respect and through institutions that work, then there may be time for the other, slower processes of cultural reconstruction to take hold.

In the second part of this book, I deal, first, with the immediate events of the last 25 years and a projection of the next 25, in order to single out the structural from the transitory elements that are responsible for societal instability. In the second essay, I return to the major cultural theme of hedonism in a political context, and I then propose some means of reconciling political liberalism, as a crucial value for a just modern society, with the necessary communal features of societal management, an idea which I call the *public household*.

Unstable America: Transitory and Permanent Factors in a National Crisis

I

FOR ANYONE considering the State of the Union at the opening of the 1960s, a question about the sources of political and social instability would have seemed an improbable one. The United States was then seemingly at the height of its powers. The Communist world, after the 1956–1957 convulsions in Poland and Hungary, was apparently falling into disarray. Domestically, there had been eight years of relatively high prosperity at stable prices. The threat of radical-right extremism, embodied by Senator Joseph R. McCarthy, had faded away. The social justice movement for the blacks was under way, beginning with the epochal Supreme Court decision of 1954 (*Brown* v. *Board of Education*), which had legitimated the black claim for integration; and the Eisenhower administration itself had taken the highly symbolic step of sending federal troops into a Southern community (Little Rock, Arkansas) to protect the right of black children to enter white schools. Like the public personality of President Eisenhower himself, the country seemed bland, self-assured, and eager to advance the broad, if platitudinous, conceptions of universalism in foreign affairs and progress at home.

There were some small clouds on the horizon. Economic growth had slowed down, so that by the end of the 1950s it was no longer rising at a rate sufficient to match the increases in the labor force and in productivity. From 1953 to 1960, the labor force grew at a rate of 1.5 percent a year, while productivity was rising at a rate of 3.2 percent. It would have required a growth in GNP of about 4.5 percent to provide the necessary number of jobs to meet these growths; but output, which had been as high as 5.2 percent per year between 1947 and 1953, slowed to 2.4 percent between 1953 and 1960, and the result was an increase in unemployment. By the end of the decade, unemployment had risen to more than 6 percent of the labor force. But because the greater number of the unemployed were black or unskilled, with little means for becoming politically effective, the unemployment situation, for the while, was ignored. Toward the end of his term, President Eisenhower began running a large budget deficit to increase demand, but the effort did not reach a growing number of "hard-core" unemployed.

In the foreign field, the victory of Fidel Castro in Cuba, and the inability to reach an accord with him (a matter as much the fault of Castro as of the fumbling State Department), gave rise to apprehensions about a possible Soviet foothold in the western hemisphere. And the United States began to organize clandestine efforts to overthrow him.

The paradox of the Kennedy administration was that its very élan and activism—the need to seem and to be effective—both in the foreign field and at home, stimulated and unleashed the forces of turbulence which racked the United States in the 1960s. In foreign affairs there was, first, the disaster at the Bay of Pigs—the humiliation of American power and a new raising of the question of American will. At Vienna, Khrushchev throught he had taken the measure of John F. Kennedy and was emboldened to place missiles in Cuba, a confrontation from which he backed down, thereby restoring Kennedy's credit. In Vietnam, where Eisenhower had shied away from large-scale commitments (despite the pressure of Secretary of State John Foster Dulles and Chief of Staff Radford), Kennedy made the fateful decision, after the fall of Diem, to step up American activity in the field and to move American advisors and weapons into direct action.

In the domestic field, the Kennedy administration began a helter-skelter effort to improve the lot of the poor and the blacks; but one of the paradoxical consequences of those efforts, notably in the poverty program, was to provide a large number of jobs and to create small political bases and machines for activists who would use their positions to organize community-action groups and to increase po-litical agitation in the black and poor communities. A revolutionary movement always has the problem of how to finance its activities and to provide time for functionaries to ply their agitation.[1] One of the astonishing effects of the Kennedy (and Johnson) "War on Pov-erty" was to facilitate the growth of a movement which would, in part, mount political pressure, if not a political war, on the adminis-tration itself.

It would be absurd to assume that such agitation and turbulence might not otherwise have come to the fore. The classic illustration of the trajectory of expectations, first laid down by Tocqueville and repeated tediously since then by social scientists, tells us that no society which promises justice and, having admitted the legitimacy of the claims, slowly begins to open the way, can then expect to ride out the consequent whirlwind in a comfortable fashion. But along with the rising tumult of the blacks and the disadvantaged came an ambiguous war; and the combination of the two, which reinforced each other, led to rising domestic violence, the alienation of youth, and the growing challenge to the legitimacy of the system among the intelligentsia and the leadership cadres of the young, all of which have brought into question the very stability of the system itself.

It would be equally foolish to assume that immediate and mani-fest causes, important as they are, can wholly disorient a society as large and powerful as the United States. Underneath, there have occurred upheavals, sociological and technological, which have been reworking the social structure of the society. These four changes—the simultaneous creation of an urban society, a national polity, a communal society, and a post-industrial world—will out-last the immediate vicissitudes and continue to create deeper up-heavals and tensions in the society. And beyond these structural changes in the society lie three other areas of difficulty which pro-foundly affect the future of the United States: the relation of de-mocracy to empire, and the question of whether any democracy can maintain an imperial role; the participation revolution, with its challenge to technocratic and meritocratic modes of decision mak-

---

[1] Both Huey Newton and Bobby Seale, the founders of the Black Panther Party, were employed in the poverty program and wrote the party's manifestos, and conducted their early activities, while on the government payroll.

ing; and a profound change in the culture, with the development of a fundamentally anti-rational and anti-intellectual bias in the arts and in the modes of experience and sensibility.

Any assessment of the future of the United States would have to deal with these three dimensions: the immediate political and social upheavals, the structural changes, and the fundamental questions of value and cultural choices. Within these confines I can only be schematic about each. And if one is to consider these questions in the light of the problem of social and political instability, one must also turn, at first, to the consideration, at the level of sociological theory, of those factors which precipitate instability and revolution (or counter-revolution) in a society.

SOURCES OF INSTABILITY

The key question for any political system—this is the triumph of Max Weber over Marx in contemporary social thought—is the legitimacy of the system. As S. M. Lipset has written:

Legitimacy involves the capacity of the system to engender and maintain the belief that the existing political institutions are the most appropriate ones for the society. The extent to which contemporary democratic political systems are legitimate depends in large measure upon the ways in which the key issues which have historically divided the society have been resolved.

While effectiveness is primarily instrumental, legitimacy is evaluative. Groups regard a political system as legitimate or illegitimate according to the way in which its values fit with theirs.[2]

If one looks at Western political society in the twentieth century, one can identify at least seven factors which, in varying combinations, have resulted in the social instability of the society and the consequent loss of legitimacy for the political system.

(1) *The existence of an "insoluble" problem.* The unemployment problem of the 1930s was regarded by most societies as insoluble. Clearly few of the bourgeois democratic regimes knew what to do to reverse the Depression. Every Western society was plunged into crisis at the time. It was only the acceptance of unorthodox

[2] S. M. Lipset, *Political Man* (Garden City, N.Y.: Doubleday, 1960), p. 77.

economic policies that permitted these economies to recover. The Depression, clearly, was one of the forces conducive to fascism in the 1930s.

(2) *The existence of a parliamentary impasse.* In Italy, Portugal, and Spain, in the 1920s and 1930s, the continuation of a parliamentary impasse, created by the polarization of forces in the society, impeded any effective government and contributed to a sense of helplessness in the populace which was crystallized either in mob action, an authoritarian dictator, or a military coup.

(3) *The growth of private violence.* In Germany, and in other countries, the creation of private "armies" and the growth of open street violence, uncontrolled by the government, led to the breakdown of authority.

(4) *The disjunction of sectors.* Rapid industrialization in some areas and a large-scale agricultural lag in others have led to continuing instability.

(5) *Multi-racial or multi-tribal conflicts.* Obvious sources of instability have been the conflicts in India, between Hindu and Muslim before partition, and subsequently among different language groups; in Nigeria, between the regions representing different tribes; in Belgium, between Flemish and Walloons; in Canada, between English and French; and so forth.

(6) *The alienation of the intelligentsia.* The cultural elites carry the integrative symbols of the society, and the disenchantment of these groups has been a feature of almost every revolutionary situation. The defeat of Batista, in large measure, arose from the opposition of the middle classes in Cuban society to the regime.

(7) *Humiliation in war.* A crushing defeat often cracks a political system, as it did Wilhelminian Germany and czarist Russia, but a partial defeat (or one construed as humiliating) can be just as disintegrating. The defeat of Russia by Japan in 1905, the first instance of an Occidental power losing to an Oriental nation since the invasions of Genghis Khan and Tamerlane, represented a great psychological humiliation for the country. In Latin America, the first revolution since the Mexican overthrow of the aging dictator Profirio Díaz (in 1910) came only in 1952, with the Bolivian national revolution—despite the previous rise of socialist, Communist, populist, and *indigenista* movements between the two World Wars and during the Depression. It came after the defeat of the country in the Chaco War, a defeat which shattered the standard expectations

and values of the society and led the mass of young middle-class whites and *cholos* completely to reject traditional politics and parties.

Such a list is not exhaustive, but it does sum up the major political experience of the century. Within that framework, what can we say about the United States and, more specifically, about the factors which one can identify as the sources of instability and strain—the Vietnam war, the alienation of youth, the rancor of the blacks, and the multiplicity of social problems which derive from the structural changes in the society? Which of these are "soluble," and under what conditions? Which have a potential for further strain?

THE BREAKUP OF CONSENSUS

Let us begin with the overt and visible factors. The United States in the 1950s was a mobilized society. It was mobilized, primarily, to meet the threat of international Communism. After an initial demobilization in 1946–1947, there came a rapid buildup of arms. The Korean war brought about a vast expansion of conventional armed forces. NATO and SEATO extended these arms, under a presumed nuclear shield, around the world; for the first time in American history a permanent military establishment had been created. Science, in considerable measure, was mobilized as well. The vast revolutions in military technology—the creation of hydrogen bombs, nuclear missiles, new means of propulsion of warheads—all went hand in hand with the vast expansion of research and development and the tying-in of research institutions and universities to government.

Mobilizing a society to meet an external threat, where that threat can be unambiguously defined, unifies a country. Internal divisions are minimized or glossed over, compromises are made, and politics becomes focused on external affairs. It is striking to recall that in the 1930s the United States was riven by sharp labor struggles which in their intensity approached the classical Marxist conceptions of naked class division. Yet when World War II broke out, these divisions were subordinated to the national effort and labor was brought into the government, while industrial relations went from conflict to accommodation. In the 1950s the threat of an aggressive Communism, particularly after the Eastern European purge trials, the seizure of Czechoslovakia (and the defenestration of Masaryk), and the encirclement of Berlin, brought the liberal community to the support of the government against that threat.

By the end of the 1950s, the situation had changed. International Communism was no longer a monolith. Evil no longer seemed unambiguous. Different kinds of Communism had come to the fore. The United States was in the quixotic position of providing aid to Tito and even to Gomulka. If the Soviet Union was still expansionist, that aggressiveness was more and more defined in traditional great-power terms rather than as ideological fervor. The moralism which had animated American foreign policy for a decade, particularly in the rhetoric of John Foster Dulles, had become attenuated. Ironically, moralism, a feature of the American style, was increasingly taken over by the opponents of the society, the New Left, who began to characterize the United States in the same "totalistic" terms (as evil, sick, and bankrupt) that the United States had previously used to characterize its political enemy, and who began to picture American society itself by such monolithic terms as "the System."

The breakup of the Communist world thus made it difficult to sustain a mobilized posture on ideological grounds. The emergence of such figures as Castro and Ho Chi Minh provided ready symbols for the latent revolutionary romanticism of youth to respond to. Castro, along with Ché, had shown that the Leninist myth of a handful of dedicated revolutionaries toppling a society could, like progressive revelation, recur in a big-power world. Despite the fact that peasant uprisings in North Vietnam had been suppressed, as in 1956, and dissident radicals had been murdered, "Uncle Ho" became for many the symbol of purity and selflessness, an idealistic avuncular figure in a harsh and impersonal world.

THE TENSION OF INCLUSION

Domestically the most immediate point of strain in American society was race. The militancy of the blacks, the fact of riot, the threat of further strife became pervasive. How did it all come about?

The starting point for any social inquiry is: Why now, not then; why here, not there? The primary clue to the changing political role of the American black is a remarkable demographic shift. In 1910, about 90 percent of the blacks in the United States lived in the South. As late as 1950, 68 percent still lived there. But 1960 was the "dividing year"; at that point half the black population was in the North. The balance shifted strongly during the 1960s.

It was not only that blacks had been leaving the South; they had become urbanized as well. In 1910, just about three-fourths of the blacks lived in rural areas; by 1960, almost three-fourths lived in cities. In 1960, in fact, for the first time in American history, American blacks had become *more urban* than whites.

A significant new pattern was developing as well—the concentration of blacks in a few major cities. Thus, in 1960, there were over 1 million blacks in New York City, about 890,000 in Chicago, 670,000 in Philadelphia, 560,000 in Detroit, and more than 335,000 in Los Angeles. By contrast, the largest southern concentrations were 215,000 blacks in Houston and 186,000 in Atlanta.

These concentrations went together with another social development—the movement, sometimes a flight, of the white population to the suburbs. This meant that, within the central city limits, the Negro population began to form a significant proportion of the whole. Perhaps symbolic of the change is the fact that, by the mid-1960s, blacks constituted more than 55 percent of the population of Washington, D.C., the nation's capital.

What this population density and social weight did was to give the black community the possibility of political leverage which a unified polity could exploit effectively. This developing political power is the important background reason why the blacks became able to demand, more successfully than before, a change in the patterns of power.

This changing demographic and political map allows us to see how the black community came to mobilize effective social power. But by itself it does not explain the trajectory of the "civil rights revolution," the emergent black nationalism, or the temper of the black militants.

The turning point in the civil rights revolution was, clearly, the Supreme Court decision in May 1954 which struck down the principle of segregation in public schools. In so doing, the Court emphasized the symbol of the term *equality* as the overriding value in judging social change. It stated that blacks should have full and equal access to public facilities and services in the nation. But there were two further sociological consequences of this decision. One was the fact that the highest court in the land had *legitimated* the demands of the blacks; the second was that the moral initiative had passed into their hands. The burden of proof was now no longer on the blacks but on the whites.

What the Court had done was to admit the historic injustices done to the blacks (specifically, an 1883 Supreme Court action declaring illegal the post-Civil War legislation of Congress which, at that time, had granted full civil rights to blacks; that court action had opened the way to "Jim Crow," or segregation laws by southern states). In so doing, the Court made it difficult for any person or group to oppose the demands of the blacks even when some of these, by previous standards, might be considered "extreme" (such as preference in admission to schools, or preference in hiring). When a nation has publicly admitted moral guilt, it is difficult to say no to those it has offended. And when a nation admits moral guilt but goes slow in restitution, then the explosive mixture becomes even more inflammable.

The chief dilemma, of course, is the definition of "slow." When expectations of change rise rapidly, the pressure of hope will inevitably outstrip the reality. Just as inevitably, there will be a disjunction between objective change and the subjective assessment of change. Many blacks, for example, claimed that conditions for them had "worsened." But what they clearly meant was that they were not where they expected to be. A conservative measures social change by the distance from the past; a revolutionist from some mark in the future.

The record shows that a number of distinct gains were registered. The largest gains were made by the black middle class. In 1960, 36 percent of the black males and 63 percent of whites over 25 years of age had completed high school; by 1966 the figures were 53 percent for black and 73 percent for white males. In higher education, in 1960, 3.9 percent of black males and 15.7 percent of whites had completed college. In 1966, 7.4 percent of black males and 17.9 percent of whites had completed college, an increase of nearly 90 percent in black college graduates over the period.

The factors we have enumerated involve changing demographic and political weights and the legitimation of demands. To this one has to add, of course, a major consideration regarding any social movement—the nature of its leadership. The rising new leadership of the blacks was young, militant, and aggressive. In this there is a curious psychological paradox, in that a second generation which has *not* experienced the kind of direct humiliation inflicted on its elders—and which has often (as in the case of literary intellectuals) received special largesse—is psychologically more assertive and more outspoken and extreme. There are several intertwined reasons for this. The elders, facing more difficult circumstances, had to be more accommodating in order to achieve gains, and in the process often acquired an inner stoicism; the young can be more extreme because there are fewer "penalties" and, indeed, more rewards in acting out their anger. Since the overall society is, in principle, receptive to change, individuals can more easily outbid one another in being more "left" and more extreme. More important, perhaps, in the effort to achieve an internal cohesion and a group identity, the assertive emphases on nationality, on a common past, and on the positive features of Negro life become necessary means of achieving a sense of psychic independence. And raucous as this process may make people, it is a necessary one for any group which seeks to achieve a coherent sense of itself as a group.

And yet, the major thrust of the blacks in American life, in politics and in economic life, has not been an effort to overthrow the society, but an effort to change the class balance. It has been a drive for inclusion, paced by a cultural and psychological mood which emphasized revolutionary rhetoric. By the 1970s that revolutionary rhetoric had subsided. In the 1960s, however, it was far from clear that it would.

THE CRISIS IN CREDIBILITY

A sense of disorientation became widespread in the United States in the 1960s. The rapidity of social change is always unsettling to large masses of the population, and the sense of rapid social change, technological and sociological, was perceived everywhere. To see if the mood was transient or not, it is more useful not to go to the areas of tumult, which inevitably reveal alienation, but to the *traditional* sectors of society. These—most especially religion—are the source of stability in any culture. Now, while interpretation of polls is notoriously difficult, they can be a useful indicator of change in attitudes, if the same question is asked over a period of time. At various intervals from 1957 to 1968 the Gallup Poll asked this question: "At the present time, do you think religion as a whole is increasing its influence on American life, or losing its influence?" What is striking, of course, is that this shift of mood parallels the

The Influence of Religion

	LOSING	INCREASING	SAME
April 1957			
National Sample	14%	69%	10%
Protestant	17	66	10
Catholic	7	79	8
April 1962			
National	31	45	17
April 1965			
National	45	33	13
April 1967			
National	57	23	14
Protestant	60	21	13
Catholic	48	31	16
April 1968			
National	67	19	8
Protestant	69	17	8
Catholic	61	24	8

years of the Kennedy and Johnson administrations, the years of the New Frontier and the Great Society. The singular quality of the New Frontier was its sense of promise, symbolized in the vibrant words of the Kennedy inaugural speech and in the ardor that characterized the arrival of a "new" generation in politics.

How does one account for the change of mood in this decade? One can only be schematic, and indicate four factors:

(1) *The multiplicity of social problems.* The remarkable performance of American industry (and the psychological lift occasioned by the fact that there was no economic depression after the war, though one had been widely forecast by economists) seemed to indicate that economic growth would, in time, solve all social problems. The term "affluent society," as used by J. K. Galbraith, seemed to affirm this possibility.

The other side of Galbraith's argument, that public squalor was increasing while personal consumption was rising, was for a long time neglected. It was the rising sense of public squalor which in large measure became responsible for the growing sense of dismay. The Kennedy administration turned its eyes more readily than the previous Republican administration to domestic affairs. It sought to make a record in the domestic field. But that very effort itself fo-

cused public attention on questions that previously had been ignored: poverty, housing, education, medical care, urban sprawl, environmental pollution, and the like. Whether such problems are
"solvable" is moot. But what is clear is that the rapidly heightened
awareness of these multiple social questions was instrumental in
creating a sense of unease in the society.

(2) *The black riots and crime.* From 1963 to 1967 there were
five "hot summers" in which, each year, there was a crescendo of
rioting that, beginning in the South, passed quickly to the North, so
that in Watts, Detroit, Newark, and Washington, D.C., whole sections of each city went up in flames. The Kerner Commission reports showed that *none* of these riots was organized. In each instance, a small event, usually an instance of police brutality, or
alleged police brutality, sparked wild rumors, and the tinderbox
exploded. As in any social movement, wild, episodic, rampaging
behavior signals a first phase of action. The next phase is an effort to
create more disciplined militant actions. In the black communities
many contradictory currents were at work. There was black nationalism, which sought to build distinctive black institutions, and
made militant demands for resources toward those goals. But there
were also movements, such as the Black Panthers, which emphasized guerrilla tactics and which were ready to link up with white
radical movements.[3]

The growth of black militancy itself created covert white "back-
lashes," a mood expressed most vividly, in the Wallace movement.
Typically, the support for George Wallace in the North came
mainly from blue-collar workers, and the ethnic groups in which
they predominate. Adjacent in status, to the blacks, they felt the
most threatened. In becoming upwardly mobile, these workers had
bought their own homes in their neighborhoods, and they felt that
these status gains were threatened by the blacks.

---

[3] After 1970 the Panthers split. One faction, led by Eldridge Cleaver, advocated
insurrectionary tactics, and Cleaver himself fled to Algeria to organize such actions
from abroad. The other faction, led by Newton and Seale, opted for political action
within the system and to build institutions within the black community.

Any extreme movement, at a crucial juncture, always faces such choices. The
trajectory of militancy forces a movement to more and more extreme actions, in
order to maintain zeal and cohesion. Yet if the situation is not "ripe" for revolutionary
action, the movement is threatened by disintegration unless it makes the necessary
volte-face and begins to work within the system. For a discussion of the parallel
problem that confronted SDS and the extremist student movements, see my essay,
"Columbia and the New Left," in *The Public Interest*, no. 13 (Fall 1968): 61–101.

Many of these fears were summed up in the phrase "law and order," and were focused principally on crime. To what extent the amount of crime actually increased is difficult to determine. The FBI crime index is notoriously unreliable and statistically inadequate. Though we cannot measure the actual increases in the extent of crime, it is clear that a disproportionate number of crimes have been committed by blacks. This, in itself, should occasion no surprise. Crime is a form of "unorganized" class struggle, and the lowest groups in the society have always committed a disproportionate number of crimes. What was in the past true of the Irish and the Italians is true of the blacks. But black crime is more "visible," because of the urban concentrations, and thus the degree of apprehension has risen very sharply.

(3) *The alienation of youth.* One can find many sources for the growing alienation of youth in any advanced industrial society. The common structural source, I believe, is the dropping of an "organizational harness" on youth, and at an earlier and earlier age. The student resentments were, to simplify, the initial "class struggles" of the post-industrial society, just as the machine-wrecking movements of the period from 1815 to 1840 presaged the worker-employer class conflicts of industrial society.

There were, equally, some singular features. There was a striking change of cohort, a numerical increase of about 50 percent in the one decade, and a consequent sense of increased competition for place.[4] There was a reduction in the status of a college education. One generation earlier, going to college had still been a distinctive status feature. But in the elite schools, more than 85 percent of the graduates were going on to some postgraduate work, so that in these places the college became simply a way station. In the large public universities, to use Martin Meyerson's phrase, the "elect" became only the "electorate." And all this meant increasing pressure on the young. In secondary school there arose the anxiety: "Will I get into college? Will I get into a good college . . . ?" In college there was the question: "Can I get into graduate school . . . ?"

In a previous time, possessing a college degree was an assurance of place in society. Yet in the modern technological revolution, a

---

[4] From 1940 to 1950, there was no increase in the age cohort of 14 to 24, the number remaining at 27 million. From 1950 to 1960, the number also remained constant. But in the 1960s, reflecting the postwar baby boom, the numbers increased, like a tidal wave, to 40 million youngsters.

college degree is no longer the means of stepping on to the high plateau of society. Advancement involves a continual process of professional training and retraining in order to keep up with the new techniques and new knowledge being produced. In short, much of the alienation of the young was a reaction to the social revolution that had taken place in their own status.

(4) *The Vietnam war.* If there was any single element which was the catalyst of social tensions in the United States, and perhaps even in the world, it was the Vietnam war. The war was without parallel in American history. It was perceived as morally ambiguous, if not dubious, by a large portion, perhaps the majority, of the population. And in the conduct of the war there arose a critical problem of credibility which threatened the very legitimacy of the office of the presidency.

In most countries, there is a distinction between the nation and the administration in office. One can be opposed to a *government*, yet not call into question one's allegiance to the *nation*. In the United States, the distinction has never been necessary because the government reflected a broad consensus. Yet during the Vietnam war, the rejection of the government led many to reject the nation.

It began as a question of credibility. This question arose in the first instance because the official optimism of the Johnson administration (particularly during 1964 and 1965) was increasingly belied by events. The decisions to increase the number of troops (to a total of a half-million Americans), to bomb the North, and to refuse to negotiate were continually justified on the ground that "one more step" would move the United States to victory. To some extent, the personality of President Johnson was a factor, in that his secretiveness led to many deceptions. At one point the credibility of the Council of Economic Advisers as a source of economic data was imperiled because the president withheld from the council information on spending in Vietnam, and the public estimates of the council, in consequence, misled the business community.

But it was not a problem of credibility alone. There was the moral question of the relation of disproportionate means to the ends. The mass bombing, the defoliation of large areas, the resettlements of population, the large number of deaths, all raised crucial moral issues which the administration by and large avoided.

The final element in the *dégringolade* of the Johnson policies was the evident impotence of the military strategy. The bombing was highly ineffective. The "search-and-destroy" tactics extended the American lines and left the cities vulnerable to the stunning Tet offensive, which erupted simultaneously at almost 100 points. For the American right, this impotence was especially infuriating. It therefore demanded, as did General Curtis Lemay the vice-presidential candidate on the Wallace ticket in the 1968 election campaign, the extension of aerial bombing and the destruction of Haiphong, on the ground that only more massive action would win the war. Yet the administration did not pursue this line, for the reason that a further escalation from the American side would be matched by an equal escalation of North Vietnamese manpower and Soviet arms. But this very admission could only heighten the sense of a stalemate, and of American impotence.

For the young, the Vietnam war was the single most direct source of alienation. The rising draft calls increased anxiety about careers and the future. Service in the armed forces was regarded at best as a waste of years, at worst as an immoral complicity. Impotent themselves to affect the course of national policy—or so they thought—the students turned their fury against the university as a symbol of the society.

The war produced an estrangement of a large section of the future elite from the society. Whether that estrangement can be overcome is one of the large questions about the future strength—and will—of the United States as a great power.

THE STRUCTURAL REVOLUTIONS

The discussion of any society risks seduction by what is transient and tumultuous. Such issues engage our energies and our passions; they absorb us in the present. Some of these issues are consequential for the future; some blaze forth, yet quickly turn to dry ashes.

Any meaningful discussion of a society has to try to identify deeper, persistent elements which are the shaping forces of the society. These are in three realms: values, the legitimating elements of the society; culture, the repository of expressive symbolism and sensibility; and social structure, the set of social arrangements concerned with the distribution of persons in occupations and in the polity, and with the allocation of resources to meet stipulated social needs. In this essay, I shall concentrate on the deeper-running currents in social structure; necessarily, again, I have to be schematic.

Of the four major structural changes in the society, the first is the demographic transformation, the second, the creation of a national society, the third, the emergence of a communal society, and the fourth, the development of a post-industrial society. All these have been taking place almost simultaneously. It is the synchronic conjunction of these multiple revolutions which has generated so many strains in the society.

THE DEMOGRAPHIC TRANSFORMATION

From the end of World War II, to 1970 there were three major demographic changes in the United States. The first was a large population expansion, the second, the rapid urbanization of the country, and the third, the racial transformation of the central cities of the major urban areas.

In the decade from 1950 to 1960, almost 28 million persons were added to the population, a figure as large as the entire population increase in the *seven* decades from 1790 to 1860. From the end of World War II to 1970, the population went from 140 million to 200 million, an increase of more than 42 percent in less than a quarter of a century. Ninety million children were born; subtracting for deaths, the net increase was 60 million.

In the first half of the nineteenth century, the average increase of the population, per decade, was about 25 percent. The increases after World War II were about 20 percent a decade. Yet, sociologically, there were two crucial differences between the earlier and later periods. One was a *change of scale*. The population increase from 5 million to 7 million between 1800 and 1810 was a large one for the country in percentage terms. Yet the growth from 150 million to 180 million from 1950 to 1960, while smaller in percentage terms, represented an enormous change in scale. The second difference was a change in institutional structure. The early increases in population were largely segmental, in that the new units simply extended the chain of the society in different spatial directions. The new increases were *pyramidal*: they come on top of the existing population and added new interdependencies.

This concentrated population growth was compounded by an

extraordinary and largely unnoticed fact, a revolution in the area of agricultural productivity. From 1900 to the mid-1940s, agricultural productivity had increased fitfully at about a 2 percent rate. During World War II, largely under the stimulus of demand, but even more because of the new and extensive use of fertilizers and nitrates, productivity on the farm went up to about a 6–8 percent rate annually. As a result, more than 25 million persons left the farms in the quarter of a century and moved to the cities.[5]

In consequence of these demographic changes (plus the shrinkage in the number of coal miners), large sections of the center of the country, from the Dakotas down to west Texas, lost population. Families moved to the "rims" of the nation. Of the 3,000 counties in the United States, 1,000 lost population in the period from 1960 to 1970, and the gainers were largely the urban metropolitan centers on the coasts and on the Great Lakes.

A high-consumption society, built on a complex infrastructure, creates vast new demands for services, such as medical care, playgrounds, schools, and transportation. It has been estimated (by the New York Regional Plan Association, in 1968) that it takes $18,000 per person, as a capital cost, to provide infrastructure services—roads, sewerage, water, schools, housing, and so forth. More than 40 percent of the postwar population was under 20 years of age. The increase in this large cohort, plus the migrations impelled by the agricultural revolution, gives one some sense of the huge capital and other social costs that were required to absorb the large population changes in the quarter of a century after World War II.

If there was a population "explosion," there was also, so to speak, a population "implosion," an ingathering of the population into the metropolitan areas. By 1970 about 70 percent of the population lived in urban areas. (By 1980, 75 percent of the people in the United States will reside in urban areas. There will be 165 cities with a population of 100,000 or more, compared with 100 in 1960. As a corollary, the number of automobiles in use may rise from 59 million in 1960 to 120 million in 1980.) Within the central cities there were equally important shifts. From 1960 to 1966 there was an *absolute decline* in the white population in the central cities (by 0.3 percent); the white population of the suburbs increased 21.3 percent. In the same period, the nonwhite population in the cen-

[5] One consequence was the vast reduction in the number of black sharecroppers, from about 4 million to 500,000. And these, too, moved to the cities.

tral cities increased by 23.9 percent, and in the suburbs by 10.1 percent.

Even though the birthrate began to slow down after 1956, the expansion of the U.S. population has continued. For one reason, there were fewer spinsters. In 1950, about 15 percent of females had never married; two decades later, only 7 percent had stayed single. For another, there was an increase in immigration, particularly after the reform of the immigration law in 1965 to permit about 400,000 persons a year to enter legally. And, finally, because of the postwar boom, the base of the population itself expanded. Though the growth *rate* has slowed down, it is likely that by the year 2000 the U.S. population will reach about 280 million.

THE NATIONAL SOCIETY

In the quarter of a century after World War II, the United States became, for the first time, a national society. It had long been a "nation," in the sense of achieving a national identity and a national symbolism. But it is only in that period that, because of the revolution in communication and transportation, the United States became a national *society*—in the fundamental sense that changes taking place in one section of the society began to have an immediate and repercussive effect in all the others.

One can understand this transformation by comparing it with a previous change, namely the emergence of a national economy. Between 1910 and 1930, the United States became an effective national economy; but it had few institutional mechanisms to deal with an economy of that scope. In historical retrospect, the salient meaning of the New Deal was the creation of institutions to undergird and manage a national economy. What Franklin D. Roosevelt did was to match the scale of economic activities with a new political scale. Financial markets were regulated by an SEC; union activities and labor relations, by an NLRB; the flight of capital, by exchange controls and the abandonment of gold; the maintenance of employment, through the use of fiscal policies and government deficit financing.

The emergence of the national society after World War II posed social problems for which there have been no corresponding institutional mechanisms on a national scale. And one of the problems that have beset the polity is that the Kennedy, Johnson, and Nixon administrations singularly failed in the effort to create such mechanisms, particularly in the areas that enhance the quality of life—health, education, social opportunity, and recreation and land use.

There are three broad problems which one can identify as a consequence of the emergence of a national society.

First, there is the fact that social problems have become national in scope. The ease of migration throughout the country and the variability in conditions add burdens to particular areas. One can see this in the growth of welfare rolls in New York City. In 1959, there were 240,000 persons on welfare, at a cost of $325 million dollars. By 1968, almost 1 million persons were on welfare, at a cost of $1.7 billion. Without national standards, New York must carry the burdens of a large part of the country.

Second, there is the inadequacy of the present administrative structure. The United States is composed of 50 states which, under the Constitution, have responsibility for the health, education, and welfare of their citizens. But what, in a national society, is the rationale for such small entities as Rhode Island, Delaware, New Jersey, and Maryland, which have small tax bases, whose populations tend to work in other states, and whose costs of administration remain high? At the other end of the scale there are 80,000 municipalities in the United States, each with its own tax and sovereign powers. This is not decentralization, but disarray. The extraordinary fact is that while the United States has the most modern economy in the world, its polity remains Tudor in character, antiquated, and top-heavy with a multiplicity of overlapping jurisdictions—townships, counties, and cities, plus special entities like health districts, park districts, sewage districts, water districts, and so forth. The failure of an efficient administrative structure has been itself a contributing element to the inability of cities or regions to have any effective planning.

Third, there is the rise of plebiscitary politics. In the United States there has been an eclipse of spatial distance. One of the consequences is to make Washington the central cockpit for all political argument and to mobilize pressures on a single area.

If one compares the history of the United States with that of Europe, there has probably been more labor violence in America than in any country on the Continent. Few statistics are available, but if one takes such rough indicators as the number of persons killed, the number of times troops have been called in, the number of strikes, and the number of man-days lost, it is evident, I think, that there has been more violence in the United States, but with less political and ideological effect than in Europe. One of the reasons for this is that in the United States, unlike Europe, much of this violence took place at the perimeters of the society, rather than the center, and it took considerable time for these effects to take hold. Today, labor issues have been institutionalized. But other fractious problems remain. And the possibilities for "mobilization politics," of organizing direct pressures, are high. To make one comparison: in 1894, in the midst of a severe economic depression, a group of unemployed, the so-called "Coxey's Army," began a march on Washington from Massillon, Ohio. Ten thousand men started out, but by the time they reached Washington some weeks later the ranks had dwindled to a handful. In 1963, Martin Luther King and A. Philip Randolph called for a march on Washington; within a week almost a quarter of a million persons had descended on the nation's capital.

Given the fact that political conflicts are bound to multiply—for reasons spelled out in the next section—the increased possibility for mass pressure as a means whereby any group can obtain its demands becomes a further source of structural strain in the system. Given the possibilities for violence which have been endemic in the system, a new source of great strain has been created by the emergence of a national society.

THE COMMUNAL SOCIETY

The emergence of a communal society derives from the growth of non-market public decision making, and the definition of social rights in group (rather than individual) terms. In scale, both are distinctly new on the American scene, and both pose new kinds of problems for the society. By non-market, public decision making, I mean simply the growth of problems which have to be settled by the public authorities rather than through the market mechanism. The laying out of roads, the planning of cities, the organization of health care, the financing of education, the cleaning up of environmental pollution, the building of houses all become matters of public concern. No one can *buy* his share of "clean air" in the market; one has to use communal mechanisms in order to deal with pollution.

The virtue of the market is that it disperses responsibility. When a "decision" is reached by the multiple choices of thousands or millions of individual consumers, acting independently in the market, there is no one person or group of persons to blame for such decisions. If a product does not sell, or there is a shift of taste, and firms or even entire industries fail because of such market decisions, no single group can be saddled with the charge of being responsible. But with non-market public decisions, the situation is entirely different. The decisions are visible, and one knows whom to blame. In effect, decision making has become "politicized" and subject to all the multiple direct pressures of political decision making.

The simple point is that as non-market public decision making becomes more necessary, for there are tasks which the individual cannot do for himself, such new mechanisms multiply the potentialities of community and group conflict. When one "burdens" the polity with more and more political issues, when housing, health, education, and the like become politicized, strains are compounded. The simple prediction I first made in the report of the Commission on the Year 2000 (1967) is that in the coming years there will be more and more group conflicts in the society.

By group rights, I refer to claims on the community which come to be decided on the basis of group membership rather than on that of individual attributes. The American value system has been predicated on the basis of individual achievement and equality of opportunity as given to individuals. In the past, various functional groups have been recognized as having collective character (e.g., trade unions), and rights were given to the group (e.g., a union shop). But these groups are voluntary associations, and a man loses those protections when he changes his status. The recent issues arise from the demands of blacks for rights as a "property" of their color. The paradoxical fact is that the argument that black lawyers used before the Supreme Court in 1954 was that "separate but equal" was discriminatory and that blacks were entitled to be treated as *individuals* (and to achieve equality on that basis) rather than as a *category*. But the slowness of integration and the psychological assertiveness of a group identity have changed the character of black demands. The blacks have moved from a claim of equality of opportunity to equality of result. And this can be obtained, they argue, only through special quotas, preferential hiring, compensatory education, and the like.

The demand for group rights will widen in the society, because social life increasingly becomes organized on a group basis. The need to work out philosophical legitimations and political mechanisms to adjudicate these conflicting claims is another source of strain in the society in the coming years.

THE POST-INDUSTRIAL SOCIETY

In a post-industrial society, which, I suggest, is only now beginning to emerge, we may see fundamental changes in the stratification system, principally in the bases of class position and the modes of access to such position.

In my last book I explored five different dimensions of a post-industrial society.[6] Here let me emphasize just two of them. The first is the centrality of theoretical knowledge as the source of innovation and policy analysis in the society.

The university, because it is the place where theoretical knowledge is codified and tested, increasingly has become a primary institution of the society. To that extent, the university has become burdened with tasks greater than it has ever had to carry in its long history. It has to maintain a disinterested role as regards knowledge, yet be the principal service agency of the society, not only in training people, but as the source of policy advisers as well.

The second change is the shift from a goods-producing to a service society. In the United States, by 1970, about 65 percent of the labor force was engaged in services. But the central fact is the

[6] *The Coming of Post-Industrial Society* (New York: Basic Books, 1973). I should emphasize the fact that a post-industrial society does not "displace" an industrial society, or even an agrarian society. Food is still the foundation of all society, but what the introduction of industry meant was that one could reduce the number of persons engaged in agriculture and increase the yields because of chemical fertilizers. A post-industrial society adds a new dimension, particularly in the management of data and information as necessary facilities in a complex society. One can see the differences between the social structures—they are ideal types—in the following schematization:

	PRE-INDUSTRIAL	INDUSTRIAL	POST-INDUSTRIAL
Resource	Raw materials	Energy	Information
Mode	Extractive	Fabrication	Processing
Technology	Labor-intensive	Capital-intensive	Knowledge-intensive
Design	Game against nature	Game against fabricated nature	Game between persons

emphasis on technical and professional services, and on human services. And it is the expansion of these sectors which accounts for the major transformation of the occupational structure of the society.[7]

In the most fundamental ways, a post-industrial society begins to reshape all modern economies. The emphasis on education as the mode of access to skill and power, the role of technical decision, the conflicts between skill groups and new elites (e.g., the scientific community and the military) all presage new kinds of difficulties for advanced Western societies, and for the United States in particular.

THE FUTURE IN THE SHORT AND LONG RUN

The immediate questions before the society by the end of the 1960s were the issue of the blacks and the alienation of the sensitive young. In the 1970s, however, the manifest issues of the previous decade—the blacks and youth—have diminished.

The drive of the blacks was and still is for inclusion in the society, even though many want this on their terms (e.g., an education adapted to "black needs"), and the problem remains the transfer of resources to meet those demands.

The mood of the young was more diffuse and inchoate. They adhered to no single coherent ideology, other than, for many in the elite universities, a generalized attack on prevailing middle-class values—which, in bourgeois terms, meant delayed gratification, psychological restraints, and rationalistic and technocratic modes of thought. A tiny number became completely alienated and ready even to become "urban guerrillas" in an effort to destroy the society. The youth cohort, as a whole, is now moving through the age cycle, and is becoming preoccupied with the problems of jobs and family. As a cohort, they are more liberal than their fathers, but not revolutionary.

[7] For an extensive discussion of the role of human services, see Alan Gartner and Frank Riessman, *The Service Society and the Consumer Vanguard* (New York: Harper & Row, 1974).

The problems deriving from the structural changes in American life remain. These include the reorganization of the governmental administrative structure of the society; the creation of national health, education, and welfare policies appropriate to a national society; the reconciliation of conflicting rights of the communal groups; and the creation of a comprehensive science and research-and-development policy that can advance the better features of a post-industrial society. Without these resolutions, the ongoing political life of the society will be more difficult.

Beyond these, however, are four more generalized problems which a troubled society has only begun to be aware of and has yet to confront.

The relation of democracy to empire. The United States after World War II could not go back to its earlier status of a parochial power, with its national life dominated (as in the 1920s and before) by the small-town mentalities which had ruled it for so long. A new metropolitan and world outlook had emerged, and American policy increasingly became shaped by considerations of empire. The United States became an imperial power less for economic motivations than because of the fact that, as the strongest power, it was drawn (and went) into the ensuing contest of will in all areas of the world. Thus the United States began to exert a predominant influence, if not hegemony.

In times of trouble, it is instructive to read Thucydides, and one is struck in this instance by the situation of Athens after the Persian wars. Thucydides posed the dilemma of a democracy which chooses empire rather than retreating to a provincial role.[8] Though no parallels are exact, the problems of Athens and the Delian Confederacy are extraordinarily suggestive of the situation of the United States vis-à-vis its own allies, and its problems with the Soviet (Spartan) bloc. But the real problem is whether a democracy, potentially riven by discord between factions, can sustain a unity, especially in defeat, or whether even in victory it can sustain an expansive role as a leader and protector of other states without

[8] There is also in Thucydides, especially in his description of the Corcyrean events, a forewarning of what happens in any society when violence unleashes civil passions. "In the confusion into which life was now thrown in the cities, human nature, always rebelling against the law and now its master, gladly showed itself ungoverned in passion, above respect for justice, and the enemy of all superiority; since revenge would not have been set above religion, and gain above justice, had it not been for the fatal power of envy;" *The Peloponnesian War* (New York: Modern Library, 1934), p. 191.

being driven (as was Cleon, the successor to Pericles, whom one can compare to Lyndon Johnson) to the temptations of large-scale risks.

An imperial role is difficult for any nation, since it means the commitment of large-scale resources, of men and wealth, which, if not returned with profit, cause deep strain within. The relation between democracy and empire is especially trying, and increasingly one can see that the imperial role is not one that is fitting, in political structure and national style, for the United States.

The creation of a new political elite. An elite, at best (as in an Establishment), serves as a source of moral authority and political wisdom. What was important about the United States in the decade and a half following World War II was that a more or less coherent political elite emerged, providing a consistent leadership in the area of foreign policy.

An elite is sometimes defined by its structural position in a society, but the fact that men possess economic or political or military power, or stand at the pinnacle of an organization, does not necessarily mean they are an elite, in the sense that their leadership is followed. In the United States the elite that emerged was defined more by outlook—a cosmopolitan and worldwide vision—than by structural position alone. Men such as General Marshall, Henry Stimson, John McCloy, Robert Lovett, Dean Acheson, Douglas Dillon, and others of the "foreign policy establishment" were drawn primarily from the New York financial community, but it was not their *interests* that defined them as an elite, but their character and judgment. The important consideration was that their opinions had weight because they were respected. Reciprocity between judgment and respect is a necessary condition if policy is to be tempered by the weight of elite opinion.

American foreign policy after World War II was primarily oriented toward Europe because the tasks of reconstruction were most necessary there. But the policies that emerged, principally the Marshall Plan, arose, too, because of the experience and interests of these men in European affairs. There never was a similar elite group with comparable experience and judgment about Asia, and one of the failures of American foreign policy, to that extent, derives from this lack.

In the last decade, the influence of that major political elite has been disappearing, and no comparable elite has arisen to temper

policy and to provide a source of judgment. The Kennedy administration sought, self-consciously, with its panache and élan, to constitute itself as an elite, and among the intellectuals and the young
it gained an enthusiastic following, if not a moral authority. But
this ended with the Vietnam war.[9]

If one follows the wisdom of a Bagehot, the existence of such an
elite is a necessary element in the creation of political authority in
the society. Without such an elite there is a problem of authoritative leadership. Given the divisions in the society, the question of
whether an elite can emerge is moot.

The failure of liberalism? To a considerable extent, liberal social policy was associated with the rise of Keynesianism and macro-
economic planning. Just as the New Deal was the haven, in large
measure, of young lawyers because of the role of regulatory agencies (the symbolic godfathers being Felix Frankfurter and the
Harvard Law School) the New Frontier and the Great Society in
its early days became associated with economists and political
scientists.

Under the leadership of Walter Heller, the Council of Economic
Advisers was transformed into a professional body whose advice on
policy, particularly after the resounding economic success of the tax
cut in 1962, became highly influential in government. But economists
were more than economists. They became managers as well. The
"McNamara revolution" in the Pentagon, for instance, was principally
the work of economists led by Charles Hitch.

In recent years there has been a growing skepticism about the
ability of economists to manage the economy. In England, during
the 1960s, the Labour government, despite the advice of a number
of distinguished economists, such as Nicholas Kaldor and Thomas
Balogh (a "plague of economists," Michael Postan has called them)
were unable to to solve Britain's difficulties. Professor John Vaizey,
an English Labourite economist, writing of the "incoherence in post-
Keynesian thought," ends pessimistically: "Reluctantly, I think, one
must conclude that running an economy to order may be beyond

[9] It would be more accurate to say that the Vietnam war discredited the nascent
political elite that was emerging in the 1960s. As one of my Harvard colleagues, who
had been an important government adviser, put it, inelegantly but succinctly: "We
blew it. There was a challenge to create a sustained Establishment as in Britain, and
it all went." Whatever one can say about the factual accuracy of its reportage, the
fact of failure is summed up in the sardonic title of David Halberstam's book *The
Best and the Brightest.*

the power of analysis of present-day economists." In the United States, fiscal policy, the tool of Keynesianism, began to lose its luster long before the recession of the 1970s.

In social policy, particularly in the United States, the record of social scientists is even more dismal. In the areas of education, welfare, and social planning, social scientists have reluctantly begun to admit that the problems are more complex than they thought. The failure of liberalism, then, is in part a *failure of knowledge*. This is not an answer to the liking of the New Left, which still presses for the easy simplicities. Yet this failure of knowledge, too, is a source of intellectual disarray and concern when one realizes that a large, complex society, especially one that necessarily has to be future-oriented, requires social planning in order to meet the onrush of social change.

The participation revolution. What is evident everywhere is a society-wide uprising against bureaucracy and a desire for participation, a theme that is summed up in the phrase "People ought to be able to affect the decisions that control their lives. . . ."

This upheaval from below takes many forms. In part, it is a revolt against the idea of a meritocracy in which technical achievement alone becomes the criterion of place in the society; in part (as in the case of the blacks) it is a form of community self-assertion.

To a considerable extent, the Democratic administrations of the 1960s did go far in the creation of new social forms to involve people in crucial decisions. The poverty program called for the creation of community-action groups. (In New York, for example, 26 neighborhood community councils were created through the poverty program, which became the source of a new political base —principally for Mayor Lindsay—in the city.) The Model Cities housing program called for community participation in the planning of new neighborhoods. The large Community Mental Health programs require the participation of local bodies in the planning of policies and programs. In education, decentralization programs in many cities have widened the scope of community control.

To a considerable extent, the participation revolution is one form of reaction against the professionalization of society, and against the emergent technocratic decision making of a post-industrial society. And every advanced industrial society will have to confront this phenomenon. What began years ago in the factory, through the trade unions, has now spread to the neighborhood—because of the onset of the communal society—and will, in the coming years, spread to organizations as well.

Yet "participatory democracy" is not the panacea its adherents make it out to be, no more than were the earlier efforts at creating plebiscitarian political mechanisms (e.g., initiative, referendum, and recall). With all the furor about participatory democracy, it is curious that few of its proponents have sought to think through, on the most elementary level, the meaning of these changes. Certainly, if individuals are to affect the decisions that change their lives, then segregationists in the South would have the right to exclude blacks from the schools. But one would have to say that the South is not an independent political entity but part of a larger polity, and thus has to comply with the moral norms of the society. Similarly, should a neighborhood group be allowed to veto a city plan which takes into account the needs of a more inclusive polity?[10]

In short, participatory democracy is one more way of posing the classical issues of political philosophy: namely, who should make, and at what levels of government, what kind of decisions for how large a social unit? And there are no clear-cut answers to these questions. But the tensions remain, and they will become exacerbated.

Any estimate of the ability of a society to meet its problems depends, as we know from a long series of political manuals, from Thucydides to Machiavelli, on the quality of its leadership and the character of the people. With all our attention to social forces, only a fool would say (as have some Marxists like Georgi Plekhanov) that the individual does not count and that history throws up a leader appropriate to the situation. As Sidney Hook pointed out in *The Hero in History*, there are "event-making men" as well as eventful men, and the event-making man can create a turning point in history. It was the unshakable will of Lenin and his tactical sense of timing that were decisive for the victory of the Bolshevik forces in October 1917. On a different scale, it was the force of Charles de Gaulle's authority that turned back the threat of the French Army's seizing power in Algeria in 1958, when a Guy Mollet surely would

---

[10] In 1974 the Irish residents of South Boston violently resisted busing on the ground that the breakup of neighborhood-based schools would mean the breakup of traditional neighborhoods as well. Should South Bostonians have the right to control the decisions which affect their lives?

have faltered. So one of the imponderable, though crucial variables is the character of leadership in the decade ahead.

But the ability to intervene into events, and to control them, depends upon the context in which one lives. What has become decisive for the rest of the century is that the context of decision is no longer the national situs, no matter how powerful a nation seems. We have moved completely into world economy. It is this point that brings into question the ability of American society to solve its own problems in the decade ahead.

I I

IN FUTURIST STUDIES we make a distinction—an arbitrary one, to be sure—between *prediction* and *forecasting*. Prediction is the stipulation of "point events," i.e., that something will occur at such time and place. Forecasting is the identification of structural contexts out of which problems arise, or the trends which may be realized. A set of events—which is what one seeks to predict—is often the conjunction of structural trends with particular contingencies. Since such contingencies are not forecastable (they cannot be subject to rules, or formalized in an algorithm), one can invoke "intelligence" (inside information), shrewd guesses, or wisdom, but not any social science methodology in making predictions. In short, one can deal with conditions, but not precipitating factors; with structures, not contingencies. This is the limitation of any forecast, if not of analysis.

In the decades after World War II, the major structural contexts which framed the emergence of social problems in the United States were, as I indicated earlier, the creation of a national society as the new arena of decision and conflict for domestic forces, and the sudden, violent thrust of the United States into a paramount role in world political society, as it took over a policing role in Asia, Africa, and the Middle East which had been forfeited by the British and the French. By the early 1970s it had not yet solved any of the questions of the national society, particularly the creation of national systems to manage the problems of health, education, and welfare; and it had begun a headlong retreat from its previous role as the paramount political power in *all* parts of the world. Yet what was becoming most clear, for the decade and beyond, was that the structural context of decisions was becoming enlarged and that most of the significant questions confronting the society, particularly the economic ones, were no longer solely within the power of America to decide.

In this section, I want to consider the two major changes which confront the United States for the remainder of the century. One is the new role of the international arena as the relevant structural context; the other is that of an American "climacteric," and the possibility of an irreversible slide in the degree of American economic and political power in the world. Since my focus is on *structural* contexts, I have left aside the important, but highly contingent political issues, such as oil or other commodity cartels.

THE INTERNATIONAL CONTEXT

The economy. The most fundamental fact about the context of economic decisions is that the determination of such decisions is no longer in the hands of any single country, no matter how large or powerful; thus the economic fate of each country is increasingly beyond its own control.

From 1830 to 1930 there was, broadly speaking, a "self-regulating" international market based on gold. National economies were subject to the discipline of that market. If prices rose too high, there would be a fall-off in trade, a deficit in the balance of payments, an outflow of gold, a fall in prices, and a new balance. Inevitably, the "price" of such adjustment was a decline in employment. Theoretically, then, in a self-regulating market, capital and labor would migrate to new opportunities. But a flow of capital endangers the economy of a society, and countries seek to halt it if they can; and while migration of workers was a safety valve, after World War I such migration was virtually halted. Individual nations began to seek "exemptions" fom the hazards of market-induced adjustments by reducing free trade and by intervening in the domestic economy in order to maintain employment. The main casualty of such measures was the international economy. Great Britain's adoption in 1930 of a system of imperial preference for the import of goods was the first signal. The abandonment of the gold standard the next year by England, followed by the United States, heralded the new era of economic nationalism.

Out of the experiences of the 1930s, national governments learned, more or less, how to manage national economies through fiscal and monetary mechanisms. But since the end of World War II, and particularly since the 1960s, with the full economic reconstruction of Western Europe and Japan, the expansion of world trade and of worldwide investment has brought the international economy squarely back to the center of decisions.

A number of crucial changes have created a new set of instabilities and problems for all the advanced economies. For 20 years, the international economic system was based on the strength of the dollar, and on the convertibility of other currencies into dollars, as the medium of international exchange and settling of balances. But that stability foundered as the United States found itself with a large balance-of-payments deficit of its own, and as other countries became uneasy about holding so many dollars.[11]

A second factor was the emergence of the multinational corporation as one of the main actors on the world scene. It is indicative of the size of these corporations—if one takes the big 300—that their combined production of goods and services is higher than the GNP of every country in the world except the United States, and that, if one projects the present rates of growth, multinational enterprises will account for as much as one-third of all world production by the end of the century. The chief effect of the multinational corporations is in transferring capital, technology, and managerial skills (but not skilled workers; hence the opposition of unions) on a global scale. The markets are no longer national markets. Hedges against currencies are made not to protect a nation's money but to protect a corporation's balances. The plans of the multinational corporations do not always coincide with the economic interests of any single country.

A third element is the internationalization of the capital market;

---

[11] One cannot miss the irony of the situation, for in the years immediately following World War II the concern of many economists was with the problem of how there could be *any* world trade, since so few countries had dollars, and so many would not have any. So the various reform schemes for international trade proposed the use of commodity reserves as the backing for international currency units, to give those countries some basis for the acceptance of their currency in international trade.

the world horizon becomes a single canvas, as financial capital, increasingly sensitive to differentials in yields, quickly crosses national boundaries in order to obtain better returns on its money. Even national stock markets, subject as they are to diverse influences, have shown an increasing parallelism of movement during the past decade. As Richard N. Cooper has observed:

This growing interdependence can be confidently projected into the future (in the absence of strong government action to retard the process) because its source is those technological advances in transportation and communication which increase both the speed and reliability of moving goods, funds, persons, information, and ideas across national boundaries —in short, the same forces producing the much-touted smaller world, in terms both of economic and psychological distance.[12]

Such economic mobility erodes the ability of a national government to pursue its own economic objectives. A contractionary monetary policy can be circumvented by corporations or banks borrowing from abroad, rather than from domestic sources. Earnings can be shifted about, through differential price transactions, so that taxes are reduced. Regulatory policies can be evaded by operating through subsidiaries.

Inevitably, national governments must seek to defend themselves against both the independence of multinational corporations and the instabilities which are generated by the imbalances of payments. Countries may resort to unilateral actions of devaluation or seek some means of working in international concert. But who is to set the international objectives?

In a logical sense, three alternatives are open. Nations can seek to reduce their dependency on the world economy by seeking to restrict capital outflows, impose import quotas, limit the number of foreign workers, and the like. A second effort (by a nation, like the United States, in a position to do so) would be to extend aggressively the controls over home-based multinational corporations, or to seek the maintenance of a singular standard of world currency (the dollar). A third path would be the creation of an international authority with governmental powers, on some broader scale, to define common economic mechanisms and policies.

Illogical as it may be, most countries will seek, in different areas,

[12] Mr. Cooper has elaborated the argument in his book *The Economics of Interdependence* (New York: McGraw-Hill for the Council on Foreign Relations, 1968) and in some unpublished papers for a study group of the Council on Foreign Relations.

a combination of all three. National autonomy is not quickly forgone, as even the European Community has learned. Individual countries, by bilateral action, will become more aggressive in international economic affairs. And the powers of international agencies, such as the International Monetary Fund, will probably be increased. The major question will be whether some cooperative relationships can be established which, even though they may not be able to maximize a common set of economic objectives, will minimize the frictions which occur as incompatible policies are pursued.[13]

The society. One major social process in most countries in the last 25 years has been, because of the revolutions in transportation and communication, the creation of national societies. In the next 25 years, this process of enlargement will repeat itself on an international scale.

The revolutions in transportation and communication are at hand. The multiplication of jumbo jets and the eventual use of Concorde-type airplanes will increase the number of travelers throughout the world and reduce the times elapsed. The extension of international communication satellites will speed the spread of low-cost international data transmission and expand international television exchanges, especially for "real-time" events. Inevitably, such structural change carries the potential for contradictory effects. On the one hand, the extension of communications networks allows for greater degrees of centralization and control, both territorially and functionally. On the other hand, it becomes increasingly difficult for any society to wall itself off from the rest of the world. When Condorcet, in his *Sketch of the Progress of the Human*

[13] Let me emphasize that I deal here with the problems and strategies of Western industrial economies, or in a quick shorthand, the OECD countries, and not the world as a whole. Inevitably, there is the larger context of the Comecon countries, the Middle East with its new larger amounts of income, and the less developed countries.

Equally, one can only sketch a general context, yet particular contingencies may distort the situation enormously. Thus there is the question of the fate of the monies flowing to the Organization of Petroleum Exporting Countries, which rose by $50 billion in 1973. If one "projects" the present curve of demand and prices, the OPEC investable surpluses would total $100 billion by the end of 1974 and cumulate to $500 billion by 1980 and more than $600 billion by 1985, amounts which would almost absorb the entire world monetary system. Yet here, too, there is clearly a fallacy in extrapolation. Demand for oil might fall, the producer cartel might break up and prices could fall, or alternative energy sources (oil, coal, nuclear power, and the like) could significantly alter the balances. With all that, the major structural change remains the centrality of the international context of economic decisions.

Mind (1793), made some predictions about the spread of equality and democracy in the world, the major instrument of change, he pointed out, was cheap printing. Today, with international radio and television, despite censorship, news and ideas come through.

The effects of this process are equally apparent. With the new transportation and communication come more interactions between people, more exchanges, a greater number of ties, an increase in what Émile Durkheim, who charted this process, called the "moral density" of the society. Yet again, a double, often contradictory, set of effects ensues. On the one hand, there is an increase in the character and multiplicity of "shocks" as events are speedily reported, and there is also a shortening of "reaction time" as individuals respond to these events. There seems to be some evidence that the daily visualization of the Vietnam battlefield on American television screens was a factor in the turn of attitudes and revulsion of the people against the war. On the other hand, there is the possibility that such a multiplicity of shocks and on-screen visualizations results in a distancing of oneself from the events and an anesthetizing of feeling. A bomber crew, flying 30,000 feet high, does not feel the shock of the bombs. Scenes of destruction on TV as a daily diet can dull the capacity for emotional response. In short, as in so many other aspects of society, there is the potentiality for overload; in this case, of sensory overload.

What is clear, though, is the reduction of distance. In military terms, it means that tens of thousands of soldiers can be airlifted quite readily to almost any part of the globe, and control of operations remains in the political center at home. Economically, it means that countries can import large amounts of resources from distant sources of supply at relatively lower costs, as Japan did for example, in buying large amounts of coal from the United States, over 10,000 miles away. Psychically and socially, one can see the spread of "contagion effects" as, in the case of the youth movements of the 1960s, new issues, themes, and tactics are picked up readily and applied in diverse situations.

What all this has meant, institutionally, is the vast multiplication and spread of *international* and *transnational* organizations on an extraordinary scale. (An organization is international if the control is explicitly shared among representatives of two or more nationalities. An organization is transnational if, even though the control is within a single nation, it carries on operations in the territories of two or more nation states.) Both kinds of organizations have always existed, and it is obvious that on both governmental and non-governmental levels we have had an enormous increase in international organizations. But the major change has been in the scope and character of transactions. As Samuel P. Huntington has observed:

During the twenty-five years after World War II, however, transnational organizations: (a) proliferated in number far beyond anything remotely existing in the past; (b) individually grew in size far beyond anything existing in the past; (c) performed functions which they never performed in the past; and (d) operated on a truly global scale such as was never possible in the past. The increase in the number, size, scope, and variety of transnational organizations after World War II makes it possible, useful, and sensible to speak of a *transnational organizational revolution* in world politics.[14]

The growth of a world economy and a world society makes central the problems of resource management on an international scale. There is the general question of the effects of technological and similar processes on the environment and the need for international monitoring of changes in the environment, which was raised at the UN conference in Stockholm in 1972. But there are the new and more difficult questions of international authority over resources common to all. Three issues are especially important: the oceans, the weather, and energy.

A UN Law of the Seas Conference, which opened in Caracas in 1974, will have to decide, in effect, how some 70 percent of the earth's surface is to be owned and controlled; whether national sovereignties are to extend either 12 miles or 200 miles from the shore is one question. More diffuse questions, particularly in the light of world shortages of protein, are the scope and extent of fishing rights, and of the impending destruction of the world's whale and seal population. How are these questions to be managed?

More uncertain is the question of weather. In the next 25 years there may be large technological advances in the modification of weather, from cloud-seeding to changing ocean currents by melting ice caps or by blocking certain arctic straits and changing the saline proportions of the waters. Will these be left to individual countries to try, or will there be some international authority?

[14] Samuel P. Huntington, "Transnational Organization in World Politics," *World Politics* 25 (April 1973):333.

Third is the question of the pooling of energy. This can take the form of sharing of stocks, such as oil; or of more complicated yet potentially more important system, such as worldwide "energy grids" that would allow for the shift of electrical energy use from one part of the world to another, as one part sleeps and the other works. But none of this is possible without some international mechanisms, such as in communications.

Inevitably—because of the questions of resources, environment, spillover effects, and densities—ours is a world that will require more authority and more regulation, everywhere. By the end of the century, a single time-space framework will finally be in place, engirdling the entire world. We will have reached the great *Oekumene*—the single household economy—which the Greeks had envisioned as the boundary of the civilized world. In principle, many of the problems which beset the Greek world confront us as well. The crucial difference—it is this which distinguishes a modern from an ancient world—is *scale*. How much can be managed from a single center? How large can a political or economic enterprise be, without becoming a behemoth that falls of its own weight? How many nations can be effective participants in a world assembly? The major question before the international society is the construction of new forms proportionate to the scale on which we now live. The major question posed by the extension of international society in the next 25 years is the management of scale.

AN AMERICAN CLIMACTERIC?

The world economy. The hazards of prediction are nowhere more evident than in the wildly swinging assessments of American power, economic and political. Nearly ten years ago Jean-Jacques Servan-Schreiber wrote a European best-seller, *The American Challenge*, which pictured a powerful, almost omnipotent American business class exploiting a widening technological lead and utilizing its superior management ability and large-scale organizational capacity to become the dominant presence in the European market. Within a few years, the "technology gap" had almost disappeared, and the United States was desperately trying to climb out of a deep balance-of-payments chasm by devaluing the dollar, and seeking to stem the tide of Japanese and European goods (autos, radios, typewriters, television sets, optical instruments) that were flooding the

American market. In fact, today, one thinks of an American climacteric, a critical change of life, as being the nodal point for the future—carrying the implication that the U.S. economy (and its superior advantage in the world economy) has passed its peak, that the "aging" process is real and the loss of leadership irretrievable.[15]

The idea of a climacteric is, admittedly, an elusive one. The metaphor is biological, and it is difficult to conceptualize societies (*pace* Spengler) in terms of a life-cycle idea. Yet it is quite clear that some economies are overtaken by others; that rigidities or ossifications, old habits or rooted ways, do take hold; and that economies begin to lose out to more aggressive competitors. The idea of an economic climacteric was first applied to Great Britain to signify that point in time—it is now usually set in 1890—when it became apparent that the United Kingdom could not turn back the economic challenge of Germany. Even so, it takes a long time for the crossover points to become manifest. In the 1890s, Britain was growing at a rate of only 2–3 percent per annum, as compared with 6 percent for Germany, but Britain was still far ahead of Germany in income. And yet it took Germany almost 70 years (largely due to setbacks in two wars) to pull ahead of Britain in output and, finally, in per capita income.

The main argument was laid out a long time ago by Thorstein Veblen in his book *Imperial Germany and the Industrial Revolution* (1915). An aggressive country, entering later into the industrialization cycle, is able to take advantage of newer technologies and other countries' experiences in plant layout and design, while countries that industrialized earlier have older and more inefficient plants that are not fully amortized. The argument was generalized in recent years by Raymond Vernon in his analysis of the "product cycle" in the international economy. A country that innovates has a comparative advantage only so long as it has a monopoly of the new technology. The technology is diffused first to the most adept imitators and ultimately to the world (as in cotton textiles). But when the technology is sufficiently widespread, then the traditional "factor-proportion" advantage—a country exports those goods based on the factors is has in abundance—comes into play.

As Kindleberger points out, the U.S. product cycle in foreign trade started in the 1860s and the 1870s with exports of the revolver

[15] See, for example, Charles P. Kindleberger, "An American Climacteric?," in *Challenge*, January–February 1974. I follow here Kindleberger's argument.

and the rifle, the sewing machine, then the reaper and the combine, the typewriter and the cash register. During the 1920s and 1930s, the newer advantages were in automobiles, motion pictures, and radios. After World War II the technological lead of the U.S. was in pharmaceuticals, television equipment, semiconductors, computers, and airplanes.

Except for computers and airplanes, where it has about 75 percent of the world market, the United States has begun to lose ground in these advanced areas, and there seems to be a dearth of new products to take their place. It may be that as we exhaust easily usable resources, the new and necessary dependence on high technology to create new energy sources—e.g., nuclear energy, extraction of oil from shale, gasification of coal—may give the United States some new advantages, but this is problematic.

But the question is more than one of high technology alone. In the next decades, U.S. industry will need large amounts of new capital to increase primary processing capacity, and the problem of a capital shortage—because of a low rate of household savings and because of declining profit margins of U.S. firms—may be a real one. In many crucial areas, American industry has lost its product advantage (e.g., automobiles, television equipment, household appliances), so that the United States not only has lost ground in markets abroad (as in automobiles) but now finds itself "invaded" by such products. Given the new, higher costs of raw materials that have to be imported, it is not clear that the present edge in high technology outweighs the other losses in dollar volume, so that a deficit in the balance of trade may be a continuing problem for the 1970s.

But larger than the deficits in the balance of trade have been the large gaps in the balance of payments, deficits created by the expansion of investments abroad, but more importantly by the huge costs of maintaining an American military presence in so many parts of the world. Until the early 1970s, the use of the dollar as an international reserve currency—the willingness of other countries to hold excess dollars—had meant that the United States was not subject to balance-of-payments discipline. But the United States received a rude shock in 1973, in the literal—and symbolically even greater—fact, discovered by American tourists, that hoteliers and shopkeepers abroad would not accept dollars in payment of their bills. The dollar had lost its magic. And it could no longer be the monetary standard for the world.

Whether Japan is the country that will overtake the United States as the dominant economic power in the world is moot. One can extrapolate the comparative growth rates (10 percent for the decade 1960-1970 for Japan, 3 percent for the United States) and find the cross-point in the future when that symbolic event might take place. One is mindful, too, of the fallacy of extrapolation, since "exogenous" political events, such as the change in oil and energy prices, can equally change the slope of a growth curve.

Yet the sense remains that the period of American economic dominance in the world has crested and that, by the end of the century, the United States, like any aging *rentier*, will be living off the foreign earnings on the investments its corporations made in the halcyon quarter century after World War II. Will the other countries, particularly in the "Third World," allow this condition to go on for long, without taking steps, as the oil-producing countries have, to control those investments?

The world polity. Writing in 1966, but from the assumed vantage point of the year 2000, Samuel P. Huntington remarked that the dominant feature of international politics during the 30 years after World War II was neither the U.S. confrontation with the Communist countries, nor the tensions between the developed and underdeveloped countries, but the expansionist move by the United States "into the vacuums that were left after the decline of European influence in Asia, Africa, and even Latin America." The English, the French, and the Dutch were almost completely out of Southeast Asia; the English were out of the Middle East and Argentina; the French were largely out of North Africa. "The decline of Europe and the expansion of American influence (political, economic and military) went hand-in-hand."

By the year 2000, however, the American hegemony will have begun to come apart. Huntington describes the process:

... in the year 2000 the American world system that has been developed during the last twenty years will be in a state of disintegration and decay. Just as American influence has replaced European influence during the current period, so also during the last quarter of this century American power will begin to wane, and other countries will move in to fill the gap. Among those that will play a prominent role in this respect will be China on mainland Asia, Indonesia in Southeast Asia, Brazil in Latin America, and I do not know what in the Middle East and Africa. Unlike the end of the European empire (which was relatively peaceful), the decline of American influence will involve numerous struggles because the relationship between the rising powers and the U.S. will be much less close (in terms of values and culture) than was the relation between the U.S. and the European powers; and because there will be fewer common interests against a third power than existed when the U.S. and Europe stood against the Soviet Union. The struggles accompanying the disintegration of the American world order will have profoundly stimulating effects on the political development in the participating states. These struggles are, indeed, likely to play a major role in generating national cohesion and institutional development. At the same time, the decline of American influence will tend to undermine and disrupt American politics. The American political system could be less likely than that of the Fourth Republic to adjust successfully to the loss of empire.[16]

By the mid-1970s, however, a quarter of a century before the year 2000, the process of disintegration was already under way. U.S. influence in Southeast Asia, from Indochina to India, had become badly blunted. After a brief foray into the Congo in the mid-1960s, the United States seemed to have withdrawn almost completely from sub-Saharan Africa. In the Middle East, while there was a seesaw with the Soviet Union as to influence in the Arab world, the main fact that emerged out of the Yom Kippur war—and the concerted action of the oil-producing countries to regulate the world supply of oil by political fiat—was the growing autonomy and power of these countries as independent actors. In 1956—the year of Suez—England and France could engage, covertly, in joint action with Israel, to overthrow the Egyptian regime (only to find themselves stymied by the United States); but by 1974, that kind of "gunboat diplomacy" by any of the major Western powers was no longer thinkable.

In his "retrodictive" view, Huntington did not explain why the American hegemony would begin to disintegrate. It may well be, as André Malraux once remarked, that the Americans lack an "imperial style" and never could run an empire. Yet, as Denis Brogan remarked as long ago as 1952, the United States had always been guided by a "myth of omnipotence." It had regarded itself as the fair-haired child of God whose large and marvelous continent

[16] Samuel P. Huntington, "Political Development and the Decline of the American System of World Order," in *Toward the Year 2000*, ed. Daniel Bell (Boston: Houghton Mifflin, 1968), p. 316.

would be the scene of the unfolding of His historic design. Americans were always the "biggest" and the "best," and their energy, like that of the Asiatic and Turkic tribes which swept over the Eurasian steppes and the Middle East to create the classic warrior empires, had carried the United States to its enormous industrial power by the middle of the twentieth century.

The "myth of omnipotence" was first warped in 1952, when the United States was held to a virtual stalemate in Korea. Twenty years later, it had suffered a humiliating defeat in Vietnam. The Vietnam war was a blow in two ways. It showed that a big country could not use its power to enforce its will against a small country: public opinion, within the United States and throughout the world, and the possible threat of retaliation by the Communist powers limited U.S. firepower, which could have been used to destroy Hanoi completely; so the limited force, and the political disadvantages in supporting an unpopular regime, effectively crippled U.S. policy. Domestically, the war unleashed a large wave of protest and discontent, a questioning of the legitimacy of the country and the institutions of authority, whose effects are still to be gauged.

The test of any country, as I have pointed out in the first section of this essay, is its ability to survive humiliation in war, and the United States will have to grapple in the next decade with the effects of its involvement in Vietnam. But what does seem likely is that, despite the rhetoric of any president, the experience in Vietnam will effectively limit the ability of the United States to impose its "will," and to employ force in any test of strength, or any challenge to its power, in the world. And without "will" and the threat of force there is no possible hegemony.

The next decades, therefore, for political and economic reasons, may see the retreat of the United States from the center of world power. What the shape of any new world system may be is difficult to say because so much, especially in the next decade, depends upon contingencies: the political succession in Communist China and the possibility of overt conflict or rapprochement between the major Communist powers; rising political discontent in Latin America, which would preoccupy the United States and force its attention largely to hemispherical hegemony; the political stability of India; the spread of Communist power in the Mediterranean Sea and the balance-of-peace in the Middle East. All of these are problematic.

For the foreseeable future, the United States may still be the paramount power, but it cannot be the hegemonic power, either from any altruistic, Wilsonian vision as the "world's policeman," or from the cold, manipulative view of "capitalist economic domination." It will have difficulty enough—as the next essay discusses—in maintaining its own political stability.

The most striking feature of the 1970s—because of the multiplication of economic and social problems, and the inability of societies to manage them—may well be the centrifugal forces which will tear apart established national societies. In the 1975–1985 decade we may see the breakup of the United Kingdom, as long-dormant parochial nationalist sentiments swell up, as in Scotland, and demand some independence (particularly economic independence) from Westminster. In Yugoslavia, it is unclear whether the Federal Republic will hold together after the death of Tito, because of the existing tensions between the constituent republics. In China, the lack of a firm political infrastructure—since neither the Party nor the Army now has sufficient authority—may stimulate the growth of a new regionalism, a military dictatorship, or the wild, gyrating swings of renewed cultural revolutions, until some new authority emerges. In the Soviet Union, the slowdown of productivity, the difficulty of managing a large, complex society, and, most important, the increasing salience of ethnic identity and the change in the proportions of Great Russians to Ukrainians to Uzbeks and other minorities (because of differential birth rates) all may create huge political strains. Whether India, facing large crop setbacks—in part because of the inability to manage scale, in part because of the rapid rise of oil prices, which has reduced the availability of energy and fertilizer—can manage without large-scale disruptions is debatable. In Italy and Great Britain, labor troubles, low productivity, large imbalances in trade and payments, and double-digit inflation may bring both countries to the edge of national bankruptcy—and polarized social conflicts.

In the face of this dismal scenario—which is not a prediction, only a possibility—the conditions of the United States may shine by comparison. The United States can achieve a considerable measure of economic independence—at a cost. The prime economic problem of inflation can be brought under some control. The major sociological difficulty is that the United States, so strongly individualist in temper, and so bourgeois in appetite, has never wholly mastered the art of collective solutions, or of readily accepting the idea of a public interest, as against private gain.[17] In the end, I would argue, the ability of the United States—or any democratic polity—to deal with its problems adequately depends on the ability of the polity to come to some conception of a "public household." And it is to that question that I now turn.

[17] I have explored the question of an American "climacteric" within the context of American history and expectations in an essay "The End of American Exceptionalism," *The Public Interest*, no. 40 (Fall 1975).

The Public Household: On "Fiscal Sociology" and the Liberal Society

I

IN THE classical tradition of economics there are two realms of
economic activity. There is the *domestic household*, including farms,
whose products are not valued (a housewife is not paid; the produce
consumed on the farm is not always measured in GNP) because they
are not exchanged in the market. And there is the *market economy*,
where the value of goods and services is measured by the relative
prices registered in the exchange of money. But there is also now a
third sector, more important than the other two, which has come to
the fore in the last 25 years, and which will play an even more crucial
role in the next 25. This is the *public household*.[1] For reasons that I

[1] The phrase "the public household" was commonly used by German and
Austrian sociological economists in the 1920s in dealing with problems of state
finance. Friedrich von Wieser, the noted Austrian economist, wrote, in a classic
essay originally published in 1924: "It is common usage to speak of the public
economy as the national household, or, as the case may be, the county household,
city household, or generally the public household . . . . the state economy is essentially
one of common expenditure; as such, it does at any rate have some resemblance with
the private household and to this extent the current term of public household is not
inappropriate." Friedrich von Wieser, "The Theory of the Public Economy," in
Classics in the Theory of Public Finance, ed. Richard A. Musgrave and Alan T.
Peacock (New York: St. Martin's Press, 1964).

The idea of the public household is the organizing concept used by Richard A.
Musgrave in his standard work, *The Theory of Public Finance* (New York:
McGraw-Hill, 1959).

seek to make clear below, I prefer the term "public household," with its sociological connotations of family problems and common living, to the more neutral terms such as "public finance" or "public sector."

The public household, as expressed in the government budget, is the management of state revenues and expenditures. More broadly, it is the agency for the satisfaction of public needs and public wants, as against private wants. It is the arena for the register of political forces in the society. As Rudolf Goldscheid, a socialist economist, wrote almost 60 years ago, "the budget is the skeleton of the state stripped of all misleading ideologies."

Yet the extraordinary fact is that we have no sociological theory of the public household. We do have a comprehensive theory of the domestic household. Aristotle's *Politics* opens, in fact, with "the theory of the household": *oikonomia*, or household management, is the basis for his discussion of the domestic and the political economy and the principles appropriate to each. For the market economy, we have a theory of the firm, a general equilibrium theory to explain the clearing of all markets, and a set of philosophical justifications—the enhancement of individual benefit through the mutuality of exchange—in the writings of John Locke and Adam Smith. Yet we have no integrated theory of the economics and politics of public finance, no sociology of the structural conflicts between classes and social groups on the decisive question of taxation, no political philosophy (with the recent exception of John Rawls, but nothing from socialist writers) which attempts a theory of distributive justice based on the centrality of the public household in the society.[2]

[2] Richard Musgrave has said: "Economists have paid much attention to the formulation of theories that examine the problems of consumer households, business firms, cooperatives, trade unions and other decision-making units in the economy. While much remains to be done, we can boast of a fairly adequate framework in which to explore these matters. No such success can be claimed for occasional attempts to develop a corresponding theory of the public sector." (Ibid, p. 4.)

Since his work, there have been an increasing number of studies in "fiscal politics," the most noteworthy of which is Aaron Wildavsky's *The Politics of the Budgetary Process* (Boston: Little, Brown, 1964) and William Niskanen's *Bureaucracy and Representative Government* (Chicago: Aldine, 1971). Such studies have dealt largely with the "internal" politicking of budget setting, with the emphasis largely on the behavior of bureaucratic agencies, but they have not tied these issues to the broader problems of economic and social policy or to the impacts on social groups in the society.

The most ambitious attempt to develop a "sociology of fiscal politics," is James O'Connor's *The Fiscal Crisis of the State* (New York: St. Martin's Press, 1973). O'Connor writes from a Marxist point of view. ("The volume and composition of government expenditures and the distribution of the tax burden are not determined

These distinctions of domestic household, market economy, and public household, and the distinctive principles underlying each of them, are, I believe, crucial for understanding the fundamental political and sociological dilemmas of advanced industrial societies.

The nature of a household consists in sharing things in common —the domestic goods, the village green, the defense of the city— and necessarily has to come to some common understanding of the common good. But it is more than that. As Aristotle observes in Book I, Chapter 13 of the *Politics*: ". . . the business of household management is concerned more with human beings than it is with inanimate property; it is concerned more with the good condition of human beings than with a good condition of property (which is what we call wealth). . . ."

In the ancient world there is no *economic* principle, in the modern sense of the term.[3] The aim of the domestic household is production for use, for self-sufficiency. There is no effort to calculate whether one would be better off with specialization, or with division of labor. The artisan or craftsman produces on order, for a specific customer, tailoring the product to his size or shape, rather than generalizing production for abstract "customers" or market.

The distributive principle is simple. The head of the household makes the necessary decisions, but at the table there is simple sharing. No one is given food in exact proportion to what he has con-

---

by the laws of the market but rather reflect and are structurally determined by social and economic conflicts between classes and groups" [p. 2].) It is, surprisingly, one of the few Marxists efforts to grapple with the crucial role of state finance in reshaping societal configurations. As is evident from my discussion of his argument below, I have serious disagreements with his formulations. Yet I have profited greatly from his efforts and from the readings, particularly in Goldscheid and Schumpeter, that he suggested.

[3] For an elaboration of this argument, see M. I. Finley, *The Ancient Economy*, (London: Chatto and Windus, 1973). Professor Finley writes: "[Alfred] Marshall's title [*Principles of Economics*] cannot be translated into Greek or Latin. Neither can the basic terms, such as labour, production, capital, investment, income, circulation, demand, entrepreneur, utility, at least not in the abstract form required for economic analysis. In stressing this I am suggesting not that the ancients were like Molière's M. Jourdain, who spoke prose without knowing it, but that they in fact lacked the concept of an 'economy' and, *a fortiori*, that they lacked the conceptual elements which together constitute what we call 'the economy.' Of course they farmed, traded, manufactured, mined, taxed, coined, deposited and loaned money, made profits or failed in their enterprises. And they discussed these activities in their talk and their writing. What they did not do, however, was to combine these particular activities conceptually into a unit, in [Talcott Parsons'] terms into a 'differentiated sub-system of society.' Hence Aristotle, whose programme was to codify the branches of knowledge, wrote no *Economics*" (p. 21).

tributed (though the head of the household may take the lion's share). Each is given in accordance with his needs.

The controlling idea is that of *needs*. According to Aristotle, men have natural needs: sufficient food, clothing, shelter from the elements, care during sickness, sexual intercourse, companionship, and the like. But these needs, biologically derived, are limited and satiable. The art of household management, for the domestic and the political economy, entails the observance of these natural limits. Acquisition has a limit in size, determined by the purposes (i.e., the natural needs) of the household. The acquisition that is unlimited, that is directed largely to selfish monetary gain, Aristotle calls *chrematistic*; it is "unnatural" precisely because it is unlimited. (In the literal Greek, it might be noted, the root *chremata* means things.)

In a market economy, one defined by the principle of consumer sovereignty, what is to be produced is determined by the aggregate decision of individuals or households, as consumers, in accordance with their taste. In a capitalist market economy—private or state— the profits from such production are not used for personal or sumptuary purposes, but are reinvested into productive equipment to provide more or cheaper products for more consumers. In a private enterprise economy, such decisions as to the use of capital are made by individuals in accordance with their judgments as to the best return; in the public enterprise economy, such decisions are made by elected or political officials.

It is important to realize that the market economy, though it is associated historically with the rise of modern private capitalism, is *as a mechanism* not necessarily limited to that system. Such writers as Enrico Barone and, later, Oskar Lange argued that a socialist market economy was entirely possible, and that the market would operate more efficiently under socialism than under modern capitalism, where its operations were consistently distorted by monopoly or oligopoly.

What is distinctive about the modern market economy, sociologically, is that it has been a *bourgeois* economy. This has meant two things: first, that the ends of production are not common but individual; and second, that the motives for the acquisition of goods are not needs but *wants*.

In bourgeois society, the individual, not the state, is the unit whose purposes are primary for the society. That was the nineteenth-century conception of liberty: to be free of the ascriptive ties of family, community, or state; to be responsible for oneself; to make or even remake one's self in accordance with one's ambition. In economic terms, each man worked and saved for himself, for ends chosen by himself (or often, if he was of the middle class, for ends imitative of the higher classes).[4]

But like the expanding geographical horizons, his sense of what he wanted became unlimited. In bourgeois society, psychology replaced biology as the basis of "need" satisfaction. It is no accident, so to speak, that the philosophy of bourgeois society was utilitarianism, a hedonistic calculation of pleasure and pain, or that Bentham, the founder of utilitarianism, coined the heavy-handed neologism *maximumization*. In Aristotle's terms, *wants* replaced *needs*—and wants, by their nature, are unlimited and insatiable. When the Protestant ethic, which had served to limit sumptuary (though not capital) accumulation, was sundered from modern bourgeois society, only the hedonism remained. The economic principle—the rational calculation of efficiency and return—has been operative in the choice of means, in order to increase production (e.g., the most efficient combinations of labor and capital, or the specialization of tasks and functions), but the engine which began to drive the socio-economic system (in its Soviet Communist as well as its Western bourgeois form) has been the prodigal idea of private wants and unlimited ends.

The public household (as against the market, which seeks to serve diverse private wants) has always existed to meet common needs, to provide goods and services which individuals cannot purchase for themselves, e.g., military defense, roads, railways, and so forth.[5] In the last 40 years, however, it has been transformed by its commitment to three new tasks.[6]

[4] But that economic freedom, particularly after the reform in England of the Poor Laws in 1834, was a form of coercion as well. With the end of parish relief, especially after the Speenhamland experiment, an individual was forced to go to work, or starve. English divines such as T. R. Malthus or William Townsend believed that without such scourging hunger men would remain indolent and lazy and lack individual responsibility. Whigs such as Burke held a "household" view of the society, and believed it the responsibility of the country to care for its poor.

[5] Public goods and services, in the economists' use of the term, derive not from psychological preferences of individuals, nor from the ideological demands of groups, but from the technical character of production. These are goods and services that are not divisible to individual preferences, or which arise where large externalities require public action.

[6] No process is so abrupt, and a sociologist invariably must infuriate the historian with these somewhat arbitrary trichotomies. Large-scale government action in the

The first was the task of establishing normative economic policy in the 1930s. The existence of the Depression made it clear that only conscious action by governmental authority could rescue the country from the crisis which engulfed it. Since then, the direction of the economy has become a central government task. Government spending controls the level of economic activity; tax and monetary policies direct the timing of investment; transfer payments effect the partial redistribution of incomes through social security, subsidies, revenue sharing, and the like. In general, all modern polities are involved in the functions of allocation, redistribution, stabilization, and growth.

The second task, which emerged in the 1950s, was the underwriting of science and technology. While much of this was linked to defense, through the revolutions in military technology, the more fundamental fact was the centrality of science and the systematic use and application of research, from basic science to systems analysis, to economic innovation (i.e., the development of science-based industries like computers, electronics, optics, and polymers) and to managerial and economic policy. The linked relation of science to technology is now inextricable. (It had not been so during the industrial revolution.) The expansion of the technical and administrative classes in the society is largely irreversible, though its rate of growth may have slowed down. In consequence of these changes, the government has become directly involved in science policy (it has been estimated that about two-thirds of all work in science, both expenditures and personnel, is directly or indirectly dependent on government) and in higher education. Who shall be educated, and how far; how much should be spent for graduate training, and in what fields—this is no longer, in its magnitudes, a matter of individual choice but of government policy.

The third task was the commitment to normative social policy in the 1960s. This included civil rights, housing and environmental policy, health care and income support (the more genteel term, these days, for welfare policy—though the implications are much

United States was undertaken to open up waterways, public land, and grants for railways in the early nineteenth century. The trust-busting of Theodore Roosevelt marked a significant intervention in the economy in the first decade of the twentieth. But I date the transformation in the 1930s largely as the conscious effort by government to begin to *manage* the economy; and one can take the violent hostility of big business to the New Deal, and to Franklin D. Roosevelt, as an index of the significance of that change.

broader than merely helping the indigent). While much of this came pell-mell and piecemeal, what was not completely recognized, and still is not, is that the government had made a commitment not only to create a substantial welfare state, *but to redress the impact of all economic and social inequalities as well*. Much of this was faltering; in actual fact, little as yet may have been accomplished. But the historical watershed is the fact that a normative societal commitment has been made, and it, too, is largely irreversible.

These commitments are creating new and deep dilemmas for the society. To begin with, all issues and conflicts become explicit and focused. No one "voted in" the market economy and the industrial revolution, but today issues of direction of the economy, costs, redress, priorities, and goals all have become matters of conscious and debated social policy.[7] Moreover, the public household now becomes the arena for the expression not only of public needs *but also of private wants*. This takes the form of governmental responsibility for economic growth, or of various social claims on the community, such as higher education for all. Above all, the basic allocative power is now *political* rather than *economic*. And this raises a fundamental question of restraints. The economic constraint on private wants is the amount of money that a man has, or the credit he is able to establish. But what are the constraints on political demands?

"One of the great puzzles of the 20th century," Charles Lindblom has observed, "is that masses of voters in essentially free democratic societies do not use their votes to achieve a significantly more equal distribution of income and wealth, as well as of many of the other values to which men aspire. . . . What needs explaining is why they do not try." My argument is that such an effort will now be made. Until now the public household has not been the arena where such action could be effective. But today the public household is more than a third sector; increasingly in the modern polity it absorbs the other two. And the major aspect of the public household is the centrality of the budget, the level of government revenues and expenditures, as the mechanism for reallocation and redress. How

---

[7] One may also note, however, that the changeover in the conception of taxes—and the state budget in general—from revenues and the payment of the costs of government, to a fiscal instrument for economic direction and redistributive purposes, itself came gradually, and without plan, and was not subject at its inception to a conscious public policy debate either.

much the government shall spend, and for whom, obviously is the major political question of the next decades.

The fact that the public household becomes a "political market" means that the pressure to increase services is not necessarily matched by the mechanisms to pay for them, either a rising debt or rising taxes. What one finds, therefore, is that the new central issue for social analysis is "fiscal sociology" (the term is Schumpeter's), and that the new field of class struggle is tax conflict (the thought is Marx's).

THE EMERGENCE OF
FISCAL SOCIOLOGY

In a remarkable but neglected article published in 1918, "The Crisis of the Tax State,"[8] Joseph Schumpeter argued that the fiscal history of a society provides insight "into the laws of social being and becoming and into the driving forces of the fate of nations, as well as into the manner in which *concrete* conditions and in particular, organizational forms, grow and pass away." He further stated:

The public finances are one of the best starting points for an investigation of society, especially though not exclusively of its political life. The full fruitfulness of this approach is seen particularly at those turning points . . . during which existing forms begin to die off and to change into something new, and which always involve a crisis of the old fiscal methods. . . . Notwithstanding all the qualifications which always have to be made in such a case, we may surely speak of a special set of facts, a special set of problems, and of a special approach—in short, of a special field: fiscal sociology, of which much may be expected (p. 7).

The modern tax state, which for Schumpeter was the heart of "fiscal sociology," arose in the sixteenth century and after, primarily out of the needs of the princes and monarchs of the European states

---

[8] The essay, translated by W. F. Stolper and R. A. Musgrave, is reprinted in *International Economic Papers*, no. 4 (New York: Macmillan, 1954), pp. 5-38, The editors, in an introductory footnote, make a relevant observation: "*The Crisis of the Tax State* has been the least accessible of Schumpeter's major socio-economic writings and the only one which remained to be translated into English. It combines a historic analysis of the origin and nature of the modern democratic state with a sociology of taxation, outlines a theory of taxable capacity, and advances . proposals for the prevention of post-war inflation caused by the realization of liquid assets, which bear a striking resemblance to the currency reforms of recent decades."

to pay the expenses of war, especially as the breakdown of the feudal system of vassalage made it imperative to hire mercenary armies to do the fighting. Taxes thus came to be levied, and a bureaucratic administrative system arose to collect, and then to spend, these monies. And as the newly emergent state acquired a solid framework, taxes came to be used for purposes other than the original ones.[9]

It would be impossible to trace here the vicissitudes of the state —its extension in the monarchical societies and its decline in the bourgeois societies, which wanted a "poor" state. But the general process that Schumpeter describes as the origin of the system is, clearly, as a sociological process, a recurrent possibility. As Schumpeter wrote:

It goes without saying that there is more to the state than the collection of taxes necessitated by the common need that was their origin. Once the state exists as a reality and as a social institution, once it has become the center of the persons who man the governmental machine and whose interests are focused upon it, finally once the state is recognized as suitable for many things even by those individuals whom it confronts— once all this has happened, the state develops further and soon turns into something the nature of which can no longer be understood merely from the fiscal standpoint, and for which the finances become a serving tool. If the finances have created the modern state, so now the state on its part forms them and enlarges them—deep into the flesh of the private economy.[10]

The power of the state (and, indeed, its possible autonomous role) is the central fact about modern society. Yet to an extraordinary degree this role of the state, especially in economic matters,

[9] As Schumpeter adds, "This is why fiscal demands are the first sign of life of the modern state. This is why 'tax' has so much to do with 'state' that the expression 'tax state' might also be considered a pleonasm. And this is why fiscal sociology is so fruitful for the theory of the state" (p. 19).

It is no accident that the modern tax state appeared first in Central Europe, where the patrimonial households of the princes and monarchs became transformed into the public household, where bureaucracy thus first appeared, and where the state, in contradistinction to Anglo-American experience, took the lead in building the industrial society.

[10] Ibid., p. 19. Schumpeter also commented: "Taxes not only helped to create the state. They helped to form it. The tax system was the organ the development of which entailed the other organs. Tax bill in hand, the state penetrated the private economies and won increasing dominion over them. The tax brings money and calculating spirit into corners in which they do not dwell as yet, and thus becomes a formative factor in the very organism which has developed it. The kind and level of taxes are determined by the social structure, but once taxes exist they become a handle, as it were, which social powers can grip in order to change the structure" (p. 17).

played almost no part in Marx's discussion of capitalism. As the Marxist writer Rudolf Goldscheid observed 50 years ago:

Fiscal exploitation is the oldest form of exploitation besides outright slavery . . . . nearly all the privileged classes' privileges were tax privileges, the classes were largely tax classes. . . . In all these original forms of exploitation and early forms of capitalism, public finance and the tax system played a decisive part. Marx recognized this very clearly when he described public debts as the lever of original capital accumulation. Strangely enough, however, he failed to build this profound insight functionally into his whole doctrine.

. . . Indeed Marx so completely neglected the State in his conclusions, that he failed to observe how its expropriation helped the private expropriators.[11]

The reasons for this neglect, and they are central to the understanding of the limitations of Marxist theory, are twofold. First, Marx regarded society (the economic substructure), not the state (a political superstructure), as the true locus of social relations. The economic relations in production were decisive for the understanding of power. The state was the reflection of underlying economic forces and would be the instrument of the dominant economic classes. The state which had emerged in the seventeenth century was an aspect of monarchical feudal order that would become subordinate to bourgeois society.[12]

Second, Marx felt that bourgeois capitalism would solve—had solved—the problems of production and had created the necessary mechanisms, if not the economic fact, of abundance. For Marx, the contradiction of capitalism was the discrepancy between social labor and private property, between the cooperative nature of production and individual ownership. This is why, in the course of social evolution, socialism was the necessary next stage *after* capitalism. Socialism, in the conception of the first generation of Marxist writers, was a *distributive* concept, not a theory of how to manage an economy. Administration was thought to be a simple matter, so

---

[11] Rudolf Goldscheid, "A Sociological Approach to Public Finance," in Musgrave and Peacock, op. cit., pp. 204, 208.

[12] The one place where Marx wrestled with the problem of the state was the brilliant pamphlet *The Eighteenth Brumaire of Louis Napoleon.* The question he had to explain was how, in a bourgeois class-dominated society, an "adventurer" could arise who could seize state power and manipulate one class against another in the name of civil order. Marx makes the distinction between political power and economic power, and he acknowledges that while Louis Napoleon was able to break the political power of the middle classes, he did not challenge their "material" (i.e., economic) power.

simple—as Lenin thought in *State and Revolution*—that any shoe-maker could, in turn, take a hand in managing administrative matters. (His model, after all, was the post office.)

In a fundamental sense, these two theorems of Marx are irrelevant. The problem of *capital*—of raising it and spending it—is still very much with us, in the advanced industrial societies as well as the underdeveloped economies. In economic fact, it will *always* be with us. As Goldscheid said quite rightly:

> Every social problem and indeed every economic problem is in the last resort a financial problem. Whatever question is under discussion, whether it be intensification of agriculture to exploit the astonishing potentialities opened up by the progress of chemistry, or rationalization of industrial production, or an attempt to avoid the enormous waste of human life and health in our cultural progress—always we need capital, to be advanced for equipment which can yield a return only later. In this sense capitalism is an eternal economic category and it is immaterial whether the tasks are those of public economy or private economy (p. 212).

Furthermore, we have witnessed the "return" of the state. Marx—and orthodox Marxists—had felt that the state could not intervene in the inevitable crises of capitalism to provide economic stabilization and direction. In fact, when socialists were in office during the Depression, in Germany and in England (including the redoubtable Austro-German socialist economist Rudolf Hilferding, the author of the socialist classic *Das Finanzkapital*), the governments took no steps to manage the crisis (other than the classic capitalist response of deflation, which deepened the crisis) because the "overproduction" crisis had to run its course. That was what Marxism taught.[13]

James O'Connor, seeking to build a Marxist theory of the state in relation to the centrality of the state budget, based on Goldscheid, has posed the dilemma this way:

> Our first premise is that the capitalistic state must try to fulfill two basic and often mutually contradictory functions—*accumulation* and

[13] For a discussion of socialist economic policies during the Depression, see Adolf Sturmthal, *The Tragedy of European Labor* (New York: Columbia University Press, 1943), chaps. 4–10.

Yet as Goldscheid observed in his essay, written in 1925 but ignored at the time: "It is . . . both absurd and very strange that nearly all the leading socialist theoreticians from Marx to our days, who otherwise so despise bourgeois economic and financial theory, should agree with it so completely on the one point that tax reform and public finance reform can by and large alter nothing in the existing social order and that fiscal policy can contribute little or nothing to the solution of the social question" (p. 209).

legitimization. This means that the state must try to maintain or create the conditions in which profitable capital accumulation is possible. However, the state also must try to maintain or create the conditions of social harmony. A capitalist state that openly uses its coercive forces to help one class accumulate capital :* the expense of other classes loses its legitimacy and hence undermines the basis of its loyalty and support. But a state that ignores the necessity of assisting the process of capital accumulation risks drying up the sources of its own power, the economy's surplus production capacity and taxes drawn from this surplus (and other forms of capital).[14]

O'Connor is half right. This is a central dilemma of the capitalist state. But it is also true of *all* industrial or industralizing societies in which the state has taken a directive role; it is as true for the Soviet Union as for Algeria. Each state has to balance the calculation of capital accumulation (and the restriction of consumption) against the social needs and demands of the population. In this respect, the Soviet Union, too, is a state capitalist society, as are Algeria and most of the other countries that call themselves socialist.

The essential difference between the so-called socialist states and the Western capitalist states is less the question of property relations (though private property has given a dominant economic class a disproportionate degree of political power) than the character of the polity, the way the citizenry conceives of the public household. O'Connor writes that "a capitalist state that openly uses coercive forces to help one class accumulate capital at the expense of other classes loses its legitimacy and hence undermines the basis of its loyalty and support." But it is not the "capitalist state" that runs that risk, it is the *democratic* polity. In the Soviet Union, coercion is openly used to accumulate capital (wages are held down, strikes are forbidden), and a new bureaucratic class has benefited. The Soviet Union has been able to do this because of the combination of ideology (the promise of a Communist utopia) and terror (the secret police) which a totalitarian or quasi-totalitarian state can employ. (With the current waning of ideology, and in the inability to maintain total terror, the Communist Party risks losing its legitimacy unless it can find new ways of expanding its base of power and including other members of the managerial class in the crucial decision making.)

The sociological fact about modern Western democratic polities

[14] James O'Connor. *The Fiscal Crisis of the State* (New York: St. Martin's Press, 1973), p. 6. Italics in the original.

is that the political system is a wider arena in which all kinds of interests—ethnic, economic, functional (e.g., military), bureaucratic—are claimants. The political and philosophical problem of the public household derives from the fact that the state has to manage the double function of accumulation and legitimization: to provide a unified direction for the economy, in accordance with some conception of the common good (as well as to have some unified conception of the national interest in foreign policy); and to adjudicate—on the basis of power, or by some normative philosophical criterion—the conflicting claims of the different constituencies. In its first task, it has an autonomous function of leading and directing; in the second, it is at worst an arena of power, at best a normative umpire.

The sociological dilemma for the modern public household is that it not only has to provide for *public needs* in the conventional sense, but it has also become, inescapably, the arena for the fulfillment of *private and group wants*; and here, inevitably, the demands cannot easily be matched by the revenues, or by the sociological knowledge adequate to these demands. In this first respect, it was Schumpeter, 55 years ago, who uttered these prescient words:

> The fiscal capacity of the state has its limits not only in the sense in which this is self-evident and which would be valid also for a socialist community, but in a much narrower and, for the tax state, more painful sense. If the will of the people demands higher and higher public expenditures, if more and more means are used for purposes for which private individuals have not produced them, if more and more power stands behind this will, and if finally all parts of the people are gripped by entirely new ideas about private property and the forms of life—then the tax state will have run its course and society will have to depend on other motive forces for its economy than self-interest. This limit, and with it the crisis which the tax state could not survive, can certainly be reached. Without doubt, the tax state *can* collapse (p. 24).

THE REVOLUTION OF RISING ENTITLEMENTS

Condorcet and Tocqueville had argued that what was distinctive about modern society was the demand for equality. That thrust continues today, 150 years after it first emerged as a powerful political force. But in the last third of this century, the demand for equality has been broadened into a demand for a wider set of rights —political, civil, and social—as claims on the community.[15]

What is clear is that the revolution of rising expectations, which has been one of the chief features of Western society in the past 25 years, is being transformed into a *revolution of rising entitlements* for the next 25. This may take the form of a demand for a basic minimum family income, to give each family the floor of a modest standard of living; or a demand for "educational drawing rights" in which each person would be entitled to 12 or 14 or 16 years of free education, the times to be taken at the option of the individual; or a demand for the assurance of lifetime employment through a combination of private and public guarantees. The particular demands will vary with time and place. They are, however, not just the claims of the minorities, the poor, or the disadvantaged; they are the claims of *all* groups in the society, claims for protections and rights—in short, for *entitlements*.

What this means, inevitably, is an enormous expansion in services —human services, professional and technical services—in the society. In the last decade, health and education, along with government employment, have been the fastest-growing sectors in Western societies.[16] (An article in the February 22, 1974 issue of *Science*

[15] One forgets how recently the struggle for these rights began. Political rights, principally universal suffrage, were achieved for men and women only 50 or so years ago. And in several European countries (Belgium, Austria, and Germany) it took general strikes by the working class to win voting rights. In the American South, the blacks received legal voting protections less than a decade and a half ago. Civil rights include the traditional liberties of speech and assembly, but they also include right of access to all public places, right of free travel, etc.; and in many countries, these latter rights are still abridged. Social rights—economic security, social services, educational access, and the like—are still being negotiated.

[16] From 1945 to 1970, total expenditures by the U.S. government rose from 12.8 percent of GNP to 22.4 percent; that of state and local governments from 5.9 percent to 11.9 percent of GNP—in sum, government expenditures accounted for 34.3 percent of GNP—which totaled about $1.4 trillion dollars in 1974.

Since 1950, federal spending for what is defined as "social welfare purposes" has risen from $14 billion to $180 billion, or from less than a fifth of the federal budget to more than half. (Of that increase, 70 percent is accounted for by three broad areas: increases in social security, i.e., pensions for the aged; increases for veterans and for the handicapped and disadvantaged, i.e., the blind and aged; and medicaid for the poor and medicare for the aged.) If social expenditures by state and local governments are added, it appears that in 1975 the government is spending more than one-quarter trillion dollars for social programs.

In the last 25 years there has been a sizable shift in government expenditures from defense to social welfare. Between 1950 and 1960, total government expenditures rose by $81 billion, of which $29 billion or roughly 36 percent was for defense and international relations. Between 1960 and 1971, government expenditures increased pointed out that in the state of California, on any particular day, about 7.2 million of the state's 19.5 million people were under some institutional care, in day care centers, schools (but not colleges), hospitals, prisons, old age homes, and the like. That total was nearly as large as the state's entire civilian labor force that year.

The major dilemma in fiscal sociology arises from the structural imbalance between the technological (industrial and scientific) sector and the human and governmental services sector, in relation to productivity, wage increases, unit costs, and inflation. An obvious example should make this clear. Workers in the automobile industry may demand and receive a 10 percent wage increase. But labor costs are only 30 percent of the cost of producing an automobile, and the rise in unit costs is, therefore, only 3 percent. If the productivity of the industry rises 3 percent or more (and it usually does), then there is no inflationary increase and the cost of the wage in-

---

by $218.1 billion, of which, however, only $33.4 billion or roughly 15 percent, was accounted for by defense and international relations while that for domestic social programs grew by 184.7 billion. (The number of different federal grant programs for social purposes has gone from about 200 in the early 1960s, to more than 1,000 in 1975.)

The picture, in the broad view, can be seen from the following table. (I have picked five-year intervals, though in some cases inserted selected years to indicate sharp rises as in the late 1960s for the Vietnam War, and for social programs in the 1970s.)

Major Categories of Government Spending
(in billions of constant 1975 dollars)

Fiscal Year	Payments for Individuals	National Defense	Federal Non-Defense Operations	State and Local Operations
1955	$ 33	$112	$ 60	$ 76
1960	51	105	68	91
1965	66	110	92	113
1967	84	136	103	128
1968	93	151	109	134
1969	103	145	96	142
1970	110	130	97	144
1972	143	108	104	152
1974	164	91	96	164
1975	180	87	98	165

The figures here have been drawn from the tables on Governmental Revenues and Expenditures by Major Functions, *Statistical Abstract of the U.S.: 1974*, pp. 246 et seq. The table on Major Categories of Government Spending is from the Office of Financial Analysis of the U.S. Department of Treasury, and is from a memorandum by Daniel P. Moynihan on "Quality of Life of Individuals and Communities in the U.S." to the Commission on Critical Choices for Americans, June 1975.

crease can be readily absorbed. But what happens when policemen and, in tandem with them, firemen and sanitation workers also demand a 10 percent wage increase? In those instances, labor costs are about 70 percent of the cost of services, and a 10 percent wage increase translates itself into a 7 percent increase in unit costs. But productivity in such employment rises by, say, 2 percent. This means that there is a 5 percent inflationary gap as a result of the parallel wage increases. Given the fact that in the United States government employment, particularly at the state and local levels, has increased enormously (because of the greater demands for education, health care, and personal security), one has the ingredients for a deep and continuing urban crisis.[17]

Two major problems will confront the public household. One is the increasing "overload" of issues which the political system may simply be unable to manage. The virtue of the market is that it disperses responsibility for decisions and effects. The public household concentrates decisions and makes the consequences visible. The second problem is that, because of the pressure of the rising entitlements, there is a constant tendency for state expenditures to increase, requiring more taxes to pay for services, and stimulating more inflation because of the imbalances in productivity. Both are, simply, prescriptions for increased political instability and discontent.

In all this, too, there is an ideological irony. For more than 100 years—since the publication of *Capital*—Marxists have been predicting the demise of capitalism. The "first" theory predicted such a demise because the unplanned and anarchic nature of the market would lead to an excessive concentration of industry, resulting in declining profit margins (as the proportion of labor decreased) or in large imbalances between production and consumption. Where Marxists witnessed, as in the 1930s and after, extensive intervention by the state, and a redress of these imbalances, they then argued

[17] For a comprehensive discussion of this question, see William J. Baumol, "Macroeconomics of Unbalanced Growth: The Anatomy of the Urban Crisis," *American Economic Review* 62 (March 1972).

What gives added point to the entire problem is that 65 of every 100 persons in the labor force are today engaged in services (including transportation and utilities, as well as professional, business, and human services) and that by 1980 about 70 of every 100 persons in the labor force will be in services. For the general data on these macro-trends, see *The Coming of Post-Industrial Society* (New York: Basic Books, 1973), chap. 2.

that capitalists and legislators would readily vote money for armaments and defense, as a means of shoring up the economy, but not for social expenditures. Capitalism, therefore, was entirely dependent on a wartime economy. Now a third, neo-neo-Marxism, holds that the growth of the state sector, which particular emphasis on social expenditure, is necessary to the maintenance of capitalism; for as James O'Connor writes, "the fiscal crisis of the capitalist state is the inevitable consequence of the structural gap between state expenditures and revenues."

Each of the three versions held the dismal fate of capitalism to be inevitable. And at some point, since all social systems change, capitalism may expire and Marxist "theory" will claim the victory. But if the reason for capitalism's demise is the expansion of social expenditures, the labeling is a conceit. To call the heart of this argument "Marxism" is part of that incorrigible radical mythmaking which seeks to convert every crisis into proof of the validity of a (constantly redefined) ideology.[18] O'Connor remarks that "the only lasting solution to the fiscal crisis is socialism," a term that is left pristinely undefined. Yet it is unclear how "socialism," better than any other system, would decide the "efficient" allocation between "accumulation and social demands," or deal with those structural sources of inflation that derive from the imbalances of productivity in the different sectors.

Irony apart, there are real crises ahead for the public household, in all societies. But they do not derive primarily from the "iron laws" of economics; they are the recurrent dilemmas of private vices and public interests, now writ large. The resolution, essentially, can come only from a consensual agreement on the normative issues of distributive justice, in the balance to be struck between growth and social consumption. But can there be growth?

---

[18] If there are relevant intellectual ancestors for this present argument, they are Weber, with his conception of *legitimacy* (or the understanding of why people give assent or denial to a social system), and Schumpeter, with his conception of fiscal sociology and his insight into the social tensions generaated when a democratic polity begins to make demands which cannot be matched by the productive capacity of society.

THE DILEMMAS OF GROWTH: THE ECONOMIC CONTRADICTIONS OF CAPITALISM

The heart of all modern industrial societies, capitalist or Communist, is the ability to use a substantial portion of net national product for purposes of investment and economic growth. Apart from the question of the possible reduction of capital accumulation because of the rise in social expenditures, the commitment to economic growth, or even the ability of advanced economies to sustain growth, has been called into question for a host of other reasons, among them the adequacy of resources and the spillover effects on the environment.

The basic framework of socio-economic policy in the next decades will be set by the interplay of resources (food, energy, materials), population, and the environment. Whether resources will be sufficient, or whether the environment (including the atmosphere and climate) will be wrecked; whether the rate of population growth, most importantly in Asia and Latin America, can be slowed; these are questions on which the experts divide.[19] From a sociological perspective, however, one can make three observations about the character of "economic growth" in its relation to Western societies—and perhaps all societies, with the possible exception of China and the smaller tribal countries of Africa.

First, economic growth has become the secular religion of advancing industrial societies: the source of individual motivation, the

---

[19] The review studies prepared for the United Nations Symposium on Population, Resources, and the Environment in Stockholm, 1973, indicate that the *physical* magnitudes of minerals, energy, water, and land *are* sufficient on a global scale to sustain current growth rates for the next two or so decades. And a detailed inventory or resource availability of the major mineral reserves provides "clear evidence . . . that the future will not be limited by sheer availability of important materials . . ." For the UN studies, see Roger Revelle, "Will the Earth's Land and Water Resources Be Sufficient for Future Populations?" and D. B. Brooks and P. W. Andrews, "World Population and Mineral Resources: Counterintensive or Not?" *UN Symposium on Population, Resources, and Environment* (Stockholm, 1973). For the inventory of resource availability, see William D. Nordhaus, "Resources as a Constraint on Growth," *Proceedings of the American Economic Association*, 64 (May 1972).

The real economic problem—and the drag on economic growth—will be the increase in costs of extracting these minerals, or the payment of "monopoly" prices, such as the price of oil, to producer cartels. The rate of economic growth will depend largely on the rising costs of these primary products.

basis of political solidarity, the ground for the mobilization of society for a common purpose. A hundred or more years ago, as I pointed out, nobody "voted in" the Industrial Revolution, in the way various political assemblies proclaimed a French Declaration of the Rights of Man, a Constitution for the United States, or a program for the Soviet Union. But as the standard of living kept rising, societies became conscious of the steady possibilities of economic growth, and what had been largely an uncoordinated market process now became the object of concerted government policy. In one sense, economic growth, by holding out a promise of plenty for the citizenry, has been the "moral equivalent" of war that William James once sought. Previous wealth had been gained by plunder, annexation, expropriation; now societies were being mobilized for a concerted internal effort, rather than for war against a neighboring state. While economic growth has never had the emotional power of nationalism, or of other ideological appeals that have been used to mobilize societies, it has become an important creed for Western industrial societies. If there is no commitment to economic growth, what can the Soviet Union—or Japan, or the United States—hold out as a social goal for its people?

The second fact is that economic growth has been a "political solvent." While growth invariably raises expectations, the means for financing social welfare expenditures and defense—without reallocating income (always a politically difficult matter) or burdening the poor (which has become almost an equally difficult affair)—have come essentially from economic growth. In a trillion-dollar economy, an increase in the economic growth rate of 1 percent means a net addition of $100 billion by the end of a decade. And as the Kennedy and Johnson administrations found out (until Vietnam war expenditures began to escalate), the Congress was more willing to vote for the social welfare costs of the New Frontier or the Great Society, so long as economic growth provided additional fiscal revenues, than to reform the tax structure or increase the weight of taxes in the society.

And yet, paradoxically—and this is the third point—economic growth may be the source of a distinctive "contradiction" of capitalism, a contradiction which may be the cause of its economic undoing. For economic growth has been inextricably linked with inflation, and it seems unlikely that any democratic political economy can abolish its inflation without disastrous political consequences.

The inflation which has been plaguing the industrial economies for the past several years seems to be a compound of several convergent factors: a simultaneous increase in demand on a worldwide scale; shortages in primary commodities and raw materials (e.g., food); shortages in primary processing capacity (e.g., steel, paper); wage-cost inflation as a function of shifts in employment from the industrial to service sectors and the reduced productivity in services; and the inability of governments to reduce expenditures. Some of these, presumably, are temporary—so we are told about the shortages in primary commodities and primary processing capacity. Some of these are inherently structural; this is certainly the case in the differential productivity between the industrial and service sectors.

But underneath all this is a basic change in the character of society which makes it difficult for any polity to use the traditional modes of restraint or "discipline" (in the archaic use of the term) to hold down demand, to increase unemployment, or to reduce governmental expenditures. In the last two decades, economic growth has been tied to various social objectives, the chief of which has been full employment and a steady increase in consumption. In sum, the Keynesian revolution—for this is the simplest, symbolic shorthand for the change—has meant a powerful and irreversible revolution in social expectations as well. Put simply, where workers once feared losing a job, which was the common experience of the Depression, they now expect a job and a rising standard of living. And no government can deny that expectation.

What this has meant, practically, is that governments necessarily will increase spending, and run larger budget deficits, if unemployment tends to rise; equally, governments are called upon to increase social expenditures, particularly in the areas of health, welfare, social services, and the like. Meanwhile, trade unions, for both defensive reasons (when prices are rising) and for aggressive reasons (to share in the economic growth), maintain steady pressure for wage increases. So a steady albeit manageable, inflation of 4 to 5 percent a year—becomes an inevitable concomitant of economic growth, and this becomes the "price" the polity pays for social peace. But where such inflation conjoins with other structural or contingent elements to create an inflationary spiral—such as the double-digit inflation that many Western societies now face—then the "normal" economic tools which are available to government become ineffective. The normal responses are to reduce the money supply (but this creates liquidity crises and possible bankruptcies for firms and, more broadly, tends to hurt crucial sectors such as construction and home building, which are highly sensitive to interest rates), or to reduce heavily the level of government expenditures. But governments find it difficult to do either, since a major consequence of such deflation is a rise in unemployment—and to levels which are politically unacceptable. An alternative is to institute an "incomes policy" which seeks, by administrative fiat, to establish levels of equity in the polity; but without a heavy tax load on the wealthy, an incomes policy is unacceptable to unions. And, finally, one can seek strong wage and price controls, with consequent distortions of the economy and often, in the end, wholesale evasions. But the simple point is that no one wants to pay for the inflation, and modern democratic governments find it politically difficult to assess any particular group for the costs.

And yet a fundamental dilemma exists. A persisting double-digit inflation wrecks the middle class. A strong deflationary policy creates rising unemployment and succeeds only at the expense of a portion of the working class. The only way out, if *both* continue, would necessarily have to be strong wage-price controls, and an incomes policy to adjust inequities. Yet such controls, to be effective, would require a strong regulatory body with policy powers to halt any widespread evasions. And if such controls remained for a long period of time, as they might, crucial decisions on investment would necessarily become a matter of government say as well. In short, that way out of the dilemma, without recourse to a class war, would mean the transformation of the private enterprise economy into a corporative society. Where inflation continues rampant, a new class war takes place, not primarily between employers and workers in enterprises, but between the middle class and the working class, in the arena of the state budget.

Schumpeter once remarked that stationary feudalism was an historical entity, stationary socialism an historical possibility, but stationary capitalism an historical contradiction in terms. It was the central insight of Marx that a capitalist economy had to keep expanding, by accumulation and by the reinvestment of capital. Proponents of a "stagnation" thesis in the late 1930s argued that a capitalist economy would necessarily reach a finite limit of expansion because of the exhaustion of investment opportunities, a belief that was belied, as Schumpeter again was the first to point out, by the "open seas" of technology and technological innovation. But the major problem regarding growth is that when there is a persistent inflation, the economy has a chronic shortage of capital, and corporations find themselves in recurrent liquidity crises as the money managers, in an effort to curb inflation, hold down the money supply.

Obviously, if a society expects sustained inflation, few people will save (since the money will steadily lose value) or commit their money to long-term investments in bonds or equity shares. Corporations, in turn, must increasingly resort to bank loans, commercial paper, or other short-term credit instruments not only to raise working capital but also to pay for longer-term needs.

The major consequence of inflation is that the capital burden falls increasingly on the banks, or on the government. In the United States, the Banking Act of 1933 separated investment banking and commercial banking precisely to limit bank control of large corporations, as had happened in the 1920s. The passage, though, of new legislation in 1970 allowed the major banks to establish bank holding companies which moved heavily into consumer credit, financing of real-estate construction, and even into long-term corporate credit. To raise their own capital, banks competed for money, "buying" corporate certificates of deposit, Eurodollar deposits, and idle reserves of smaller banks. In the early 1970s, the banks found themselves strapped as they became overextended on loans, particularly in the real-estate field. In consequence, the government has become more central, not only as a "bail-out" for corporations, but even, as has been proposed by a number of sophisticated financiers, as a direct source of equity capital for industries, such as utilities and housing, that cannot get funds in the regular capital markets.[20]

[20] See Felix G. Rohatyn, "A New R.F.C. Is Proposed for Business," *New York Times*, December 1. 1974, sec. 3, pp. 1, 12. As Mr. Rohatyn, a partner in Lazard Frères, observes, in the past ten years the debt-equity ratio of individual corporations has gone from 25 percent to 40 percent, under the pressure of inflation and the collapse of the equity markets. The New York stock exchange has estimated that corporations will require about $50 billion a year in new equity capital for the next decade, but in 1974 there was only about $5 billion forthcoming in equity capital. Since the banks themselves are overextended, the only solution, Rohatyn contends, is a government corporation, similar to the Reconstruction Finance Corporation (RFC) set up during the Depression, to provide that money. Nor does Mr. Rohatyn shrink from the implications of his proposal: "There can be no denying that such an organization . . . can be perceived as a first step toward state planning

In England, the Labour government had to step in and bail out the Leyland Motors Corporation, England's largest auto firm, and Burmah Oil, which had opened up the North Sea explorations, when both companies found themselves in difficulties. The French government rescued Le Nickel, the world's second-largest nickel company, in 1974 by buying a half-share of the company's operations in New Caledonia, which, though in the Pacific, is part of metropolitan France. And in the United States the government has been of direct or indirect help to the railroads, the aerosapce industry, and even the automobile industry, by indirect tax benefits or direct capital infusions.

Whether by becoming the "investor of last resort," or by influencing the capital market through credit allocation (e.g., directing banks to allocate monies specifically to certain industries, such as housing), or by investing directly in firms (taking a strong equity position through shareholding), government will inevitably extend its power in the capital markets. At what point one would call this "state capitalism," or a "corporative economy," may be more a matter of semantics than of reality. The basic point is that the scope of private corporate control of its own affairs in this most crucial of all matters—the management of capital—is increasingly diminished. What counts more and more is the nature and quality of state policy, and the degree of public voice in setting societal goals.

But there is a larger "cultural" question in which these economic issues are embedded. American capitalism changed its nature in the 1920s by heavily encouraging the consumers to go into debt, and to live with debt as a way of life. In the 1960s, the basic financial structure of the economy became transformed when sharp individuals began to realize that considerable fortunes could be created through "leverage," that is, by going heavily into debt and using that borrowed money to underwrite finance companies, create real estate investment trusts, and increase the debt/equity ratio of corporations, rather than expand out of internal financing or by equity capital. The changes in the banking laws allowed bank holding

of the economy. Yet the time may have come for a public debate on this subject. . . . What many will call state planning would, to the average family, be no more than prudent budgeting. . . . There are many who believe that long-range economic planning at the Federal level will become a necessity. . . . The RFC could be one of the key instruments in this kind of approach. By injecting equity capital where none is available in quantity, it could facilitate major restructuring for the public purpose."

companies to extend, in rickety ways, the financial structure of the economy. But it was a highly leveraged economy—an economy built on a mountain of debt. An incomes statement, which deals with revenues and profits (much of these from "accounts receivable") is of interest to an accountant, and for a strong company, to an investor. But the key variable, where there is a mounting debt, is the "cash flow," the monies coming in, either from current income or from borrowing, to pay for the rising costs. When money becomes tight, cash flow becomes a problem, and there ensues a liquidity crisis. And again, out of this leverage and liquidity one finds an additional inflationary pressure.

Just as families have to learn to live within their means, the question is whether the economy can be "disciplined"—and the master has to be the government—to live within the actual cash flows available, and to forego debt. But if one foregoes debt—either in consumption or in investment—what happens to growth in the economy? Necessarily, it has to slow down.

Economic growth and inflation thus involve a peculiar contradiction in capitalist democratic economies. In the Communist states such as the Soviet Union, economic growth has gone largely into expanding the heavy industry sectors, rather than into consumption; workers' wages and demands are controlled; and the inflation, which does exist, is disguised by the underemployment of labor or by chronic shortages.

Marx had argued that capitalism had to keep on expanding or it would collapse. For him the internal dynamism of the system was the competitive effort of capitalists to maintain a rate of surplus value by increasing the ratio of technology to labor. Capital accumulation thus was seen as the motor of the system. But the irony is that economic growth, which is the fruit of capital accumulation, has created a set of economic and cultural expectations which the system finds difficult to reduce, and which, when coupled with other erratic factors (such as the wild yet recurrent inflations that come from a spurting world economy), creates conditions of economic and political instability that governments increasingly find difficult to manage. And all of these lead to disorientations and insecurities which shake the faith of individuals in their societies.

THE CRISES OF BELIEF

Crises of belief are recurrent in human history, which does not make them less significant, even if the topic risks becoming banal. The invitation to despair arises because the consequences are real, if not always immediate, and yet no one can do very much about them. Gadgets can be engineered, programs can be designed, institutions can be built, but belief has an organic quality, and it cannot be called into being by fiat. Once a faith is shattered, it takes a long time to grow again—for its soil is experience—and to become effective again.

In the Soviet Union, where a messianic creed sought to embody itself in a people, the crisis of belief is threefold: most persons no longer believe in the creed (would one dispute the end of ideology in the Soviet Union?); there is a loss of faith in the leaders (the denigration of Stalin, and the admission of *his* crimes by his heirs, effectively broke the feet of that idol); and few persons seem to believe in "the future"—it no longer works.

In the United States there has been a loss of nerve on the part of the establishment; in fact, the chief characteristic of the establishment is its eagerness to repudiate its own existence. There is a widespread questioning of the legitimacy of institutions, especially on the part of the young who would normally move into elite positions. In the population at large there is a loss of confidence about the future of the country.

In Japan, a "frame," or a complicated set of reciprocal obligations between individuals in a group situation, has held the institutions of the society together. Japanese religion has been an extension of such mediating ties between persons, not a belief in transcendence as in the West. Those ties, before World War II, were centered in the nation (and the army) and in the emperor, as the embodiments of the religion. Those ties were transferred, after a shattering military defeat, into the mundane tasks of economic reconstruction and growth. But a double problem emerges: if economic growth falters, what could replace it (the reassertion of an aggressive nationalism?); or if economic growth increases affluence, will the discretionary social behavior that accompanies it tend to dissolve the frame?

The major consequence of this crisis—I leave aside its deeper cultural dilemmas—is the loss of *civitas*, that spontaneous willingness to obey the law, to respect the rights of others, to forgo the temptations of private enrichment at the expense of the public weal —in short, to honor the "city" of which one is a member. Instead, each man goes his own way, pursuing his private vices, which can be indulged only at the expense of public benefits.

The foundation of any liberal society is the willingness of all groups to compromise private ends for the public interest. The loss of *civitas* means either that interests become so polarized, and passions so inflamed, that terrorism and group fighting ensues, and political *anomia* prevails; or that every public exchange becomes a cynical deal in which the most powerful segments benefit at the expense of the weak. Yet even where a sense of *civitas* remains, as in England, the ruts into the future may have been cut so deep from the past—the constraints may be so large, the freedom to maneuver and change so narrow, the institutions, particularly the economic ones, so encrusted—that no regime can substantially stop the slide, and a sense of weariness and despair takes over. These are the grays on gray, the crises of the political order, of the next 25 years.

Several generations of idealists, like many younger people today, saw socialism as the answer to bourgeois society. Yet the death of socialism is the unrealized political fact of this century. In the Soviet world we have seen the cruel falsification of the communal dreams of the nineteenth-century radicals. The "socialism" of most of the third-world countries is a deceit in that liberty and freedom are denied while new elites drive the people in the name of economic development. And in China the people are fused into a single "moral personality," embodied in the thought of Mao, so that all ego is erased and all individual voices of expression, especially in culture, are suppressed. Whether this will take hold as a new "religion"—or whether, after the death of Mao, new forces of individuation will appear—remains to be seen.

In the Communist countries of Europe, the decline of faith makes the question of *civitas* more salient; inevitably, *civitas* becomes identified with public liberties. For the Communist countries, the problem is that there are no institutional outlets for dissent, no public debate, no accessible arena where "factions" (I use Madison's sense of the term, not Lenin's) can declare their interests. Yet a complex society inevitably multiplies constituencies and interests, and one has to provide some legitimate arena for the mediation of their claims. In the Soviet Union, in the next 25 years, the two major political problems may be the reassertion of demands by the nationalities for greater autonomy (and a sharing of power) and the broadening of the political system.

In the West, in the next decade, we will probably see the increasing frustration of the middle classes, with political effects difficult to detail. Higher-salaried workers are beginning to resent the narrowing of differentials in pay, as a result of egalitarian tendencies; was the strike of the higher Swedish civil servants in 1973 the harbinger of more such action to come? The rising cost of services means a curtailment of everyday amenities, including mail delivery and garbage collection.[21] But these are petty frustrations as against the double impact of inflation and taxes.

The middle class suffers for a double reason: the increase in prices requires an increase in income to keep pace;[22] but the increased income puts the middle-class person in a higher tax bracket where the new "bite" is more than proportional to the increase in income, so the erosion becomes steeper. If the inflation is rapid, and the tax system unchanged, the spiral becomes a geometric progression. As the *Economist* commented: "If you earn £10,000 a year, and if the present 19 percent annual inflation rate and the 1974–75 tax rates continue, you will need £40,000 a year by 1978 merely to maintain your present living standards. You won't get it."

The irony of all this is that inflation becomes a ready means of financing new public expenditures, as larger proportions of individuals move automatically into higher tax brackets. And, as has been said, to an even greater degree the basic resources of the society will go into the purchase of public goods. But as Anthony Downs has pointed out, it is often difficult to convince a public of the worthwhileness of such goods, since they are uniform and rarely

[21] Herman Kahn has proposed a "law" that as the income per capita in any society approaches $4,000 a person, the standard of living of the upper middle class falls: one cannot find porters at railroad stations (*pace* Tokyo Central Station); page boys to deliver books in a library (*pace* the New York Public Library); shoeshine boys in a shoe-repair shop; or more than once-a-week garbage collection in Cambridge, Massachusetts.

[22] In the United States, as late as 1940, 26 percent of the population was self-employed; as small businessmen or independent artisans or professionals, people could try to increase their own prices in the effort to beat inflation. But today 85 percent of the labor force is on wages or salary, locked into incomes which can only move on a step-plateau basis. A large portion of union wages are "indexed," i.e., adjusted automatically to cost-of-living escalation, but most salaried workers, particularly middle-class professionals, are not so covered, and therefore the lag is greater.

adapted to individual taste; and as Mancur Olson has noted, since a collective good has to be available to all, many individuals hold back from paying for it in the hope of gaining a "free ride."[23] But the main point is that the expansion of such goods and the increases in governmental costs and services have to come, in the end, from taxes. And for most persons, taxes are seen not as the necessary purchase of goods which the individual cannot purchase for himself, but as a reduction in personal income. Private consumption is a matter of individual choice, public consumption a matter of legislative fiat; most persons regard the latter as an abridgment of their "freedom to spend."

When the effective tax rate in a society rises to 35 percent or more of an individual's income, and he becomes increasingly aware of these increases, one has a further recipe for discontent, unless the reasons for such taxes are clearly spelled out. But few politicians usually have that courage, and it is easier to pander to the discontent.

The consequence is a sharp increase in political instability. In the next decade we may see the breakup of the party systems as we have known them in Western societies. There seems to be, especially among the middle classes, a revulsion against politics, a mood which, in the past, has led to the weakening of strong party rule and the fragmentation of legislative bodies. What is striking is that, as of 1974, no party held a majority in the legislatures of Norway, Sweden, Denmark, France, West Germany, the Netherlands, Belgium, Italy, or Great Britain.

In Denmark, Norway, and Sweden, which for 40 years gloried in the "middle way," there has been a sharp polarization of the electorate that is alarming to the established parties. In Denmark and Norway anti-tax parties have emerged in protest against high taxes, "indulgent" welfarism, the growth of governmental bureaucracy, aid to developing countries, and even high defense expenditures. Throwing the traditional conservatives into disarray, Mogens Glistrup's Progress Party came from nowhere in the 1973 elections to form the second largest group in the Danish Parliament. And in Norway a similar party, led by Anders Lange, achieved a striking electoral success. The reaction of the Social Democratic parties in

[23] See Anthony Downs and Joseph Monsen, "Public Goods and Private Status," *The Public Interest*, no. 23 (Spring 1971): 64–77; and Mancur Olson, *The Logic of Collective Action* (Cambridge: Harvard University Press, 1965).

both countries was to claim that these protests were "populist" in their aims and demagogic in their methods, appealing to people's worst instincts and behaving in a truly un-Scandinavian manner!

In the United States, the political party is in a state of decay. Most party machines are weak in finances, personnel, and resources. Party identification has weakened. Forty percent of the electorate designates itself as "independent," and fewer and fewer persons take the trouble to vote.

True, party systems are deeply embedded in the institutional life of Western societies: they are often legally reinforced, as is the two-party system in most U.S. state voting laws; and they have patronage and cadres. But it is likely that there will be more "invasions" of the parties by extremist factions, as in the case of the McGovern "new politics" in the Democratic Party, or the Young Socialists in the German SPD. And it is likely that we shall see larger swings between parties in elections, or the recourse to extra-political party organizations.

In all this, there is a double danger. Politics is always a compound of interests and symbolic expressions (ideologies or emotional attachments to individuals or institutions). One may forgo interests yet still retain beliefs; or lose beliefs yet still have an interest stake in the society. But where trust in society and its institutions is battered, and where interests fail to gain the recognition they feel entitled to, there is an explosive mixture ready to be set off. Individuals cannot stand too much uncertainty in their lives, and the direst measures of uncertainty are the rapid and fluctuating loss in value of the money people use for exchange (the aggravating discrepancies between income and what one has to buy, the erosion of the wealth one has painfully accumulated) and fluctuating unemployment. It is in these circumstances that the traditional institutions and democratic procedures of a society crack, and the irrational, emotional angers and the desire for a political savior come to flood tide. The decline of liberal democracy—especially in Europe—and a shift to the political extremes may well be the most unsettling fact of the last quarter of the century.

The economic dilemmas confronting Western societies derive from the fact that we have sought to combine bourgeois appetites which resist curbs on acquisitiveness, either morally or by taxation; a democratic polity which, increasingly and understandably, demands more and more social services as entitlements; and an individualist ethos which at best defends the idea of personal liberty, and at worst evades the necessary social responsibilities and social sacrifices which a communal society demands. In sum, we have had no normative commitment to a public household or a public philosophy that would mediate private conflicts.

It is too easy to say, as many radicals do, that this is all a consequence of "capitalism." And even more deceptive is the implied answer that there is a normative alternative called "socialism" which is economically viable and philosophically justifiable. All that the radicals have done is to beg the question. Whether socialism is economically viable in an advanced industrial society and a democratic polity that is responsive to the diverse needs and desires of diverse groups, *without coercion and the loss of liberty*, is quite debatable. And other than the promise of an "abundance" that would dissolve all social conflicts, we have not had any political or philosophical schema in the name of socialism that justifies the new distributive rules of such a society.[24]

[24] Within the framework of political theory, the problem can be looked at not only in terms of consensus but also in terms of legitimacy, a concept which goes to the root values of a society.

Jürgen Habermas, the leading Marxist scholar today, locates the "legitimation" problem primarily in the conflict between a capitalism founded on private, individual motives, and one which inexorably becomes a state capitalist society where the individual cannot be motivated or rewarded in individual terms. While I think that the ground of the argument is correct, what troubles me about the way Habermas formulates it is that in his language, systems become "reified"; that is, the systems create or compel behavior, or manipulate persons, and the recalcitrances of individual societies, or the character of people or traditions, disappear under the monolithic weight of the term "system."

Thus, in dealing with the question of the rising, competing social demands which place heavy burdens on the polity, Habermas writes: "We would still have to explain why late-capitalist societies even bother to retain formal democracy. Merely in terms of the administrative system, formal democracy could just as easily be replaced by a variant—a conservative, authoritarian welfare state that reduces the political participation of the citizens to a harmless level; or a Fascist authoritarian state that keeps the population toeing the mark on a relatively high level of permanent mobilization."

Habermas explains that such solutions are less possible today because "the socio-cultural system creates demands that cannot be satisfied in authoritarian systems." And he continues: "This reflection leads me to the following thesis: Only a rigid socio-cultural system, incapable of being randomly functionalized for the needs of the administrative system, could explain how legitimation difficulties result in a legitimation crisis. This development must therefore be based on a *motivation crisis*—i.e., a discrepancy between the need for motives that the state and the occupational system announce and the supply of motivation offered by the socio-cultural system."

And he concludes: "If no sufficient concordance exists between the normative

Any society, in the end, is a moral order that has to justify (in the sociological jargon, to legitimate) its allocative principles and the balances of freedoms and coercions necessary to facilitate or enforce such rules. The problem, inevitably, is the relation between self-interest and the public interest, between personal impulses and community requirements. Without a public philosophy, explicitly stated, we lack the fundamental condition whereby a modern polity can live by consensus (and without it there is only continuing conflict) and justice.

In the United States, in the past, there was an "unspoken consensus," and the public philosophy did not need to be articulated. There was, as Louis Hartz has pointed out, a liberal tradition, derived from Locke, that shaped the political system. Lacking a Robespierre, it also lacked a de Maistre, so that both revolution and reaction as contending forces never found fertile soil in American life. The American style was one of ad hoc compromise. In American political debates, except for the Civil War, there was rarely an appeal to "first principles" as, say, in France, where every political division was rooted in the alignments of the French Revolution. In

---

structures that still have some power today and the politico-economic system, then [capitalism] can still avoid motivation crises by uncoupling the cultural system. Culture would then become a nonobligatory leisure occupation or the object of professional knowledge."

I do not think that "formal democracy" in countries such as Sweden, England, and the United States can "easily" be replaced. The strength of democracy derives from an autonomous tradition of liberty, not the "needs" of the capitalist system. Paradoxically, the only societies capable of maintaining a permanent mobilization of the population are not the "late [i.e., advanced] capitalist" societies, but the revolutionary societies, which are the authoritarian ones.

Further, I do not think that there is a unified politico-economic system, since the polity is both the regulator of the economy and the wider arena for claimants of rights; and while I would agree that there is a disjunction between the motivations demanded in the economic and production systems and the life-styles which are sought in the culture, I do not believe that culture can be "uncoupled" (and by whom?) and remain as an area where people harmlessly discharge their impulses, sexual and otherwise. As I have argued in the first chapter, it is precisely in the realm of culture that capitalism becomes undermined and its "hegemony" is virtually destroyed. On that score, therefore, I am more pessimistic than Habermas about the long-run ability of capitalist society to maintain its vitality as a moral and reward system for its citizens. And yet, the grounds for legitimacy may rest in the values of political liberalism *if* it can be divorced from bourgeois hedonism. This is the issue I address in the next section of this essay.

For Habermas' argument, see "What Does a Crisis Mean Today? Legitimation Problems in Late Capitalism," *Social Research* 40 (Winter 1973): 643–667. This essay appears as Part Two of Habermas's book *Legitimation Crisis* (Boston: Beacon Press, 1975).

the United States, there were three unspoken assumptions: that the values of the individual were to be maximized, that rising material wealth would dissolve all strains resulting from inequality, and that the continuity of experience would provide solutions for all future problems. Abundance, too, was the American surrogate for socialism.

Yet all those assumptions have now broken down. Groups, and the community, have their claims. Rising wealth has not redeemed inequalities and has brought new problems in its wake. Experience is no longer a sure guide to the complex, technical problems of a modern society. And the values underlying the assumptions of material well-being and achievement are now also being called into question.

Some new purposes have to be established. Some new assumptions have to be laid down. The implicit agreements of the past were a great strength, for articulation always lays bare the contradictions between ideology and reality, and calls for a resolution which cannot always be given. Yet such a task cannot be evaded. The consumer-oriented, free-enterprise society no longer morally satisfies the citizenry, as it once did. And a new public philosophy will have to be created in order that something we recognize as a liberal society may survive.[25]

II

THE PUBLIC PHILOSOPHY

The centrality of the public household in a modern interdependent economy is inescapable. Moreover, as I have tried to show, the public household is not just "the government," or a public economic sector alongside the market economy and the domestic household;

[25] In this discussion of the national style, I have drawn on some paragraphs from an earlier essay, "The Disposessed—1962," in *The Radical Right* (Garden City, N.Y.: Doubleday, 1963), pp. 14-15. For the argument on the "unspoken consensus," see Louis Hartz, *The Liberal Tradition in America* (New York: Harcourt, Brace and World, 1955), Pt. 1; and on the characteristic American mode of compromise, the essay by W. W. Rostow, "The National Style," in *The American Style*, ed. Elting E. Morison (New York: Harper, 1958).

it is now prior to both and directive of each. It is the *polis* writ large. Yet we do not have any theoretical underpinning for this state of affairs—a political economy of the public household that joins the economic and the political dimensions, or a political philosophy of the public household that provides decision rules for the normative resolution of conflicting claims and a philosophical justification of the outcome. Walter Lippmann has observed wryly that "there are those who would say . . . that it is the characteristic illusion of the tender-minded to believe in philosophy." Yet the point of philosophy is that it states a rational standard, provides for consistency of application so that actions are not arbitrary or capricious, and establishes a normative justification which satisfies men's sense of fairness. Only on that basis are some consensual principles of political life possible; without them, there is only brute power. People obey might but respect, and voluntarily agree to, right.

The political philosophy of the classical *polis* was set forth by Aristotle. Its model was the family: just as there is the natural authority of the parent, so there is the natural authority of those most fit to rule, the rational men. The basis of the *polis* is the satisfaction of natural needs. Unlimited acquisition can only be destructive of the household; the aim of household management, therefore, is restraint of desire. This is a point of view distinctly uncongenial to a democratic ethos and to the modern temper.

Such issues apart, the sheer sociological limitation to the Aristotelian *polis* is *scale*. A society where individuals seek to help one another, and to share on the basis of some common principles, requires that individuals know one another well and can express their concern for each other; the basis of such a society is mutual love or mutual trust. This is why Rousseau, in *The Social Contract*, argued that the moral society could only be a small one, and why Freud, in *Civilization and Its Discontents*, argued that Communism, or equal sharing, was impossible in the larger society, since the love which held persons together was only meaningful if it was direct and specific to each, rather than "aim-inhibited" and generalized to all "humanity." As Leo Strauss put it: "Only a society small enough to permit mutual trust is small enough to permit mutual responsibility or supervision—the supervision of actions or manners which is indispensable for a society concerned with the perfection of its members; in a large city, in 'Babylon,' everyone can live more or less as he lists."²⁶ (Modern society, as F. Scott Fitzgerald also knew, is Babylon.)

In contrast to this communitarian ethic are the justifications of the liberal society laid down by Locke, Adam Smith, and Kant. Central to Locke's thought is the doctrine of individual property. Property is the extension of one's own labor; it provides protection from exploitation by others; it is the corollary of the right of self-preservation. For Adam Smith, individual exchange, in which each man pursues his own self-interest, is the basis of freedom, self-satisfaction, and mutual advantage; when rationally pursued through the division of labor, it is also the basis of accumulation and wealth. For Kant, the character of public law is primarily *procedural* rather than substantive; its purpose is to define the rules of the game within which men can freely compete for what they want, rather than to prescribe specific outcomes.

The logic of all three arguments is, in the words of Adam Smith, "within the system of natural liberty" to limit the public household to three tasks: protecting the society from violence and invasion by other societies; providing internal security and the administration of justice; and "erecting and maintaining certain public works and certain public institutions, which it can never be for the interest of any individual, or small number of individuals, to erect and maintain; because the profit could never repay the expense to any individual or small number of individuals, though it may frequently do much more than repay it to a great society."

The "great society," a phrase which occurs thrice in *The Wealth of Nations*, in its context (which is established at the conclusion of Book 5, Chapter 1) means the "whole society."²⁷ Yet more and more, since the initial prescriptions, the establishment of "public works and public institutions" has become a larger and larger task for the "great society," and today the balance has shifted drastically in that direction. But this new "collectivist" reality exists in a theoretical vacuum.

Socialism—I think primarily of the Marxist tradition—has never found it necessary to provide a normative justification of its philos-

---

²⁶ Leo Strauss, *Natural Right and History* (Chicago: University of Chicago Press, 1953), p. 131.

²⁷ Adam Smith, *The Wealth of Nations* (New York: Modern Library, 1937), p. 651. (See also pp. 681, 647 for discussions of the "great society.")

ophy, even though it claims to be the doctrine of the public household par excellence. This is in part because it was conceived in an evolutionary frame, in which socialism was seen as the next, higher stage of consciousness or rationality; and in part because for Marx the precondition for Communism was *the abolition of economics itself*. The source of evil in the world for Marx is scarcity, for this gives rise to envy and competition, and the murderous pursuit of private advantage. Nature, in Marx's view (following Hegel), is necessity; economics is the labor necessary for wresting goods from nature. As man gains technical powers over matter, he moves out of nature into history; and the end of history, that final independence from nature, is freedom. When man does not have to labor, when there is abundance for all, the superstructure is, so to speak, cut loose, and man can move where he will, free of necessity and constraint. Under Communism, in effect, there are no problems of allocation.[28]

But the ineluctable fact about any society, as we now recognize, is that there is no escape from "economics." Men constantly redefine needs so that former wants become necessities. The constraints of resources are tangible, and while the amounts needed may not become physically exhausted, the costs of using these rise, and relative costs, not physical quantities, become the measures of scarcity.[29]

[28] In a curious sense, this is the argument of Locke as well. Restrictions on acquisitiveness were required in the state of nature because the state of nature is a state of penury. They can safely be abandoned in civil society because civil society is a state of plenty. And this became the justification of "bourgeois" acquisitiveness, the expansion of "wants."

The utopian socialist doctrines of Fourier and Saint-Simon were anchored, however, in a theory of human nature. Fourier felt that men differed significantly in temperaments and appetites (much like Jung's division of psychological types), and that the communitarian colony would match the contrasting and complementary temperaments to produce harmony. Saint-Simon thought that men differed in talents and competences, and that occupational divisions in the socialist society would be in "chambers" that would group these different competences in a rational division of function See my essay "Socialism," in the *International Encyclopedia of the Social Sciences* (New York: Macmillan, 1968), and my essay, "Charles Fourier: Prophet of Eupsychia," in *The American Scholar* 38 (Winter 1968–1969).

[29] The turn from political economy to economics, so to speak, comes not with Adam Smith but with Ricardo. For Ricardo, there were natural limits to capital accumulation set by resources; therefore the subject matter of economics had to be not the means of the accumulation of wealth, which it was for Adam Smith, but allocation within restricted means, or distribution: "the laws which determine the division of the produce of industry among the classes who concur in its formation."

For Ricardo, economic growth was limited by the scarcity of natural resources (principally land); as entrepreneurs sought to extend the use of resources in the face of declining yields, the rate of profit inevitably would have a tendency to fall with the rising capital invested per worker. Marx took over from Ricardo the idea of the

And it is against the recurrent restraint of "scarcity," rather than the release of abundance, that the modern public household has to provide a normative political philosophy for its two tasks:

(1) The definition of the common good, the classical problem of the *polis*; and

(2) The satisfaction of private rights and wants, claimed by individuals and groups.

The classic doctrine of the *polis* emphasized civic virtue, a chief element of which was moderation of needs and limitation of acquisition; liberty was a subordinate good. The philosophy of modernity emphasized liberty, or the pursuit of pleasure and happiness without limit; the public interest became a subordinate good.

This feature of modernity was first recognized by Rousseau, and it is at the heart of his efforts to reformulate a philosophy for the public household. The problem, as Rousseau put it, was that in modern society man was both *bourgeois* and *citoyen*. As a citizen he had public duties, but as a bourgeois he pursued private interests, appetites, and passions. Rousseau sought to overcome this bifurcation in *The Social Contract*—the condition of which was not prior to society, but arose after man came out of nature into society—by the denial of all private individual interest, the erasure of all ego into the single moral personality which would be the community or general will. Without self-interest, each person would be equal to every other in all respects. In contemporary life, this alternative is exemplified in Communist China, and its civil religion—which Rousseau also thought necessary as a binding belief—in the deification of Mao's thought.

Modern Western society went in a different direction than Rousseau had sought: toward the pursuit of individual, acquisitive interests in the *economy*, and the enhancement and enlargement of the self in the *culture*. The private economic interests of accumulation were pursued in the market, often at the expense of the public household. The "making" of one's self became the free choice of a personal life-style from the repertoire of the world's cultures, the

---

tendency of the rate of profit to fall, but linked it not to the question of limited yield of resources, but to the narrowing of the base of labor and the extraction of surplus value. As to the need for rising yields (which a socialist society would have to encourage) rather than the dimishing returns of nature, Marx placed an unexamined faith in the power of technology.

mingling of different artifacts as if these were independent modules of culture, free from the continuity of the past and its traditions. In both cases, in economy and culture, there was a search for the satisfaction of appetite, whose ends were unlimited.

Today—and this is the distinctive change in the idea of rights, particularly the right to happiness—the satisfaction of private wants and the redress of perceived inequities are not pursued individually through the market, but politically by the group, through the public household. Liberalism had justified the individual pursuit, free of the *polis*. Classical political theory, and its modern reformulation by Rousseau, sought to justify the primacy of the *polis*. The modern appetite wants to enhance some individuals at the expense of others, and to aggrandize all, through the public household.

But the difficulty is that the public household in the twentieth century is not a community but an arena, in which there are no normative rules (other than bargaining) to define the common good and adjudicate conflicting claims on the basis of rights. The question again is: What can be the political philosophy of the public household?

Any inquiry into philosophical rules has to begin with substantive issues, and for this we have to take up the claims—the issues of redress and justice—against existing distributions of privileges and rights, and adjudicate them. In the wider methodological sphere, given the nature of a pluralistic society, we have to accept the differences between men and to establish which differences are relevant and legitimate for the normative functioning of the public household.

In this matrix of economic and philosophical questions, there are four issues I would single out as ones that have to be resolved:

(1) What are the relevant units of the public household, and what are the balances of rights among these?

(2) What are the tensions between liberty and equality as people seek to enhance one or the other of these somewhat incompatible values?

(3) What is the balance between equity and efficiency in the competition between social claims and economic performance?

(4) What are the dimensions of the "public" and the "private" spheres, both in the economic pursuit of goods and in the realm of morals?

These four issues make up an agenda whose resolution would constitute a philosophy for the public household of modern liberal society. I cannot make any claims in pressing that resolution. What I can do is to try to sharpen the definition of these issues through the principle of relevant differences.

THE UNITS OF SOCIETY

For Aristotle the *polis* is the primary unit of society; for Catholic social theory it is the family; for classic liberalism the individual; and for modern liberalism the plural interest group. Each, in its way, has claimed priority or necessity; each has combated the claims of the others.

In Western society in the last 200 years it is the individual who has had precedence. For Jeremy Bentham, "the community is a fictitious *body* composed of the individual persons who are considered as constituting, as it were, its *members*. The interest of the community then is what?—The sum of the interests of the several members who compose it."[30]

But this nominalist utilitarianism neglects the reality of structures that necessarily stand outside individuals. A university is a changing composition of persons, yet the entity has a symbolic meaning beyond the tenure of its particular members. And this is even more true of a *people*, whether a religious-cultural group like the Jews, or a national-cultural group like the Irish and a hundred others throughout the world. Without such corporate allegiance, non-rational at its core, a faith freely given or reaffirmed, the play of interests becomes a war of each individual against the other, a war sometimes violent, sometimes not.

Yet the claims of the community, when total, become a greater monstrosity, leading to a conformity of ideological beliefs or submission to a heavy-handed bureaucratic Moloch. The idea of individualism *is* a distinctive achievement of human consciousness. As Isaiah Berlin has noted (following Condorcet), the idea of liberty as individual rights

was absent from the legal conceptions of the Romans and Greeks; this seems to hold equally of the Jewish, Chinese, and all other ancient civilizations that have since come to light. The domination of this ideal

---

[30] Jeremy Bentham, *An Introduction to the Principles of Morals and Legislation*, ed. J. H. Burns and H. L. A. Hart (London: University of London, Athlone Press, 1970), p. 12.

has been the exception rather than the rule, even in the recent history of the West. Nor has liberty in this sense often formed a rallying cry for the great masses of mankind. The desire not to be impinged upon, to be left to oneself, has been a mark of high civilization both on the part of individuals and communities. The sense of privacy itself, of the area of personal relationships as something sacred in its own right, derives from a conception of freedom which, for all its religious roots, is scarcely older, in its developed state, than the Renaissance or the Reformation.[31]

The freedom to live as one prefers is supported by a number of philosophical and economic justifications. If this value is confirmed, it guards against the tyranny of the community (even if sanctioned by a majority vote). If the necessary institutional arrangements are observed, it divides political from social institutions and prevents the fusion of political powers within any single body. If individual initiative is respected, it gives free play to entrepreneurs, economic and intellectual, to create those products and institutions (from automobiles to "free schools") which are responsive to those who want them and will pay for them, privately or through the public household. Yet it is that very individualism, so rampant in the United States, which has also led to the spoliation of the environment and has been at the roots of the neglect of social services and other community needs.

Continental liberal theory, from Montesquieu to de Tocqueville to von Gierke, has recognized a different social unit—the *Gemeinde*, the smaller communities that go back to the medieval social order, the corporation (such as a university or a religious foundation), the "guilds" of merchants and artisans (we would now call them professional associations). These were self-ruling corporate bodies within the larger society which lived according to their own codes and were privileged in their powers. For someone like Durkheim, these professional bodies and occupational communities appeared as the necessary anchorages for civic morals in the large-scale modern society, standing between the unchecked egoism of the individual and the enormous and threatening power of the state.

Whether such intermediate groups can serve this purpose today is debatable; the groups have become rampant claimants in their own right. Yet what is clear in a modern pluralistic society is that the existence of groups with defined claims is a sociological fact whose legitimacy must be taken into account. The extent and vari-

[31] Isaiah Berlin, *Four Essays on Liberty* (London: Oxford University Press, 1969), p. 129.

ety of such groups are astonishing. They comprise functional economic groups (business, labor, farmers); symbolic status groups (religious, national, racial); socially disadvantaged groups (poor, aged, handicapped); culturally expressive groups (women, youth, homosexuals); civic-purpose groups (civil rights organizations, consumer and environmentalist groups); economic special-purpose groups (taxpayers' associations, veterans' lobbies); cultural special-purpose groups (universities, scientific and professional associations, art associations); functional political associations (conferences of states, or city or municipal organizations), and 57 other varieties.

Because of the multiplicity of such groups, it is doubtful that a single issue today could polarize an entire society. The peculiar strength of a modern democratic polity is that it can *include* so many interests. True, the very increase in their number and their concentration in the political arena lead to an overload, a fragmentation, and often a politics of stalemate. Yet the nature and character of the diverse group interests cannot be denied, for such is the character of a contemporary democratic polity.

Where, then, does that leave us in seeking a normative philosophy of the public household? The answer, difficult to spell out in detail, is that there cannot be *one* overriding interest whose claims take precedence at all times—neither the individual, his property or his rights; nor the state, with its claim to direct and control economic and social activity, or to regulate morals or private conduct; nor the plural groups with their claims for redress and protection. Rather, we have to consider those rules, rights, and situations which apply to *all* persons irrespective of any differences, and also those rules, rights, and claims where there are *relevant* differences (in need, in grounds for redress, in burdens to be borne) between groups—and allocate accordingly. The distinction cannot be applied in any formal fashion; it can only be made meaningful in practice.[32]

---

[32] Injustice arises, says Aristotle, when equals are treated unequally, and also when unequals are treated equally. Yet such formulations are formal and abstract. As Morris Ginsberg points out, "The statement that equals should be treated equally and unequals unequally throws no light on what is to be done by, to, or for equals and unequals"; *On Justice in Society* (Baltimore: Penguin, 1954), p. 7.

Yet there is a different distinction in Aristotle that is applicable, the distinction between "arithmetic equality," which is applied to all, and "proportional equality," which is based on differences in merit. It is this distinction that I shall use as a starting point for the principle of "relevant differences" as the measure for justice.

LIBERTY AND EQUALITY

In a long and thoughtful discussion of egalitarianism in *Dissent* (Fall 1973), Michael Walzer concludes that "liberty *and* equality are the two chief virtues of social institutions, and they stand best when they stand together." Yet the liberal tradition beginning with Kant, and the most thoughtful critics of mass society in the nineteenth century (de Tocqueville and Burckhardt), posed the issue as liberty *versus* equality. And I think that, in the form the debate has been taking in recent years, the problem is the contrast and not the conjunction.

Classic liberalism defined equality as equality before the law. The definition rests on the distinction between the rule of law and the rule of men. The rule of law sets the rules of the game which apply generally to *all* players; within these rules, individuals are free to strike their own bargains, make their own choices, determine their own actions. Under the rule of men, a governor or judge may set forth determinations which single out some, but not others, for obligation and redress. Often this may be for reasons of justice and fairness, but an element of arbitrariness and coercion remains.

The bias of liberalism was for the first, even though an inequality of outcome might result, because its overriding value was the reduction of coercion by government and the rule of free bargain. The bias of social intervention was, and is, the element of redress in the name of some other value. The heart of the liberal argument is that men differ in their capacities, needs, aptitudes, and talents. Thus one has to distinguish between *treating people equally* and *making them equal*. The effort to make people equal must lead to some determination by an administrative body of the degree of differences, and the degree of redress. It therefore means treating people *unequally*. The logic is inescapable.

Now, for a variety of reasons one may have to treat people unequally. The most important, perhaps, is that any single value, whether it be freedom or justice, when taken as absolute and overriding, and applied in an exacting way, can lead to excess. No single value can satisfy what are inherently incompatible objectives, even when most men desire the incompatible. So one has to be clear as to what one is forgoing, in the effort to resolve the incompatibilities. In his *Four Essays on Liberty*, Isaiah Berlin has summed this up brilliantly:

. . . nothing is gained by a confusion of terms. To avoid glaring inequality or widespread misery I am ready to sacrifice some, or all, of my freedom: I may do so willingly and freely: but it is freedom that I am giving up for the sake of justice or equality or the love of my fellow men. I should be guilt-stricken, and rightly so, if I were not, in some circumstances, ready to make this sacrifice. But a sacrifice is not an increase in what is being sacrificed, namely freedom, however great the moral need or the compensation for it. Everything is what it is: liberty is liberty, not equality or fairness or justice or culture, or human happiness or a quiet conscience. If the liberty of myself or my class or nation depends on the misery of a number of other human beings, the system which promotes this is unjust and immoral. But if I curtail or lose my freedom, in order to lessen the shame of such inequality, and do not thereby materially increase the individual liberty of others, an absolute loss of liberty occurs. This may be compensated for by a gain in justice or in happiness or in peace, but the loss remains, and it is a confusion of values to say that although my "liberal," individual freedom may go by the board, some other kind of freedom—"social" or "economic"—is increased. Yet it remains true that the freedom of some must at times be curtailed to secure the freedom of others. Upon what principle should this be done? If freedom is a sacred, untouchable value, there can be no such principle. One or other of these conflicting rules or principles must, at any rate in practice, yield: not always for reasons which can be clearly stated, let alone generalized into rules or universal maxims. Still, a practical compromise has to be found.[33]

How do we determine what to forgo? In regard to equality, we turn to the principle of relevant differences. Let us take the examples of crime and taxes. Two men both commit the same crime. Under the law, they are treated as arithmetically equal, even though each may be able to bear the punishment differently (both are fined $100 for speeding, yet one is a millionaire, the other a pauper; or both men lose their driving licenses, but one can engage a chauffeur, the other cannot). Yet in the case of taxes, not only do two men of unequal incomes *not* pay the same amount in taxes, or even the same proportion of income, but the wealthier pays a progressively rising tax as his income goes up. Yet we recognize the actions in both instances as just.

Where individuals are to be deprived of liberty, or punished for committing a crime, we tend to reduce the administrative discretion in order to avoid favoritism or abuse of power. (And when discretion is used, as in giving leniency to a young offender, it has to be justified.) The bias is in favor of *equal treatment*. Yet in the in-

[33] Berlin, op. cit., pp. 125–126.

stance of taxes, of obligations to support the financial burdens of a society, we recognize that those most able to bear the burdens shall do so.[34] These individuals are treated unequally (in the formal sense), and we recognize that it is right to use such methods *to tend to make* persons more equal. Yet there is no overriding principle of equality, in one or another of these forms (arithmetic or proportionate), that holds under *all* circumstances.

In this respect, the classic liberal and the classic socialist tradition are one. Equality in the socialist tradition was never "leveling," in the sense of aiming at the attainment of equality under all conditions and in all respects. This is what Marx once contemptuously called "raw communism," and viewed as the lowest stage of human society. What Marx wanted was the abolition of *class privileges* and *class distinctions*, i.e., socially imposed and socially enforced *arbitrary* distinctions between persons; when these were removed, the natural differences would still remain. Yet if one man had more than another, so be it, so long as these differences were *earned*, a reward according to work. This was Marx's definition of socialism.[35]

The question of equality has become a central issue for the public household today. Yet rarely is it clear what the disputes are about—how much equality, in what areas, and so forth. We have been discussing *principles* (i.e., standards) of equality (arithmetic and proportional) and the elimination of arbitrary (e.g., class) distinctions, so that natural differences (in talent, etc.) remain. But these only gain meaning when they are applied to substantive issues in society, particularly the relevant redress of those inequalities that have been socially patterned.

There are, logically speaking, three dimensions of equality: *equality of conditions, equality of means,* and *equality of outcomes.*

[34] And this is the principle we clearly should apply to the question of bearing the burden of inflation.

[35] The references to "raw communism" are in the *Economic-Philosophical Manuscripts* (London: Lawrence and Wishart, 1959). The discussion of equality and natural differences is in the "Critique of the Gotha Programme," in *Selected Works* (Moscow, 1935) vol. 2, pp. 564–566. Under socialism, Marx writes, "*equal rig't* . . . recognizes no class differences, because everyone is also a worker like everyone else, but it tacitly recognizes unequal individual endowments and thus productive capacity as natural privileges. *It is, therefore, a right of inequality, in its content, like every right.*" Thus, under socialism each person is paid according to his contributed labor, and such payments will differ. Under Communism, the "higher stage" of society, when abundance has been achieved, each person would receive "according to his need."

Equality of conditions, by and large, refers to equalities of public liberties. These include equality before the law, equality of movement in public places, the principle of one man, one vote—the cluster of liberties which we call political and civil rights. The guiding principle here, indisputably, is equal treatment by a common standard. Where individuals, in these instances, are unequal because of public discrimination, we try to *make* them equal, so that they can be treated equally. We do so in order that each person can fully exercise his rights as a citizen of the polity.[36]

Equality of means has meant, both in the liberal and socialist traditions, equality of opportunity—equality of access to the means of securing the unequal outcomes. This has signified, historically, the elimination of public positions reserved on some ascriptive basis (e.g., officers' positions in the army for sons of the aristocracy, inherited trades through guild restrictions), and the provision for free access in and out of the economic marketplace and equal access to education, where education is the means of acquiring competences necessary for higher positions.

Equality of opportunity has been the overriding definition of equality in the liberal societies of the West which have established individual social and geographical *mobility* as a value. By and large, this principle has been unchallenged. When it has been seen that equality of opportunity is a *formal* fact, but that certain groups have been historically disadvantaged and in poor position to compete "fairly" for position, there have been good grounds for compensatory action to redress these inequalities. Yet the principle remains: Individuals are to be treated equally in their efforts to achieve what they can through their "natural" abilities and individual efforts.

The outcomes of the competition between individuals are disparate degrees of status, income, and authority.[37] These disparate

[36] Public liberties, it should be noted, antedate modern democracy and are, logically and philosophically, independent of democracy. Briefly, liberty is *how* one rules; democracy is *who* rules. A democracy can, by majority vote, suppress liberty and install tyranny. Public liberties have existed and flourished in aristocratic societies: e.g., the pervasiveness of the common law and legal rights before universal suffrage in England; the existence of public liberties, such as academic freedom, in Wilhelminian Germany. By and large, the *extension* of public liberties has come about in modern democracies most recently through the pressure of groups that had been excluded (e.g., workers, blacks, women).

[37] Let me emphasize here that I define the outcomes as income, status, and *authority*; and thus I distinguish normatively between *authority* and *power*. Authority is a competence based upon skill, learning, etc., and is a functional component of an

outcomes have been justified on the ground that they are freely gained and earned by effort. This is the basis of the idea of a "just meritocracy" and, historically, of the striving to realize both liberty *and* equality. But in recent years there has been an outcry that the disparate outcomes are too large and unequal, and that public policy ought to seek greater equality of outcomes—in short to *make* persons more equal in income, status, or authority. Yet such efforts can be achieved only by restricting other individuals' access to position or the disposition of their achieved outcomes (e.g., the use of wealth to gain other privileges). In short, the effort to reduce disparities of outcomes means that the liberty of *some* is qualified or sacrificed in order to make *others* more equal to them.

Now, it would be foolish to argue that no value can ever be qualified. Now would I say, of course, that today most of the disparate outcomes of status, income, and authority are justly earned. But what we are arguing is a normative principle—the just rules of a public household. And the difficulty with the current argument for greater equality of outcomes is that such equality can be achieved only by administrative determination, by the enhancement of bureaucratic power in society. In its own simple overriding claim to make all men equal, it ignores the principle of relevant differences.[38]

Let me illustrate the difficulties by a brief discussion of one current issue as it relates to status. I refer to the question of quotas.

In the demand for greater equality of outcomes, some egalitarians have argued for quotas for minority students in admissions to

---

institutional position. Power is the ability to command, which is backed up, either explicitly or implicitly, by force. In a society, power can legitimately be exercised by a government to maintain security and order; but *within* a society, one seeks to reduce power (coercion) and expand authority. When people lack authority, especially for redress, they seek to invoke power.

[38] One of the more ludicrous aspects of this argument is the claim that a society ought to insist on "cultural equality" as well. Thus Herbert Gans writes, in *More Equality* (New York: Pantheon, 1968) that "a culturally equal society would . . . treat all ways of expressing oneself and acting as equal in value, status and moral worth . . . [because] they express the differing aesthetic standards of people in different socioeconomic and educational circumstances."

But this relativism establishes a hopeless confusion between preferences and judgments. Any person or group is entitled to his or its own *preferences* in music, poetry, art, etc. But it is ridiculous to assume that *any* aesthetic expression is of equal "value" with any other. When public monies are to be spent, is everybody to be subsidized on the ground that any artistic production is of equal value with any other? One of the very real difficulties today in a national arts policy is that, because of the "populist" pressures in Congress for distribution of monies across-the-board, artistic centers of importance are neglected while Podunk receives its share. In such instances, excellence is sacrificed for equality.

universities and professional schools, and for quotas for women and blacks in professional positions in universities, hospitals, governmental agencies, and the like. But in the course of making this argument, they tend to overlook the relevant distinctions, namely the qualifications and competences that apply at different stages.

In admissions, colleges have used criteria other than grades. In Ivy League schools, children of alumni are given preference to maintain tradition; geographical quotas are established to insure diversity; talented athletes are given special scholarships in order to fill the needs in competitive sport. Yet two things are apparent. First, these modifications are within *some* range of grades (not everyone is admitted, and academic achievement, even if stretched, is still a controlling principle); and second, as one proceeds into graduate and professional schools, these extraneous criteria are narrowed and the focus is largely on academic achievement. One further consideration should be noted. Admission to school is an entry point into the system; yet by itself it does not guarantee the outcome. To that extent it is still within the purview of equality of opportunity. So when, for valid social reasons, one wants to expand the number, say, of black doctors or black lawyers, there is a case, within limits, for giving preference to minority students in admission to schools. (The greater difficulty comes later: does one bend the standards all along the way? In Pennsylvania, a disproportionate number of black students failed the state bar examination; in consequence there was some demand for a special examination for blacks.)

But in the appointment of individuals to professional positions, none of the modifications can hold. A professor or a doctor or an administrator is tested by the competence appropriate to the position, and the idea of "group representation" has little meaning. The criterion, necessarily, has to be competence, not representation, if the sense of appropriateness is to be maintained.[39] If discrimination (sexual or class) is arbitrary, so is the demand for equality of status on the basis of sex or class; and both have to be rejected.

Let us take a different issue, which involves not status but wealth

[39] Aristotle makes an interesting observation: "civil discord arises not only from inequality of property, but also from inequality of the office which men hold. But here we must note a difference. The distribution of property works in the opposite way from the distribution of office. The masses become revolutionary when the distribution of property is *equal*. Men of education become revolutionary when the distribution of office is *unequal*"; *Politics*, op. cit., p. 65. Italics in the original.

and the access to health care. In the United States, health care is given largely on a fee-for-service basis, and thus provides an advantage for those with higher incomes; they can command better surgeons and doctors, better nursing care, and the like. One may say that if a man has earned his money it is his right, if he so chooses, to spend his income for what he desires most. Yet one balks at the idea that something as fundamental and cherished as health should be "rationed" primarily on the basis of differential income. If not income, by what other criteria? One can say, by the criterion of merit—for those most socially deserving. In the Soviet Union, for example, there are special hospitals and special medical facilities for the high Party functionaries. And to some extent this is true in the United States for army and high government officials in such institutions as Walter Reed Hospital in Washington, D.C. Yet here, too, though one recognizes a somewhat juster rule—better care for the more socially valuable (or socially-defined valuable!) persons—there still remains a nagging sense of injustice.

The problem is analogous to that of military service: are all men to be called equally, or should there be exemptions for the talented who could contribute their services to society in some other way? In the American Civil War, men could still buy their way out of the draft by money; that was done on an individual basis by paying a substitute, but today it is done on a collective basis, by raising military pay to attract volunteers, instead of a draft.

There is no single principle of justice or sacrifice. What is striking is that individualist and liberal societies tend to argue, in the case of military service, for equal risk for all, while Communist countries, where the primacy of society is the overriding value, more readily adopt the differential principle of exemptions from service for the talented.

In the instance of health, however, the problem is clearer. Our sense of fairness, of the idea of the equal worth of life, tells us that we need to find some way of equalizing health services, of insuring everyone's access to adequate medical care, despite income or status. But surely the response should be not to restrict individuals from spending money for individual care (e.g., private rooms, special food), as some trade unions in Great Britain have proposed (and even struck for), but to upgrade the services for all.

Let me turn now to the third outcome, authority. What does "equal authority" mean, and in what spheres? In September 1973 the Danish parliament, in order to achieve "a more perfect combination of freedom and equality" in the university community, enacted a law abolishing the existing faculties and stipulated that decisions on academic questions leading to degrees in all disciplines be made by elected councils composed of 50 percent teachers, 25 percent students, and 25 percent non-academic personnel (a category embracing everyone from registrars to janitors). Similar situations exist in a number of German universities (though more often the councils are a tripartite body of senior professors, junior professors, and students). Moreover, in various hospitals, newspapers, and publishing houses (more often in Europe than in the United States), similar councils have been demanded. In these, all policy decisions would be made by the constituent groups: in the hospitals by the doctors, nurses, orderlies, and in some instances the "community"; in the newspapers by publishers, editors, and reporters; in the publishing houses by publishers, editors, and authors. These demands are justified on the ground of "equal participation" by all those in the enterprise. In older guises, this was a demand in factories for guild socialism, industrial democracy, or "workers' control."

This is not the place to deal with the entire range of issues of "participatory democracy," from large industrial enterprises, to local neighborhoods, to hospitals, and so forth.[40] Yet one can take the simple example of the university to illustrate a principle.

The purpose of a university is defined by its educational policy. It has to be responsive to an intellectual tradition, to the standards of learning and cultural heritage that it transmits; it is accountable to the society for the encouragement of talents, and it is responsible to the student body which is enrolled in the quest for knowledge. But the formulation of policy (what is to be taught and by whom, the standards of judgment and the criteria of achievement) is not the right and responsibility of the society, or of the student body; it is

[40] On the questions of workers' control in industry, see my essay "Work, Alienation and Social Control," *Dissent* (Summer 1959), reprinted in their twentieth anniversary issue (Spring 1974).

One can also observe that there is often little to stop a group of authors or reporters from starting their own publishing houses and newspapers as "collectives," and running these on principles of equal authority. Yet the vicissitudes of such enterprises, as the "underground" papers in Berkeley, Boston, and New York have shown, do not encourage such hopes. The sociological law of "faction formation and fission" has been destructive of almost all of these enterprises, for there is no "system overload" so great as that piled on by the high density of radical activist talkers, and no enterprises so prone to splitting as the free collective enterprises.

the responsibility of those qualified by earned authority to decide, that is, the faculty. On this basis, therefore, students do not "vote" on their own degrees, junior faculty members do not vote on the tenure of the senior faculty.

Yet educational policy is not the whole of a university. Student life is its own sphere, and that is why parietals and similar direct controls on student life are legitimately suspended. A university engages in research, in service to government, corporations, or communities, and the responsibility for the balancing of these activities is that of the university administration. There is, in all this, an operative principle—namely, to respect the character of the different spheres, and to limit the privileges of each sphere to those dimensions appropriate to its character.

If this principle of relevant differences is observed, we have the basis for a more general approach to the question of equality. We know that even when arbitrary differences such as class or sexual privileges are eliminated, there will be differences in income, status, and authority between persons, differences arising out of talent, motivation, efforts, and achievements. And individuals will want to exercise the rewards and powers of those achievements. "The question of justice arises," as I wrote in an earlier essay on meritocracy and equality, in *The Coming of Post-Industrial Society*, "when those on top can convert their authority positions into large, discrepant, material and social advantages over others."

In an area such as health care, we can say, quite rightly, that access to services should not be determined on the basis of differential income. It is appropriate to our sense of individual worth that all persons should be assured of adequate care, despite income or status. For this reason I would share Michael Walzer's argument that a relevant principle is "*the abolition of the power of money outside its sphere* . . . a society in which wealth is no longer convertible into social goods with which it has no intrinsic connection." Since money and, to a different extent, power are easily convertible (i.e., they can command privileges, such as better health care, quite readily), Walzer assumes that it would be difficult to prevent that undue exercise of influence without a "radical redistribution of wealth." My own sense is that a "radical redistribution" is the most politically difficult task of all, and that the objectives we mutually desire might be achieved by selective taxes on consumption and by upgrading those necessary social services which are appropriate to all.

If our criterion, then, is the reduction of undue and illegitimate influence and command of resources, the relevant principle of liberty and justice would be: to each according to his earned effort; to each according to the powers and privileges appropriate to each sphere.

EQUITY AND EFFICIENCY

The issue of equality and liberty is the question of the disparities *between persons* and the role of the government in reducing these disparities or containing their undue influence. The question of equity and efficiency is the problem of balance between the "economizing mode" of the society—the doctrine of productivity, or the effort to achieve increased output at lesser cost—and the social criteria of non-economic values. In another sense, it is also the question of the balance between present and future: how much does the present generation have to forgo (in consumption) to insure a higher rate of capital stock for future generations? And, conversely, how much of exhaustible resources can the present generation use up at the expense of the next generations?

The economizing mode[41]—the exact calculation of monetary costs and returns—has been an efficient organizer of production but has had two large social costs: treating people as things within the sphere of production, and using the environment as a "free good," and therefore recklessly. To this extent, the balance today has begun to shift, slowly, away from the economizing mode. The satisfaction of men in work—where they spend most of their time and seek to fulfill their capacities—becomes a valid claim on the enterprise, even when this may be at the expense of efficiency. And the environment is no longer a free good, in that producers and users are now "taxed" and forced to clean up the pollution they have engendered, even at the expense of making certain capital assets "non-productive."

[41] I prefer the term "economizing mode" to "market economy." The market is only one aspect of economizing. While the market, when measured by price and return on capital, exacts a financial discipline on an enterprise, industrial society also comprises the rationalization of work, which derives from the engineering mentality, exemplified by Frederick W. Taylor. To that extent, the economizing mode and its reduction of men to things is as characteristic of the Soviet industrial economy as of the capitalist market economy. For the distinction between the economizing and sociologizing modes, see *The Coming of Post-Industrial Society*, chap. 4.

Where there is a relatively clear-cut confrontation between the claims of efficiency and those of equity, the former are being bent; and the arguments are accepted, if not in the society as a whole, then by the intellectual community. (And the thoughts of the present generation of "academic scribblers" will influence social and economic policy tomorrow.) But many of the political issues in a society are claims of rival equities, and the difficult question is whether there is a general principle of adjudication. In locating a new airport, for example, how do we balance the longer distances that travelers may have to cover (and the costs of roads or rails) against the noise of the planes in a location closer to the city? In planning a roadway, how do we trade off the social and psychological costs of disrupting existing communities (and how large do these have to be?) against the economic costs of longer highway loops? In arguing for mass transportation, how do we tabulate the savings in materials and energy against the increased travel time and decreased mobility (having to meet standardized commuter schedules) of forgoing private cars? How do we establish "just" differentials in pay, between highly skilled and low-skilled, between doctors and nurses, if relative scarcities or length of training—the criteria of the market—are no longer employed?

Inevitably, in all these matters, we move from complete laissez faire to negotiated decisions. But on what principles? Always to help the less advantaged? Or by the criterion of social costs and benefits?

Is there a general rule for equity? On social-welfare questions, economists have usually held to some version of Pareto-optimality: the distributional principle that as some persons become better off, no one should be worse off. More recently, John Rawls has proposed a maximin criterion to replace the principles of utility, and it is this principle which today is receiving intense philosophical scrutiny.[42]

The maximin principle insures that all persons would receive a

[42] See John Rawls, "Some Reasons for the Maximin Criterion," *American Economic Review* 64 (May 1974, Proceedings issue): 141–146.

Rawls begins with the assumption that "injustice exists because basic agreements are made too late." Since individuals know their social positions and their relative strengths, bargaining in the social system becomes distorted. But what if they were back in the "state of nature," behind a "veil of ignorance," knowing nothing about each other (whether one's neighbor was weaker or stronger, more talented or less talented)? What common rules would then be established in order to assure each person that he would be well-off on some minimal basis, consonant with every other person's being as well-off as himself? This is the basis of the maximin rule.

minimal share. Individuals would freely choose this arrangement, Rawls believes, because they would want to minimize the risk of losing out altogether; so they would opt for a "maximum" consonant with that "minimal" risk. Thus Rawls arrives at his "difference principle" based on a maximin criterion. As he puts it:

Social and economic inequalities are to meet two conditions: they must be (a) to the greatest expected benefit of the least advantaged members of society (the maximin equity criterion) and (b) attached to offices and positions open to all under conditions of fair equality of opportunity.

Since this would have been the "original" principle of justice, freely accepted in the state of nature, it can now be used as a principle of redress in social policy.

There have been a number of criticisms of the maximin criterion. It assumes that individuals are "risk averse" and would want to minimize their chances of loss. This might be true of one's life, yet much less so of one's goods; many individuals might risk the loss of a bicycle in order to have a chance for an auto, even if the outcome could mean they would have to walk. The notion of "benefits" is ambiguous. It is accepted that we cannot compare interpersonal utilities, so we need some objectively measurable index, such as income or wealth; but many social benefits involve complex trade-offs which defy measurement.[43] And most ambiguous is the definition of "least advantaged." If income is used as the criterion, does this mean that everybody earning less than the median income (i.e., the lower *half* of persons in the country) is disadvantaged? Or is it the lower fifth, or the lower tenth; and on what basis? And if some other criterion (the destitute, the unskilled, those from broken homes), what would that be?[44]

[43] Let me give a composite example from current U.S. government housing policy. On a desirable river site, 25 percent of the regular housing units are reserved for low-income families who may pay much less rent than is paid by high-income tenants for a comparable apartment. The site is high-cost, and the subsidy, accordingly, is large. For the money involved, the government could build more housing for the poor than the existing units. At the same time, if the river-site units were fully occupied by high-rental tenants, the taxes on those units would finance more municipal services. So there is a double "loss." Yet the government has decided, as a matter of social policy, that there is greater "benefit" in mixing housing projects than in segregating by income groups, even at the expense of more housing. How does one decide which "benefit" is greatest? What is equity? What is the efficiency in allocation?

[44] I leave aside here the most trying question of redistributing wealth between rich and poor nations. If we can see how difficult it is to establish normative rules within a polity that has common laws, and mechanisms to enforce social decisions, how much more difficult is it to deal with relations between nations where there is no common frame of law.

And yet there is a virtue to this approach. For what it involves is the "buying off" of the disadvantaged. If we wanted to locate an airport nearer to the city in order to save time and travel costs, we would then ask those who would have to endure the noise how much money they would accept as the price of noise in order to put the airport close in. The market, in those circumstances, would have depressed the value of their homes; the social welfare criterion increases the return. Or, if there is a firm or industry with an aging labor force that is increasingly inefficient, we would then ask the employer (as in the longshore men's and typographers' union agreements) how much he would pay to "buy out" these workers, in order to retire them.

The crux of the problem, however, is not the *degree of redistribution*—let us say of income and wealth, for these are the most important and most easily measurable items—*but the balance between redistribution and growth*. The distribution of income influences the rate of growth of an economy, as the rate of growth influences distribution. Any large-scale redistribution of income inevitably increases the slope of consumption at the expense of investment. Yet the maximin principle, Rawls admits, "is unsuitable for determining the just rate of savings; it is intended to hold only within generations."

But that is exactly the prior question. What is the proper rate of economic growth for a society? How is this growth to be financed? How are the fruits to be distributed? Rawls's maximin criterion is a principle for equity in "the stationary state." Yet it is not clear that the society—American, Russian, or any contemporary society—would vote for the stationary state.

In the stationary state, net savings are by definition zero. Why forgo consumption now, if the later returns will not be greater than at present? But since resources are exhaustible—by the laws of entropy (even in recycling we lose some portion of the original amounts by heat dissipation) if not by direct physical use—we either have to make some investment to find new resources (or to make existing ones more capital intensive), or reduce the consumption of those exhaustible resources in order to husband the amount for our own future, or for future generations. As Robert M. Solow has remarked: "We have actually done quite well at the hands of *our* ancestors. Given how poor they were and how rich we are, they might properly have saved less and consumed more. No doubt they never expected the rise in income per head that has made us so much richer than they ever dreamed was possible. But that only reinforces the point that the future may be too important to be left to the accident of mistaken expectations or the ups and downs of the Protestant ethic."

Do we want our children—and theirs—to be less well off than we are? What is a just "time preference" for society? How much do we have to save or forgo in order to transmit the economic capacity we have inherited? An individual's decision to save is determined by his discount of the future. The technical superiority of future goods over the present (productivity) would increase more than proportionally the value of his holdings; in the stock market of the 1960s, this lure led investors to seek capital gains, not immediate returns. A rising uncertainty over the future diminishes such expectations, and investors may then seek dividends or immediate returns, rather than wait for the future. In an analogous sense, the rate of use of exhaustible resources is also a function of such equilibrating forces —of future expectations against present returns. In a striking metaphor, Leon Walras called the process of achieving equilibrium *tâtonnement*, the trial-and-error search, a tapping like that of a blind man with a stick toward a goal he cannot see.

Yet it is not clear that a social decision is best served by the sum of individual decisions, especially when a few individuals hold a disproportionate amount of the resources. As Solow, again, has remarked: "The pure theory of exhaustible resources [tells] us that . . . the balance between present and future is more delicate than we are accustomed to think . . . and the choice of a social discount rate is, in effect, a policy decision about inter-generational distributions [of income and welfare]."[45]

What we owe to the future is a capacity to produce. What made the ideology—and the experiences—of Soviet Communism so terrifying was the ruthless notion that the present generation was expendable for the sake of the future, so that during the Stalinist years Russia engaged in a brutal form of "primitive accumulation" which led to the sacrifice not only of living standards but also of millions of human lives for the sake of "production." What makes

[45] Robert M. Solow, "The Economics of Resources or the Resources of Economics," *American Economic Review* 64 (May 1974, Proceedings issue): 1–14; see also his "What We Owe to the Future," *Nebraska Journal of Economics and Business* (Winter 1974).

the spectacle of Western bourgeois society so repulsive is the waste and squander of resources on needless products of status or display (e.g., the large, heavy automobile; the extravagant packaging of consumer items) for the sake of consumption.

The social discount of the future has to be a social decision, an allocative rule under the principle of equity, as to how to increase the productive capacity of a society on the basis of the restriction of some kinds of consumption. And that, necessarily, brings us to the question which is at the heart of a liberal society: the balance between the public and the private, and the definition of their appropriate spheres.

THE PUBLIC AND THE PRIVATE

The liberal theory of law, as codified by Kant, has two postulates: that law is to be formal (i.e., procedural), not substantive; and that law is separate from morality.

The view of law as primarily procedural derived from the emergence of bourgeois society as a separate sphere in which the satisfaction of individual wants, not the wealth of the state, was the goal of economic activity. It posited a basic equality between the competitors, and ruled out interference because it would upset that equality. Where there were to be restrictions on liberty and property, they would have to be general and calculable, and apply equally to all. In this conception, the basis of law is formal rationality.

The distinction between law and morality derived from two sources. One was the philosophical view of man's will as *autonomous*, as self-determining, not as heteronomous or dictated from external sources such as nature or custom. (As Kant said: "No man may compel me to be happy in his way.") The second was the historical experience of the wars of religion in the seventeenth century, which led to the resolution that no group could impose its own private beliefs on others through the secular arm of the state. One could prosecute crime, but not sin; one could enforce rights, but not righteousness.

In effect, the liberal theory accepted the distinction between the public citizen and the private individual which had so bothered Rousseau, and reinforced it. This theory did not want the individual to be swallowed up in the general will of the state; nor did it want to dissolve the state into the atomistic world of private interests. It sought to maintain, difficult as it was, the separation of relevant spheres.

In every society, principles are bent for the sake of interests, and the liberal theory of freedom has been so bent. In the United States at the turn of the century, individual freedom was the criterion by which the Supreme Court struck down a state statute limiting the hours of work in hazardous occupations (*Lochner* v. *New York*, 1905), stating: ". . . There is no reasonable ground for interfering with the liberty of the person or the right of free contract . . . in the occupation of a baker. . . . These are grown and intelligent men. . . . They are in no sense wards of the State." Yet, at the same time, there was considerable regulation of personal morals, from Sunday blue laws to prohibition of liquor; presumably these were not "grown and intelligent men."

There was, then, a double standard: the conservatives wanted economic freedom but moral regulation. Today there is an odd crossover and another double standard. Contemporary liberals want economic regulation and moral freedom. They want active state intervention in economic affairs, yet decry any interference with individual morals under the flag of privacy.

Are there any general rules which we can apply? Or is each social group to press its own interest? What are the relevant spheres of the public and the private in economics, and what are the relevant spheres in morality?

In the 1930s, in the great flush of the vogue for economic planning, it was argued that the government ought to nationalize all industries in order to insure "production for use rather than production for profit." Lewis Mumford (in his *Technics and Civilization*) proposed that "a normal standard of consumption" be defined by biologists, moralists, and men of cultured taste, and that the goods be "standardized, weighed and measured," and supplied to all members of the community; he called this "basic communism." We are far from such simplicities. The performance of nationalized industries in almost every country has not been demonstrably better than that of private or mixed enterprises; as Michael Polanyi once observed, the workers in England no more feel that they own British Railways than that they own the British Navy. And as Walter Lippmann observed in the 1930s, "the difficulty of planning production to satisfy many choices is the rock on which the whole conception founders."[46] If there are significant variations in desires, tastes, and choices, only the market is sufficiently flexible to respond to these differences. This, however, does not negate the contention that there needs to be *some* social-decision mechanism to provide adequate social services for all and to set a social minimum that gives people sufficient goods for a sense of self-dignity.

If there is a new emphasis today, it is a retreat from the older visions of centralized public ownership, with the bureaucratic overload that early proponents so rarely took into account. It is an emphasis, as Alice Rivlin has put it, not on *public provision*, but on *public financing* of care. The government's primary role, in the older conception, was to provide "public goods"—housing, hospitals, and other services. Now it is to set standards and provide resources, and the recipients can buy their own housing and pay for their own health care.

What some liberals and some New Leftists have rediscovered are the virtues of decentralization and competition. Without competition, one is left at the mercy of the indifferent private monopoly or the slovenly bureaucratic agency. Without the separation of powers one is left, in the case of employment, at the mercy of a single power, whether it is a private corporation or the state. Yet without public mechanisms for the transfer of payments and the setting of standards, one cannot use such effective power for the achievement of social ends. What is needed is that balance of the private and public spheres—of public care for private needs—which enhances liberty and equity.

What is morality? Are there to be no legal restraints? Is everything to be permitted—obscenity, pornography, incest? In his essay *On Liberty*, John Stuart Mill remarked that there was a propensity to "extend the bounds of what may be called moral policy until it encroaches on the most unquestionably legitimate liberty of the individual." And it was this "moral police" that had to be resisted at all costs. Yet the great historic religions of the West share a com-

---

[46] Walter Lippmann, *The Good Society* (Boston: Little, Brown, 1947; orig. ed., 1937), p. 97. As Lippmann points out: ". . . if Mr. Mumford has in mind a guaranteed minimum income which may be spent freely, then he has no ways of knowing whether the consumers will have Mr. Mumford's own excellent tastes, and go to the stores demanding what he thinks they should demand. But if they do not wish to buy what he would like them to buy, then his planners are bound to find that there is a scarcity of some goods and a glut of others."

mon judgment of the nature of man: When there is no restraint, when mere experience is the touchstone of what should be permitted, the impulse to explore everything, to seek all sensations, even when sanctioned on aesthetic grounds, leads to debauchery, lust, degradation of others, and murder. The lesson they all have drawn is that a community has to have a sense of what is *shameful*, lest the community itself lose all sense of moral norms.

What is shameful? An exact line is impossible to draw. For some it is nudity, for others homosexuality, for others pornography. And even the notion of "community standards" may be of little help, since the community itself is often divided. But what *can* be defined is a different distinction of *public* and *private*, and a wall can be set up between them. Thus, there can be a prohibition on public display of pornography, obscenity, and those prurient elements which degrade the human personality; but behind the wall, what consenting adults do is their own business.

Where does this leave us? With public virtue, and private vices. A tribute—in a different sense of the word—that hypocrisy pays to the double nature of man. A difficult formula, but perhaps the only one which limits the "moral police" of the Mrs. Grundys and the "love's body" of a Norman O. Brown.

What these four arguments add up to, in their socio-philosophical consequences, is the rejection of bourgeois hedonism, with its utilitarian emphasis on economic appetite, yet the retention of political liberalism, with its concern for individual differences and liberty. Historically, political liberalism has been associated with bourgeois society. It was assumed that freedom in the economic realm was the precondition for freedom in all other realms. (As the old saw had it, "free markets make free men.") But economic liberalism has become, in corporate structure, economic oligopoly, and, in the pursuit of private wants, a hedonism that is destructive of social needs. The two can be sundered. We can reject the pursuit of bourgeois wants, as lacking a moral foundation for society, and insist on the necessity of public goods. Yet we need political liberalism to assure the individual of protection from coercive powers and, within appropriate spheres, of rewards for his own efforts and merits. And the arbiter of both cannot be the market—which has to be seen as a mechanism, not a principle of justice—but instead must be the public household.

A REAFFIRMATION OF LIBERALISM

The argument for the public household rests, at bottom, on the need for a restatement of what is legitimate (the grounded values) in a society. Legitimacy shapes the continuity of institutions and the willing responses of persons. The idea of the public household is, then, an effort, in the realm of the polity, to find a social cement for the society.

The centrality of the public household does not necessarily mean the expansion of the governmental economy or the administrative sector. It is, to go back to Aristotle, "a concern more with the good condition of human beings than with the good condition of property." It is a recognition of the distinction between ends and means and the reinstatement of social purposes as the "good condition" which public policy has to seek. It is the centrality of conscious decisions, publicly debated and philosophically justified, in the shaping of directions for the society. Where bourgeois society separated the economy from the polity, the public household rejoins the two, not for the fusion of powers, but for the necessary coordination of effects. The public household requires a new socio-economic bill of rights which redefines for our times the social needs that the polity must try to satisfy. It establishes the public budget (How much do we want to spend, and for whom?) as the mechanism whereby the society seeks to implement "the good condition of human beings."

But there is, too, a qualification, for there is not a single right that takes "just precedence" (in Locke's phrase) over any other. The common thread of classical, Catholic, and Communist doctrine is to fuse law and morality, to insist that there is a single overriding principle (though they disagree sharply as to what this is) to which all persons, as members of the community, must subscribe. And traditional Catholicism and contemporary Communism, since they claim the possession of truth, define all those outside the faith as victims of error and heresy who must be combated.

Liberalism rejects this doctrine because it emphasizes not the common aspects of men but their diversity as individuals and as groups. In a homogeneous society, one might insist on the obligation to respect the common beliefs, but in a pluralistic society, composed of diverse groups and separate creeds, the imposition of one set of belief as articles of faith becomes intolerable. As Isaiah Berlin has remarked:

The notion that there must exist final objective answers to normative questions, truth that can be demonstrated or directly intuited, that it is in principle possible to discover a harmonious pattern in which all values are reconciled, and that it is towards this unique goal that we must make; that we can uncover some central principle that shapes this vision a principle which, once found, will govern our lives—this ancient and almost universal belief, on which so much traditional thought and action and philosophical doctrine rests, seems to me invalid, and at times to have led (and still to lead) to absurdities in theory and barbarous consequences in practice.[47]

Liberalism accepts the tension of the public and the private, the dual roles of person and citizen, individual and group. The questions are: how to find common purposes, yet retain individual means of fulfilling them; and how to define individual (and group) needs and find common means of meeting them. Can these tasks be accomplished in a society where "interest" alone rules?

"The public philosophy," Walter Lippmann has written, "is addressed to the government of our appetites and passions by the reason of a second, civilized, and therefore acquired nature. Therefore the public philosophy cannot be popular. For it aims to resist and to regulate those very desires and opinions which are most popular."

In the classical view, as we have noted, a public philosophy could only be achieved in a republic of small size, since, as Montesquieu said, "in a small republic, the public good is more strongly felt, better known and closer to each citizen." Alternatively, some pessimists today hold that prodigalities of appetitie (resources and population) can only be controlled by the iron hand of a centralized regime.

When the first issue was debated by the Founding Fathers, Madison wrote the sophisticated rebuttal to the classical view, by turning it completely around. A supreme danger in any democracy, Madison agreed, is the possibility that "a passionate majority" might "sacrifice to its ruling passion or interest both the public good and the rights of other citizens. To secure both the public good and private rights against the dangers of such a faction, and at the same time to preserve the spirit and form of popular government, is then

[47] Berlin, op. cit., pp. iv–vi.

the great object to which our inquiries are directed." Whereas a small direct democracy along classical lines "can admit of no cure for the mischiefs of faction, a representative republic opens a different prospect and promises the cure for which we are seeking." The greater the size, the greater the "variety of parties and intersts," and hence the smaller the probability "that a majority of the whole will have a common motive to invade the rights of other citizens; or if such a common motive exists, it will be more difficult for all who feel it to discover their own strengths, and to act in unison with each other...."[48]

There were—and are—two corollaries to the propostion: first, that all interests are to be included; and second, that all issues should be negotiated.

Yet amid such diversity, negotiation alone may not suffice, and the multiplicity of interests can lead to fragmentation. Out of the living experience of creating a representative, national republic, the United States also forged a second instrument, a Supreme Court which would be the repository of legitimacy and whose verdicts would seek to redefine the common rules and equitable distributions of a heterogeneous society. The U.S. Supreme Court is unique in the acceptance by the entire polity of its rule as the normative arbiter.

In the liberal philosophy which framed the republic, private property was conceived of as an "absolute right," the third, along with security of the person and the liberty of the individual, of those necessary to a civil society. And yet, over the last century, the Court has redefined that right by pointing out that the *uses* of property are not abolsute, since grave dangers to neighbors and society can result from reckless use, and that while there are legal rights to the use and enjoyment of property, there are no absolute rights that contravene common social purposes. Again, neither in the original Constitution nor in the Bill of Rights does the word "equality" appear. It only emerges in the Fourteenth Amendment, which stipulates "the equal protection of the laws," and in the Fifteenth Amendment, where it is tied to race, color, and previous servitude. Yet equality today, in education, voting, and the like, has become a central concern of the public philosophy.

[48] These questions are cogently explored in Robert A. Dahl and Edward R. Tufte, *Size and Democracy* (Stanford, Calif.: Stanford University Press, 1973), from which these quotations are taken; see pp. 7, 10, 11.

The mechanis ns of compromise and adjudication thus still exist. The question is whether there is a common will. Here, too, there is a prior condition—the need for some transcendent tie to bind individuals sufficiently for them to make, when necessary, the necessary sacrifices of self-interest.

Historically, what has united a people has been a ruler, a doctrine, or a destiny—and in the great periods of a people or a nation, a fusion of the three. A charismatic figure offers a people the psychological tie of identification and fulfills a need for submission and awe. A doctrine provides people with a set of explanations and justifications for their place in the world. A destiny gives them a surge of power and self-confidence, if not self-aggrandizement, that enhances the psychological tie of allegiance.

In the United States, what gave purpose to the republic at its founding was a sense of destiny—the idea, expressed by Jefferson, that on this virgin continent God's design would be unfolded. On a virgin continent, men could be free, prodigally so, to pursue their individual ends and celebrate their achievements. Its doctrine was shaped by a Protestantism which emphasized sobriety, work, and resistance to the temptations of the flesh. By and large, the belief in the "great man" was more muted in the United States than in other societies, though it is striking that, in fact, ranked by profession, the largest number of presidents in American history have been generals who distinguished themselves in war.

In the heyday of the imperial republic, the quiet sense of destiny and the harsh creed of personal conduct were replaced by a virulent "Americanism," a manifest destiny that took us overseas, and a materialist hedonism which provided the incentives to work. Today that manifest destiny is shattered, the Americanism has worn thin, and only the hedonism remains. It is a poor recipe for national unity and purpose.

Yet in trial and defeat—and there has been defeat—a virtue emerges: the possibility of a self-conscious maturity (which the stoics called the tragic sense of life) that dispenses with charismatic leaders, ideological doctrines, and manifest destinies, and which seeks to redefine one's self and one's liberal society on the only basis on which it can survive. This basis must be created by conjoining three actions: the reaffirmation of our past, for only if we know the inheritance from the past can we become aware of the obligation to our posterity; recognition of the limits of resources and the priority of *needs*, individual and social, over unlimited appetite and wants; and agreement upon a conception of equity which gives all persons a sense of fairness and inclusion in the society and which promotes a situation where, within the relevant spheres, people *become* more equal so that they can be *treated* equally.

This would be a kind of social compact, but a social compact that, though renegotiated in the renewable present, does not, cannot, ignore the past. It was the hubris of classical liberalism, and of socialist utopianism as well, to believe that in each new generation, in a new social contract, men could start afresh, discard the past, and redesign institutions anew. Within limits, men can remake themselves and society, but the knowledge of power must coexist with the knowledge of its limits. This is, after all, the oldest and most enduring truth about the human condition—if it is to remain all too human.

Afterword: 1996

Now THAT THE moral and economic contradictions of Soviet communism have been concluded—is that the end of History or only of utopianism?—all that remains are the cultural contradictions of capitalism.

This book—published twenty years ago—had three themes:

(1) *The tension of asceticism and acquisitiveness.* Modern capitalism, according to the reiterated thesis of Max Weber, was made possible by the asceticism sanctioned by Calvinist and early Protestant thought, which exalted work as a calling and encouraged savings by the delayed gratification of impulses. To be in debt was something a frugal individual feared. Yet over time, the drive to acquisitiveness has won out. In fact, contemporary capitalism can exist only if the machinery of gratification and instant demand is well oiled, usually with cosmetic fragrance. (It is striking that in every major city in the world, from New York to Helsinki to Tokyo, every large department store one enters displays cosmetics and fragrances spread across its ground floor.)

(2) *The tension between bourgeois society and modernism.* Though both were born in the same womb, so to speak—the rejection of the past, the commitment to ceaseless change, and the idea that nothing is sacred—the fratricide was there (as it has been in so many founding situations) from the start. Bourgeois society feared modernism in its cultural impulses to explore the tenebrous; modernism despised the cramped character of bourgeois life. Yet over time, the culture of bourgeois society (the realism of a Norman Rockwell or a Grant Wood) faded and the culturati embraced modernism (except in music, which was too difficult to listen to) and flaunted modernist products on its shelves and walls. Since the midcentury, modernism has become exhausted—in the novel, with its breakup of narrative time; in poetry, with its broken syntax; in painting, with the end of illusionism and the

Author's Note: I wish to thank Paul Golob for his tactful suggestions and thoughtful editing.

spread of abstraction and formalism; in architecture, with its spare geometric forms. In its place, we have seen the rise and spread of postmodernism (noted on pp. 50–55), over the past twenty years. In postmodernism's cultural forms, Foucault and his followers continued the attack on bourgeois society and humanism. In its literary modes—poststructuralism and deconstruction—there has been the denial of authorial intention; of an objective reading of a text; of the primacy of the critic's response to the meaning of a text; and, in the curriculum, of the existence of a canon, or a body of work, philosophical and literary, that commands authority by virtue of its transcendental greatness. On the vulgar level, PoMo, as postmodernism is now called, is the creed of pastiche and parody, of the idea that anything goes, of the enthronement of popular and low culture, and of exhibitionism—in body art, performance art, the cross-dressing of a Madonna or the androgynous appearance of a Michael Jackson, and the transgression of the blasphemous—all of which is intended to, and does, shock "traditional" bourgeois morality and has given rise to a political reaction and a set of cultural wars that has tended to polarize the polity.

(3) *The separation of law from morality.* This theme, less explicit than the previous two, is one that becomes increasingly important, especially since the market has become the arbiter of all economic and even social relations (as in corporate obligations to employees) and the priority of the legal rights of ownership and property over all other claims, even of a moral nature, has been renewed.

The source of this separation, which began in the seventeenth century, was that morality, as it was then understood, was primarily religious and did not cover the private conduct of individuals, as it does today. The religious wars of the seventeenth century were tearing societies apart until various kinds of accommodations were reached. Initially, it was *cujus regio, ejus religio;* one took the faith of one's ruler, and on this basis, there were exchanges of populations. Later, as in England, a principle of toleration was extended. In the United States there was a formal separation of church and state and the principle, "violated" by the Eighteenth Amendment (Prohibition), that no single group could impose its morality on the entire society.

But it was in the economic realm that the separation of law from morality had its greatest impact. Law was to be formal and procedural, not substantive, and this separation meant that the state would not interfere in economic contracts arrived at between negotiating parties. This was the principle laid down by the Supreme Court decisions of the latter decades of the nineteenth century, under Justice Stephen J.

Field, from *Mun. v. Illinois* to *Lochner v. New York* (when Justice Oliver Wendell Holmes, in a famous dissent, stated that the Court was enacting Herbert Spencer's *Social Statics* as the law of the land). And under the Court's rulings, the corporation was declared to be a "legal person" entitled to all the protections of the rights of property.

During the New Deal years and after, the economic relation was transformed somewhat, especially under collective bargaining with the trade unions, to become a social relation that institutionalized rights other than property in union contracts. But in recent years, the social realm has been shrinking and the "naked" economic relation has been assuming priority, especially in the rights of the "shareholder" (even though the shareholder is an individual who moves in and out of a company quickly, seeking the highest financial return) as against the "stakeholder," who may be an individual who has worked for a company for twenty years only to find his or her place wiped out overnight. The issues of relative rights and of the moral boundaries of property rights, especially in the period of mergers and acquisitions, downsizing, and the like, are crucial sociological issues for the society.

The elaboration of these issues is the text of this Afterword.

I

THE DOUBLE BIND OF CAPITALISM

Capitalism in the cultural sense, as a mentality or spirit, rather than just an economic mode of organization, began with two juxtapositions: the rising awareness of and excitement about new worlds open to exploration and wealth beyond the confined spaces of the older Europe, and the emphasis on the individual, rather than on the collectivity, as the relevant actor on the historical stage.

The new worlds, conceived as paradise on earth, quickened the imagination, much as the revelation of John had given early Christians a vision of a new heaven and a new earth. But these new earths were here or just beyond a horizon that loomed up, rather than faded away, as one approached it. Rabelais's Pantragruel journeyed westward to the oracle of Babuc, reaching Canada and blazing a trail for Shakespeare's Prospero. His younger contemporary, Montaigne, in his *Essays* (quoted by Shakespeare in *The Tempest*), wrote a *Livre des Coches*, derived from some travel writing on Brazil. Cyrano de Bergerac (the seventeenth-century writer, not the character by Edmond Rostand) wrote a fanciful *Voyage dans la lune*. And in *Voyage autour du Monde*, Bougainville described an actual circumnavigation of the globe, which provoked great excitement about the sexual habits in Tahiti, the island he named New Cythera (the epithet of Aphrodite); prompted by this account, Diderot wrote the extraordinary *Supplement au Voyage de Bougainville*, which explored both the nature of pleasure and the limits of sexual conduct.[1]

What emerged from all this was a sense of openness to change, the detachment from place and time, of social and geographic mobility, and a readiness, if not eagerness, to welcome the new, even at the expense of tradition and the past. It was the proposition that there are no ends or purposes given "in nature," that the individual and his or her self-realization (though *her* came later) is the new ideal and imago of life, and that one can remake society and remake oneself in an effort to realize new individual goals.

The rise of individualism, particularly in the early nineteenth century, provoked a strong reaction from Catholics and socialists. In France, Bonald and de Maistre, both theocrats, militantly attacked "political protestantism" and asserted that man exists only for society. During the Restoration, after Napoléon, French writers of both a conservative and a liberal bent—Lamartine, Balzac, Sainte-Beuve, Lammenais, and de Tocqueville—expressed alarm about *l'odieux individualisme*, the pernicious view that they held responsible for the disintegration they said was occurring in their society. And against the atomization and egoism of society, the followers of Saint-Simon called for socialism as a new order based on association, harmony, and altruism.[2]

There are two sources, one theological and the other institutional, for the rise of individualism. The first, clearly, is the Protestant Reformation of Luther and Calvin. The core of Protestantism is that it is *anti-institutional* and *antinomian* (and, to that extent, even anti-intellectual). Against the authority of the church as the custodian of sacraments and the medium of salvation, the Reformation placed the individual and his conscience as the source of judgment. And against the intellectualism of Thomism and other doctrinal interpretations, the Reformation placed the Bible (which Luther translated) and literalism as the source of faith.[3]

[1] For an enchanting little volume on the expansion of the European imagination inspired by the encounter with other lands, see Henri Baudet, *Paradise on Earth: Some Thoughts on European Images of Non-European Man* (New Haven, Conn.: Yale University Press, 1965).
[2] For an exposition of this debate, see my essay, "Socialism," in the *International Encyclopedia of the Social Sciences* (New York: Macmillan Co., 1968), Vol. 14, pp. 506–34.
[3] The explosive nature of those sources of justification fueled such revolutionary movements

The institutional source of the rise of individualism was the claim of private enterprise, not birthright, as the basis for position and privilege in society. The success of private enterprise was the profit of the firm, not the mercantilist wealth of the Crown. The social mobility it stimulated challenged the older hierarchical order of society. A new class was coming to the fore.

With all this came revolutionary upheavals in political theory, the full implications of which are still not resolved some two to three hundred years later. For Jeremy Bentham, the community was a "fiction," and only individuals were the units of society. In the utilitarianism that Bentham formulated, a hedonic calculus would measure the pleasures and pains (profits and losses) gained or suffered by individuals in their efforts to "maximize" (a word he coined) their advantages. And social welfare was the sum total of such a hedonic calculus.

Capitalism thus embodied the idea of the modern, the ceaseless surge of change, and the emergence of the individual from the Protestant Reformation and the spirit of enterprise. But these were also the sources of the cultural contradictions of capitalism, which I sought to explore in these pages.[4]

Weber's *The Protestant Ethic and the Spirit of Capitalism*, written in 1904–05, is probably the most important sociological work of the twentieth century.[5] But its title—and the later mythmaking about "the Protestant ethic"—has obscured the intention explicit in the author's introduction, namely, to explain the historical puzzle of the past five hundred years, the question why a total revolution in the organization of society—law, administration, the economy, the arts and religion, and the development of science—occurred only in the West, not in other sections of the world. That revolution was the *rationalization* of life.

The impulse to profit and gain is found in all societies, but only in

as the Anabaptists in Germany and later the Fifth Monarchy Men in the Cromwellian revolution in England (Oliver Cromwell was briefly a Fifth Monarchy man), to bring the kingdom of God to earth. However, though Luther and Cromwell recoiled from the radical implications of the new beliefs, the idea of the individual remained sovereign.

[4] I make a distinction, difficult as it may be, between "modernity," "modernism," and "modernization." *Modernity* is a *spirit*, an outlook, a worldliness, and even a cosmopolitanism, that can be found even in Greek and Roman life (in the skeptics and the Epicureans); in the humanism of the Renaissance; in the robustness of Elizabethan life; and as an "official" view today, when it has become routinized and even banal. I define *modernism* as a *cultural* movement promoting experimentation, the "eclipse of distance" I have discussed in these pages, and the declaration of the authority of the artist to define what is art. *Modernization* is a set of institutional changes, particularly on the economic and governmental levels, to adapt the society to new technological innovations and to spur economic development.

[5] Max Weber, *The Protestant Ethic and the Spirit of Capitalism*, trans. Talcott Parsons (London: G. Allen & Unwin, 1930).

the West did capitalism, as a rational organization of production and the calculable balance sheet of costs, take hold and develop in the extraordinary way that it did. It was the effort to explain "rational economic conduct" that led Weber to the study of religion. Weber's question was: How did modern economic life supersede the traditional mode, the Catholic ethic of a fixed order based on the scholastic theory of the just price and the just wage? And for Weber, the answer lay in "the rational ethics of ascetic Protestantism."[6]

What Weber was saying was that at its beginning, modern capitalism required a certain type of character that matched the capitalist enterprise itself—the methodical, disciplined, work-oriented individual. To use Weber's phrase (adapted from Goethe), there was an "elective affinity" between character and material interests.

But character alone could not break the bonds of the past. What was also required was a religious ethic that provided justifications for conduct and sanctions for lapses. In the Protestant worldview, all work (from the highest to the lowest) was a "calling" and thus sanctified, as against the view that work was a punishment for man's sin of disobedience. The idea of a calling, then—which Weber argued did not exist in previous religious or ethical codes—is a moral obligation that projects religious behavior onto the everyday world.

But there was also another source, which Weber did not develop—the Puritan New Model Army of Cromwell. This was one of the most unusual armies in the history of warfare, one that emphasized self-discipline and asceticism and levied punishments for drunkenness, looting, or rape that were vigorously enforced. The discipline of this army, it may be said, passed over into the factory. The logic of industrial society, the purposeful rationality of means–ends behavior, established the boundaries for economic behavior.[7]

[6]But as Weber also emphasized, "thus we treat here only one side of the causal chain." As he wrote: "Not ideas, but material and ideal interests directly govern man's conduct. Yet very frequently the 'world images' which have been created by 'ideas' have, like switchmen, determined the tracks along which action has been pushed by the dynamic of interests."

Weber's synoptic statements about the rationalization of modern life can be found in his last lectures (1919–20) and were published as *General Economic History*, Frank H. Knight trans. (London: Allen & Unwin, n.d.), especially Part 4. The quotation on "the switchmen" is from Weber's *Religionssoziologie*, and can be found in the introduction to H. H. Gerth and C. Wright Mills, eds., *From Max Weber* (New York: Oxford University Press, 1946), pp. 63–64.

[7]The change from a military to an industrial society was first proposed by Saint-Simon, who coined the term "industrial society" to designate the new society run by engineers and entrepreneurs, and developed by August Comte, who had served as secretary to Saint-Simon. The Saint-Simonians promoted much of the industrialism in France in the nineteenth century, and the flagship of the steamship line, the Compagnie Générale Transportation was named the S.S. *Saint-Simon*.

The theme of a changeover from a military to an industrial society was laid out by Herbert Spencer and elaborated on by Raymond Aron as his master scheme of sociology. It was meant, in a way, as orthogonal to Karl Marx's notion of the change from feudal to capitalist society.

The Protestant ethic as a way of life, then, was one of piety, frugality, discipline, prudence, the strenuous devotion to work, and delayed gratification. As to the stirrings of the body, "along with a moderate vegetable diet and cold baths, the same prescription is given for all sexual temptations as is used against religious doubts and a sense of moral unworthiness: 'work hard in your calling.' "[8]

The restraint on consumption leads to capital accumulation, a way of life, as Weber pointed out, of moneymaking as an end in itself that "was contrary to the ethical feelings of whole epochs." Yet, as Weber stated, "The capitalistic system so needs this devotion to the calling of making money, it is an attitude toward material goods . . . which is intimately bound up with the conditions of survival in the economic struggle for existence."

The Protestant ethic, then, particularly in its Calvinist form, supplies the moral energy and drive of the capitalist entrepreneur. Weber spoke of Calvinism as having an "iron consistency" in the bleak discipline it demands of adherents. The accumulation of wealth was morally sanctioned insofar as it was combined with a sober industrious career. Wealth was condemned only if employed to support a life of idle luxury or self-indulgence. As Calvin wrote in a commentary on Isaiah: "For it too often happens that riches bring self-indulgence, and superfluity of pleasures produces flabbiness as we can see in wealthy regions and cities (where there are merchants). Now those who sail to distant places are no longer content with home comforts but bring back with them unknown luxuries . . . household furnishings . . . pictures . . . expensive tapestries like Phrygian embroidery and vases molded with exquisite art."

Weber's formulation of the Protestant ethic, it must be stressed, is *not* a historical or descriptive account of specific national developments in a specific time and place, but an "ideal type," a construct or collage drawn from diverse and even startlingly different writers, such as Calvin, the English divines Thomas Hooker and Richard Baxter, and the American moralist Benjamin Franklin. It is a heuristic device for creating a distinctive religious ethic that could be compared to other types constructed in the past or in other cultures and societies.[9]

---

[8]Weber, *The Protestant Ethic.*

[9]The ideal type, as Weber used it, "can only be an historical individual, i.e., a complex of elements associated in historical reality which we unite into a conceptual whole from the standpoint of their cultural significance."

In using Benjamin Franklin as an exemplar of the prudence, industry, and frugality typical of the Protestant ethic—in fact, he cited Franklin more often than Calvin and Baxter—Weber was misled and misled his readers about Franklin, the man. Franklin, printer and publisher, wrote popular homilies as formulas for success, especially about money begetting money. He was, in a way, writing for "the market." But Franklin, the man, was a shrewd and

But such a methodology has its risks. For one, as has been evident in the United States in recent years, it has been invoked as an ideological weapon in the cultural wars, when polemicists decry the loss of the Protestant work ethic as if it had literally existed here. For another, any actual application shows how misleading the construct may be in dealing with history.

This mistaken use of ideal type for history is vividly exemplified in Simon Schama's brilliant *The Embarrassment of Riches*, a cultural exploration of the Dutch republic—the first capitalist nation in the world—during its "golden age" in the seventeenth century. The Dutch had been told by the humanists and Calvin that great wealth was a test of moral fiber. Yet in this "ordeal of prosperity," the Dutch burghers succumbed to the lure of pageantry and display. As Schama wryly noted, republics rarely live up to the innocence of their origins; if born in austerity, they invariably flourish amidst pomp: "At the zenith of its power and brilliance, in the mid-seventeenth century, the Dutch republic was no more immune than any other from acts of elaborate self-congratulation. The Flemish towns . . . had married the Burgundian taste for opulence with their own vernacular tradition of civic pomp to produce Renaissance ceremonies of unrivalled splendor in the north." Thus, one part of Weber's proposition that the Protestant ethic restrained consumption to the advantage of capital accumulation, Schama concluded, "does not hold true for the Netherlands, the most formidable capitalism the world had yet seen."[10]

What Weber thought might be true for the *origins* of capitalism, he knew did not hold true after its success. As he wrote, in a mixture of resignation and despair, in the concluding pages of his magisterial book:

Since asceticism undertook to remodel the world and to work out its ideals in the world, material goods have gained an increasing and finally, who knows?—has escaped from the cage. But victorious capitalism, since it rests on mechanical foundations, needs its support no longer. . . . In the field of its highest development, in

---

cosmopolitan individual. He was, for his day, a good scientist, and he took his pleasures, siring some illegitimate children with a housemaid, a common enough practice for the age, emulated even by Hegel and Marx. And in Paris, when Franklin was American minister to France, he was quite the bon vivant. He once sought to seduce Mme. Helvetius, the widow of the famous philosopher. As the story is told, he approached her one evening at a ball and said: "Mme. Helvetius, last night I had a dream. I dreamt I was at the gates of heaven and saw there my late wife. I approached her eagerly, but when she saw me she turned her back on me and walked off with M. Helvetius. Come, Madame: let us take our revenge on them." The story is told in Sainte-Beuve's portrait of Franklin in *Portraits of the Eighteenth Century* (New York: Frederick Ungar, 1964), Vol. 1, p. 323.

[10]See Simon Schama, *The Embarrassment of Riches* (New York: Alfred A. Knopf, 1987), p. 224, for the quotation on the "power and brilliance" of the Dutch republic; pp. 322–23 for the discussion of Weber's thesis; and p. 289 for the quotation from Calvin on wealth, which Schama used as an epigraph for Chapter 5.

the United States, the pursuit of wealth, stripped of its religious and ethical meaning, tends to become associated with purely mundane passions, which often actually give it the character of sport.[11]

If this has been the fate of asceticism, one has to turn to the other chord in this polyphony to understand the cultural contradictions of American capitalism. The theme of acquisitiveness was the leitmotif of the other major early historian of capitalism and the antagonist of Weber—Werner Sombart. Sombart is rarely read today because of the sprawling, paradoxical, inconsistent, and contentious style of his works (and, perhaps, because his 1930 book, *A New Social Philosophy*, was pro-Nazi). Yet it was Sombart who coined the term "capitalism" (Marx never used it) to designate an interdependent *system* organized around the role of capital in accordance with a definite plan and applying definite technical knowledge in providing for material wants. Paradoxically, his own exposition of the development of capitalism and its central features was completely unsystematic and often contradictory.[12]

For Sombart, greed and gold were the *fons et origo* of capitalism—as of all human endeavor: "The love of money is one of the founders of human society; it arranges marriage, produces treaties, sets up states

[11]*The Protestant Ethic*, pp. 181–82. What Weber meant by "the cage" was "the technical and economic conditions of machine production which today determine the lives of all the individuals who are born into this mechanism, not only those directly concerned with economic acquisition, with irresistible force." This conclusion led Weber to one of his most powerful statements of cultural despair, which has often been cited by radical as well as reactionary critics of modern life:

> No one knows who will live in this cage in the future, or whether at the end of this tremendous development entirely new prophets will arise, or there will be a great rebirth of old ideas and ideals, or, if neither, mechanized petrification, embellished with a sort of convulsive self-importance. For the last stage of this cultural development, it might well be said: Specialists without spirit, sensualists without heart; this nullity imagines that it has attained a level of civilization never before achieved.

[12]Sombart's major work, *Der Moderne Kapitalismus*, was first published in 1902, with numerous editions and revisions and expansions published in 1916–17 and the final version, in six parts, published in three volumes, in Munich, 1921–27. There is no English translation, though a large abridged and paraphrased summary was published by F. L. Nussbaum as *A History of the Economic Institutions of Modern Europe: An Introduction to Werner Sombart's Der Moderne Kapitalismus* (New York: F. S. Crofts & Co., 1933).

Sombart's most interesting book, *Der Bourgeois*, was translated and edited by M. Epstein as *The Quintessence of Capitalism: A Study of the History and Psychology of the Modern Business Man* (New York: E. P. Dutton & Co., 1915). The third German edition was published in 1923.

The maddening *Die Juden und das Wirtschaftsleben*, with its identification of Jewish merchants and bankers on the basis of physiognomy, was translated in 1913 by M. Epstein as *The Jews and Modern Capitalism*, and a critical edition, with an introductory essay by Bert F. Hoselitz and an extended bibliographical note by Hoselitz and Benjamin Nelson, was issued by the Free Press (of Glencoe, Ill.) in 1951 and reissued in 1962 by Collier Books.

A neglected book, on the nature of the court and secular love, prompting the demand for luxury goods by women, quite at variance with Sombart's other work, was published in 1913 as *Luxus und Kapitalismus* and issued in 1967, in English, by the University of Michigan Press.

Sombart's most succinct statement about the nature of capitalism is "Capitalism" in the *Encyclopedia of the Social Sciences* (New York: Macmillan, 1942), Vol. 3, pp. 195–208.

and cities, provides honour and renown . . . stimulates commerce, alchemy, and medicine. . . . The art of war is likewise sustained by money-getting; and the discovery of new lands, too, as Queen Isabella and King Ferdinand, no less than Columbus, found out."

But it was the discovery of gold in the New World that unlocked the floodgates to Western economic development. "If not the whole of European history, then surely at least the history of the capitalist spirit, must begin with the struggle . . . for the possession of that accursed thing, gold."[13] And in *Der Bourgeois*, Sombart sought to limn the psychology of the new men who now roamed the new geography of the fabled lands of Cathay and Imago Mundi. For him, these men— freebooters, adventurers, and entrepreneurs—were intermingled. The Elizabethan John Hawkins, the captain of a "pirate" ship and a trader, was no different from Cecil Rhodes, wielding sword and rifle, playing the stock exchange, and becoming a capitalist entrepreneur who exercised brute force. ("It is strange to find in [Rhodes] even one iota of the Puritan spirit.") The modern businessman he found in America "unites within himself . . . the freebooter, unscrupulous calculator, landlord and speculator all in one. Any trust magnate will serve as an illustration." And it is clear that the man Sombart had in mind was John D. Rockefeller, a man who knew "how to glide over every moral restraint with almost childlike disregard."

What is new in all this is its "boundlessness," the falling away of natural limits. "There are no absolute limits to acquisition, and the system exercises a psychological compulsion to boundless extension. . . . The abstract, impersonal character of the aim indicates its limitlessness. . . . Profits, no matter how large, can never reach a level sufficiently high to satisfy the economic agent. The positive drive toward boundless acquisition is grounded in the conditions of management. . . . Acquisition therefore becomes unconditional, absolute. Not only does it seize upon all phenomena within the economic realm, but it reaches over into other cultural fields and develops a tendency to proclaim the supremacy of business interests over all other values."

The limitation of both Weber and Sombart is that they dealt primarily with the origins of capitalism, but not with its structural transformations. Modern capitalism began with the Industrial Revolution two hundred years ago, with the technological changes of the creation of machinery

[13]One may say that in his writings, Sombart developed Marx's ideas and anticipated those of Joseph Schumpeter. In *Capital*, Marx wrote: "The discovery of gold and silver in America, the extirpation, enslavement, and entombment in mines of the aboriginal population . . . the conquest and looting of the East Indies . . . signalled the rosy down of the era of capitalist production."

for the mechanical production of goods, the laying of thousands of miles of track for the railroads, the invention of steamships that could move faster than wind, and the sociological migration—a total change of life— of hundreds of thousands of persons into cities. All these were a transformation of life hitherto unknown in human history.

The emphasis on production meant an emphasis on renewable enterprise: the greater need for capital and a closer measure of its return; the large-scale organization of labor, the attention to markets and distribution, and an awareness of technology as the source of change and of heightened competition.

But twentieth-century capitalism wrought in some ways an even more startling sociological transformation—the shift from production to consumption as the fulcrum of capitalism. This was the rise of consumer durables: automobiles, refrigerators, television sets, washing machines and dryers, and the like. And all this created the revolution in retailing, particularly, as I noted, the invention of the installment plan, the most "subversive" instrument that undercut the Protestant ethic. Against the fear of going into debt, there was now the fear of not being credit worthy. Instead of saving for the good things of life, one could buy them now and pay later. Marketing and hedonism, as I argued, became the motor forces of capitalism. What we have here is the extraordinary change, far beyond the "civilizing process," that, as Schumpeter said, brought silk stockings to the shop girl and luxury to the masses.

In his marvelously fetching and quirky book, *Luxury and Capitalism*, Sombart made the idiosyncratic argument that illicit love and the style of life it produced gave rise to luxury—and capitalism. By "illicit love," he meant that of the mistress and the courtesan in the life of the Court, particularly the Court of Louis XIV, with the deer park in which its courtiers gamboled.[14]

If these were the only extravagances, astonishing as they may be, of a court grandly exhibiting its wealth to the world, it would be a curio for the history books. But they were not. What they signified was the transmutations in the history of sensibility. "This purely hedonistic conception of woman," as Sombart put it, was in direct opposition to the religious and institutional restraints that the Church had placed on

[14]The symbol of all this was Madame de Pompadour, the mistress of Louis XV, who set the style of living and shaped the tastes of her day. The accounts of another courtesan, Madame du Barry, have been preserved in their entirety. Her bills from the goldsmiths and jewelers; the silk merchants and lace dealers; the perfumers and hatters; the sellers of furniture, pictures, and vases; the tailors and embroiderers, the carriage makers and horse traders, the painters and sculptors, the makers of gardens and fountains, and on and on totaled 12,481,803 livres. At that time, an individual living in genteel poverty managed on 700 livres a year.

women until those times. But the sensual encounters celebrated at the court, sometimes in refinement, sometimes in debauchery, were "an emancipation of the flesh."[15]

The sequel to the flaunting of illicit love was the establishment of fashion. The mistress was not just a figure at the court but the actress, the cocotte, the *amant*, the *demoiselles de moyenne vertu*, the kept woman, the woman of the town. In France, almost every grand politician (down to Mitterrand in our day) had an acknowledged mistress, and well-known authors, such as Chateaubriand, were famous for establishing the practice of *cinq à sept*. The *grandes cocottes* were often the featured attraction at the spring races in Paris, their costumes, vying with one another for striking display, were carefully observed by other women and, at a distance, by the wives who did not wish to be left out. A gorgeous theatrical version of this scene is in the musical *Gigi*, the education of a young courtesan.

The exigency of all this was that all the follies of fashion, luxury, splendor, and extravagance first exhibited by the courtesans became the style that was copied, albeit not in such a flamboyant form, by the young women and middle-class wives who also wanted to be smart and join the fashion parade. And if these women could not go to the spring races, they could soon, in the twentieth century, peruse the huge number of women's and fashion magazines—with such names as *Glamour*, *Vogue*, *Cosmopolitan*, *Mademoiselle*, and even *Seventeen*—that would quickly bring the new styles to their audiences in full, gorgeous color by the smartest photographers, in a style that also became, in the work of Richard Avedon and Irving Penn, an "art form." And designers, such as Hubert de Givenchy, Coco Chanel, Christian Dior, Yves St. Laurent, and Oscar de la Renta, soon became celebrities and marketable names for cosmetics.[16]

All modern advertising is geared to this task of selling illusions, the persuasions of the witches' craft. That is a contradiction of capitalism, one that remains true today. Two films exemplify these themes in dif-

---

[15]See Sombart's *Luxury and Capitalism*, pp. 63–77, for the detailed expenditures at the French court. On the romantic and troubadour conception of romantic love, see Denis de Rougemont, *Passion and Society* (London: Faber & Faber, 1956). As de Rougemont wryly remarked apropos of the nineteenth-century novel—such as *Anna Karenina* and *Thérèse Raquin*—every woman had a husband and desired a lover.

[16]What are cosmetics, and what do they mean for personality? The story is best told by the remarkable psychologist Jean-Jacques Rousseau in *The First and Second Discourse*, edited by Roger D. Masters (New York: St. Martin's Press, 1964), pp. 155–56. Rousseau related what happened in that mythical moment when young men and women, growing up, began to meet around a large tree or campfire, to sing and dance and be "true children of love and leisure." But when "each one began to look at the others and wanted to be looked at himself," public esteem became a value. "The one who sang or danced the best, the handsomest, the strongest, the most adroit, or the most eloquent, became the most highly considered; and *that was the*

ferent ways. One is *Wall Street*, in which the protagonist, Gordon Gekko, an investment pirate, played by Michael Douglas, addresses a meeting of wary stockholders and proclaims the virtues of greed in a loud, triumphal voice. The other is Robert Altman's *Pret à Porter (Ready to Wear)*, in which a fashion show in Paris, exhibiting the latest styles of the great houses of fashion, ends with the display by a couturiere tottering on the verge of bankruptcy, who brings the house down by having her models walk down the runways—in the nude! These are the clothes of the emperor.

How far this is from the Protestant ethic!

II

THE END OF MODERNISM

Bourgeois capitalism sought initially to unify economy, character structure, and culture in a common frame. The first contradiction, as I just reiterated, is that the unfolding of capitalism destroyed the keystone of that character—the sober, prudential, delayed gratification of the Protestant ethic—with the acquisitive impulses unleashed by the technological revolution of the consumer-durable culture, aided by the sociological innovation of the installment plan and consumer credit.

The second contradiction was the surrender of prudential bourgeois culture to cultural modernism. In these pages, I have sought to relate cultural modernism to changes in social structure: The openness to change, the social and geographic mobility, and the immediacy of experience all created a common syntax that I called "the eclipse of distance"—of aesthetic distance, social distance, and psychic distance—as spectators were drawn into and enveloped by the scenes they beheld. In all this there was a turning away from the "rational cosmology" that had defined Western culture since the Renaissance: that of spatial foreground or background in painting through mathematical perspective; of beginning, middle, and end as the ordered chronology of time in novels; of the "correspondence theory" of truth in the semantic relation of words to objects.

---

first step toward inequality and, at the same time, toward vice." Those who had lost out, so to speak, began to dissemble, to adorn themselves, to wear plumage, to be sly or boisterous; in short, "for one's own advantage . . . to appear to be other than what one in fact was, to be and seem to be become two altogether different things; and from this distinction [arises] conspicuous ostentation, deceptive cunning, and all the vices that follow from them."

Where the aesthetic was joined to politics, particularly in the twentieth century, the "worldview" of modernism had been (until World War II) primarily reactionary or revolutionary: whether Stefan George or Gottfried Benn in aesthetics, or the German expressionists in theater and art; whether Ezra Pound, T. S. Eliot, William Butler Yeats, and Wyndham Lewis or the early revolutionary voices of W. H. Auden and Stephen Spender in poetry.

Bourgeois culture found few defenders. In its style it had been partial to realism or had appropriated the romantic and decorative modes of the past (particularly in architecture and painting). But in literature and painting—the experimental novels of Gertrude Stein, Virginia Woolf, James Joyce, and Marcel Proust or the cubism and primitivism of Pablo Picasso and Georges Braque, for example—the older bourgeois culture collapsed and, in an astonishing tour de force, modernism was first resisted and then eagerly sought by museums, corporate patrons, and publishers. The further irony was that cultural modernism was smashed by fascism and communism, both of which sought inflated exaggerations of the baroque in architecture or socialist realism in painting and literature. In the end, cultural modernism could find an audience and patronage only in liberal bourgeois society, particularly when the advanced art became a status badge for display and for discussion by the culturati, the new class of consumers.

And yet, in its worldview, there is something of historic significance in modernism. The crucial point is that modernism disrupts mimesis—the exact "copy" of the external world. It is experimental, emphasizing in spatial terms multiple perspectives and different angles of vision, and in its breakup of time, the flow of consciousness and the emphasis on *durée*, rather than metric chronology. Thus it breaks the ordered coordinates of space and time. But modernism is still linked to *traditional* art and culture in its search for (and, indeed, in some arts, the centrality of) *form*. The "realization of form" (to use the key term of Aristotle) is the *zwang* or pull to completeness, if not perfection. It is not the traditional "realist" form of genre, as a "true" copy of the world is. Nor is it the *immanent* unfolding of a logic (as in the sonata form in music) or the "emergence" of a figure out of the stone, as in sculpture; rather, it is the *constructed* entity, reworked by the will and imagination of the artists in different spatial forms, as in the multiple depictions of Mont Saint-Victoire by Cézanne, the flatness on the same plane of different views. And apart from content, there is a preoccupation with materiality—the texture, the thickness or thinness of paint, the stroke of the brush (or the drip), as ends in themselves, as elements in the aesthetics of modernism.

The search for order is the search for underlying forms in the formalist poetics of Roman Jakobson; the structural anthropology of Claude Lévi-Strauss, with its imposition of binary codes on the diversity of myth; or the formalist criticism of Clement Greenberg in painting. Yet, as against the contemplative nature of classical art, it is also a movement from what is *known* to the *knower*. For classical philosophy, knowledge is in the predicate; subjectivity is contingent or wayward and cannot be knowledge in itself. But the movement from the known (Plato's sense of preexisting forms) to the knower is the starting point of constructed knowledge in modern thought. The turn comes with Immanuel Kant in his remarkable statement that *"the understanding does not derive its laws (a priori) from, but prescribes them to, nature."* It is the movement from "reason in nature" to "reason in mind."[17]

In modern analytic philosophy and in the formalist elements of modernism, there remains the centrality of reason in constructing our pictures of the world "out there." Yet in this retreat from the primacy of materialism—the basis of a "copy" theory of knowledge or of a correspondence theory of truth (of word to object)—a new rift is opened. And if mind is superseded by language as our means of knowing, then the very waywardness of language introduces a larger degree of uncertainty in our epistemological theories of knowing. And given this centrality of language as the frame of understanding, for some writers, "anything goes." The latter becomes that realm of the strange phenomenon of the past twenty years designated (I cannot say "known") as *postmodernism.*

What is it? Everyone who has written a book or article on postmodernism begins with an apology for the inability to define the term. This is understandable, for if one could define it, it would not be postmodernism, since it would then have an identifiable referent.

I want to make a distinction, quite arbitrary, between postmodernism and PoMo, as a way of sorting out the quiddities of the phenomenon. I distinguish postmodernism as a somewhat serious effort to define a new style originally in architecture or new techniques of literary analysis, from PoMo, which is its vulgar form, exhibited in fashion and display and a new jargon by a culturati to maintain an adversary stance against the society to which these writers think that modernism has surrendered.

Postmodernism, in the past two decades, has become a sweeping attack on the grounds of all knowledge—epistemology, literature, and the arts. It has been able to do so because it has "hitched" a ride on a num-

---

[17]Immanuel Kant, *Prolegomena to Any Future Metaphysics,* Carus translation revised by James W. Ellington (Indianapolis: Hacket Publishing Co., 1977), p. 62. Emphasis in the original.

ber of philosophical developments that have become the center of "discourse." It has drawn from the powerful attacks of Nietzsche and Heidegger on traditional metaphysics; from the pragmatism of Dewey, with his theory of truth rooted in practice; from the anti-foundationalism in analytical philosophy of Quine and Goodman, which denies fixed points of reference; and from Wittgenstein's reversal of his older picture-theory of language in favor of the (often misunderstood) idea of "language games." As Richard Rorty put it: Of course, there is a world "out there," but the ways of knowing it are not out there.

Yet all these efforts have been rooted in some ontological quest, whether the narrow "physicalism" of Quine or Dewey's emphasis on method or the "many faces of realism" of Hilary Putnam. Postmodernism is a flight from philosophy—I think of Foucault or Derrida or Rorty—into cultural history, rhetoric, or aesthetics and the denial, if not the subversion, of universalist and transcendental values. Combined with the sociology of Pierre Bourdieu, it continues the "exposé" of humanism and morals and power relations initiated by Nietzsche, though, unlike Jürgen Habermas, it does not present an alternative normative value system to be counterposed to the humanism of Western individualism. (Rorty, in partial exception, presents a strange combination of social democratic politics combined with the antimetaphysics of Heidegger).[18]

PoMo is the perfect pleonasm. It is the all-purpose adjective, adverb, noun, verb, pronoun (but not Subject), object, conjunction, disjunction, and descriptive and prescriptive term. In the august Paris *Le Monde* (reported in the *New Yorker*), the mandarin French philosopher Alain Finkelkraut attacked a jury at the Cannes film festival for praising the movie *Underground* by the Yugoslavian director Emir Kasturica, which he called "a rock postmodern, over the top, hip Americanized version of the most drivelling and lying Serbian propaganda." An issue of the Mexican magazine *Universidad de Mexico* featured an article, "El futbol: simbolo de la sociedades postmodernas?" And a full-page advertisement in the *New York Times Magazine* featured three bold horizontal lines

---

[18]Earlier, I declared my own triune views of being a socialist in economics, a liberal in politics, and a conservative in culture. In the past year or more, I have come to work out a new conception of "natural law" that differs from the classical, Thomist, or early liberal thinkers to provide an ontological foundation for a conception of "human rights" and "crimes against humanity" that liberal theorists of rights, such as Ronald Dworkin, have failed to provide. I have been influenced, to a considerable extent, by Lloyd L. Weinreb's *Natural Law and Justice* (Cambridge, Mass.: Harvard University Press, 1987), though Weinreb is still uncertain about the possibility of an ontological foundation. My argument is laid out in an unpublished paper, "The Re-birth of Utopia: The Path to Natural Law," originally presented as a lecture at the Club de Debate of Complutense University, Madrid, April 25, 1996.

with the words "[Living] [Without] [Boundaries]" and underneath, "S A F A R I For Men, by Ralph Lauren, clearly a postmodern fragrance."

In his *Idea of the Postmodern: A History*, Hans Bertin wrote: "Daniel Bell's mid-1970s attempt to sketch the sociological background of postmodernism . . . was not immediately followed up by other sociologists. With few exceptions, the social sciences ignored the debate on the postmodern until the mid-1980s."[19] Since then, the issues have swamped the intellectual scene. Given the cacophony that has made any thoughtful exploration nigh unintelligible, I would like to single out some of the diverse strands that have emerged in these past two decades.[20]

The first public awareness of the term "postmodernism" was, surprisingly, in architecture, where it was used as a straightforward *rejection* of modernism. Architects had begun to tire of the machine aesthetic of the Bauhaus and Le Corbusier or the spare, geometrical forms of Mies van der Rohe and wanted to return to the liveliness of the vernacular and the "ordinary" life of what Jane Jacobs called the mixed vitality of the neighborhood. As Robert Venturi, who led the way, remarked:

Architects can no longer afford to be intimidated by the puritanically moral language of orthodox Modern architecture. I like elements which are hybrid rather than "pure," compromising rather than "clean," distorted rather than straightforward. . . . I am for messy vitality over obvious unity. I include the non sequitur and proclaim the duality.

Whereas Mies van der Rohe had proclaimed that "less is more," Venturi retorted, "less is a bore."

[19]London: Routledge, 1995, p. 209.
[20]There are, inevitably, confusions and overlaps and misconceptions about the relationship of the terms "postindustrial" and "postmodern." In my 1974 book, *The Coming of Post-Industrial Society*, I sketched an "ideal type" of post-industrial society along several dimensions: the change from a goods-producing to a service society in occupations; the role of coded information as a new control system for production and communication; and the codification of theoretical knowledge as the new source for the applications of science and technology in the economy. I stated explicitly that these were changes in the techno-economic dimensions of society and that technology did *not* determine the other sectors, political and cultural, of the society. Where I discussed postmodernism, as I have in this book, it was as the working out of and reaction to the nature of modernism, *in the culture*.
The French writer Jean-François Lyotard picked up my theme of postindustrialism and joined it to postmodernism by linking the role of knowledge in the two. I find his attempts confusing. As I have argued in these pages, culture and technology follow different logics, and while there are some reciprocal influences (such as the role of technology in graphic images or in the production and amplification of sound), the two spheres are quite separate. In technology, there is a linear principle of substitution, in that a more efficient or productive technique replaces another. In culture, there is no such principle of change, for the new developments widen the imaginative repertoire of culture. For an excellent and clear discussion of these distinctions and a good guide to the various theorists, see Margaret Rose, *The Post-Modern and the Post-Industrial* (New York: Cambridge University Press, 1991).

If one wonders why this movement developed in architecture, ahead of other art forms, Charles Jencks, a "theoretician" of the movement, remarked that architecture had "succumbed to the alienating effects of modernization." As he wrote in his book *What Is Post-Modernism?*, "Modernism failed as mass housing and city building because it failed to communicate with its inhabitants and users who might not have liked the style, understood what it meant, or even known how to use it."[21]

Once the strictures of modernism were broken, postmodernism became a wildly fanciful game of styles. Venturi adopted the exuberant neon birds of paradise of Las Vegas. There is the baroque postmodernism of Michael Graves, the rococo postmodernism of Charles Moore, the neoclassical postmodernism of Aldo Rossi, and the post-industrial postmodernism of Piano and Rogers in the Pompidou Center in Paris, as well as the disjointed postmodernism, each plumb line askew, of Frank Gehry. In a serious spirit, Jencks said that postmodernism is a form of "double coding, not the elimination of the high and the low, the elitist and the everyman, but juxtapositions which bring these different styles together in a variety of ways."

Yet one can also say that postmodernism also becomes *pompier.* Philip Johnson, who had been one of the theorists of modernism as an associate of Mies van der Rohe, but was always ready to lead the fashion parade, designed the AT&T building on Madison Avenue in New York, whose top is a broken pediment in Chippendale style. What we find here is a trajectory, repeated in field after field, that what begins as a serious endeavor (even if sometimes in a jokey style) ends in kitsch.

Postmodernism in architecture was a straightforward confrontation with a previous historically unified style. Yet in the flapping winds of intellectual fashion, the term veered off into the wild blue yonder and became the zeitgeist of any and all ready-made "discourses."

A useful starting point in identifying the varied themes of postmodernism is Lyotard's *La Condition postemoderne*, published in Paris in 1979, though not translated into English until 1984. Lyotard, like the sociologist Jean Baudrillard (who has written copiously on the consumer society), was a member of *Socialisme ou barbarie*, a small Marxist group in Paris in the 1950s, led by Cornelius Castoriades, one of whose chief purposes was to expose the Stalinist system as a form of state capitalism. Lyotard abandoned traditional Marxism and embraced the con-

---

[21]As Jencks remarked apropos an American experience: "Modern architecture died in St. Louis, Missouri on July 15, 1972, at 3:32 P.M. (or thereabouts) when the infamous Pruitt-Igoe scheme, or rather several of its slab blocks, were given the final *coup de grace* by dynamite." Pruitt-Igoe had been given an award by the American Institute of Architects when it was designed in 1951. Its purist style was meant to instill, by example, corresponding virtues in the inhabitants. Yet over the years, it produced a crime rate higher than any other public-housing development.

cept of postindustrial society, in which information, not production, became the control system of the economy. In the analysis of culture, Lyotard made his own contribution. An idée fixe, simple but didactic.

Modern culture, says Lyotard, is organized around grand Metanarratives, terms such as Progress, Emancipation, or Enlightenment that establish the values of the society. Each of these Metanarratives has its form of legitimation, which is also its armor. The political form, derived from the Enlightenment, is the moral armor of universal freedom. The philosophical one, drawn from German idealism, sees history as the realization of Reason, or universal knowledge.

These legitimations, Lyotard argues, have lost their power, though it is not entirely clear whether it is the intellectual underpinnings that have been undermined or the beliefs held of them in the modern world. What remains, in its privileged place, is science. And here Lyotard joined with Jürgen Habermas in arguing that science has become equated with instrumental rationality (as a servant to power) and that instrumental rationality has come to dominate all other forms of reason. It is Weber redivivus and denatured.

In place of Metanarratives, all that remains are language games in which the rules are set by the social institutions within which the languages are embedded. Thus the question is: How do we break out of these walled-off cities? For Habermas, the task is to engage in "communicative action," to end all ideologies (including science) that inhibit us from reaching rational agreement or consensus. For Lyotard, the task is to encourage dissensus and conflict. Modernist science sought to establish timeless representations as truths of the world. Postmodern science, Lyotard says, needs to be antirepresentational, a continuing permanent revolution (the Cheshire trace of the old Trotskyism, one might say) against the "truths" of the Established.

If I adopt Lyotard's simple strategy, I can identify two metanarratives that became the intellectual overpinnings and the terrible simplifications of the ideology of postmodernism. One is the attack on the Enlightenment, the other the attack on "bourgeois humanism." These are the themes to be found in the twenty-year reign of French structuralist, deconstructionalist, and poststructuralist thought, proclaiming, in stupefying terms, the Death of Man, the Death of the Subject, the Death of the Author, the Death of Meaning, and the Death of the Self, heralded by the iconoclastic gurus (an oxymoron, to be sure) Foucault, Derrida, Barthes, and Lacan.

Michel Foucault burst on the French intellectual scene (in *Les Mots et les Choses*, 1966) with the declaration of the end of the concept of Man and its replacement by language in understanding mind or consciousness. In itself, there was little novelty in the latter assertion: with Frege and Russell, Carnap and Quine, logical positivism and analytical philosophy, the study of language as the medium through which concepts were expressed had become central to the philosophical effort to understand the reality "out there."

What gave Foucault's work its radical "spin" was the grandiose prediction of the Death of Man, and the statement of a new method of philosophical analysis. The new methodology argued that each period of philosophical thought had its distinctive *episteme*, or a cultural code that orders human experience—linguistic, perceptual, and practical. Between each *episteme* there was a radical rupture that changed the ordering principle of each code. The idea of *episteme* had been proposed by the French philosopher Gaston Bachelard (1884–1962), but Foucault gave it a historicity that Bachelard's work, which dealt with images and archetypes, never developed.

For Foucault, the contemporary epistemological rupture was with the Enlightenment concept of Man, who was identified in sociohistorical terms as the bourgeois subject and in psychological and philosophical terms as ego and cogito. Therefore, Foucault mounted a challenge to the tradition of Western humanism and the role of human agency in the direction of history. "As the archeology of our thought easily shows," Foucault wrote, "man is an invention of recent date, [and] one can certainly wager that man would be erased like a face drawn in the sand at the edge of the sea." And this is an "eventuality" to be welcomed rather than dreaded. The "void" left by the disappearance of man does not create a lacuna to be filled. It is a space in which "it is once more possible to think. To those who wish to talk about man . . . or his liberation," to all those "warped and twisted forms of reflection, we can only answer with a philosophical laugh." Thus, Foucault dismissed bourgeois humanism as a passing episode of history.[22]

Foucault's laughter at "the subject"—the Cartesian cogito whose unyielding doubt that he could not doubt was the Archimedean point in the axis of knowledge—would have remained a flamboyant gesture, except for the fact that from diverse sources, new developments in philosophy, literature, anthropology, and linguistics had signaled a new turn (the word "rupture" would be too extreme because these forces

---

[22]Michel Foucault, *The Order of Things* (London, 1970), p. 387. I am indebted to Richard Wolin's essay "Modernism vs. Postmodernism" (*Telos*, No. 62, Winter 1984–85) for his discussion. For a cogent explanation of the philosophical foundation of Foucault's early philosophical thought, see the essay by George Canguilhem, Foucault's teacher at the École Normale Supérieure, on "The Death of Man, or Exhaustion of the Cogito," in *The Cambridge Companion to Foucault*, edited by Garry Gutting (New York: Cambridge University Press, 1994), chap. 3. This is the first English translation of Canguilhem's informative essay.

did not cohere) as a new "paradigm," to use the Kuhnian equivalent of *episteme*.

Classical philosophy had always emphasized the *known*, not the knower. Knowledge was in "the predicates," the qualitative essences within the types that marked off one sphere of knowledge or one discipline from another (the differences, for example, between physics and biology and psychology). The knower was simply contingent; his or her sensory perceptions were accidental or irrelevant to what was known. But René Descartes introduced the radical distinction between *res cogitans* and *res extensa*, and for him, knowledge began with the knowing subject beholding the world. From Descartes on, the problem for philosophy was how one creates "objective" pictures of the world if one begins from a subjective point of view. Later Continental philosophers attempted to do so by "eliminating" the subject by seeking structural or phenomenological modes of explanation that concentrated on the *system* of relations, or *structures* of language and social ties between individuals, and on categories of experience (logic), rather than the content of experience (psychology) itself.

The three modes that became influential at the time were the phenomenology of Edmund Husserl, the structural anthropology of Claude Lévi-Strauss, and the structural linguistics of Ferdinand de Saussure, whose lectures between 1907 and 1911 were published posthumously (as the *Course de Linguistic générale*) in 1916, and rediscovered in recent decades, with the interest in signs and semiotics as ways of dealing with meaning.

The phenomenology of Husserl and the structuralism of Lévi-Strauss and de Saussure were efforts to find invariant and universal rules of thought, language, and social relations, independent of subjectivity. With the writings of Derrida, structuralism was rejected—deconstructed, so to speak—and the question of meaning and reference was withdrawn from the "world" and lodged in "the text."

In itself, the idea of pure textual criticism is an old one, which, in contemporary literary criticism, was exemplified by "close reading," such as William Empson's demonstration that a word-by-word analysis of a poem is necessary to reveal the ambiguity (and its seven types) that exists in poetry; I. A. Richards's "practical criticism" to elucidate the four different kinds of meaning in a poem (sense, feeling, tone, and intention); or, in the United States, the New Criticism of John Crowe Ransom, Cleanth Brooks, and others of that school who sought coherence in the interrelated meanings of words and phrases fused in a poem.

But all such efforts, Derrida would say, are attempts to *fix* the meaning of a text and are derived from traditional concepts and categories of Western reason since the Greeks. Derrida called them "the metaphysics of presence," the search for some unifying transcendental reference point that can uncover an ultimate intelligibility rooted in philosophy. Such efforts to find an *arché* and *telos*, some notion of an entelechy, or the inner design of a project, from its origins to conclusion, he thought, were only "the last dream of humanism."

Derrida wanted to reject philosophy, its search for an ontological center and an authority guaranteed by some transcendental concept. Instead of philosophy (or, in his language, "the signified"), there is only literature, and in literature there is only text, and in text there are only signs.

Although Derrida has been perceived as the voice of wild interpretive freedom, he is anything but. His methods and his categories are as schematic as those of a scholastic schoolman. His all-purpose tool is the technique of "deconstruction." Yet any effort to pin down the meaning of the term is invariably elided by the fact that Derrida refuses to assign any fixed meanings for terms, including, apparently, his own.

In the end, textual analysis for Derrida is not concerned with "the fetishism of Meaning," which is a relation to a referent, or an outside reality. One reason Derrida is attractive, especially to literary theorists, who find their subject now designated the central focus of all inquiry, is that deconstructionism blows apart all systems in favor of a method that is also an antimethod. Derrida has it both ways. As Barbara Johnson, a second-generation deconstructionist, described Derrida's method in his *Disseminations*:

> Consider the following passage from Derrida's *Dissemination:* "It is thus not simply false to say that Mallarmé is a Platonist or a Hegelian. But it is above all not true. And vice versa." Instead of a simple either/or structure, deconstruction attempts to elaborate a discourse that says *neither* "either/or," *nor* "both/and" nor even "neither/nor," while at the same time not totally abandoning these logics either.[23]

The parade marches on. With Barthes, one finds a rejection of the historical or biographical contexts of literary criticism, since they deal primarily with an *author*. For Barthes, the author does not have a "privileged" position in determining the meaning of his or her work. Meaning is encoded in language, and there are not only formal systems of language (as with Saussurian linguistics), but also class or cultural codes that seem "natural" to the author but are only conventional or

[23]In Jacques Derrida, *Disseminations*, trans. Barbara Johnson (Chicago: University of Chicago Press, 1981), p. 207, as cited in John M. Ellis, *Against Deconstruction* (Princeton, N.J.: Princeton University Press, 1989), pp. 5–6.

stereotypical, what Barthes called *"mythologies."* And the author may be trapped unknowingly within them.

Meaning, for Barthes, arises from the signs (both linguistic and cultural) that they seemingly refer to and from the "mythological" responses of the readers who provide significance to the text. The reader's response, not the author's writing, then, is the arena of meaning. But since the text is not a fixed object, but an event that changes over time, the temporal responses of different readers invariably annihilate the preceding responses—ad infinitum?

And from the "author" to the "self." Freud constructed psychoanalysis on the argument that the self, the ego, was not an autonomous subject, but was driven by unconscious impulses and repressed memories that had to be kept at bay for the individual to function in the world. For Freud, there is no sense of time in the unconscious, which is why memories and fears are always below the surface and lead to neuroses unless they are displaced or subjected to rational control or the tight authority of a superego, parental or institutional.

It was Lacan who drew the most radically antihumanist consequences from Freudian theory. The fundamental premise of humanism that Lacan radically called into question was that individuals have the capacity to function as the subjects or authors of their own acts. Yet, Lacan noted, "the subject does not know what he is saying, and for the best reasons—because he does not know what he is."

The idea of the ego, Lacan stated, is a mistake, purely and simply, *"méconnaissance."* As Richard Wolin explained: "Since the self can never be anything but a patchwork of artificial linguistic constructs that serve to cover up and distort the unconscious, the "true" subject is unattainable, since the attempt to reach it is mediated by language, which is a falsifying medium of representation. The honest approach to subjectivity would be to embrace its primordial fragmentation."[24]

If this is what we are, can one have a conception of moral responsibility once the idea of human agency is rejected as a form of "metaphysical illusion"?

For a phenomenon as pervasive as postmodernism, the question inevitably arises, What is its relation to other dimensions of society. For

[24]See Richard Wolin, "Antihumanism in the Discourse of French Postwar Theory," *Common Knowledge*, 3 (Winter 1994), pp. 70–71. Freudian analysis aims to strengthen the ego, whereas Lacanian analysis aims to deconstruct the ego to undo the repressions that begin when "the mirror state" of infancy, the sense of the I and the me, take hold.

the Marxist literary critic Frederic Jameson, postmodernism is a "new social formation," the "cultural logic of 'late capitalism,'" driving from a break in social development" so that postmodernism is a new "cultural dominant and a new socioeconomic stage of capitalism." As Douglas Kellner describes it: "Commodification and capitalist exchange relations have penetrated the spheres of information, knowledge, computerization, and consciousness and experience itself to an unparalleled extent." That is the postmodern condition. For the English sociologist Scott Lash, what is occurring is a conflict between the settled bourgeoisie, the middle classes of *industrial* capitalism, whose tastes run to high modernist art, and the new *postindustrial* bourgeoisie who are asserting themselves and seeking to replace the allegiance to high modernism with its own postmodernist culture. And for cultural theorist Mike Featherstone, postmodernism as a sociological fact is identified with the "lifestyle" of the "new middle class," which he defined as the "new cultural intermediaries" and the "helping professions."[25]

So runs the gamut of sociology.

It is foolish to seek to locate postmodernism or PoMo as either "right" or left."[26] What we have here is the working out of the logic of modernism (its anticognitive and anti-intellectual modes) and consumerism (its acquisitiveness) in a world where the culturati find their own worldviews incoherent—because of the absence of a secure foundation in traditional morality or in a liberalism that found it difficult to set limits on permissible behavior—and have welcomed the cultural anarchism and the transvaluation of values that postmodernism set loose.

As an intellectual endeavor, postmodernism is fading. Foucault and Derrida have lost their allure. Lacanian analysis is fractured among competing sects, since they are unable to find a common language, even among the master's *écrits*. Barthes, sadly, is largely forgotten. In

[25]Jameson's essay, "Postmodernism, or the Cultural Logic of Late Capitalism," appeared in the *New Left Review*, No. 146 (1984); Kellner's "Postmodernism as Social Theory," appeared in Featherstone, *Consumer Culture and Postmodernism* (London: Sage Publications, 1991), p. 258; Lash's theory is presented in his *Sociology of Postmodernism* (London: Routledge, 1990) and Featherstone's is in his *Consumer Culture and Postmodernism*.

[26]In his Adorno Prize lecture in 1980, Jürgen Habermas denied the claims of a postmodern break in history and attacked postmodernism as a form of neoconservative ideology. In another paper, he wrote of a line leading from George Bataille via Foucault to Derrida as representing a "young conservative" tradition whose members "on the basis of modernistic attitudes . . . justify an irreconcilable antimodernism." A few years later, in 1985, however, he stated that he now found "certain affinities between the negative dialectics of Adorno, the archeologies of Foucault, and the deconstructions of Derrida." Quoted in Rose, *The Post-Modern and the Post-Industrial*, pp. 55, 225.

France in the past several years, we have seen the rise of a new liberalism and conservatism in political philosophy that seek to remain resolutely secular and modern and to formulate "a modern humanism that is neither naively metaphysical nor flatly historicist." These writers are attempting to return to "the subject" (though not to an individualism that isolates the person) and to make universal political and moral judgments possible without appeals to religion, tradition, or human nature. It is not the individual who is the source of such rights, it is contended, but a civic republicanism rooted in the obligations and reciprocity of citizens to one another.[27]

Yet many of the diffuse themes live on, especially in university courses, for postmodernism's appeal is adversarial and the philosophy finds a wider public audience on themes that sound some resonant cultural chords. Given their importance, I single out three themes here for a brief discussion: the attack on science and technology, the elimination of the distinction between high and low culture, and the relativism that has pervaded much of social analysis.

Derogation of science has become a vogue. For Lyotard, science is a narrative, so that Descartes's *Discourse on Method*, his discovery of doubt, is a bildungsroman. For the literary critic Stanley Fish, science is a rhetoric, no more "privileged" than any other rhetoric, and contains no objective tests of truth. For Wendy Kaminer, an observer of PoMo, rationality has been out of fashion in recent years; as she wrote in *It's All the Rage:* "New-agers condemn it as left-brain thinking; some feminists consider it male-identified, while radical academics dismiss it as a pretense of objectivity."

A more troublesome expression is the view of Vaclav Havel, who, in a widely quoted essay, called communism the realization of science. The fall of communism, he stated, can be regarded as a sign that modern thought—based on the premise that the world is objectively knowable—has come to a final crisis. Furthermore, he noted:

Modern science . . . abolishes as mere fiction even the innermost foundation of our natural world. It kills God and takes his place on the vacant throne . . . as its sole legitimate arbiter of all relevant truth. For after all, it is only science that rises

[27]For a useful guide to this thinking, see *New French Thought: Political Philosophy*, edited by Mark Lilla (Princeton, N.J.: Princeton University Press, 1994). The key figures in this enterprise are Luc Ferry and Alain Renault. With respect to some of the writers discussed here, see the essays in that volume on Lévi-Strauss by Tzvetan Todorov and on Foucault by Ferry and Renault. Independently of the French, one can find a vigorous defense of civic republicanism in the writings of Quentin Skinner and on rights by Ronald Dworkin.

above all individual subjective truths and replaces them with a superior trans-subjective truth which is truly objective and universal.[28]

Against modern science, Havel wants "the authority of 'personal experience,'" the experience of mystery and of the absolute, to achieve a "new postmodern face for politics." When pressed to explain his conception of postmodernism, Havel wrote, in "The End of the Modern Era" (on the OpEd page of the *New York Times*, July 8, 1994), that "our lost integrity" might be renewed by "a science that is new, postmodern, such as the anthropic cosmological principle and the Gaia hypothesis," the idea that the earth is alive. To which Nicholas Wade, a science writer on the *Times*, wrote: "A view of the world built on the anthropic principle and the Gaia hypothesis would not be postmodern science but rather a throwback to the numerology and astrology from which the era of rationalism has still not fully rescued us."

Havel's need for "individual spirituality . . . and above all to trust one's own subjectivity as the principal link with the world" is completely understandable in light of his firsthand experience with a Communist regime that sought to flatten all critical thought with the hammer of ideology and his vocation as a playwright, with its emphasis on the particularity of character. But the equation of communism with science is grotesque. In Stalinist Russia, physicists could not openly espouse Albert Einstein's theory of relativity or modern quantum mechanics, since these theories were deemed to be idealist and probabilistic and hence to violate the precepts of Lenin's *Materialism and Empirio-Criticism*, with its copy theory of knowledge and deterministic, mechanistic view of the world. And worse, leading biologists and geneticists were imprisoned and even executed when they opposed Lysenko's charlatan championing of Lamarckian evolution.

But what is more important are the misconceptions of science by Havel and others who hold the romantic view that has emerged so strongly in recent years. One is the misconception of how science "works." The other is the misconception of the relation of science to the arts and other realms of experience.

Regarding the first, one must distinguish between science as an institution and the *findings* of science. The institutions and the applications are often subject to "outside" control and even direction. But crucial to science are the *findings*—the structure of matter, from atoms to quarks or the double helix of DNA. Here we find a "republic of sci-

[28]Jan Vladislav, *Vaclav Havel, or Living in the Truth* (London: Faber & Faber, 1987).

ence." No single person has the papal authority to declare the truth. Findings must be verified openly and by procedures (and notebooks) that are subject to public scrutiny. Science is the only genuine permanent revolution in human affairs, since it is committed to challenging the findings of its forebears. It is, following Weber in "Science as a Vocation," a charismatic community.[29]

The different argument, common to those who counterpose the humanities to science, is that science has usurped primacy "over other types of cognition and experience." But as Victor Weisskopf, a passionate physicist and musician, put it: "Art and music on the one hand and science on the other are fundamentally different approaches to human experience, and each have their own claims. 'In the morning I turn from mystery to reality, and in the evening I return from reality to mystery.' "[30]

There is no reason to consider a Gothic sculpture better than a Romanesque one or to judge the music of Mahler more valid artistically than that of Mozart. Such changes in the arts widen the aesthetic and moral repertoire of mankind. Unlike technology, the arts are not erased, but become a permanent depository from which individuals can draw to renew and remold an aesthetic experience. But there is "progress" in science. Classical physics and quantum theory describe two "different" physical worlds. We know more about the structure of matter from the later work of Murray Gell-Mann and Richard Feynman than we did from the earlier work of Ernest Rutherford and Max Planck. We know the double character of light as both wave and pulse. Einstein's theory of gravity is a revision of and an advance over Isaac Newton's. We also now understand the genetic code and the mechanisms of heredity. And evolution and natural selection undergird our understanding of species. The twentieth century revolutionized, in fact, our conceptions of physics, chemistry, and biology for better or worse, but their truths cannot be denied.

For several hundred years, a sharp distinction has been made between high culture and low (or popular) culture. Herbert Marcuse maintained that art is the negation of restraint. This distinction was not always made. In Catholic culture, the liturgy and litany, expressed in soaring architecture, had instilled a sense of awe that was felt by all

[29] I elaborated on this point in the section on "the ethos of science," in *The Coming of Post-Industrial Society*, pp. 378–86.
[30] Victor F. Weisskopf, *The Joy of Insight: Passions of a Physicist* (New York: Basic Books, 1991), pp. 301, 313.

worshippers. In Elizabethan England, the bawdiness of the plays, as in Shakespeare's, mingled the high and the low.

High culture, especially in the nineteenth century, was of two kinds. One can best be described by the German word *Bildung* (literally formation or education), which means cultivation—the cultivation of taste and the appreciation of the classics. The other was what Carl Schorske called "Biedermeier" culture, or the gilt-bound volumes of the classics, such as by Schiller or Goethe, that lay behind the glass doors of heavy Biedermeier bookcases.

High culture has always had an aristocratic bias, as T. S. Eliot pointed out. Yet with the growth of the middle class, the spread of literacy, and the mechanical reproduction of art, concern arose about the fate of "culture." The fears were addressed most directly by Matthew Arnold in *Culture and Anarchy* (1869). For Arnold, with the decline of religion, culture was the remaining moral force to define what it meant to be civilized. But how was culture to be received in the England of his day? Lacking a precise scientific vocabulary, as he noted ironically, he responded to the different modes of behavior by inventing three distinct terms, "Barbarians," "Philistines," and "Populace," "to denote roughly the three great classes into which our society is divided."[31]

Arnold's terms have largely disappeared, except for "philistine," which remains a term of opprobrium. But what has been crucial is Arnold's conception of culture as the lodestar of civilization and the recurrent fear that the distinctions between high and low culture will be erased.

In the postwar American years, the issues were sharpened by Dwight Macdonald in a famous monograph, *Masscult and Midcult*, which launched a withering assault not only on the mass culture being produced by movies and television, but also on the "middlebrows" who, by producing a simulacrum of culture, were claiming to be the bearers of culture and imposing their standards on the society. Macdonald

---

[31]The Barbarians were the aristocrats, the manly individuals "of good looks and fine complexions" who were capable of reinvigorating and renewing "our worn-out Europe." (What we have here is the "myth" of the English public-school boy, derived from the experiences of Arnold's father, Dr. Thomas Arnold, the famous headmaster of Rugby.) Then there were the Philistines, the middle classes, "particularly stiff-necked and perverse, who do not pursue 'sweetness and light' " and who prefer "that sort of machinery of business, chapels, tea-meetings . . . which make up the dismal and illiberal life." And finally there was the Populace, the working class, raw and half developed among their poverty and squalor, now issuing from their hiding place "to assert an Englishman's heaven-born privilege of doing as he likes . . . bawling what [they like], breaking what [they like]." "Barbarians, Philistines and Populace," chapter 3 of *Culture and Anarchy*, edited by J. Dover Wilson (Cambridge: Cambridge University Press, 1960), pp. 98–118.

did not evince an Arnoldian belief in culture: "Most High Culture has been undistinguished since talent is always rare." High Culture, "however inept," is an expression that is idiosyncratic, "and the audience similarly responds to [these expressions] as individuals." But Masscult is bad in a new way. "It is not just unsuccessful art. It is non-art. It is even anti-art." Masscult is a manufactured culture, packaged to a formula. It is impersonal, lacks standards, and is in "total subjection to the spectator."

The true enemy, however, was not Masscult but Midcult—a corruption of High Culture that seeks to pass itself off as "the real thing." As examples of Midcult, Macdonald cited the Revised Standard Version of the Bible, instead of the King James Version; the Museum of Modern Art film department's tribute to Samuel Goldwyn for making "higher-quality" films; and, for more extended analyses, Ernest Hemingway's *The Old Man and the Sea*, Thornton Wilder's *Our Town*, Archibald MacLeish's *J.B.*, and Stephen Vincent Benét's *John Brown's Body*.

Whether Macdonald's distinction remains valid today is difficult to say, for when parody and pastiche have taken over the novel, as with those of Tama Janowitz or Jay McInerny, and Woody Allen becomes the icon of the culturati, the distinction is blurred.[32]

The phrase that most sharply defined the distinction between high culture and low culture was the title of Clement Greenberg's 1939 essay, "Avant-Garde and Kitsch," in which Greenberg sought to define the "extremes" of artistic phenomena.

"Avant-garde" was that which was genuinely ahead of the times. And "Kitsch," a German word, meant trash and, in a cultural context, the gaudy and decorative, like the Victorian figurines that decorated the windowsills in Brighton, England. In the American context, Greenberg labeled popular commercial art, such as Busby Berkeley movies and cutesy dolls, Kitsch.[33]

And then there is Susan Sontag's famous, quite brilliant "Notes on 'Camp'" (1964), which revealed a mode of sensibility that had led, until

---

[32]Macdonald's essay *Masscult and Midcult* was published as Number 4 in a series of independent monographs by *Partisan Review*. The neologisms of the title may need explanation today. Macdonald was adopting a device that was common in radical "discourse" of his day—shortening terms, as hard Bolsheviks would do, to a slogan. Thus, as proletarian literature was always shortened to *proletlit*, similarly, Macdonald shortened the phrases "mass culture" and "middlebrow culture" to Masscult and Midcult.

[33]The French have a phrase, *nostalgie de la boue*, the taste for the gutter, but this has always been a taste of the *raffiné* for "rough trade," or the equivalent of "going slumming." And many "high artists," notably Henri Toulouse-Lautrec, have specialized in "low subjects."

then, an underground existence. Sontag declared that the crucial point about Camp "is that it totally elides the distinction of high and low and provides a new standpoint, that of the non-conformist spectator, who wants to substitute enjoyment for seriousness, and still think of that in aesthetic terms. Camp is a form of mockery, bitchiness, yet also an aesthetic judgment by the outsider." It is no accident, Sontag noted (somewhat cautiously for the time), that there is a "peculiar affinity and overlap" between homosexuality and Camp. "Camp is the triumph of the epicene style." As she wrote, "The connoisseur of Camp has found more ingenious pleasures. Not in Latin poetry and rare wines and velvet jackets, but in the coarsest common pleasures, in the arts of the masses. Mere use does not defile the objects of his pleasures, since he learns to possess them in a rare way. Camp—Dandyism in the age of mass culture—makes no distinction between the unique object and the mass-produced object. Camp taste transcends the nausea of the replica."

Camp, then, is a "third way [with] different standards [that] apply than to traditional high culture." And yet, so voracious are the appetities of the culturati to embrace the new, so as not to be bored with the old, that even Camp has now become a tired cliché, a fate that Sontag well knew when, as she said, she took the risk of writing about it at all.[34]

Here we have a different cultural contradiction—a culturati, often drawn from the "sensibility of the sixties" but now ensconced in comfortable chairs in universities, promoting PoMo in the recherché literary quarterlies and the arts. Postmodernist critics decry the elitism of the arts. They advocate "audience-centered" aesthetic theories. And they want neoconservatives to stop denigrating popular culture. Even Grant Wood and Norman Rockwell, once described as bathetic, are artists whose virtues have been rediscovered. PoMo has become an "aesthetic" of a counter-elite, those who conflate high art and Kitsch.

In the art world in the 1980s, sculptors like Jeff Koons created what Michael Brenson called "art that looked like trash and trashes high art," such as the porcelain bust of the Italian porn star Cicciolina (later Koons's wife) who mocked politics by running for the Italian Parliament, attracting crowds by baring her breasts—and getting elected. Keith Haring did graffiti in the subway, then became an artist by drawing simple stick figures, and claimed mockingly that what he was doing

---

[34]Susan Sontag, "Notes on 'Camp,' " in *Against Interpretation* (New York: Noonday Press, 1966), pp. 275–92, esp. 289–90.

was what was found in the cave paintings of Lascaux. He drew and re-drew his images on T-shirts, buttons, and banners in the thousands to sell in the consumer culture. Cindy Sherman reproduced images by Leonardo da Vinci and other painters and simply signed her name on top of theirs as an aggressive gesture of appropriation.

The great genius of PoMo was Andy Warhol. Warhol produced por-traits of Mao Zedong, Marilyn Monroe, and Jacqueline Onassis and multiplied these images in changing phosphorescent colors, like frozen strobe lights, as silk screen. But his greatest stroke of genius was to paint 100 Campbell soup cans as a literal representation of those stacked ob-jects. Marx wrote of the "fetishism of commodities," in which the worker is separated from the product he has made. With Warhol, the artist appropriates the commodity and sells it to the bourgeoisie.

"When we think of our times as 'Postmodern,' " wrote the British critic Malcolm Bradbury in *Dangerous Pilgrimages* (1995), "what we generally mean is this sense of ever-refracted, depthless, despatialized history, this sphere of random and pluralistic quotation, this merging of myths and motifs that suggests we live in a culture beyond culture."

There may be much truth to this description, but what is puzzling is the use of the word "pilgrimage." A pilgrimage is a journey to a shrine like a peregrine seeking a sacred grove. In John Bunyan's *The Pilgrim's Progress* (1678), the greatest literary expression of the Puritan sensi-bility, Christian goes through the danger and distraction of the Slough of Despond (and other places, high and low) to reach the Celestial City. But where does the PoMo pilgrim go in his heedless hum, a stranger to culture?

The culture of the Enlightenment constructed the ladder to the city of heaven with the rungs of rationality and reason. Man, on his ascent, would leave behind fear, superstition, myth, and the unknown. The new anthropology, replacing the old theodicy, was progress. For Hegel, as for Marx who followed him, there were Historic Nations and Back-ward Nations, the latter frozen in time or tribe or caste, incapable of becoming modern. But who, today, would think of calling any nation "backward," retarded by culture, rather than a victim of colonialism and imperialism? To do so would be plainly Eurocentric. And so we go from History to Epistemology, to Culture and to the Social Con-struction of Reality. As Ernest Gellner mordantly traced this:

We are castigating a whole culture . . . , we are consigning it to a lower level in virtue of being backward. . . . This is no longer to be tolerated. So what is the al-ternative? To recognize that all cultures are equally valid, that they carry their own norms of validity with them, and that to judge them and damn them from the outside in the name of putatively universal norms (which, in reality, are tools of domination and exploitation) is wrong. So respect for others entails relativism.[35]

What all this signifies (signifier and signified both) is the end of the avant-garde, a proud idea that has been the banner of modernist culture for the past hundred and fifty years. Modernism, like Marxism, sought the radical transformation of reality, which is why cultural periodicals, such as *Partisan Review*, or critics such as Irving Howe could embrace the contradictory two. Postmodernism does not wish to "transform" reality, but to retreat from it, as in some hermetic deconstruction of texts; to mock it by pastiche and parody; or to gibe at its commercialism by being commercial.

Modernism was difficult because of the unity of revolutionary form and multiple content in the advance or denial of the history of its genres. But the history was always there. PoMo is formless because it turns its back on history. The avant-garde, despite the military metaphor of being in "advance" of society, was in contradiction to the existing modes. PoMo is not opposition, but the appropriation of everything, not an attack on older philosophical or literary categories, but the dissolution of classifications, an *olla podrida* of discourse. William James once said that concepts without percepts are empty, and percepts without concepts are blind. One can only say, recalling what Samson did with the temple, that postmodernism is eyeless in Gaza. We seem to have seen the exhaustion of Modernism and now, also, the exhaustion of Culture. The only contradictions remaining are the contradictions of politics.

III

THE STATE OF THE UNION

The Cold War has ended and the United States remains—but for how long?—the paramount power in the world. Ideological conflicts—at least those derived from nineteenth-century claims to the possession of the future—have disappeared, leaving capitalism seemingly unchallenged. This situation has led to the view by Francis Fukuyama of

[35]Ernest Gellner, "Anything Goes: The Carnival of Cheap Relativism Which Threatens to Swamp the Coming *Fin de Millenaire*," *Times Literary Supplement* (London), June 16, 1955, p. 6.

"the end of Histc y," a thesis one can hold only if one believes that History is the working out of an idea that is translated into materiality (a theme Marx reversed; Marx believed that the course of materiality gives rise to ideas). Henry Luce believed in the "idea" of the American Century, a belief he soon surrendered, perhaps too soon, when the United States found its military power mired in Vietnam and its economic power challenged by Japan. And there is a sinking sense today that the wave of History is moving to the Pacific Rim and that the twenty-first century will be the Asian century or, more specifically, that of China, if that nation is able to hold itself together—a billion and one persons under one Party-dominated roof—and make the transition to a market economy.

Leaving such metamorphic issues aside, I wish to explore further the changes in American society in the twenty years since that chapter was written. I spoke then of an "unstable America." Today I would have to deal with a confused, angry, uneasy, and insecure America. There are three themes I would single out as the foci of these discontents:

- the unraveling of the middle class and the fear of individuals that they are losing a secure place in the society and control over their future
- a set of culture wars—populism versus elitism—that is politicizing moral issues and polarizing the society through the mobilized disruptions of activist groups
- a rising distrust of politics—and even of the political system—and with it, the loss of *civitas*, which makes respect for the law possible.

And below these overt manifestations are the structural changes in the society. These changes do not determine political and social attitudes, for these are shaped by values that are derived from traditions and history, from religious or philosophical credos. But structural changes define the problems that have to be met; set the contexts of economic opportunity, occupational advancement, and social mobility that give people the resources to sustain or challenge their attitudes; and provide windows onto the world that make one aware of other cultures, other values, and other responsibilities.

The first major context is the rise of the global economy. In this century, we have seen the move from a regional to a national to an international economy. And each of these changes involved new roles for the government and for the large economic enterprises that have become multinational in scope. But a global economy differs from an international economy, which is a worldwide division of labor between raw materials and manufacturing, and in which national firms become multinational yet retain a national allegiance.

A *global* economy is a *single* market for capital, commodities, skilled labor, and technical knowledge, crossing boundaries easily through communication systems and in which (to the extent that sovereign nations permit) these factors cross borders and seek the highest returns for their investments or profit for their products. Given the relative ease with which the production of goods can be standardized, when labor costs become a factor in final prices, the pull of the market becomes massive in the shift of jobs. Furthermore, given the revolution in materials technology, one is no longer even dependent on raw-material sites, since one can make synthetics, composites, alloys, and other "material transsubstantiations" and be free of cartels and other groups that, in the past, sought to control these materials. Inevitably, then, there are large shifts of the economic tectonic plates with which the politics of each national society has to contend.

The second major context is communication: the worldwide crisscrossing that creates the "global village" through television; the wiring of the world through fiber optics, which expands the bandwidths for the transmission of messages; cable television, which multiplies channels and breaks the older systems of governmental monopolies; satellites, which elude any national controls; and networking, such as the Internet and Web sites, which allow for the rapid exchange of messages or access to information set forth by providers.

The third major context is technology, which drives the global economy. But technology has the further impact of breaking down the walls between activities and making them fungible. Thus, in the past twenty years, the distinctions among banks, insurance companies, brokerage houses, mutual funds, real estate companies, and the like, have tended to diminish, since all have become "financial assets" and are assessed as such. Similarly today, the lines between movie companies, CD-ROMs, on-line magazines, and such have all become entertainment and information, and new conglomerates such as Time Warner or Disney-like sponges absorb any and all of them.

As the older lines of demarcation begin to break down, firms that were once separate are thrown into a giant bag labeled "mergers and acquisitions" and get shaken up and redistributed. In all this, the traditional features of American capitalism are changing beyond recognition.

Broadly speaking, technology takes three "paths" in the logic of its

development: *tra* *nsforming technologies, extension technologies,* and *niches.*
A telephone is a transforming technology, and cellular or mobile
phones are extension technologies. Local-area networks or private
branch exchanges are niches.[36] The computer is a transforming technology. Networks (ISDN systems)—integrated services digital systems that make voice (telephone), data (computers), text (facsimile),
and image (television) compatible within a single channel—are extension technologies; and software and applications are niches.

The major consequences of such changes are the *downsizing* of the
large corporations and the development of extension and niche capa-
bilities. IBM, which had as many as 400,000 employees a dozen years
ago, will have shrunk to little more than 200,000 before the end of the
decade as it becomes a service, rather than a hardware, company. In
1996, AT&T announced plans to retire 40,000 employees, most of
whom (as is also the case with IBM) are midlevel managerial, technical, and white-collar administrative employees.

This is the source of the unease and insecurity that affect the middle class in the United States today. There is one telling statistic: In
the 1991–93 recession, more than 45 percent of the unemployed were
white-collar workers, or double the number in the previous recession
ten years before. In the past, it was the blue-collar or hourly workers
who were usually laid off. Firms had an "investment" in the training
and experience of their technical and managerial staffs. This is no
longer the case, particularly since many of these functions have been
"computerized" and applications software can take over many of the
tasks. And it is not just economic but psychological damage that is
wreaked by this discharge. Traditionally, when a blue-collar worker was
laid off, he could, and would, double up with his family or extended
kin. But the middle-class person, particularly one who has risen out of
the working class, has broken such ties and finds the experience of seeking help humiliating, especially when he or she is threatened with the
foreclosure of a car or home. In many cases, after some delay, these
managerial persons, if young, can find new employment in niche firms.
But niche firms, by their nature, are highly competitive with one another, and many start-ups fail. So the fear and insecurity remain.

If there is one telling statistic, there is one telling anecdote—the experience of the Harvard Law School class of 1985. Of the class of ten
years before, almost all the graduates who had gone into large or

---

[36]This discussion of the nature of technological change is taken from my unpublished manuscript, "The Breakup of Space and Time: Technology and Society in a Post-Industrial Age."

medium-sized firms had become partners within a decade. At the tenth reunion of the class of 1985, only 15 percent had achieved such status. As one lawyer remarked: "I was watching my peers getting fired. It was gut-wrenching. It suddenly brought home that there was no security. I thought, 'It could happen to me next, and all the Harvard diplomas in the world might not save me.' " Many of these 1985 graduates had never experienced failure and presumed that their elite degrees would be lifetime annuities, but they were not.[37]

Every generation of Americans had expected that they would build a better life for their children than they themselves had. This may no longer be the case. What we have is not the fear of "proletarianization" that wracked the German middle class in the 1930s. It is, instead, the fear of the end of "the American dream."

The facts and sources of the sense of insecurity are clear. What is also present, though its nature is more ambiguous, is the charge of moral decay in the country. William Bennett, who was Secretary of Education under President Ronald Reagan, drew up a set of "cultural indicators" in which he found, among other things: "What is shocking is just how precipitously American life has declined in the past 30 years. . . . There has been an increase in violent crime, a 419 percent increase in illegitimate births, a quadrupling of the divorce rates, a tripling of children living in single-parent homes . . . a drop of 80 points in SAT [Scholastic Aptitude Test] scores."

And the "reasons" were stated quite stridently by the Republican Speaker of the House Newt Gingrich, when a three-year-old in Los Angeles was murdered as a by-product of a street shooting: "Now we have had, since Lyndon Johnson created the Great Society, a 30-year experiment in destroying America. For some 30 years we have liberated prisoners, tolerated drug dealers, put up with violence, accepted brutality, and done it all in the name of some kind of bleeding-heart liberalism which always had one more excuse, one more explanation, one more rationale."[38]

Leaving aside (for the moment) the factuality of these charges, there are three themes that are crucial for understanding the social divisions in American society. One is the "society" versus the "culture." The terms are arbitrary, but the distinction can be made clear. The "social

---

[37]The experience of the Harvard Law School class of 1985, related at their tenth reunion, was reported in the *Wall Street Journal*, May 8, 1995.

[38]Quoted in "Speaker Gingrich Lashing Out, in His Own Words," *New York Times*, December 17, 1995, p. 34.

structure" of the United States today (in the mundane sense of work and daily life) is largely bourgeois, moralizing, and cramped. This is the "moral majority," rooted in Protestant evangelicism, who seek to hold on to "traditional values," by which they mean, more often than not, the literalism of the biblical word. The "culture" is liberal, urban, cosmopolitan, trendy, fashionable, endorsing freer lifestyles, and permissive—and often unable to establish limits to that permissiveness (in violence in movies and on television, pornography, and sexual behavior).

This is an old division in American life, responsible in the past for Prohibition, the Hays code in the movies, and the local censorship of libraries. This division has returned with even greater virulence today and is embodied in the culture wars.

The political embodiment of the cultural division is populism versus the elites. Populism was an agrarian movement at the turn of the century by farmers who felt they were being exploited by the bankers, from whom they borrowed money for planting; by the railroads that carried their grain at exorbitant rates; and by the corporate monopolies that charged high prices for farm equipment. All these forms of exploitation were dramatized in Frank Norris's novels *The Pit* (on the Chicago grain market) and *The Octopus* (about the railroads) and, most starkly, in John Steinbeck's *The Grapes of Wrath* (about the Great Depression).

The original cry of populism was *for* governmental regulation of the monopolies, rural electrification, mortgage protection against foreclosure of farms, and so forth. The cultural contradictions of populism were summed up by the career of William Jennings Bryan, who ran for president as a radical on the Democratic ticket in 1896, thundering against the "cross of gold" on which the farmers were being crucified and defending Creationism against evolution in the Scopes trial in Tennessee in 1924.[39]

Much of populist thinking was expressed in conspiracy theories about the secret forces that manipulated people's lives. (The populists believed that it was not the "market" that set their prices through supply and demand, but the "manipulators," and sometimes they were right.) Just as the English essayist William Cobbett had thundered in the nineteenth

[39]United on the agrarian issues, populists often divided on other issues. In the Republican Party in the Midwest, there were such progressives as George W. Norris of Nebraska and William E. Borah of Idaho, and in the Democratic Party in the South, there were Democrats, such as John Rankin of Mississippi, the sponsor of the Tennessee Valley Authority for cheap electricity, and Theodore Bilbo, also of Mississippi, both of whom were anti-Semitic and antiblack.

century against "The Thing," and reactionaries believed that it was the Freemasons and Jews who were behind both the French and the Russian revolutions, so American populists denounced "Wall Street" (as against "Main Street") and, later, "Madison Avenue." The rhetoric of conspiracy carries over today against The Media, The Liberals, and The Beltway, as if these were all monolithic entities acting in unison.

In the political climate of the present day, the conspirators are the elitists and the intellectuals. (It may be a form of sociological reductionism to point out that the intellectual leaders of the Republican Right—Phil Gramm, Richard Armey, and Newt Gingrich—held marginal positions in second- and third-rate colleges and universities, but this was true as well of Democratic liberals like George McGovern and Hubert Humphrey.) However, the anti-intellectual rhetoric is palpable. When Gingrich designated Stephen Hanser, his closest friend and a retired professor of West Georgia College, as his personal historian, Hanser said sarcastically to the *Wall Street Journal:* "Look, my non-credentials are in order: I have nothing to do with Harvard, Yale, Princeton, Stanford, ABC, CBS, NBC, the New York Times, the Wall Street Journal, and any of you other dinosaurs of the discredited elite."

The third theme is government. The refrain was sounded by President Reagan: Don't trust government. Not bad government, or even big government, but just plain vanilla government. Now, a case can surely be made against "big government"—except, of course, when one's own subsidies, such as tobacco, sugar, maritime support, governmental guarantees against the expropriation of investments abroad, and the like—are jeopardized. It was a strong theme of Students for a Democratic Society in the 1960s, in favor of participatory democracy and the right of people in local communities to affect the decisions that control their lives (except, later, perhaps, for the South Boston Irish who did not want black youths bused to their schools). But the denunciation of government in the last decade has also fostered extremist militia movements whose members are willing to take up arms against federal law-enforcement officials. The bombing of the Federal Building in Oklahoma City in 1995, in which several hundred persons were killed, brought to the fore the end product of those fantasies.

Ideologically, the country is being polarized. To those on the Right, we are two nations: the moral and the immoral, the traditional culture and the counterculture. To those on the liberal Left, the United States is a society that is increasingly being riven by the rising inequalities of wealth and income and in which the poor, black and white, are being left behind by the lack of economic opportunity. These propositions do not directly confront one another, and we need some relevant distinctions to sort out the multifarious differences in American life and illuminate the different modalities.

The first distinction is that if we "subtract" the black situation and the plight of the central cities (all of which are more than 50 percent black and Hispanic), then we see two different crosscutting pictures.

Blacks are more than twice as likely as whites to be jobless, and among teenagers, four times. Nearly a third of all blacks, as against 10 percent of whites, live below the poverty line, and this proportion becomes three in four among black children. Among black women, the rate of out-of-wedlock births went from 45 percent in 1972 to 68 percent in 1992. About 23 percent of all black men aged 20 to 29 are in prison, on probation, or on parole.

The issue that many Americans single out as the basis for fear, especially in the urban centers, is crime. Yet the striking fact is that the overwhelming number of crimes are committed not by blacks against whites but by blacks against blacks.[40] With regard to homicide, a black man is six times as likely to be murdered as is a white man. Most suburbs in the United States, where the majority of whites live, are relatively free of violent crime. The disjunction between reality and apprehension can only be explained, perhaps, by the repeated focus on blacks and crime in the visual media or in political speeches without the clarifying context of statistical facts.

The socioeconomic disparities between blacks and whites are well known. Yet what is less well known is the rise of the black middle class. In 1980, 20 million whites over the age of twenty-five (out of 115 million) had completed college, or little more than 17 percent. By 1993, the number had risen to 31 million whites (out of 140 million), or about 22.5 percent. At the start of the same period, 1 million blacks (out of nearly 13 million) had completed college, or about 7 percent of the black population. In 1993, the number had doubled (2 million out of 17.7 million), or about 12 percent. In the thirteen-year period, each group of middle-class persons had increased by about 5 percentage points. Roughly, then, by the end of the decade, one-fourth of the white population was "safely" upper middle class, compared with 15 percent of the black population.

[40]As John J. DiIulio, Jr., of Princeton University reported in the Fall 1994 issue of *The Public Interest*, the chances of black male teenagers' being violently assaulted are more than six times those of white adult males, 7.5 times those of white adult females, nearly 20 times those of elderly white males, and 37.5 times those of elderly white females—who often express the greatest fear of being assaulted.

As with every dimension of postindustrial society, education is the dividing line between those who are able to get ahead and those who are not. Welfare—the governmental program of Aid to Families with Dependent Children (AFDC)—has become the symbol, particularly to conservatives, of all that is wrong with the black community. AFDC provides cash assistance to low-income families in which one parent (invariably the father) is absent. About 4.5 million adults and 9.5 million children are now on the nation's welfare rolls. In the legislation to which both parties have agreed, welfare is to be turned back almost completely to the states, and women who have not gone to work after two years would find themselves struck off the welfare rolls.

What is striking in all this is that those who argue most strongly that the plight of the black family is a *cultural problem* want to use *economic sanctions* to end welfare. (As the black economist Glenn Loury told a congressional committee, cutting off benefits would not "teach" poor women to stop having babies.)

Out-of-wedlock births and the breakdown of the family have been the most salient issues in the conservative brief on moral decay. The problem was first highlighted by Daniel Patrick Moynihan in 1965, when as Assistant Secretary of Labor in the Johnson administration, he wrote the report on "The Negro Family." Yet thirty years later, in a reprise (in *The American Enterprise*, January–February 1995), Senator Moynihan pointed out that by the year 2000, 40 percent of *all* births in the United States will be out of wedlock and, to the surprise of many, *the figures will be the same for England and Wales*. Furthermore, in a comparison of twelve industrial societies, he noted that five—Iceland, Sweden, Denmark, France, and the United Kingdom—had *higher* rates of out-of-wedlock births than did the United States.

It is quite evident that divorce has become common in almost all modern societies (except Japan and nominally Spain and Italy, as Catholic countries). In the United States, only 15 percent of the white women who married in the early 1940s eventually divorced, whereas almost half the white women who married in the early 1970s have already been divorced. In all, 30 percent of all women in the United States today have been divorced, but more than half of them remarried within five years of the divorce. So, if men and women divorce, they also remarry. The two-parent family makes up about 80 percent of all households (compared with half of black families).

And if the maintenance of family values is the trumpet call of conservative causes, one can also point out that the only president of the

United States to have been divorced was Ronald Reagan, with children from both marriages to whom he was indifferent. (And he never went to church.) In the 1996 electoral campaigns, it may also be pointed out, the presidential candidates Robert Dole and Gramm have been divorced. And Republican Speaker of the House Newt Gingrich went through a messy divorce himself. But all this is also the triumph of rhetoric over reality.[41]

The focus, then, on the United States as an example of moral decay because of out-of-wedlock births and family "breakup" crumbles in the face of similar situations in all Western European nations, Catholic as well as Protestant. A major change has been taking place in the most primordial of institutions: Marriage is no longer a sacrament but a matter of choice, which for most persons is a definition of freedom (though sometimes of license as well).

There is a pervasive sentiment, as indicated in the rise of conservative voting, that something is morally wrong with this country. The focus has been on drugs, crime, violence, and teenage pregnancy. And much of this (using code words about blacks) has been blamed on the government and "failed" governmental policies.

But what about the role of the free market in fostering "decay"? The market is mechanism, yet its operations—what is bought and sold—are guided by the values in the society. One example is the phenomenon called "gangsta rap," the hard-core incitement to violence against the police, which makes explicit and degrading remarks about women and espouses sadistic and other forms of kinky sex (titles like "[Expletive] the Police" and "To Kill a Hooker") and whose featured singers have done time in prison for various crimes. One of the leading companies, Death Row Records, started in 1992 by a twenty-nine-year-old gang leader named Suge Knight and a singer, Dr. Dre, has sold more than 15 million records and grossed more than $100 million. The buyers (as is also evident at Death Row concerts) are white, suburban, male youths, and the singers are black, inner-city thugs.

After William Bennett charged the record industry with fostering immoral behavior, Time Warner sold its lucrative interest in a company, Interscope. Yet a few months later, when much of the publicity had died down, MCA, now owned by Seagram, signed a $200 million deal to acquire 50 percent of Interscope, whose latest record in the

---

[41]For a more detailed analysis of the issue of "moral decay," see my essay "The Disunited States of America," *Times Literary Supplement* (London), June 9, 1995.

week of the deal, Tupac Shakur's *All Eyz on Me*, sold 500,000 copies and became Number 1 on the charts of *Billboard* magazine.[42]

The Protestant ethic decries not only promiscuous sex but also gambling. As recently as 1988, casino gambling was legal in only two states, Nevada and New Jersey. By 1994, casinos were operating in twenty-three states—apart from the state governmental gambling, lotteries, and betting on horse races—and the firms engaged in these ventures had a stock-market capitalization (as of February 1996) of more than $30 billion. As Robert Goodman reported in *The Luck Business:*

> In the early 1990s, revenues in the gambling industry were climbing about two and a half times faster than those in the nation's manufacturing industries. . . . By the beginning of 1995, legal gambling in the United States [including lotteries] was generating over $37 billion in yearly revenues—more than the total amount Bill Clinton promised to use during each of his first four years in office to help rebuild America's transportation system, create a national information network, develop technology to help clean up the environment, and convert the defense industry to a peacetime economy.

Records and gambling are at the margins of American life. The corporation is at the center. Yet the most "subversive" book about American capitalism that I know is Bryan Burrough and John Helyar's *Barbarians at the Gate*, the story of the battle for RJR Nabisco, which at $25 billion, was the largest corporate takeover in American economic history, and a fitting symbol of the Reagan era.

RJR Nabisco, primarily tobacco and foods—Winston, Salem, and Camel cigarettes; Oreo cookies, Ritz crackers, and Life Savers—was the nineteenth largest industrial company in the United States and employed 140,000 individuals. The story began with a proposal by Ross Johnson, the chief executive officer of the firm, to initiate a leveraged buyout, or LBO. In an LBO, a group of senior executives, with the aid of a Wall Street banker, proposes to buy the company from the public shareholders, by using massive amounts of borrowed money—"other people's money," in the old phrase of Louis D. Brandeis—from Wall Street brokerage houses, banks, pension funds, and the like. To pay off the ensuing mountain of debt, the company must sell off different parts of the firm, issue "junk bonds" that would be sold by Wall Street firms to savings-and-loan associations, or cut research and similar budgets. It is one version of Schumpeter's "creative destruction," except that what is destroyed are often plants of the company and the

---

[42]*New York Times*, February 19, 1996. As the *Times* reviewer, Jon Pareles, remarked about the album, "It is slick, cocksure, and utterly unrepentant."

towns where they are located, the funds that hold the junk bonds, the small-town charities and foundations that received money for community projects, and the like. And the executives become rich. In Johnson's LBO proposal, he would personally pocket about $100 million.

What was also revealed was the fabulous lifestyles of the executives, paid for by the company, including vacation homes in Acapulco and ski chalets in Colorado, all to entertain clients and executives. At a golf-show extravaganza where Frank Sinatra was singing and Bob Hope was joking, "attendees gained admission to events by flashing the $1,500 Gucci watch each was given." The pride of the company was its private air fleet known as the RJR Air Force, consisting of thirty-six corporate pilots and ten planes. When Johnson ordered a new hangar to house the fleet, it was, when finished, "the Taj Mahal of corporate hangars, dwarfing that of Coca-Cola next door."

All this, of course, was at the expense of the stockholders. But an LBO would mean even greater profits for the small inner-circle group. The first estimate was an LBO of $17.6 billion, which would be worth $2.5 billion to Johnson's group in five years. But once word went out that RJR Nabisco was "in play," a feeding frenzy began from a half dozen of the leading merger-and-acquisition firms on Wall Street, including Kohlberg Kravis Roberts, Shearson Lehman, Forstmann, and Drexel Lambert (where Michael Milken was a partner).[43]

In the rounds of bidding, the "value" of the company went from the initial level of $17.5 billion, by increments of a billion, to the final figure of $25 billion won by Henry Kravis and his associates. Each billion dollars of added debt, which was what the figures represented, meant, in the calculation of each bidder, one more company plant to be sold off or more junk bonds to be issued. At this point (as Linda Robinson, the wife of the former head of American Express and a

[43]Writing before the Civil War, George Fitzhugh, an apologist for the South, attacked the capitalist North because, "in such a society virtue loses all her loveliness because of her selfish aims . . . self-promotion and self-elevation." Writing more than a century later, Irving Kristol commented:

Suffice to say that, with every passing decade, Fitzhugh's charge, that "virtue loses all her loveliness because of her selfish aims," becomes more valid. From having been a *capitalist, republican community*, with shared values and a quite unambiguous claim to the title of a just order, the United States became a *free democratic society* where the will to success and privilege was severed from its moral moorings.

And Kristol continued: "But can men live in a free society if they have no reason to believe it is also a just society? I do not think so."

See Irving Kristol, " 'When Virtue Loses All Her Loveliness'—Some Reflections on Capitalism and the 'Free Society,' " in *Two Cheers for Capitalism* (New York: Basic Books, 1978), pp. 261, 262. Italics in the original.

public-relations adviser to one of the bidders, observed): "Peter Cohen and Tommy Strauss and Henry Kravis and the rest had totally lost sight of their real objective, RJR Nabisco. Their agreements had nothing to do with shareholder values or fiduciary duties. It was all a test of wills among an intensely competitive clique of macho, Park Avenue bullies in pinstripes. . . . Each was determined to be King of the Sandbox."

Apart from this psychological half-truth and *the $1 billion in fees* that the banks, brokerage houses, and lawyers received for their "work" in the deals, the contest raises, once again, the question: What is a corporation, and to whom is "it" responsible? Legally, the corporation is owned by the stockholders, whose shares are voted by the managers through proxies or are bought when there is a battle for control. But what of those "stockholders" (managers and workers) who may have spent most of their lives in the company or in the community, which may have given the company tax benefits and is supported by the money spent in the town, or those whose life savings are tied up in the homes they have bought? What rights do they have when their fates can be disposed of so casually by those who move the bidding one more notch just to gain control? Here is a cogent illustration of the problem of law and morality, in which the nature of law serves "property rights" and defines the corporation as a "legal person." That, too, is a contradiction of capitalism.[44]

If *Barbarians at the Gate* is the most subversive book about American capitalism that I know of, David Stockman's *The Triumph of Politics* is the most subversive book on American politics and the myths about policy making. Stockman was director of the Office of Management and Budget in the first Reagan administration, the key position at the time in the effort to hold down the rising budget deficits that were to quadruple in the Reagan years.

Stockman's account of his stewardship of the budget is a textbook in the labyrinth of governmental fiscal policy. But as a history of the Reagan team, it is more. What struck Stockman most forcibly was the economic illiteracy of the President's top advisers—Ed Meese, Mike Deaver, and Lyn Nofziger. Worst of all was Reagan himself. "The

---

[44]For a detailed, earlier discussion of these questions, see Chapter 4, on the modern corporation—its economizing and sociologizing modes—in *The Coming of Post-Industrial Society*, pp. 267–99.

There is a different pattern in the Rhine countries—Germany and Benelux—where worker representatives have half the seats on the supervisory boards of large companies, in a system called *Mitbestimmung*, or codetermination; the companies are regarded as social institutions; and other values than profit maximization are considered, such as job security. For an intriguing study of the "Rhine model," see Michel Albert, *Capitalism Against Capitalism* (London: Whurr Publishers, 1993).

President did not grasp the difference between constant dollars and current (inflated) dollars" wrote Stockman. And when the Secretary of Defense would seem to agree to cuts in the defense budget, the President could never follow the difference between budgetary authorizations and budgetary expenditures and thus could be easily twisted by those who would seem to agree to reductions in the one but maintain the level of the other.

Stockman's book is a detailed account of his efforts to hide the fact that budgetary deficits were rising, and inevitably so: "The massive fiscal policy error that had been unleashed on the national and world economy was beyond recall." Yet Stockman had to put his finger in the dike. Thus, he used "plug numbers," rough estimates whose exact numbers would presumably be filled in later, and "magic asterisks," footnotes stating that estimated revenues were being calculated. Finally, on page 353 of his book (but who in the press read that far?) Stockman wrote: "I out-and-out cooked the books, inventing $15 billion per year of utterly phony cuts in order to get Ronald Reagan's first full budget below the $100 billion deficit level."

Stockman, a former student at the Harvard Divinity School, was admitting, one could say unkindly, to a misprision. Yet he left the government to join a Wall Street firm, where he made a million dollars and vanished into political obscurity.[45]

Stockman's description, well intentioned as it was, was typical of the calculated chicanery, large and small, that has pervaded the political administrations in Washington in the past twenty or more years, though it is rarely, if ever, cited by those who decry the moral decay of American life—by which they seem to mean the decay only of the dispossessed and the privileged of academe.

For many persons, Watergate was some odd episode of a bungled burglary of the Democratic Party headquarters, and the resulting, clumsy coverup, the reason for Richard Nixon's resignation as president under the looming threat of impeachment. Europeans, in particular, are mystified by this seemingly "small" event. But Watergate was much more than that. Nixon, somewhat paranoid in his (sometimes justified) fear of encirclement by his enemies, had sought to enlist the FBI and the CIA in various illegal efforts to uncover plots against him or to tap the phones of members of Henry Kissinger's staff. When both the FBI and the CIA refused (though they quietly offered accessory

---

[45]David A. Stockman, *The Triumph of Politics: Why the Reagan Revolution Failed* (New York: Harper & Row, 1986).

aid), Nixon set up an investigative team in the White House, the so-called plumbers' unit, headed by E. Howard Hunt, a former CIA station chief. Hunt burgled the office of Daniel Ellsberg's psychiatrist—Ellsberg was a former analyst for the RAND Corporation and the Pentagon who was suspected of leaking "The Pentagon Papers," Robert S. McNamara's secret review of the failures in Vietnam, to the press. The burglary at Watergate was an effort, seemingly—though the full motivation has never been entirely revealed—to find out the relation of Lawrence O'Brien, the director of the Democratic National Committee, to the reclusive Howard Hughes, who had once given money to Nixon and employed Nixon's brother.

But Watergate was even much more than that: It was part of a pervasive effort by the Nixon administration to smear and entrap liberal political opponents in a horrendous fashion. One crucial example: John Mitchell, the Attorney General of the United States in the Nixon cabinet, the highest law officer in the land, became head of the Committee to Re-Elect the President in 1972. G. Gordon Liddy, a staff member but also a zealot and a brawler, came to Mitchell with a plan of dirty tricks. They would hire a barge in Miami, where the Democratic convention was to be held; bed it with prostitutes; take photographs of Democratic delegates in flagrante delicto; and use the photographs for blackmail. They would also firebomb the offices of the Brookings Institution in Washington and enter with the firemen to see what incriminating documents or Democratic Party research and policy papers they could find. Mitchell, until then the highest law officer of the land, only retorted: How much will it cost?

In the aftermath of Watergate, almost every top staff official of the Nixon administration—chief of staff H. R. Haldeman, chief of domestic policy John Erlichman, Attorney General Richard Kleindienst, White House counsels Charles Colson and John Dean, re-election officials Jeb Magruder and Gordon Liddy—was convicted of felonies, lying or obstructing justice, and went to jail.

Mr. Nixon, facing solid impeachment charges, resigned—the only president in American history to do so. On his death, he was hailed by Robert Dole and Henry Kissinger as a great American. *De mortuis nil nisi bonum.* But then, why speak at all?

The Reagan administration: Congress had passed a law forbidding any aid to the Contras—the group of rebels seeking to overthrow the Marxist Sandinista regime in Nicaragua. At the same time, the Iranian regime was holding Americans hostage, and through some shady back channels indicated that it would free the hostages for arms that might be supplied through Israel. A complicated scheme was set up to reach both objectives at once. Arms were smuggled into Iran, and money was deposited into Swiss bank accounts. The National Security Council, under the leadership of Admiral John Poindexter, national security adviser to the President, and its military attaché, Colonel Oliver North, was extensively involved in these Keystone Kops capers. The President claimed no knowledge of the alleged efforts. Admiral Poindexter followed the oldest rule of the staff assistant—to keep all winks and nods only for the subordinates. Both in domestic affairs and in foreign policy, there was a pattern in the Reagan administration of lying and deception. But here, as in similar matters, Machiavellian *raisons d'état* overrode common morality—even the explicit legislation of the Congress of the United States.

Thus we find a deceit. Public morality is traduced. The poor on welfare and the liberals are blamed for the "moral decay" of American society, but the men and women who levy these charges say nary a word about the incredible undermining of trust in the actions by the part in government from which they come. Hypocrisy? Or simply one further instance of cultural contradictions?

IV

CULTURE AND CLASS

Let me begin with a vision of the future:

The bourgeoisie has through its exploitation of the world market given a cosmopolitan character to production and consumption in every country. To the great chagrin of reactionaries, it has drawn from under the feet of industry the national ground on which it stood. All old-fashioned industries have been destroyed. They are dislodged by new industries, whose introduction becomes a life and death question for all civilized nations. . . . In place of old wants, we find new wants, requiring for their satisfaction the products of distant lands and climes. In place of the old local and national seclusion and self-sufficiency, we have intercourse in every direction, universal interdependence of nations.

The statement is from Marx's *The Communist Manifesto* of 1848. It is the stunning foresight of a theorist who understood the underlying logic of capitalism.[46] Yet what Marx could not have known was the

---

[46]Karl Marx, *Selected Works* (Moscow, 1969), Vol. 1, p. 112.

transformation of industrial society, the rise of a new technical class whose numbers would overpower the older industrial proletariat, and the failure of each national working class to join into a single international force.

What Marx did point to was the contradictory currents between geo-economics and geopolitics. Marxists thought that war was inevitable as a result of these clashes. (After World War I, Trotsky said that the next world war would be between Great Britain and the United States as the two competed for world hegemony.) Yet at the end of the twentieth century, it is highly unlikely that a military conflict will again break out between Russia, Germany, France, Great Britain, the United States, and Japan, as it did twice in the century. In the twenty-first century, it is clear, however, that economics will have become the continuation of war by other means.

Capitalism today is the predominant mode of production. But it is primarily a socioeconomic system, and both the political order and the culture—I speak here of high art, not the commodities of consumer culture—are not shaped by capitalism. Democracy, as a political form, is anterior to capitalism, and the desires for liberty and equality, as well as the idea of the consent of the governed, lie deep in men's conception of justice. It was the failure of Marxists to realize this fact that led the Communist movement to characterize Western democracy as "bourgeois democracy," fascism as "the last stage of monopoly capitalism," and rival Socialists as "social Fascists" and to join with the Nazis in undermining the Weimar regime, with the slogan, *Nach Hitler kommt uns* (After Hitler, we come).

That Marx never had a theory of culture was the greatest weakness of his system. According to Marx, culture was part of the "superstructure," but he never specified, nor has almost any Marxist, exactly how the "substructure"—the prevailing mode of production—gives rise to distinctive cultural patterns. In fact, as Marx wrote immediately after the statement quoted earlier: "And as in material, so also in intellectual production. The intellectual creations of individual nations become common property. National one-sidedness and narrow-mindedness become more and more impossible, and from the numerous national and local literatures there arises a world literature."

Class culture makes little sense. The phrases "bourgeois literature" and "proletarian literature" could mean only that such literature arises from individuals in each "class" or that the literature buttresses existing class rule or operates as a revolutionary force. And what sense does it make to lump together the large formal experiments in the novel—

the stream of consciousness, the disjunction of time, and the play of memory—that one finds in the novels of Virginia Woolf, James Joyce, William Faulkner, and Marcel Proust as "bourgeois" or of a "late capitalist" faction?

The idea that "social factors" influence the development of science and culture ignores the primary role of "internal" forces in the unfolding of research programs in science that seek to answer why and how theory accounts for empirical variations or anomalies, or the immanent explorations of combinations *in form* that are the constraints set by the genre within which the artist is working, such as a sonata in music or the multiplicity of different angles of vision on a single picture plane, as in cubism. When Marx was asked why, in the age of science and new material forms of production, we still appreciate Greek art and tragedy, he replied that it was because the Greeks represented the childhood of the human race, and we are captured by its artfulness.[47]

Most important, perhaps, Marxism cannot explain the survival to this day of the great historic religions—Buddhism, Hinduism, Confucianism, Judaism, Christianity, and Islam—over millennia of time, when the great political empires and the large economic systems have crumbled, if each mode produces different cultural styles and history can be marked off by distinctly different periods.

These are not the cultural contradictions of capitalism but the cultural contradictions of Marxism as a "total theory" of society.

Let me turn to the interplay of social structure and polity. For more than a hundred and fifty years in the West, *class* has been the defining term of social divisions in the society. Classes still exist, though their contours are changing.[48] Yet in the fragmentations of societies arising in the wake of the last empires (the former Soviet Union and the former Yugoslavia), in the clan and tribal societies of Africa whose nationhoods are falling apart, and in the social divisions within the ad-

[47]On the question of "internalist" and "externalist" developments in science and culture and on the autonomy of ideas, see my essay "The Misreading of Ideology," in the *Berkeley Journal of Sociology*, Vol. 35, 1990. Marx himself was a great lover of the "highest masters" of literature—Goethe, Lessing, Shakespeare, Dante, and Cervantes—whose works he reread often and whose phrases and metaphors peppered his writing. These works, he believed, were the heritage of the race. One would have to say, therefore, that Marx's theory deals primarily with the *production* of culture (inadequate as it is), not the large repertoire that remains as the deposit of the human imagination. For an excellent discussion of Marx's appreciation and tastes in culture, see S. S. Prawer, *Karl Marx and World Literature* (New York: Oxford University Press, 1978).

[48]For a description of what I have called "The Four-Tiered Class Structure" that is taking hold in the U.S. today, see my essay "The World and the United States in 2013," in *Daedalus* (Summer 1987), pp. 26–29.

vanced industrial societies, *cultural conflicts* have become the salient axes of division.

In this context, I use "culture" in the broader anthropological sense, not in Arnold's or Eliot's usages of the term as the products of the imagination. Cultures here are the binding fidelities of consciousness, rooted in history and tradition, kinship and race, religion and nationality, that shape the emotional consanguinity, literal or fictive, among individuals and make them one. In his remarkable explication of Weber's idea of "rational capitalism," Benjamin Nelson gave his own book the subtitle *From Tribal Brotherhood to Universal Otherhood.*[49] This is the paradox: that although formal and universal rules remain the impersonal mode of the *economic* relations among individuals in contractual exchanges, the ascriptive and primordial ties have become the cohesive *social* bonds in almost all societies today, capitalist and noncapitalist.

Historically, the sociological change in most societies has been the move from kinship to the polity as the basis of membership in a society—though in the early days of capitalism, one still had family businesses, family farms, and family occupations, especially when property, rather than education, was the basis of economic and social position in the society. The return to kinship or primordial attachments as the basis of bonding is, in a sense, the return to the *premodern* modes of social structure. Class, one would say, is the basis of *modern* modes of salient division in society, particularly when the classes make claim to a universal status for their members. In that context, the politics of identity is the *postmodern* style of synonymy in contemporary society.

The politics of particularity crosses the axes of Left and Right and is based on identity and culture. On the Left, in the United States, identities are race, gender, sexual identity, and ethnic identity. Gender stresses the role of women's rights, but sexual identity puts forth the demands of gays and lesbians for recognition of their rights. Ethnic identity stresses the need for multiculturalism in the schools and affirmative action in the polity.

On the Right, the issues of abortion, school prayer, "family values," crime, out-of-wedlock births, and individual freedom, the latter defined as the right to keep guns and to oppose the demands of gay men and lesbians, have become the salient political issues that rally followers. Behind much of these issues on the political level is the Christian Coalition, an assembly of fundamentalist and evangelical groups—in 1986, it won control of the Southern Baptist Convention, the largest

[49]See Benjamin Nelson, *The Idea of Usury: From Tribal Brotherhood to Universal Otherhood,* 2nd ed. enlarged (Chicago: University of Chicago Press, 1969).

Protestant denomination in the United States, with more than 15 million members—which is a dominant force in the Republican Party in about eighteen states. Its key spokesman has been Pat Robertson, who ran in the Republican primaries for president in 1988 and who has espoused anti-Semitic conspiracy theories (of international bankers and behind them, Jewish financiers) and has cultivated Jewish intellectual neoconservatives by declarations of support for the state of Israel.

Some sociologists, especially in Europe, have seen the rise of "new social movements" (such as the green movement) and new postmodern issues, such as the environment and nature, as the basis of postindustrial politics. But these, I would say, overdraw the cultural dimension of politics. In Western societies, culture *and* class remain the salient axes because issues of income inequality and the defense of the welfare state—the main achievements of postwar social democracy—remain, but so do issues of culture.

More than thirty years ago, in the volume *The Radical Right*, Richard Hofstadter, Seymour Martin Lipset, and I proposed a scheme of "double axes"—of culture and class—as ways of understanding the changing saliencies of political alignments in the United States.[50] For most of the century, class, or economic issues, had been the main division that most historians and sociologists used to understand the history of American politics—in large part because of the economic interpretation of the Constitution by such influential historians as Charles A. Beard and the virulence of the labor issue, which arose after the 1890s and resulted in an extraordinary amount of violence (more than in any European country) and clashes with the corporations and in the the New Deal's redressing, somewhat, of economic power.

Yet such analyses ignored the periods, such as the 1920s and the 1950s, when "status politics," the anxieties of cultural groups, dominated the times. And one could then look at American politics along one or the other of the two axes and locate different groups within these boxes. So, for example, most writers thought of labor as being "on the Left" because of the salience of economic issues, yet Lipset could also write on "working-class authoritarianism" because of the conservative attitudes of blue-collar workers on cultural issues.

What has occurred—at least in the American polity today—is the fusion of these issues—primarily because politics has become the cockpit in which these questions are now fought out—in the demands for rights; in the legalization of abortion; in the claims for advantage,

[50]Daniel Bell, ed., *The Radical Right* (Garden City, N.Y.: Doubleday and Co., 1963).

such as affirmative action; in the efforts to institute prayer in public schools (as against the Constitutional separation of church and state), and so on.

The result has been a blurring of lines within the old party divisions. Thus, there are economic conservatives who want greater "fiscal responsibility" and reduced governmental powers but are also "liberal" on social issues, such as abortion or gay rights. There are social conservatives who want a reduction of taxes to stimulate economic growth (the so-called supply-side theorists), yet who want *more* governmental tutelage on morals and the behavior of teenagers in the name of "family values." Libertarians such as Milton Friedman, who believes that free markets make free men, would extend their libertarian doctrines to legalize (some) drugs and allow abortion. Yet radical communitarians would limit the right of corporations to relocate plants and factories when doing so would destroy communities. Radical feminists, such as Catherine McKinnon and Andrea Dworkin, want legislation to outlaw pornography because they believe it is degrading to women, a move endorsed by social conservatives. Patrick J. Buchanan ran for president in the 1996 Republican primaries as a populist in economics, attacking the large corporations, while virulently espousing all the cultural causes of the Christian Right (one of the main themes in the Iowa caucuses was an attack on "same-sex" marriage, as undermining the values of the Republic).

What is Left and what is Right and what is liberal and what is conservative have all become jumbled as different political candidates rapidly shift ground, especially when, looking at public opinion polls, they claim to be responsive to the volatile expressions of voters. And all this is magnified by television (where Benjamin Franklin's Protestant adage, "Time is money," receives its most meaningful expression). Politics is summed up in "sound bites," a time compression that television uses more readily than do other media because of its brevity. (A study by Kiku Adatto, of Harvard University, found that the average sound bite on television of statements by presidential candidates went from 42.3 seconds in 1968 to 9.8 seconds in 1980 and 8.4 seconds in 1992.) And the candidates and their "spinmeisters," the advisers who try to control the way the messages are used by the media, are more often concerned with the way a message will be perceived than with what is actually said. As the conservative political analyst William Kristol observed during the 1996 primary campaign in New Hampshire: "It is, of course, very postmodern. There are no real events any more, just the image of events. Years ago genuine photographs of

334

events were translated into photo ops. Now I suppose one could say the campaign itself is being transformed into a 'campaign op.' "

What does this mean for democracy?

Democracy is coterminous with the public sphere. It is the sphere of open and informed debate in which values are translated into public policy. The force of public opinion was recognized long ago, when Niccolò Machiavelli called attention to *publicca voce e fama*, the tribute a ruler, especially one who had seized power, as so many condottieri did, had to pay to *virtu*, rather than accede to power by birth. And John Locke, in his *Essay Concerning Human Understanding*, added to divine law and civil law "the law of opinion or reputation," by which men judge the rectitude of actions.

Public opinion, in the modern sense, however, was a product of the Enlightenment, with the demand for the public communication of governmental acts *(Offentlichkeit)* so as to provide for the accountability of governments. And one of the first writers to popularize the term "public opinion" throughout Europe, on the eve of the French Revolution, was the intellectual Jacques Necker, who, as minister of finance under Louis XVI, understood the need for a favorable view of "public credit."[51]

But the idea of a "public sphere" gained irreversible status from the three great revolutions that shaped modern society: the English Revolution of 1688, the American Revolution of 1776, and the French Revolution of 1789. What these revolutions did was reverse the order of state and society, to institute the idea of *rights* as the foundation of legitimate government and to emphasize the centrality of liberty.

Before these revolutions, the central idea of the relation of subject to ruler was obligations, and rights were only prescriptive rights granted by the ruler to his subjects. But as Article 2 of the French Declaration of the Rights of Man and of the Citizen stated: "The aim of every political association is the preservation of the natural and imprescriptible rights of man. These rights are liberty, property, and resistance to oppression."[52] The second, overriding theme, the idea of

[51]"Necker's great contribution to the history of public opinion was to publish his fiscal statements so that the merits and faults of government policy could be appraised in public. He did so to calm the public which began to distrust the administration of finances and feared that the income of the treasury would not offer any security to the capital and interests of its creditors." See Hans Speier, "The Historical Development of Public Opinion," in *Social Order and the Risks of War* (New York: George W. Stewart, 1952), p. 328; the article was first published in the *American Journal of Sociology*, January 1950.

[52]In *The French Idea of Freedom: The Old Regime and the Declaration of Rights of 1789*, edited by Dale Van Kley (Stanford, Calif.: Stanford University Press, 1994), p. 1. Article 1 stated: Men are born and remain free and equal in rights. Social distinctions can be based only on public utility.

liberty, was the defense of each individual against arbitrary power, which was outside the rule of law.

All modern political theory is framed by the debate on the meaning and applications of these terms—other than those, such as Leo Strauss and his followers, who seek to justify classical natural right (see pp. 162–63 and 252–53 of this volume). The difficulty is that few of the theorists, searching as they do for universal common rules, philosophically grounded, take into account the most notable fact about modern societies: their diversities and contradictions.

Most societies that have a founding myth, or a written constitution, have a framework of shared values and common procedures. But every society is also a plural society with individuals who occupy, within their own lives, multiple and different positions and have various identities and interests that change over time. Moral ideals are not societal ideals, and often the two clash when embodied in actions. Values clash when the order of priorities changes, as interests are affected. And there are "structural disjunctions" when in culture, the value is "the realization of self" while the economy practices the "segmentation" of the person into roles.[53]

If we are to manage in a pluralist society without tearing the society apart, there are some relevant distinctions that we need to observe. One is the distinction between the *common good* and the *public good*. The common good is, understandably, a minimal guide, for there are not many *substantive* values and interests that all persons have in common. Defense and security, as Adam Smith noted, are common goods, usually against defined enemies. The *public good* encompasses activities that provide all individuals with an identity as citizens—a principle of inclusion. As Aristotle wrote in *Politics* two thousand years ago—the equal participation of a citizen in a self-governing community depends on the dignity of a person and his or her self-esteem and gives each a sense of personal responsibility. But the basis of such personal responsibility is having a job that provides a reasonable standard of living; and if that is so, is not full employment, not deprivation of welfare, the basic consideration for the good society? That is the theme of the "public household" that I raised in this book. That is why I remain "a socialist" in economics.

The second distinction is between the *public* and the *private*. I maintain that distinction not only on liberal philosophical principles—the creation of a personal area outside the prying and prurient intrusions of "the state"—but for prudential reasons as well. The most destruc-

---

[53]I have tried to outline a matrix of such issues, for social theory, in my essay "Social Science: An Imperfect Art," *The Tocqueville Review*, No. 1, 1995.

tive conflicts in a society arise from the politicization of moral and cultural issues because such beliefs tend to be "absolute" (held à outrance) and are nonnegotiable. One of the successful transitions of modern industrial society was to translate the labor dispute from an ideology into an interest and make it negotiable. The labor issue tore the society apart for more than fifty years, yet with the institution of collective bargaining, a structure of social peace was created.

But moral issues—such as abortion—are not easily or at all negotiable. The solution, it would seem, is to "privatize" the issue by making choice a private decision—without the use of public funds. The choice of having an abortion would then become a private right. An individual being "taxed" for practices abhorrent to him or her may become disruptive, but if the actions are private, protesters have no "right" to be disruptive. (And if one asks how the poor and indigent are to pay for such choices, the answer would be that foundations and other private organizations should provide financial support to those individuals.)

Finally, in this affirmation of rights, there is a need to affirm a single standard of human rights, without which no individual has recourse against the arbitrary power of the state to degrade, torture, and slaughter those who dissent from that power. "Prior to the U.N. Charter," Bryan Hehir wrote, "most legal scholars and governments took the position that human rights did not impede the right of the sovereign state to be monstrous to its citizens. As far as international law and other governments were concerned, human rights could suffocate within the boundaries of the sovereign state."[54]

No longer. The Nuremberg trials of the surviving Nazi leaders at the end of World War II established the criterion of "crimes against humanity." The actions of the Bosnian Serb leaders in "ethnic cleansing" are a mockery of the very idea of civilization itself. And the action of the Communist Chinese government in sentencing Wei Jingsheng to fourteen years in prison, for the "crime" of writing his opinions on a public wall, makes it clear that the Party leaders feared the consequences of both their own betrayal of once-proclaimed utopian ideals, and the deaths of millions as they imposed an ideology upon a recalcitrant nation.[55]

[54]In Henry Steiner, ed. *Human Rights at Harvard* (Cambridge, Mass.: Harvard Law School, 1995).
[55]I commend the eloquent statement of Susan Sontag (in the *New York Review of Books*, February 13, 1996) on the case of Wei Jingsheng:

For a long time almost all . . . thinking about China started from the assumption that China was an essentially collectivist society with no indigenous tradition of individual rights. Hence, Sinologists argued, we shouldn't expect a real movement for democracy and for individual rights as these are understood in the West to emerge in China. This double-standard thinking about China reflects the general decline of universalist moral and po-

I believe that this new emphasis on human rights and the establishment of a permanent tribunal to deal with "crimes against humanity" may well be the basis of the reinstatement of Enlightenment values and the foundation (as I wrote in this Afterword) of a new conception of "natural law."

My Foreword to the 1978 edition of this book ended with a final note on religion. So does this Afterword. Religions, in and of themselves, can be cruel and unyielding, as we have seen from the Inquisition to the *fatwa* of the Ayatollah Khomeini on Salman Rushdie. All embody the claims of believers to absolute and exclusive truths. All invoke the name of God. But the fundamental fact is that we do not know to whom God speaks.

For me, religion is not the sphere of God or of the gods. It is the sense, a necessary one, of the sacred, of what is beyond us and cannot be transgressed. In Judaism there is the concept of *Havdolah*, of separation, one that Émile Durkheim, himself the descendant of a line of rabbis, invoked—the separation of the holy from the profane, the transcendent from the mundane, the numinous from the dark. One of the charges I made against capitalism and modernism is that in their insatiable bursting of all bonds, there was "nothing sacred." The failure of capitalism and now postmodernism to establish boundaries of transgression—which is what a doctrine of "natural law" would provide—indicate that the cultural contradictions of the two modes remain.

In the West, in the economic and cultural realms, the Protestant ethic (now a mythos) has been overwhelmed by acquisitiveness, and Modernism has ended in the morass of postmodernism and PoMo. In the undertow of the global economy, capitalism has now been pulled east to the Pacific, where a new tide of acquisitiveness (and inequalities) and an ideology of neo-Confucianism (and political nationalism)

---

litical standards—of Enlightenment values—in the past generation. There is an increasing reluctance to apply a single standard of political justice, of freedom, and of individual rights and of democracy. The usual justifications for this reluctance are that it is "colonialist" (the label used by people on the left) or "Euro-centric" (the label used both by multiculturalist academics and by businessmen, who talk admiringly of authoritarian "Confucian cultures") to expect or to want non-European peoples to have "our" values. My own view is that it is precisely the reluctance to apply these standards—as if "we" in the European and neo-European countries need them, but the Chinese and the peoples of Africa don't—that is colonialist and condescending.

Those of us who are active in the human rights movement have understood that it is our duty to hold to a universal standard of individual rights and democracy, and not be talked into thinking that some cultures and societies don't need these as much as we Westerners do. . . . The recent history of the democracy movement in China has shown that notions of the individual and of democratic freedoms like ours do have Chinese roots.

have become the hallmarks of the new era. Standing proud on a stage of history may be a satisfactory-enough achievement for these Asian nations for the while—though the looming power of China may foreshadow a menace. But the deeper question remains: If one loses the anchorages of tradition and religion, what will be left of economic power and cultural syncretism for these "new" civilizations, if not some further contradictions of capitalism?

Index

zsche on, 4; post-industrial society and, 149; and postmodernism, 301–302; *see also* Knowledge; Self-consciousness

Consensus: breakup of, 182–183; "unspoken," in U.S., 250–251

Constantine, 175

Constitution, U.S., 284, 333, 344

Constructivism, 18*n*

Consumer class, 296, 330

Consumption economy or society, 64–65, 68, 193

Consumption ethic, 63

Contemplation, 106, 110–112

Content, 1960s sensibility and attack on, 122, 126, 129

Contradictions. *See* Disjunction of realms

Contras, 328

Cooper, Richard N., 208

Copernican revolution, 110

Copernican system, 109

Corporate class, abdiction of, in cultural-social realm, 77–80

Corporations: government involvement in capital market and, 242; inflation and, 241; and mergers and acquisitions, 285, 316–317, 325–326; multinational, 207, 208

Correspondence theory, 295, 207

Cosmology, rational, 295

Council of Economic Advisers, 79, 190, 202

Counter-culture, 55, 73–74, 79, 81, 143, 320–321; liberalism and, 79, 81; *see also* Nineteen-sixties, sensibility of

Cours de philosophie positive (Comte), 151–152

"Coxey's Army," 196

Creationism, 319

Creative Evolution (Bergson), 63

Credibility, Vietnam war and problem of, 190

Credit (installment buying), 66, 69

Crime, 261; during 1960s, 189; and issue of moral decay, 318, 321, 323

"Crisis of the Tax State, The" (Schumpeter), 227

Criterion (magazine), 104

Criticism, cultural. *See* Cultural criticism

Cruelty and violence, 1960s concern with, 121, 122, 141, 143

Crying of Lot 49, The (Pynchon), 138

Cuba, 178, 181

Cubism, 18*n*, 46, 62, 106; spatial and temporal conceptions of, 111, 112

Cults, 168, 170

Cultural criticism (art or literary criticism), 96; neo-classical, 109; of 1950s, 44–45, 129; 1960s sensibility and, 125, 129, 134–136

Cultural mass, 20, 81, 108

Culture, xi, xii, 10, 191, 255–256; adversary, 40–41, 45; autonomy of, 53, 54; axial prin-

ciple of, 13–14; center lacking in, 102–105; change and, 13, 33–35, 54–55, 68–69, 83; and class, 329–339; counter-, 8, 55, 73–74, 79, 81, 143; definition of, 12, 36, *see also* meaning of *below*; democratization of (democratization of genius), 1960s sensibility and, 129–136; differentiation of social structure and, 95; disjunction (contradiction) between social structure (techno-economic order) and, 14, 15, 37, 53, 85; disjunction within, 92–98; eclipse of distance and, 99–119; Hegelian view of, 8–9; incoherence of, 85, 86; legitimation and motivation crises and, Habermas on, 249*n*, 250*n*; Marxist view of, 8–9, 10*n*, 33, 330; mass, *see* Mass culture; meaning of, 36–45, 100; middlebrow, of 1950s, 44–45; modalities of, 12; Nietzsche's view of devitalization of, 4; and postmodernism, 313–314; religion and, relation between, 157–158; religion and work replaced by, as means of self-fulfillment, 156; religious, unity of, 99; return to primordial questions as principle of, 166; of the self, modernist culture as, 132; society vs., 318–319; socio-economic structure and, relation between, 33–34, 36–37, 55; specialization and strain between social structure and, 95; Spengler's view of, 8–9*n*; supremacy (primacy) of, 33–35, *see also* autonomy of *above*; tradition and, relation between, 131–132; unity of, 99, 104–105; varieties of experience in, 99–101; visual, 105–108; wars, 315

Culture and Anarchy (Arnold), 310

Culture for the Millions? (Jacobs, ed.), 45*n*, 101*n*, 105*n*

Currency exchange, 207

Cyrano de Bergerac, 285–286

Czechoslovakia, 182–183

Dada, 52, 123

Dahl, Robert A., 280*n*

Dangerous Pilgrimages (Bradbury), 313

Darwin, Charles, 9, 153

Dean, John, 328

Death of Man, 301, 302

Death Row Records, 323

Deaver, Michael, 326

Debt, capitalism and, 242, 243

Decision making, non-market public, 196–197

Decline of the West, The (Spengler), 8–9*n*

Deconstruction, 301, 304, 314

Decter, Midge, xii

De Gaulle, Charles, 204

De-definition of Art, The (Rosenberg), 126*n*

Defense, shift of government expenditures from, to social programs, 233–234*n*

Prediction, forecasting distinguished from, 205

"Preface to the Lyrical Ballads" (Wordsworth), 85

Pre-industrial society, 147, 149, 198*n*

Presidential candidates, 323

Pret à Porter (film), 295

Primitive world-view, 96–97

Principles of Psychology (James), 113

Privacy, 118*n*, 258

Private and public spheres, liberalism and, 274–277, 279–280

Private interests, 255; *see also* Self-interest

"Process" art, 126, 127

Prodan, Mario, 105*n*

Product cycle in foreign trade, 213–214

Production: and rise of global economy, 316; shift from, to consumption, 293

Productivity; agricultural, 193, 198*n*; techno-economic order and, 11, 13

Progress, metanarrative of, 301

Progress Party (Denmark), 247

Prohibition movement, 64, 77, 78, 319

Proletariat, 330

Prometheus, Faust and, 160, 161

Property, 253

Property rights, 285, 326

Prophecy, 157, 169–170

Proportion (proportionality), 109

Protestant ethic, 76, 78; capitalism as having undermined, 21; and end of modernism, 287–290, 293, 295, 323–324, 338; erosion of, 21, 55, 70, 71, 74, 75, 224; Franklin as exemplar of, 56–59; and gambling, 324; and issue of moral decay, 323

Protestant Ethic and the Spirit of Capitalism, The (Weber), 58*n*, 82*n*, 156, 287–291

Protestantism, 63–66, 70, 156, 281; and "moral majority," 319; Weber on, 287–291; *see also* Protestant ethic

Protestant Reformation, 286–287

Proteus, 161

Proust, Marcel, 107, 116, 296, 331

Psychic distance, loss of, 116–117, 295

Psychoanalysis, 72

Psychology: The Briefer Course (James), 113, 119*n*

Psychology of Crowds, The (Le Bon), 153

Psychotherapy, hedonism and, 72

Public, *see* Audience

Public and private spheres: distinction between, 336–337; liberalism and, 274–277, 279–280

Public household, 26, 83, 176, 219–282, 336; defined, 220–221; economic growth and economic contradictions of capitalism and, 237–243; equality and, 262; new tasks of, 224–226; public philosophy and, *see* Public

philosophy; revolution of raising entitlements and, 232–236; sociological theory of, lacking, 221; units of, 257–259; *see also* Fiscal sociology

Public interest, 250, 255

Public law, 25, 253

Public opinion polls, 344

Public philosophy, 249–277, 279, 280; Rousseau's, 252, 255, 256

Pudovkin, V. I., 18*n*

Puritanism, 17, 22; asceticism and, 82; attack on, early twentieth century, 61–63; core beliefs and values of, 56–61; Edwards as exemplar of, 56–58; erosion (end or breakup) of, 55, 63, 65, 71, 74, 78, 81; as ideology, 60–61; sexuality and, 56, 59, 62

Puritans, 82, 156; covenant of, 57, 59, 60; New Model Army of, 288

Putnam, Hilary, 298

Pynchon, Thomas, 137, 138, 144

Quantum mechanics, 308, 309

Quine, Willard, 298

Quotas, equality and, 264–265

Racial conflicts, 181

Radford, Arthur W., 178

Radical Right, The (Hofstadter and Lipset), 333

Radicals (radicalism), 25, 51, 137, 143*n*, 144, 145, 249; in 1950s, 42, 44, 45

Rahv, Philip, 143*n*

"Rain, Steam and Speed" (Turner), 111

RAND Corporation, 328

Randolph, A. Philip, 196

Ransom, John Crowe, 120, 129, 303

Rational and Social Foundations of Music (Weber), 37*n*

Rational cosmology, 295

Rationalism, 17, 28, 36, 53, 167; nihilism and, 3, 4, 7; *see also* Rationality

Rationality, 25, 254; breakup of cosmos of, 108–119; in Freud, 305; functional, 11, 37, 92; in Hegelian-Marxist view of history, 8; and postmodernism, 301, 304–305; spatial-temporal conceptions and, 108–116; *telos* of, 8; *see also* Rationalism; Reason

Rauschenberg, Robert, 115–116, 130

Rawls, John, 221, 270–272

Reader's Digest (magazine), 76

Reagan, Ronald, 318, 320, 323–324, 326–327, 329

Realism: and postmodernism, 298; socialist, 18*n*

Reality: idea of, 90, 149; social construction of, 313

Reason, 171; centrality of, and end of modernism, 297; 1960s sensibility and attack on, 143–144; and postmodernism, 301, 304